1965

This book may be kept

FOURTEEN DAYS

A fine of TWO CENTS will be charged for each day
the Book is kept over time.

DE 1 '66			
MR 20 '69			
MR 11 '71			
MR 9 '72			
FEB 22 '73			
MAY 3 '73			
MAY 17 '73			
MAR 24 '77			
APR 14 '77			

Library Bureau Cat. No. 1137.24

The Critical Opinions of John Dryden

The Critical Opinions
of John Dryden

A DICTIONARY

Compiled and Edited
by John M. Aden

VANDERBILT UNIVERSITY PRESS
Nashville · 1963

Library of Congress Catalogue Card Number: 63–9945
Composed, printed, and bound by Kingsport Press, Inc.
Kingsport, Tennessee, U. S. A.

To
the Memory of
My Mother and Father

Table of Contents

Preface

I have based this compilation of Dryden's critical opinions upon the whole of his prose works, including essays, dedications, prefaces, *au lecteurs*, headnotes, arguments, notes and observations, biographies, histories, and letters. In two or three instances I have drawn upon Joseph Spence's *Anecdotes* (ed. S. W. Singer, London, 1820). Criticism expressed in verse or drama I have not attempted to include, partly because such criticism is not as characteristic of Dryden as the prose, partly because its inclusion would have extended the size of the book beyond practical limits.

Within the boundaries indicated I have sought to include all significant critical opinion. In addition I have admitted some matter not strictly critical in nature, but more nearly literary or literary-historical. There is for example an entry on Charles II. And there are entries on such topics as booksellers, the Commonwealth, music, timeservers, etc. Under the heading DRYDEN I have included not only all of Dryden's self-criticism, but all of his comment on his literary activities, associations, and conduct. If, in other words, I have consciously erred in respect to content, it has been on the side of excess, in the hope of making the book more generally useful. It has not been possible, of course, to admit everything. I have not, for example, included all persons referred to by Dryden. I hope that no one important has been omitted, though perhaps no two persons are likely to agree on that. It should be noted, however, that some names, not included among the entry headings, may be traced to mention elsewhere by means of the index at the end of the volume. Thus Poussin, for whom there is no entry in the text, may be traced, by this means, to his mention under the heading POETRY AND PAINTING. Of other kinds of omission more will be said below.

Contents are arranged in two ways: alphabetically by subject and chronologically within subjects. Thus FANCY will be found in its proper place in the alphabetical sequence, and under that heading Dryden's remarks on the subject in chronological order. Likewise, with a few exceptions, subdivisional headings are presented alphabetically and contents under them arranged chronologically. In some few topics, such as STYLE and TRANSLATION, I have substituted a logical for the alphabetical arrangement in order to permit certain groupings which seemed desirable. Cross references follow the chronological principle throughout.

Generally entry titles follow the logic normal in such matters, being what in their nature they could not otherwise be, such as TASTE for all content relative to that subject. But not all subjects lent themselves easily to titling, and I was occasionally driven to make shift with phrases and coinages. For Dryden's "lazar and Venus" I could think of no better title than the phrase itself, and, under POET, I was at a loss to express the idea of *nimis poeta* in any other way than by the Latin phrase itself. For the business of focusing on a principal character, either in painting or in drama, I used the term HIGHLIGHTING. And so on. I did not attempt to distinguish "poetry" in the old sense of any fiction from "poetry" in the modern sense of verse composition, but the user aware of the distinction will not, I trust, experience any special difficulty on that account. The consultant who does not immediately find what he is seeking will do well to run through the list of Topics and Authors. Once in possession of the main heading, subdivisional titles will be reviewed in course and should give no trouble. The user will also be advised, where his subject appears to elude him, to look across related titles, for it was not always easy to draw sharp distinctions or create tight compartments. The distinction among CRITIC, CRITICASTER, and CRITICISM, for instance, is necessarily arbitrary at times. The user will not need to be reminded to proceed in this way with such topics as FANCY, IMAGINATION, and WIT. As for titles of literary works, they are not, as a rule, entered in the main listing, but are confined to subdivisions under author headings. Thus, one looking for Dryden's comment on *Il Pastor Fido* will find it under GUARINI. Titles may also be searched through the index.

A normal entry contains the following elements: title or heading; any special notation, such as a general cross reference, explanatory parenthesis, or the speaker in the *Essay of Dramatic Poesy;* the quotation of the critical opinion; the source of the quotation; the year of composition (or, where that is wanting, as it is in most cases, the year of publication); and the page reference in the text used (see list of abbreviations).
Thus:

Hoi Polloi [Cf. AUDIENCE, POPULAR; VOX POPULI]
(Neander) If by the people you understand the multitude, the οἱ πολλοί, 'tis no matter what they think; they are sometimes in the right, sometimes in the wrong: their judgment is a mere lottery.

Dram. Poesy, '65. K I 100

Where more than one quotation appears under a given heading, the series is arranged chronologically and each quotation assigned a letter in the alphabetical sequence to facilitate cross reference. Since all entries are printed with paragraph indentation, quotations which represent paragraph openings in the sources are indicated by the paragraph sign in brackets: [¶].

Cross references are of three sorts: bracketed references used with the titles of entries, regular cross references within the entry, and (more rarely) cross references to sources outside the present volume. In the regular cross references, the abbreviation *cf.* indicates passages of less direct bearing on the subject than those referred to without the abbreviation. With respect to references outside the compilation itself, they are of two sorts: one to original texts (e.g., "See 'Examen of *The Silent Woman,*' K I 83 *ff.*"), the other, always appearing in footnote form, to studies dealing with the main entry topics (e.g., under PROSODY, "See R. D. Jameson, 'Notes on Dryden's Lost Prosodia,' *MP,* XX (1923), 241–53"). References of this latter type are not intended to be exhaustive. I have not sought to add bibliography to the features of this book.

Insofar as possible I have avoided paraphrasing except for purely transitional purposes, usually of an introductory nature, and I have been as sparing in the use of the hiatus as the problem of bulk would allow. Wherever possible I have given the whole useful extent of Dryden's opinions in his own words. Still, some editing was unavoidable. Longer passages containing sufficiently discrete parts are presented in successive units. An example is the extended account of poetic license appearing at the close of *The Author's Apology for Heroic Poetry and Poetic License.* In other instances, where a passage contains discrete ideas in conjunction, it is reduced to its elements and the parts distributed according to subject. Dryden observes that the French poets

are strict observers of these punctilios . . . 'Tis true, some actions, though natural, are not fit to be represented; and broad obscenities in words ought in good manners to be avoided: expressions therefore are a modest clothing of our thoughts . . .

The parts of this passage are entered under three separate headings: FRENCH AUTHORS, OBSCENITY, and EXPRESSION. Where the sequence that is lost by such separation seems important, its recovery is facilitated by cross references (e.g., See EXPRESSION, b). In passages where separation seemed infeasible, or inadvisable, main entry was by the opinion which appeared to be primary or inclusive, and the included opinions indicated by cross reference.

If the pleasure arising from comedy and satire be either laughter, or some nobler sort of delight, which is above it, no man is so great a master of irony as our author [Lucian]. That figure is not only a keen, but a shining weapon in his hand; it glitters in the eyes of those it kills . . .

Since here, the reference to irony seemed more important than that to Lucian, or than those to comedy, laughter, or figure, I entered the passage under IRONY (itself a subdivision of SATIRE) and cross-referenced the other subjects to it.

I have tried to keep Dryden's formal comparisons, such as those of Shakespeare and Jonson, Homer and Virgil, intact. To do so has necessitated comparative (and doubtless clumsy) titles, such as HORACE AND JUVENAL AND PERSIUS, CHAUCER AND OVID, and the like, but these will not, I believe, pose any problems. Where comparisons are drawn informally, entry is by primary subject with cross references, as illustrated above.

Two symbols are used with hiatuses: ⸰, and ᵠ. The first signifies that illustration follows in the original, the second that a quotation or quotations follow. Where a pronoun or other pointing word or expression within the quoted text indicates or suggests the continuation, the symbols are omitted.

The question of text has not been an issue. Quotations are based on existing standard editions (listed hereafter) and left at that. I have silently corrected two errors in Ker's edition of the essays and have, except for proper nouns and adjectives, eliminated all ligatures. Otherwise the transcripts are *verbatim, literatim*. Page division in passages occupying more than one page in the original texts (editions) I have indicated by the use of a slant line (/). Professor George Watson's edition of Dryden's essays, in the Everyman series, appeared too late for me to make the use I should like to have made of it.

Something further should be said of the selective index. It is designed to provide a key to matters not readily accessible through the normal channels of entry. For example, expressions such as "our crying sin of keeping," "makes a malefactor die sweetly," or allusions to persons and titles not found among the headings, but imbedded in the quotations (such as Raphael, Pythagoreans, and *Silenus*) are in this way made accessible. The index also includes expressions and quotations from the foreign languages, especially where these are of axiomatic, proverbial, or epigrammatic character. The index was quite deliberately made inclusive of extra-critical as well as critical reference, and is therefore an important and, I hope, usefully versatile supplement to the list of Topics and Authors and the main alphabet itself.

For permission to quote from their several editions (summarized below, with abbreviations), I am grateful to the Clarendon Press, Oxford, to Houghton Mifflin

Company, and to Professor C. E. Ward and the Duke University Press.

It is a pleasure to acknowledge the advice and encouragement of Professor Richmond P. Bond of the University of North Carolina (my guide, philosopher, and friend) and of Professor Samuel Holt Monk of the University of Minnesota; the contributions towards the Chronology of Dryden's works made by Professor C. E. Ward of Duke University, and the interest and support of Dean Leonard B. Beach of the Graduate School of Vanderbilt University. For what proves amiss in the book, I alone, not they, must stand accountable. To the Committee on Grants-in-Aid of Vanderbilt University I am grateful for awards making possible the pursuit and completion of this undertaking. Finally, I would dedicate the book to my wife, Marie, if there were not a prior claim upon it.

John M. Aden
Vanderbilt University
November 1962

List of Topics and Authors*

Academy
Act Division
Acting and Actors
Action Defined
Addison, Joseph
Admiration
Æschylus
Age, Genius of
Alexandrine
Ambition
Ancients
Anonymity
Anthology
Antony and Cleopatra
Antithesis
Archaisms
Ariosto, Lodovico
Aristophanes
Aristotle
Art
Art and Life
Arts
Astrology
Audience, Popular
Augustus
Aurelius, Marcus
Authority
Ballet
Barclay, Jean
Beaumont, Francis
Beaumont and Fletcher
Behn, Aphra
Bellori, Giovanni Pietro
Berkenhead, Sir John
Biography
Blackmore, Sir Richard
Blank Verse

Boccaccio
Boiardo, Metteo Maria
Boileau-Despréaux, Nicolas
Bombast
Booksellers
Borrowing (Verbal)
Bossu, René le
Buckingham, George Vil-
    liers, Second Duke of
Burlesque
Busby, Richard
Butler, Samuel
Camoens, Luiz de
Caro, Hannibal
Casaubon, Isaac
Catachresis
Catastrophe
Catullus
Censorship
Chapelain, Jean
Chapman, George
Character[s]
Charles II
Chaucer
Chaucer and Boccaccio
Chaucer and Ovid
Chiaroscuro
Chorus
Chudleigh, Lady Mary
Cicero
Claudian
Clenches
Clergy
Cleveland, John
Clevelandism
Coinage
Collier, Jeremy

Comedy
Comines, Philippe de
Commentators
Commentators, Dutch
Common Sense
Commonwealth Period
Conceit
Congreve, William
Consensus Gentium
Consonants
Contraction
Contrast
Conversation
Conversion
Corneille, Pierre
Corneille, Thomas
Correctness
Counterturn
Couplet
Court
Court Poets
Courtier without Wit
Cowley, Abraham
Creech, Thomas
Crites [Sir Robert Howard]
Critic[s]
Critical Tolerance
Criticasters
Criticism
Crowne, John
Cultural Interchange
Curiosa Felicitas
Dacier, André
Danish Language
Dante
Davenant, Sir William
Decay

* For persons, works, and topics not included in the following list, consult the Selective Index.

List of Topics and Authors

Decorum
Demosthenes
Denham, Sir John
Dennis, John
Description[s]
Design
Designing
Deus ex Machina
Dialogue (Dramatic)
Dialogue (Genre)
Diction
Dictionary
Digressions
Dion Cassius
Disposition
Donne, John
Dorset, Charles Sackville, Earl of
Double Plot
Drama: Epic Origins
Drama Read and Acted
Dramatis Personae
Dryden, Life
Dryden, Personal Character
Dryden, Literary Life
Dryden, Works
Dryden, Miscellaneous
Dullness
D'Urfey, Thomas
Dutch Commentators
Dutch Poetry and Song
Dutch Poets
Dying on the Stage
Eclectic School
Elegy
Elocution
Emulation
Ends of Poetry
English Composition and Speech
English Drama
English Language

English Poets: Inventive Genius
English Stage
English vs. French
Englishmen
Enthusiast in Poetry
Epic
Epic, Christian
Epic Hero
Epic Machines
Epic Poet
Epic Unities
Epic vs. Tragedy
Epicureanism
Epigram
Episodes
Erasmus
Etherege, Sir George
Ethical Function
Euripides
Expression
Fable
Fairfax, Edward
Fame
Fancy
Fancy (Responsive)
Farce
Fiction
Figures
Flecknoe, Richard
Fletcher, John
Flower and the Leaf, The
Fontenelle, Bernard le Bovier de
Fools and Fops
French Authors
French Critics
French Drama
French Language
French Nation
French Romances
Fustian

Gallicizing
Genius
Genre
German Verse
Golden Ages
Good Nature
Good Sense
Gorboduc
Gower, John
Graffing
Grammar
Greek Language
Grotesque
Guarini, Giovanni Battista
Halifax, First Earl of
Harrington, Sir John
Heightening
Heinsius, Daniel
Hemistich
Hero (Dramatic)
Heroic Play
Highlighting
Historian
Historical Poem
Historical Truth
History
Hobbes, Thomas
Hoi Polloi
Holyday, Barten
Homer
Homer and Virgil
Hopkins, Charles
Horace
Horace and Juvenal and Persius
Howard, Sir Robert
Human Nature
Humors
Hyde, Lawrence (Earl of Rochester)
Idiom
Images

xvi

List of Topics and Authors

Editions and Abbreviations

Essays of John Dryden, selected and edited by W. P. Ker. Oxford: Clarendon Press, 1926. Second Impression. 2 vols. **[K]**

The Works of John Dryden, edited by Sir Walter Scott and George Saintsbury. Edinburgh, 1882–1893. 18 vols. **[S-S]**

The Poetical Works of Dryden, edited by G. R. Noyes. Cambridge Edition, Revised and Enlarged. Boston: Houghton Mifflin Company, 1950. **[N]**

The Poems of John Dryden, edited by James Kinsley. Oxford: Clarendon Press, 1958. 4 vols. **[JK]**

The Letters of John Dryden, collected and edited by Charles E. Ward. Durham: Duke University Press, 1942. **[W]**

A Chronology
of the Sources, with Abbreviations

Arrangement is by date of composition where known or conjecturable, otherwise by date of publication. Items arranged by composition date are starred. In arriving at publication dates, I have consulted Hugh Macdonald, *John Dryden, a Bibliography of Early Editions and of Drydeniana*, 1939. Professor C. E. Ward, of Duke University, whose assistance in gathering advertising dates Mr. Macdonald acknowledges, was good enough to look over the draft of the following chronology, verify it, and make suggestions as to dates of composition. His suggestions are acknowledged by the addition of his name.

Reference to letters in the chronology are abbreviated to save space: the letter *L* followed by the surname of the recipient followed by the year written (abbreviated). L-Rochester-73 signifies the letter to John Wilmot, Earl of Rochester, dated by Malone July 1673. The letters are quoted from Professor Ward's edition (Duke University Press, 1942), and carry his numbering, both here and in the text.

All dates are New Style unless otherwise indicated.

Ded. *Rival Ladies*	Dedication of *The Rival Ladies,* pub. 1664.
Dram. Poesy	*An Essay of Dramatic Poesy,* pub. 1668. Composed probably autumn 1665 [Ward. But see E. N. Hooker and H. T. Swedenberg, Jr. (eds.), *The Works of John Dryden* (Berkeley: University of California Press, 1956), I, 260]
*Pref. *Annus Mirabilis*	Preface to *Annus Mirabilis,* pub. 1667. Composed by 10 November 1666 [as signed and dated by Dryden]
*Ded. *Dram. Poesy*	Dedication of *An Essay of Dramatic Poesy,* pub. 1668. Composed shortly before August 1667(?), when *Dram. Poesy* entered in S.R. [See Hooker and Swedenberg, *loc. cit.*]
*To Reader, *Dram. Poesy*	To the Reader, prefixed to *An Essay of Dramatic Poesy,* pub. 1668. Composed shortly before August 1667(?), when *Dram. Poesy* entered in S.R. [See above]
*Pref. *Secret Love*	Preface to *Secret Love; or, The Maiden Queen,* pub. 1668. Composed probably c. August 1667(?), when the play entered in S.R. [Hooker and Swedenberg, *loc. cit.*]
*Ded. *Indian Emperor*	Dedication of *The Indian Emperour,* pub. 1667. Composed by 12 October 1667 [as signed and dated by Dryden]
Defence of An Essay	*A Defence of An Essay of Dramatic Poesy,* prefixed to the second edition of *The Indian Emperour,* pub. 1668.
Pref. *Wild Gallant*	Preface to *The Wild Gallant,* pub. 1669.
*Pref. *Tempest*	Preface to *The Tempest,* pub. 1670. Composed by 1 De-

A Chronology of the Sources, with Abbreviations

	cember 1669 [as signed and dated by Dryden]
Pref. *Tyrannic Love*	Preface to *Tyrannic Love; or, The Royal Martyr*, pub. 1670. Composed September–October, 1670(?) [Ward]
Pref. *Evening's Love*	Preface to *An Evening's Love; or, The Mock Astrologer*, pub. 1671.
Ded. *Conquest of Granada*	Dedication of *The Conquest of Granada*, pub. 1672.
Essay of Heroic Plays	*An Essay of Heroic Plays*, prefixed to *The Conquest of Granada*, pub. 1672.
Defence of the Epilogue	*Defence of the Epilogue*, appended to *The Conquest of Granada* (The Second Part), pub. 1672.
Ded. *Marriage à la Mode*	Dedication of *Marriage à la Mode*, pub. 1673. Composed February–May 1673(?) [Ward]
L-Rochester-73	Letter to John Wilmot, Earl of Rochester, dated by Malone July 1673. [Ward No. 4 and Notes, p. 145. Ward's revision of Malone's date, as stated in his note on this letter, he now regards as too early]
Ded. *Amboyna*	Dedication of *Amboyna*, pub. 1673.
Pref. *N and O*	Preface to *Notes and Observations on The Empress of Morocco*, pub. 1674.
Postscript *N and O*	Postscript to *Notes and Observations on The Empress of Morocco*, pub. 1674.
Ded. *Aureng-Zebe*	Dedication of *Aureng-Zebe*, pub. 1676.
Ded. *State of Innocence*	Dedication of *The State of Innocence*, pub. 1677.
Author's Apology	*The Author's Apology for Heroic Poetry and Poetic Licence*, prefixed to *The State of Innocence*, pub. 1677. [See G. B. Churchill, in *MP* for October 1906, pp. 381–88]
L-Latimer-77	Letter to Lord Latimer, c. July 1677. [Ward No. 5 and Notes, p. 147]
L-Dorset-77	Letter to the Earl of Dorset, c. "late summer or early autumn" 1677. [Ward No. 6 and Notes, pp. 148–49. See also James M. Osborn, *John Dryden: Some Biographical Facts and Problems* (1940), p. 264]
*Heads of an Answer	Heads of an Answer to Rymer, composed late 1677(?) [See F. G. Walcott, in *PQ* for April 1936, esp. pp. 194–99]
Ded. *All for Love*	Dedication of *All for Love*, pub. 1678.
Pref. *All for Love*	Preface to *All for Love*, pub. 1678.
Pref. *Œdipus*	Preface to *Œdipus*, pub. 1679.
*Pref. *Troilus*	Preface to *Troilus and Cressida*, pub. 1679. [Placed before the Dedication because of Dryden's reference there (Scott-Saintsbury, VI, 253) to the "following critique" (i.e., the Preface) in such a way as to make it appear almost certain that the Preface was written first]

*Ded. *Troilus*	Dedication of *Troilus and Cressida,* pub. 1679.
Ded. *Limberham*	Dedication of *The Kind Keeper; or, Mr. Limberham,* pub. 1680. [Composed October–November 1679. Before 10 November. Ward. See also Kinsley, *Poems,* Commentary, IV, 1866–67]
Pref. *Ovid's Epistles*	Preface to *Ovid's Epistles,* pub. 1680.
Ded. *Spanish Friar*	Dedication of *The Spanish Friar,* pub. 1681.
Pref. *Absalom and Achitophel*	Preface ("To the Reader") to *Absalom and Achitophel,* pub. 1681.
Epistle to the Whigs	"Epistle to the Whigs," prefixed to *The Medal,* pub. 1682. [March]
Pref. *Religio Laici*	Preface to *Religio Laici,* pub. 1682. [November]
L-Unidentified-82	Letter to an Unidentified Person, 1682(?). [Ward No. 7. Professor Ward does not attempt to date this letter. Since it refers to a dispute over Creech's translation of *De rerum natura,* which appeared in 1682, the letter cannot antedate that year. See Scott-Saintsbury, XVIII, 96, headnote]
L-Busby-82	Letter to Richard Busby, 1682. [Ward No. 9 and Notes, p. 151]
Vindication	*The Vindication of the Duke of Guise,* pub. 1683. [Composed "Late March, early April." Ward]
Ded. *Plutarch*	Dedication of *Plutarch's Lives,* pub. 1683. [Composed "Late April." Ward]
"Life of Plutarch"	"The Life of Plutarch," prefixed to *Plutarch's Lives,* pub. 1683.
L-Rochester-83	Letter to Lawrence Hyde, Earl of Rochester, c. August 1683. [Ward No. 10 and Notes, p. 151]
Ded. *History of the League*	Dedication of *The History of the League,* pub. 1684.
Postscript *League*	Postscript of the Translator of *The History of the League,* pub. 1684.
L-Tonson-84	Letter to Jacob Tonson, c. September 1684. [Ward No. 11 and Notes, p. 152]
Pref. *Sylvæ*	Preface to *Sylvæ; or, The Second Part of Poetical Miscellanies,* pub. 1685.
Pref. *Albion and Albanius*	Preface to *Albion and Albanius,* pub. 1685.
Postscript *Albion*	Postscript to the Preface, *Albion and Albanius,* pub. 1685.
L-Etherege-87	Letter to George Etherege, 16 February 1687 [as dated by Dryden. Ward No. 13 and Notes, p. 155]
To the Reader, *Hind and Panther*	To the Reader, prefixed to *The Hind and the Panther,* pub. 1687.
L-Walsh-90	Letter to William Walsh, 1690(?). [Ward No. 15 and Notes, p. 156]

A Chronology of the Sources, with Abbreviations

*Ded. *Don Sebastian*	Dedication of *Don Sebastian*, pub. 1690. Composed January 1690 [as signed and dated by Dryden]
Pref. *Don Sebastian*	Preface to *Don Sebastian*, pub. 1690
Ded. *Amphitryon*	Dedication of *Amphitryon*, pub. 1690. Composed by 24 October 1690 [as signed and dated by Dryden]
L-Walsh-91	Letter to William Walsh, c. early 1691. [Ward No. 17 and Notes, p. 157]
Pref. Walsh's *Dialogue*	Preface to *A Dialogue Concerning Women*, by William Walsh, pub. 1691. [See Osborn, *op. cit.*, p. 212, n. 11]
Ded. *King Arthur*	Dedication of *King Arthur*, pub. 1691.
Ded. *Eleonora*	Dedication of *Eleonora*, pub. 1692.
"Character of St. Evremont"	"Character of St. Evremont," prefixed to *Miscellaneous Essays*, by Monsieur St. Evremont, pub. 1692.
Ded. *Cleomenes*	Dedication of *Cleomenes*, pub. 1692.
Pref. *Cleomenes*	Preface to *Cleomenes*, pub. 1692.
*"Character of Polybius"	"Character of Polybius," prefixed to *The History of Polybius* . . . translated by Sir H. S., pub. 1693. [Volume 2 has "Imprimatur: Edmund Bohun. November 25, 1692"][1]
Discourse of Satire	"A Discourse Concerning the Original and Progress of Satire," prefixed to *The Satires of Decimus Junius Juvenalis* . . . pub. 1693. Composed by 18 August 1692 [as signed and dated by Dryden]
Arguments and Notes	The Arguments and Notes to Juvenal and Persius, accompanying *The Satires of Decimus Junius Juvenalis* . . . pub. 1693.
L-Walsh-93	Letter to William Walsh, "May the 9th or 10th" [Dryden] 1693. [Ward No. 24 and Notes, p. 163]
Ded. *Examen Poeticum*	Dedication of *Examen Poeticum: Being the Third Part of Miscellany Poems*, pub. 1693.
L-Tonson-93	Letter to Jacob Tonson, "Aug. 30.th" [Dryden] 1693. [Ward No. 26 and Notes, p. 166]
L-Walsh-93	Letter to William Walsh, "Dec. 12th" [Dryden] 1693. [Ward No. 28 and Notes, p. 167]
L-Dennis-94	Letter to John Dennis, c. March 1694. [Ward No. 31 and Notes, p. 169]
Ded. *Love Triumphant*	Dedication of *Love Triumphant*, pub. 1694.
L-Tonson-95	Letter to Jacob Tonson, c. April 1695. [Ward No. 32 and Notes, p. 170]

[1] Since the *Polybius* is referred to in the Preface to *Cleomenes* (Advertised *London Gazette* 2–5 May 1692) as "shortly [to] be published," it is placed before the *Discourse of Satire*, which is dated by Dryden 18 August 1692. [See Scott-Saintsbury, VIII, 226] I retain the title-page date of *The Satires of . . . Juvenalis* (i.e., 1693), but place the *Polybius* first on the assumption of prior composition.

L-Tonson-95	Letter to Jacob Tonson, "Saturday June the 8th" [Dryden] 1695. [Ward No. 33 and Notes, p. 171]
Parallel	"A Parallel of Poetry and Painting," prefixed to *De Arte Graphica,* by C. A. Du Fresnoy, pub. 1695.
L-Tonson-95	Letter to Jacob Tonson, c. December, 1695. [Ward No. 36 and Notes, p. 174]
*"Life of Lucian"	"Life of Lucian," prefixed to *The Works of Lucian,* Translated . . . , pub. 1711. Composed c. 1696. [See the remark by Samuel Briscoe, publisher, in the dedication of Vol. I: Macdonald, p. 179]
Pref. *Husband His Own Cuckold*	Preface to *The Husband His Own Cuckold,* A Comedy by John Dryden, Junior, pub. 1696. [Arbitrarily placed after the "Life of Lucian"]
L-Chesterfield-97	Letter to the Earl of Chesterfield, 17 February 1697 [as dated by Dryden]. [Ward No. 41]
Ded. *Pastorals*	Dedication of *The Pastorals,* in *The Works of Virgil,* pub. 1697.
Ded. *Georgics*	Dedication of *The Georgics,* in *The Works of Virgil,* pub. 1697.
Ded. *Æneis*	Dedication of the *Æneis,* in *The Works of Virgil,* pub. 1697.
Postscript *Æneis*	Postscript to the Reader, in *The Works of Virgil,* pub. 1697.
Notes and Observations on Virgil's Works	Notes and Observations on Virgil's Works in English, pub. in *The Works of Virgil,* 1697.
L-Tonson-97	Letter to Jacob Tonson, December 1697. [Ward No. 50 and Notes, p. 179]
L-Steward-99	Letter to Mrs. Steward, "Candlemass-Day [February 2] 1698[/99]" [as dated by Dryden. Ward No. 57]
L-Pepys-99	Letter to Samuel Pepys, 14 July 1699 [as dated by Dryden. Ward No. 61]
L-Montague-99	Letter to the Right Honourable Charles Montague, c. October 1699. [Ward No. 65 and Notes, p. 184]
L-Steward-99	Letter to Mrs. Steward, "Nov: 7th" [Dryden] 1699. [Ward No. 67 and Notes, p. 185]
L-Thomas-99	Letter to Elizabeth Thomas, 12 November 1699. [Ward No. 68 and Notes, p. 186]
L-Thomas-99	Letter to Elizabeth Thomas, November 1699. [Ward No. 69 and Notes, p. 186]
L-Steward-99	Letter to Mrs. Steward, "Dec: the 14th-99" [Dryden] [Ward No. 71]
L-Steward-1700	Letter to Mrs. Steward, "Feb. 23d" [Dryden] 1700. [Ward No. 73]
Ded. *Fables*	Dedication of *Fables Ancient and Modern,* pub. 1700.

A Chronology of the Sources, with Abbreviations

The Critical Opinions
of John Dryden

❧ A ❧

Academy[*]

a. . . . I am sorry, that (speaking so noble a language as we do) we have not a more certain measure of it, as they have in France, where they have an Academy erected for that purpose . . .

Ded. *Rival Ladies,* '64. K I 5

b. [Under peace, a model leader, like Robert, Earl of Sunderland] will have leisure for the ornaments of peace; and make our language as much indebted to his care, as the French is to the memory of/their famous Richelieu. You know, my lord, how low he laid the foundations of so great a work; that he began it with a grammar and a dictionary; without which all those remarks and observations, which have since been made, had been performed to as little purpose, as it would be to consider the furniture of the rooms, before the contrivance of the house. Propriety must first be stated, ere any measures of elegance can be taken. Neither is one Vaugelas sufficient for such work. It was the employment of the whole Academy for many years; for the perfect knowledge of a tongue was never attained by any single person. The court, the college, and the town, must be joined in it. And as our English is a composition of the dead and living tongues, there is required a perfect knowledge, not only of the Greek and Latin, but of the old German, the French,

and the Italian; and, to help all these, a conversation with those authors of our own, who have written with the fewest faults in prose and verse. But how barbarously we yet write and speak, your lordship knows, and I am sufficiently sensible in my own English. For I am often put to a stand, in considering whether what I write be the idiom of the tongue, or false grammar, and nonsense couched beneath that specious name of Anglicism; and have no other way to clear my doubts, but by translating my English into Latin, and thereby trying what sense the words will bear in a more stable language. I am desirous, if it were possible, that we might all write with the same certainty of words, and purity of phrase, to which/the Italians first arrived, and after them the French; at least that we might advance so far as our tongue is capable of such a standard. It would mortify an Englishman to consider, that from the time of Boccace and of Petrarch, the Italian has varied very little; and that the English of Chaucer, their contemporary, is not to be understood without the help of an old dictionary. But their Goth and Vandal had the fortune to be grafted on a Roman stock; ours has the disadvantage to be founded on the Dutch. We are full of monosyllables, and those clogged with consonants, and our pronunciation is effeminate; all which are enemies to a sounding language. It is true, that to supply our poverty, we have trafficked with our neighbour nations; by which means we abound as much in words as Amsterdam

[*] See O. F. Emerson, "John Dryden and a British Academy," *Proceedings of the British Academy,* X (1921), 45–58; "Dryden and the English Academy," *MLR,* XX (1925), 189–190.

3

does in religions; but to order them, and make them useful after their admission, is the difficulty. A greater progress has been made in this since his Majesty's return, than, perhaps, since the Conquest to his time. But the better part of the work remains unfinished; and that which has been done already, since it has only been in practice of some few writers, must be digested into rules and method, before it can be profitable to the general. Will your lordship give me leave to speak out at last? and to acquaint the world, that from your encouragement and patronage, we may one day expect to speak and write a language worthy of the English wit, and which foreigners may not disdain to learn?

Ded. *Troilus*, '79. S-S VI 250–52

PROSODY, z. ENGLISH LANGUAGE, j.

Act Division

PLAY (PARTS). ANCIENTS, b. SPANISH PLAYS, a. ANCIENTS, c. Cf. FABLE, c. Cf. DAVENANT, d. Cf. DRYDEN, WORKS, xx. Cf. CHORUS, b. Cf. SHAKESPEARE, t.

Acting and Actors [See also DRAMA READ AND ACTED; FARCE]

DECORUM, b. PROSODY, ee. AUDIENCE, POPULAR, c.

a. . . . and suppose them [plays] ever to have been excellently acted, yet action only adds grace, vigour, and more life upon the stage, but cannot give it wholly where it is not first.

Heads of an Answer, '77. S-S XV 385

PASSIONS, e. JUDGMENT (RESPONSIVE). DRYDEN, WORKS, ee.

b. But, as 'tis my interest to please my audience, so 'tis my ambition to be read: that I am sure is the more lasting and the nobler design: for the propriety of thoughts and words, which are the hidden beauties of a play, are but confusedly judged in the vehemence of action: all things are there beheld as in a hasty motion, where the objects only glide before the eye and disappear. The most discerning critic can judge no more of these silent graces in the action than he who rides post through an unknown country can distinguish the situation of places, and the nature of the soil. The purity of phrase, the clearness of conception and expression, the boldness maintained to majesty, the significancy and sound of words, not strained into bombast, but justly elevated; in short, those very words and thoughts, which cannot be changed, but for the worse, must of necessity escape our transient view upon the theatre; and yet without all these a play may take. For if either the story move us, or the actor help the lameness of it with his performance, or now and then a glittering beam of wit or passion strike through the obscurity of the poem, any of these are sufficient to effect a present liking, but not to fix a lasting admiration; for nothing but the truth can long continue; and/time is the surest judge of truth.

Ded. *Spanish Friar*, '81. K I 248–49

LEE, a. DORSET, d. DOGGETT. POET, d-2. Cf. CHORUS, d. EPIC VS. TRAGEDY, f.

c. . . . the actors share the poet's praise. Your Lordship knows some modern tragedies which are beautiful on the stage, and yet I am confident you would not read them. Tryphon the stationer complains they are seldom asked for in his shop. The poet who flourished in the scene is damned in the *ruelle;* nay more, he is not esteemed a good poet by those, who see and hear his extravagances with delight. They are a sort of stately fustian, and lofty childishness.

Ded. *Æneis*, '97. K II 161

Action Defined

(Lisideius) 'Tis a great mistake in us to believe the French present no part of the action on the stage; every alteration or crossing of a design, every new-sprung passion, and turn of it, is a part of the action, and much the noblest, except we conceive nothing to be action till they [the players] come to blows; as if the painting of the hero's mind were not more properly the poet's work than the strength of his body.

Dram. Poesy, '65. K I 64

Addison, Joseph

The most ingenious Mr. Addison of Oxford has also been as troublesome to me . . . and on the same account. After his *Bees,* my latter swarm is scarcely worth the hiving.

Postscript *Æneis,* '97. K II 244

Admiration

OVID, b. EPIC, a. IMAGES, b. IMITATION, f. [". . . admiration . . . the delight of serious plays . . ."] Cf. SILENCE. HOMER, c. IMITATION, h. EPIC HERO, i. FIGURES, e.

Aeschylus

a. [¶] The poet Æschylus was held in the same veneration by the Athenians of after ages as Shakespeare is by us; and Longinus has judged, in favour of him, that he had a noble boldness of expression, and that his imaginations were lofty and heroic; but, on the other side, Quintilian affirms that he was daring to extravagance. 'Tis certain that he affected pompous words, and that his sense too often was obscured by figures . . .

Pref. *Troilus,* '79. K I 202

MANNERS, i.

b. Longinus . . . animadverts severely upon Æschylus, who writ nothing in cold blood, but was always in a rapture, and in fury with his audience: the inspiration was still upon him, he was ever tearing it upon the tripos . . .

Pref. *Troilus,* '79. K I 221

Age, Genius of

a. (Crites) . . . every age has a kind of universal genius, which inclines those that live in it to some particular studies . . .

Dram. Poesy, '65. K I 36

b. (Neander) For the genius of every age is different . . .

Dram. Poesy, '65. K I 99

Cf. POETIC LICENSE, e.

c. . . . Shakespeare and Fletcher have written to the genius of the age and nation in which they lived; for though nature, as he [Rymer] objects, is the same in all places, and reason too the same, yet the climate, the age, the disposition of the people . . . may be so different, that what pleased the Greeks would not satisfy an English audience.

Heads of an Answer, '77. S-S XV 385

Cf. SHAKESPEARE, f. Cf. GOLDEN AGES, a. Cf. BELLORI.

Alexandrine [See PROSODY]

Ambition

[¶] Ambition is so far from being a vice in poets, that it is almost impossible for them to succeed without it.

Ded. *State of Innocence,* '77. S-S V 100

DRYDEN, WORKS, n. IMAGINATION, e.

Ancients and Moderns [See under each]*

Ancients

a. . . . it appears plainly, that not only the bodies, but the souls of men, have decreased from the vigour of the first ages; that we are not more short of the stature

---

* See Guy Montgomery, "Dryden and the Battle of the Books," *Essays and Studies by Members of the Department of English, University of California Publications in English,* XVI (1943). 57–72.

and strength of those gigantic heroes, than we are of their understanding and their wit. . . ./[H]ow vast a difference is there betwixt the productions of those souls, and these of ours? How much better Plato, Aristotle, and the rest . . . understood nature; Thucydides and Herodotus adorned history; Sophocles, Euripides, and Menander advanced poetry, than those dwarfs of wit and learning who succeeded them . . . ?

Ded. *Plutarch*, '83. S-S XVII 5–6

Cf. GOLDEN AGES, a, b. Cf. CHAUCER, c.

Act Division

b. (Eugenius) . . . the distinction of it [Old Comedy] into acts was not known to them [the Ancients] . . .

All we know of it is, from the singing of their Chorus; and that too is so uncertain, that in some of their plays we have reason to conjecture they sung more than five times.

Dram. Poesy, '65. K I 44

PLAY (PARTS).

c. (Eugenius) But . . . when I condemn the Ancients, I declare it is not altogether because they have not five acts to every play, but because they have not confined themselves to one certain number: it is building an house without a model; and when they succeeded in such undertakings, they ought to have sacrificed to Fortune, not to the Muses.

Dram. Poesy, '65. K I 46

Authority [Cf. below, *Imitation of*]

AUTHORITY, a, b.

d. But there are some pedants, who will quote authority from the ancients for the faults and extravagances of some of the moderns . . . I speak with all due reverence to the ancients; for no man esteems their perfections more than myself, though

I confess I have not that blind implicit faith in them which some ignorant schoolmasters would impose upon us . . . [T]o some pedants every thing in them is of . . . authority. . . . I am apt to believe the same faults were found in them, when they wrote, which men of sense find now; but not the excellences which schoolmasters would persuade us: yet I must cry now—

Nobis non licet . . .

Martial, Epigr. ix. 12.

Postscript N and O, '74. S-S XV 408

See below, m. DRYDEN, WORKS, cc. OGILBY. PROSODY, x. DRYDEN, LITERARY LIFE, a. SATIRE, c. ARISTOTLE, b. AUTHORITY, f. Cf. DIALOGUE (GENRE), e.

Characters

e. [¶] For the characters, they are neither so many nor so various in Sophocles and Euripides, as in Shakespeare and Fletcher . . .

Heads of an Answer, '77. S-S XV 388

Chorus

RYMER, e.

Comedy

f. (Eugenius) [¶] Among their comedies, we find a scene or two of tenderness . . . but to speak generally, their lovers say little, when they see each other, but *anima mea, vita mea* . . .

Dram. Poesy, '65. K I 54

HUMORS, b.

Drama (GENERAL)

g. (Eugenius) . . . I never judged the plays of the Greek or Roman poets comparable to ours . . .

Dram. Poesy, '65. K I 34

h. (Crites) [¶] But if we will allow the Ancients to have contrived well, we must acknowledge them to have writ better . . .¹ I can never see one of those plays which are now written, but it increases my admiration of the Ancients.

Dram. Poesy, '65. K I 41–42

i. (Eugenius) . . . tragedies and comedies were not writ then as they are now, promiscuously, by the same person; but he who found his genius bending to the one, never attempted the other way. . . . the sock and buskin were not worn by the same poet.

Dram. Poesy, '65. K I 50

Imitation of [Cf. above, *Authority*]

j. (Crites) . . . we do not only build upon their foundation, but by their models.

Dram. Poesy, '65. K I 36

IMITATION OF MODELS, a.

k. (Crites) Those Ancients have been faithful imitators and wise observers of that Nature which is so torn and ill represented in our plays; they have handed down to us a perfect resemblance of her; which we, like ill copiers, neglecting to look on, have rendered monstrous, and disfigured.

Dram. Poesy, '65. K I 38

JONSON, e, f.

k-2. (Crites) . . . whether you consider the bad plays of our age, or regard the good ones of the last, both the best and worst of the modern poets will equally instruct you to esteem the Ancients.

Dram. Poesy, '65. K I 43

l. (Crites) Yet in the mean time, we are not to conclude any thing rashly against those great men, but preserve to them the dignity of masters, and give that honour to their memories, *quos Libitina sacravit,* part of which we expect may be paid to us in future times.

Dram. Poesy, '65. K I 55

JONSON, a. ENGLISH DRAMA, b. RYMER, c.

m. It remains that I acquaint the reader, that I have endeavoured in this play [*All for Love*] to follow the practice of the Ancients, who, as Mr. Rymer has judiciously observed, are and ought to be our masters. Horace likewise gives it for a rule in his art of poetry—

. . . Vos exemplaria Græca
. . . .

Yet, though their models are regular, they are too little for English tragedy; which requires to be built in a larger compass.

Pref. *All for Love,* '78. K I 200

SHAKESPEARE, f. OGILBY. Cf. BOILEAU, b.

n. The Method which you have taken [apparently in a projected preface Walsh was preparing for a play of Dryden's (*Love Triumphant?*) See Ward, p. 167 n.], is wonderfully good; & not onely all present Poets, but all who are to come in England, will thanke you for freeing them from the too servile imitation of the Ancients. [See ENGLISH VS. FRENCH]

Letter to Walsh, 12 December 1693. Ward No. 28, p. 61

Liaison

o. (Eugenius) [¶] 'Tis true, they [the Ancients] have kept the continuity, or, as you called it, *liaison des scenes,* somewhat better [than unity of place] . . .

Dram. Poesy, '65. K I 49

Love

p. (Eugenius) . . . for love-scenes, you will find few among them; their tragic poets dealt not with that soft passion, but with lust, cruelty, revenge, ambition, and those bloody actions they produced; which were more capable of raising horror than compassion in an audience: leaving love untouched, whose gentleness would have tempered them, which is the most frequent of all the passions . . .

Dram. Poesy, '65. K I 54

q. (Crites) Homer described his heroes men of great appetites, lovers of beef broiled upon the coals, and good fellows; contrary to the practice of the French Romances, whose heroes neither eat, nor drink, nor sleep, for love. Virgil makes Æneas a bold avower of his own virtues:

Sum pius Æneas . . .

which in the civility of our poets is the character of a fanfaron or Hector: for with us the knight takes occasion to walk out, or sleep, to avoid the vanity of telling his own story, which the trusty squire is ever to perform for him. So in their love-scenes . . . the Ancients were more hearty, we more talkative: they writ love as it was then the mode to make it . . .

Dram. Poesy, '65. K I 55

Enguish Drama, a. Love.

Poetic Justice

r. (Eugenius) . . . as they [the Ancients] have failed both in laying of their plots, and managing of them, swerving from the rules of their own art by misrepresenting Nature to us, in which they have ill satisfied one intention of a play, which was delight; so in the instructive part they have erred worse: instead of punishing vice and rewarding virtue, they have often shown a prosperous wickedness, and an unhappy piety: they have set before us a bloody image of revenge in Medea . . . a Priam and Astyanax murdered, and Cassandra ravished, and the lust and murder ending in the victory of him who acted them: in short, there is no indecorum in any of our modern plays, which if I would

excuse, I could not shadow with some authority from the Ancients.

Dram. Poesy, '65. K I 50

Plots

s. (Eugenius) . . . for the plot . . . in their tragedies it was only some tale derived from Thebes or Troy . . . which was worn so threadbare . . . that before it came upon the stage, it was already known to all the audience . . .[1] [T]hey had still the *chapon bouillé* set before them till their appetites were cloyed with the same/ dish . . .

Dram. Poesy, '65. K I 46–47

t. (Eugenius) [¶] These [the Roman] are plots built after the Italian mode of houses; you see through them all at once: the characters are indeed the imitations of Nature, but so/narrow, as if they had imitated only an eye or an hand, and did not dare to venture on the lines of a face, or the proportion of a body.

Dram. Poesy, '65. K I 47–48

Fable, b. See below, v. English Drama, a, c, g. Fable, f. Aristotle, b.

Thoughts and Words

English Drama, h.

Tragedy

Rhyme (Debate), x.

u. He who undertakes to answer this excellent critique of Mr. Rymer, in behalf of our English poets against the Greek, ought to do it in this manner: either by yielding to him the greatest part of what he contends for, which consists in this, that the μῦθος, *i.e.* the design and conduct of it, is more conducing in the Greeks to those ends of tragedy, which Aristotle and he propose, namely, to cause terror and pity; yet the granting this does not set the Greeks above the English poets.

Heads of an Answer, '77. S-S XV 381

ARISTOTLE, e.

v. [¶] Next show in what ancient tragedy was deficient; for example, in the narrowness of its plots, and fewness of persons; and try whether that be not a fault in the Greek poets, and whether their excellency was so great, when the variety was visibly so little; or whether what they did was not very easy to do.

Heads of an Answer, '77. S-S XV 382
TRAGEDY, d. ENGLISH DRAMA, g. TRAGEDY, g.

w. But the Athenian theatre (whether more perfect than ours, is not now disputed) had a perfection differing from ours. You see there in every act a single scene (or two at most), which manage [*sic*] the business of the play; and after that succeeds the chorus, which commonly takes up more time in singing than there has been employed in speaking. The principal person appears almost constantly through the play; but the inferior parts seldom above once in the whole tragedy. The conduct of our stage is much more difficult, where we are obliged never to lose any considerable character which we have once presented. Custom likewise has obtained that we must form an under-plot of second persons, which must be depending on the first; and their by-walks must be like those in a labyrinth, which all of them lead into the great parterre . . . Perhaps, after all, if we could think so, the ancient method, as it is the easiest, is also the most natural, and the best. For variety, as it is managed, is too/often subject to breed distraction; and while we would please too many ways, for want of art in the conduct, we please in none.

Pref. *Œdipus,* '79. S-S VI 133–34

Unity of Action
UNITIES (DRAMATIC), ACTION, g.
Unity of Place

x. (Eugenius) But . . . give me leave to tell you, that the Unity of Place, however it might be practised by them, was never any of their rules: we neither find it in Aristotle, Horace, or any who have written of it, till in our age the French poets first made it a precept of the stage.

Dram. Poesy, '65. K I 48
DRYDEN, WORKS, 111.
Unity of Time
EURIPIDES
Verse
RHYME (DEBATE), k.
Versus Moderns
MODERNS, f. HORACE AND JUVENAL AND PERSIUS, k. ENGLISH DRAMA, i. FRENCH vs. ENGLISH, k. SHAKESPEARE, i. PROSODY, y. FONTENELLE, b.
Wit

y. (Crites) Doubtless many things [in the works of the Ancients] appear flat to us, whose wit depended on some custom or story, which never came to our knowledge . . .

Dram. Poesy, '65. K I 42

Anonymity

[¶] True it is, that some bad poems, though not all, carry their owners' marks about them. There is some peculiar awkwardness, false grammar, imperfect sense, or, at the least, obscurity; some brand or other on this buttock, or that ear, that 'tis notorious who are the owners of the cattle, though they should not sign it with their names.

Discourse of Satire, '93. K II 24
CRITICASTERS, j.

Anthology, Greek
EPIC, j.

Antony and Cleopatra

[¶] The death of Antony and Cleopatra is a subject which has been treated by the greatest wits of our nation, after Shakespeare . . . I doubt not but the same motive has prevailed with all of us in this attempt; I mean the excellency of the moral: for the chief persons represented were famous patterns of unlawful love; and their end accordingly was unfortunate.

Pref. *All for Love,* '78. K I 191

Antithesis

Wit, a, e.

Archaisms

a. . . . the refinement of a language principally consists . . . *either in rejecting such old words, or phrases, which are ill sounding, or improper; or in admitting new, which are more proper, more sounding, and more significant.* [See Language]

Def. of the Epilogue, '72. K I 164

North's *Plutarch.* Milton, b. Opera, f. Dryden, Works, bbb. Milton, c.

b. And though, perhaps, the love of their masters may have transported both [Milton and Spenser] too far, in the frequent use of them, yet, in my opinion, obsolete words may then be laudably revived, when either they are more sounding, or more significant, than those in practice; and when their obscurity is taken away, by joining other words to them, which clear the sense; according to the rule of Horace, for the admission of new words. But in both cases a moderation is to be observed in the use of them: for unnecessary coinage, as well as unnecessary revival, runs into affectation; a fault to be avoided on either hand.

Discourse of Satire, '93. K II 29

Dryden, Literary Life, b.

c. One is for raking in Chaucer (our English Ennius) for antiquated words, which are never to be revived, but when sound or significancy is wanting in the present language. But many of his deserve not this redemption, any more than the crowds of men who daily die, or are slain for sixpence in a battle, merit to be restored to life, if a wish could revive them.

Postscript *Æneis,* '97. K II 241

Modernizing.

Ariosto

Heroic Play, c. Supernatural, b.

a. . . . Ariosto neither designed justly, nor observed any unity of action, or compass of time, or moderation in the vastness of his draught; his style is luxurious, without majesty or decency, and his adventures without the compass of nature and possibility.

Discourse of Satire, '93. K II 27

Tasso, b. French Authors, b. Epic, Christian, c. Epic, g. Epic Poet, c.

b. Ariosto, who, with all his faults, must be acknowledged a great poet . . .

Ded. *Æneis,* '97. K II 220

Epic Machines, d.

Aristophanes

Lucian, h.

Aristotle*

Play (Parts)

a. . . . some genius, as universal as Aristotle . . . who can penetrate into all arts and sciences, without the practice of them . . .

[See Critic(s), h]

Pref. *All for Love,* '78. K I 195

See *passim,* Preface to *Troilus and Cres-*

---

* See Marvin T. Herrick, *The Poetics of Aristotle in England* (Cornell Studies in English, XVII), Published for Cornell University by Yale University Press, New Haven, 1930.

sida. See *passim,* Heads of an Answer to Rymer. ANCIENTS, a.

Authority

AUTHORITY, a, b. Cf. POSSIBILITY. DRYDEN, LITERARY LIFE, j.

on *Catastrophe*

b. Aristotle, I acknowledge, has declared that the catastrophe which is made from the change of will is not of the first order of beauty; but it may reasonably be alleged, in defence of this play, as well as of the "Cinna" (which I take to be the very best of Corneille's), that the philosopher, who made the rule, copied all the laws, which he gave for the theatre, from the authorities and examples of the Greek poets, which he had read; and, from their poverty of invention, he could get nothing but mean conclusions of wretched tales: where the mind of the chief actor was, for the most part, changed without art or preparation, only because the poet could not otherwise end his play. Had it been possible for Aristotle to have seen the "Cinna," I am confident he would have altered his opinion, and concluded that a simple change of will might be managed with so much judgment as to render it the most agreeable, as well as the most surprising part of the whole fable, let Dacier, and all the rest of the modern critics, who are too much bigoted to the ancients, contend ever so much to the contrary.

Ded. *Love Triumphant,* '94. S-S VIII 374

Critic

LONGINUS, a.

on *Fault in Art*

RULES, k.

Furor Poeticus

POETRY, b.

on *Imitation*

IMITATION, h.

Institutor of Criticism

CRITICISM, c.

Poetics

RULES, a.

c. (Crites) Of that book which Aristotle has left us, περὶ τῆς Ποιητικῆς, Horace his *Art of Poetry* is an excellent comment, and, I believe, restores to us that Second Book of his concerning *Comedy,* which is wanting in him.

Dram. Poesy, '65. K I 38

UNITIES (DRAMATIC), GENERAL, a. NATURE, c. TRAGEDY, m.

d. Aristotle raised the fabric of his *Poetry* from observation of those things in which Euripides, Sophocles, and Aeschylus pleased: he considered how they raised the passions, and thence has drawn rules for our imitation. From hence have sprung the tropes and figures, for which they wanted a name, who first practised them, and succeeded in them.

Author's Apology, '77. K I 183

Tragedy, Definition of

e. [¶] To make a true judgment in this competition betwixt the Greek poets and the English in tragedy:

. . . .

. . . consider whether Aristotle has made a just definition of tragedy; of its parts, of its ends, and of its beauties; and whether he, having not seen any others but those of Sophocles [Euripides], etc., had, or truly could determine what all the excellences of tragedy are, and wherein they consist.

Heads of an Answer, '77. S-S XV 382

TRAGEDY, a.

Tragedy, Ends

TRAGEDY, f, g.

Tragedy, Preëminence

EPIC VS. TRAGEDY, d, e.

Tragedy, Words
DICTION, a.
Unity of Action
UNITIES (DRAMATIC), ACTION, e.
Unity of Time
UNITIES (DRAMATIC), TIME, e.
Wit
WIT, o.

Art

RHYME (DEBATE), g. RULES, i. Cf. THE-
OCRITUS, a.

Art and Life

a. (Lisideius: in connection with narrations and decorum] . . . a poet in the
description of a beautiful garden, or a
meadow, will please our imagination more
than the place itself can please our sight.
[See *Dram. Poesy, passim.*]
   Dram. Poesy, '65. K I 63
RHYME (DEBATE), k.

b. But he [Jonson] hath made an ex-
cellent Lazar of it [the fair, *Bartholomew
Fair*]; the copy is of a price, though the
original be vile.
   Defence of An Essay, '68. K I 115
RHYME (DEBATE), aa. See *Defence of
An Essay, passim.*

Arts [See also INVENTORS OF ARTS]

(Lisideius) But the Muses, who ever follow peace, went to plant in another country [than England, i.e., to France].
   Dram. Poesy, '65. K I 56
TRAGEDY, h.

Astrology

I dispute not here the truth or lawfulness
of that art [astrology]; but it is usual
with poets, especially the Italians, to mix
astrology in their poems. Chaucer,
amongst us, is frequent in it: but this revolution [Act IV, sc. ii., of the *Duke of
Guise*] particularly I have taken out of
Luigi Pulci; and there is one almost the

same in Boiardo's *"Orlando Inamorato."*
   Vindication, '83. S-S VII 210
CHAUCER AND OVID.

Audience, Popular [See also HOI POLLOI, VOX POPULI]

DECORUM, b. SPEECHES (DRAMATIC), b.
WIT, e.

a. [I] am often vexed to hear the people laugh, and clap, as they perpetually do,
where I intended 'em no jest; while they
let pass the better things, without taking
notice of them.
   Pref. *Evening's Love,* '71. K I 135

b. The liking or disliking of the people
gives the play the denomination of good or
bad, but does not really make or constitute
it such. To please the people ought to be
the poet's aim, because plays are made for
their delight; but it does not follow that
they are always pleased with good plays,
or that the plays/which please them are always good. The humour of the people is
now for Comedy; therefore, in hope to
please them, I write comedies rather than
serious plays: and so far their taste prescribes to me: but it does not follow from
that reason, that Comedy is to be preferred
before Tragedy in its own nature; for that
which is so in its own nature cannot be
otherwise . . . but the opinion of the people may alter, and in another age, or perhaps in this, serious plays may be set up
above comedies.
   Defence of An Essay, '68. K I 120–21

c. Yet even this [failure of audience to
laugh and be serious in the proper places in
a comedy] confirms me in my opinion of
slighting popular applause, and of con-
temning that approbation which those very
people give, equally with me, to the zany
of a mountebank; or to the appearance of
an antic on the theatre, without wit on the

poet's part, or any occasion of laughter from the actor, besides the ridiculousness of his habit and his grimaces.

Pref. *Evening's Love,* '71. K I 135

d. . . . this very play [*Evening's Love*] would rise up in judgment against me, if I would defend all things I have written to be natural: but I confess I have given too much to the people in it, and am ashamed for them as well as for myself, that I have pleased them at so cheap a rate.

Pref. *Evening's Love,* '71. K I 137

e. Yet since the common audience are much of his [Settle's] level, and both the great vulgar and the small (as Mr. Cowley calls them) are apt to admire what they do not understand (*omne ignotum habent pro magnifico*), and think all which rumbles is heroic, it will be no wonder if he pass for a great author amongst town fools and city wits.

Pref. *N and O,* '74. S-S XV 400

TRAGEDY, e.   CRITIC, h.   PASSIONS, e. BOMBAST, a.   Cf. DRYDEN, WORKS, dd. DRYDEN, WORKS, n.

f. [Speaking of the fustian of Sylvester's *Du Bartas*] . . . yet I dare not answer for an audience, that they would not clap it on the stage: so little value there is to be given to the common cry, that nothing but madness can please madmen, and a poet must be of a piece with the spectators, to gain a reputation with them.

Dedication *Spanish Friar,* '81. K I 247

ACTING AND ACTORS, b.   Cf. TRAGICOMEDY, c.

g. I am accused of ignorance for speaking [in the *Duke of Guise*] of the Third Estate as not sitting in the same house with the other two. Let not those gentlemen mistake themselves; there are many things in plays to be accommodated to the country

in which we live; I spoke to the understanding of an English audience.[1]

Vindication, '83. S-S VII 163

h. Are the audience of a play-house, which are generally persons of honour, noblemen, and ladies, or, at worst, as one of your authors calls his gallants, men of wit and pleasure about the town [Cf. Shadwell's *Epsom Wells.* Scott],—are these the rabble of Mr. Hunt?

Vindication, '83. S-S VII 166

i. To clap and hiss are the privileges of a freeborn subject in a play-house: they buy them with their money, and their hands and mouths are their own property.

Vindication, '83. S-S VII 172

DRYDEN, WORKS, aaa.   DRAMA READ AND ACTED, b.   Cf. TRAGICOMEDY, d.   PURCELL, b.   TRAGICOMEDY, e.   FARCE, d.   Cf. SATIRE, k.   Cf. D'URFEY.   Cf. ENGLISH VS. FRENCH, k.

j. However it be, I dare establish it for a rule of practice on the stage, that we are bound to please those whom we pretend to entertain; and that at any price, religion and good manners only excepted . . . [See POETASTERS] There is a sort of merit in delighting the spectators, which is a name more proper for them, than that of auditors; or else Horace is in the wrong, when he commends Lucilius for it.

Examen Poeticum, '93. K II 7

Cf. ENGLISH VS. FRENCH, v. UNITIES (DRAMATIC), ACTION, g. FARCE, f. DRYDEN, WORKS, gg. PRESENT AGE, p. POET, j. CRITIC, a.

Augustus and the Augustan Age

AUTHORITY, d.   BIOGRAPHY, c.   SENECA, c.   GOLDEN AGES, b.   BOILEAU, b.   SATIRE, z.   POET, b.   HORACE AND JUVENAL AND PERSIUS, a, g.   PROGRESS, e.   POETRY, e. HOMER AND VIRGIL, a.

I doubt not but it was one reason why Augustus should be so passionately concerned for the preservation of the *Æneis,* which its author had condemned to be burnt, as an imperfect poem, by his last will and testament, because it did him a real service, as well as an honour; that a work should not be lost where his divine original was celebrated in verse which had the character of immortality stamped upon it.

Ded. *Æneis,* '97. K II 172

PATRONAGE, c-2, d.

Aurelius (Marcus Aurelius)

. . . Marcus Aurelius, an emperor as clear-sighted as he was truly virtuous; for both which qualities we need not quote Lucian . . . but may securely appeal to Herodian, and to all the historians who have written of him,—besides the testimony of his own admirable works . . .

Life of Lucian, '96. S-S XVIII 72

Authority

a. . . . but he [Howard] must pardon me if I have that veneration for Aristotle, Horace, Ben Johnson, and Corneille, that I dare not serve him in such a cause, and against such heroes, but rather fight under their protection, as Homer reports of little Teucer, who shot the Trojans from under the large buckler of Ajax Telamon . . .

Defence of An Essay, '68. K I 122

b. Those propositions which are laid down in my discourse [*Essay of Dramatic Poesy*] as helps to the better imitation of Nature, are not mine (as I have said), nor were ever pretended so to be, but derived from the authority of Aristotle and Horace, and from the rules and examples of Ben Johnson and Corneille.

Defence of An Essay, '68. K I 125

IPSE DIXIT. ANCIENTS, d.

c. They, who would combat general authority with particular opinion, must first establish themselves a reputation of understanding better than other men.

Author's Apology, '77. K I 182

d. [¶] Virgil and Horace, the severest writers of the severest age, have made frequent use of the hardest metaphors, and of the strongest hyperboles; and in this case the best authority is the best argument; for generally to have pleased, and through all ages, must bear the force of universal tradition. And if you would appeal from thence to right reason, you will gain no more by it in effect, than, first, to set up your reason against those authors; and, secondly, against all those who have admired them.

Author's Apology, '77. K I 183

ARISTOTLE, d. NATURE, c. RULES, c, d. DRYDEN, Works, cc.

e. [Speaking of the fact that in opera the sound is more important than the sense] It appears, indeed, preposterous at first sight, that rhyme, or any consideration, should take place of reason; but, in order to resolve the problem, this fundamental proposition must be settled, that the first inventors of any art or science, provided they have brought it to perfection, are, in reason, to give laws to it; and, according to their model, all after-undertakers are to build. Thus, in Epic Poetry, no man ought to dispute the authority of Homer, who gave the first being to that masterpiece of art, and endued it with that form of perfection in all its parts that nothing was wanting to its excellency. Virgil therefore, and those very few who have succeeded him, endeavoured not to introduce, or innovate, anything in a design already perfected, but imitated the plan of the inventor; and are only so far true heroic poets as they have built on/the foundations of Homer. Thus Pindar, the author of those Odes, which are so admirably restored by Mr. Cowley . . . ought for ever to be the standard of them; and we are bound, according to the practice of Horace and Mr. Cowley, to copy him. Now . . . whosoever undertakes the writing of an opera . . . is obliged to imitate the design of the Italians, who have not yet invented, but brought to perfection, this sort of dramatic musical entertainment.

Pref. *Albion and Albanius,* '85. K I 271–72

Satire, c. Cf. Unities (Dramatic), Action, g.

f. The compositions of the painter should be conformable to the text of ancient authors, to the customs, and the times. And this is exactly the same in Poetry; Homer and Virgil are to be our guides in the Epic; Sophocles and Euripides in Tragedy . . .

Parallel, '95. K II 139

Rules, j.

❧ B ❧

Ballet

Corneille, a-2.

Barclay, Jean

Satire, pp.

Beaumont, Francis

English Drama, d.

Beaumont and Fletcher

(Neander) [¶] Beaumont and Fletcher . . . had, with the advantage of Shakespeare's wit . . . great natural gifts, improved by study: Beaumont especially being so accurate a judge of plays, that Ben Johnson, while he lived, submitted all his writings to his censure, and, 'tis thought, used his judgment in correcting, if not contriving, all his plots. . ./. Their plots were generally more regular than Shakespeare's . . . and they understood and imitated the conversation of gentlemen much better; whose wild debaucheries, and quickness of wit in repartees, no poet can ever paint as they have done. Humour, which Ben Johnson derived from particular persons, they made it not their business to describe: they represented all the passions very lively, but above all, love. I am apt to believe the English language in them arrived to its highest perfection . . . Their plays are now the most pleasant and frequent entertainments of the stage; two of theirs being acted through the year for one of Shakespeare's or Johnson's: the reason is, because there is a certain gaiety in their comedies, and pathos in their more serious plays, which suits generally with all men's humours. Shakespeare's language is likewise a little obsolete, and Ben Johnson's wit comes short of theirs.

Dram. Poesy, '65. K I 80–81

15

COMEDY, f. PLAGIARISM, b. SHAKE-
SPEARE, e. CHARACTER[s], e.

Behn, Aphra

[The translation, in *Ovid's Epistles*]
of *Œnone to Paris* is in Mr. Cowley's way
of imitation only. I was desired to say that
the author, who is of the fair sex, understood not Latin. But if she does not, I am
afraid she has given us occasion to be
ashamed who do.

Pref. *Ovid's Epistles,* '80. K I 243

Bellori, Giovanni Pietro

[¶] In these pompous expressions [K
II 117–23], or such as these, the Italian
has given you his Idea of a Painter; and
though I cannot much commend the style,
I must needs say, there is somewhat in the
matter. Plato himself is accustomed to
write loftily, imitating, as the critics tell us,
the manner of Homer; but surely that inimitable poet had not so much of smoke in
his writing, though not less of fire. But in
short, this is the present genius of Italy.

Parallel, '95, K II 123

CHARACTER[s], c.

Berkenhead, Sir John

WIT, f.

Biography [Cf. HISTORY]

DRYDEN, WORKS, jj.

a. [¶] Biographia, or the history of
particular men's/lives, comes next to be
considered; which in dignity is inferior to
the other two [Commentaries, History],
as being more confined in action . . . All
things here are circumscribed, and driven
to a point, so as to terminate in one; consequently, if the action or counsel were managed by colleagues, some part of it must be
either lame or wanting, except it be supplied by the excursion of the writer.
Herein, likewise, must be less of variety . . .

Yet . . . in pleasure and instruction it
equals, or even excels, both of them. It is
not only commended by ancient practice to
celebrate the memory of great and worthy
men . . . but also the examples of virtue
are of more vigour, when they are thus contracted into individuals. [See UNITIES
(DRAMATIC), ACTION]

"Life of Plutarch," '83. S-S XVII 59–60

b. [¶] Biographia, or the histories of
particular lives, though circumscribed in
the subject, is yet more extensive in the
style than the other two [Commentaries
and History proper] . . . The style of it
is various, according to the occasion. There
are proper places in it for the plainness and
nakedness of narration, which is ascribed
to annals; there is also room . . . for the
loftiness and gravity of general history . . .

"Life of Plutarch," '83. S-S XVII 62

c. But there is withal [in biography]
a descent into minute circumstances, and
trivial passages of life, which are natural to
this way of writing, and which the dignity
of the other two [Commentaries and general History] will not admit. There you
are conducted only into the rooms of state,
here you are led into the private lodgings
of the hero; you see him in his undress, and
are made familiar with his most private actions and conversations. You may behold a
Scipio and a Lælius gathering cockle-shells
on the shore, Augustus playing at bounding-stones with boys, and Agesilaus riding
on a hobby-horse among his children. The
pageantry of life is taken away; you see the
poor reasonable animal as naked as ever
nature made him; are made acquainted
with his passions and his follies, and/find
the demi-god, a man. Plutarch himself has
more than once defended this kind of relat-

ing little passages . . .⁹ [and see IDIOM]
"Life of Plutarch," '83. S-S XVII 62–63
PLUTARCH, f, g.

d. [¶] The writing a life is at all times, and in all circumstances, the most difficult task of an historian; and, notwithstanding the numerous tribe of biographers, we can scarce find one, except Plutarch, who deserves our perusal, or can invite a second view. But if the difficulty be so great where the materials are plentiful, and the incidents extraordinary, what must it be when the person . . . denies matter enough for a page? The learned seldom abound with action, and it is action only that furnishes the historian with things agreeable and instructive.
"Life of Lucian," '96. S-S XVIII 59

Blackmore, Sir Richard

a. The whole Faculty [College of Physicians] has always been ready to oblige me; the only one of/them, who endeavoured to defame me, had it not in his power.
Postscript *Æneis,* '97. K II 244–45
DRYDEN, LITERARY LIFE, o-2

b. [¶] As for the City Bard, or Knight Physician, I hear his quarrel to me is, that I was the author of *Absalom and/Achitophel,* which, he thinks, is a little hard on his fanatic patrons in London.

But I will deal more civilly with his two poems, because nothing ill is to be spoken of the dead; and therefore peace be to the *Manes* of his *Arthurs.* I will only say, that it was not for this noble Knight that I drew the plan of an epic poem on *King Arthur,* in my preface to the translation of Juvenal. The Guardian Angels of kingdoms were machines too ponderous for him to manage; and therefore he rejected them . . .ᴵ yet from that preface he plainly took his hint; for he began immediately upon the

story, though he had the baseness not to acknowledge his benefactor, but instead of it, to traduce me in a libel.
Pref. *Fables,* 1700. K II 271–72
CRITICASTERS, k.

Blank Verse [See PROSODY]

Boccaccio, Giovanni [See CHAUCER AND BOCCACCIO]

He [Boccaccio] and Chaucer, among other things, had this in common, that they refined their mother-tongues; but with this difference, that Dante had begun to file their language, at least in verse, before . . . Boccace, who likewise received no little help from his master Petrarch; but the reformation of their prose was wholly owing to Boccace himself, who is yet the standard of purity in the Italian tongue, though many of his phrases are become obsolete, as in process of time it must/needs happen.
Pref. *Fables,* 1700. K II 248–49
DRYDEN, PERSONAL CHARACTER, e.

Boiardo, Metteo Maria
ASTROLOGY. TASSO, b. EPIC POET, c.

Boileau-Despréaux, Nicolas*

a. . . . amongst the French, the greatest of this age, Boileau and Rapin . . .
Author's Apology, '77. K I 181

b. . . . if I would only cross the seas, I might find in France a living Horace and a Juvenal, in the person of the admirable Boileau; whose numbers are excellent, whose expressions are noble, whose thoughts are just, whose language is pure, whose satire is pointed, and whose sense is close; what he borrows from the Ancients, he repays with usury of his own, in coin as good, and almost as universally valuable:

---

* See John M. Aden, "Dryden and Boileau: The Question of Critical Influence," *SP,* L (1953), 491–509.

for, setting prejudice and partiality apart, though he is our enemy, the stamp of a Louis, the patron of all arts, is not much inferior to the medal of an Augustus Cæsar.

Discourse of Satire, '93. K II 26

EPIC, CHRISTIAN, b. HORACE AND JUVENAL AND PERSIUS, k. SATIRE, c.

c. Boileau, if I am not much deceived, has modelled from hence [*Secchia Rapita* of Tassoni] his famous *Lutrin.* He had read the burlesque poetry of Scarron, with some kind of indignation, as witty as it was, and found nothing in France that was worthy of his imitation; but he copied the Italian so well, that his own may pass for an original. He writes in the French heroic verse, and calls it an heroic poem; his subject is trivial, but his verse is noble. I doubt not but he had Virgil in his eye, for we find many admirable imitations of him, and some parodies . . .[1]/we see Boileau pursuing him . . . and scarcely yielding to his master. This, I think, my Lord, to be the most beautiful, and most noble kind of satire. Here is the majesty of the heroic, finely mixed with the venom of the other; and raising the delight which otherwise would be flat and vulgar, by the sublimity of the expression.

Discourse of Satire, '93. K II 107–8

EPIC, CHRISTIAN, c.

Bombast [See also SUBLIME (FALSE)]

SHAKESPEARE, b. SETTLE, b. Cf. AUDIENCE, e. Cf. EPIC, h. Cf. HEIGHTENING, c. PASSIONS, f. Cf. SHAKESPEARE, r.

a. [Having quoted from the play in *Hamlet*] [¶] What a pudder is here kept in raising the expression of trifling thoughts! Would not a man have thought that the poet had been bound prentice to a wheelwright, for his first rant? and had followed a ragman, for the clout and blanket in the second? . ./. Wise men would be glad to find a little sense couched under all these pompous words; for bombast is commonly the delight of that audience which loves Poetry, but understands it not: and as commonly has been the practice of those writers, who, not being able to infuse a natural passion into the mind, have made it their business to ply the ears, and to stun their judges by the noise. But Shakespeare does not often thus; for the passions in his scene between Brutus and Cassius are extremely natural, the thoughts are such as arise from the matter, the expression of 'em not viciously figurative. I cannot leave this subject, before I do justice to that divine poet, by giving you one of his passionate descriptions: 'tis of Richard the Second when he was deposed, and led in triumph through the streets of London by Henry of Bullingbrook: the painting of it is so lively, and the words so moving, that I have scarce read anything comparable to it in any other language.

Pref. Troilus, '79. K I 225–26

b. [¶] To speak justly of this whole matter: 'tis neither height of thought that is discommended, nor pathetic vehemence, nor any nobleness of expression in its proper place; but 'tis a false measure of all these, something which is like them, and is not them; 'tis the Bristol-stone, which appears like a diamond; 'tis an extravagant thought, instead of a sublime one; 'tis roaring madness, instead of vehemence; and a sound of words, instead of sense.

Pref. Troilus, '79. K I 227.

SHAKESPEARE, g. Cf. CHAPMAN, a. Cf. DRYDEN, WORKS, n. SUBLIME, b. SYLVESTER's *DuBartas.* Cf. ACTING AND ACTORS, b. FIGURES, c. ACTING AND ACTORS, c. CRITIC[s], a.

Booksellers

a. Upon triall I find all of your trade are

Sharpers & you not more than others; therefore I have not wholly left you.

Letter to Tonson, December 1695(?) Ward No. 36, p. 80.

b. [Context: reasons for poor English translations. Booksellers] are persons more devoted to their own gain than the public honour. They are very parsimonious in rewarding the wretched scribblers they employ; and care not how the business is done, so that it be but done. They live by selling titles, not books; and if that carry off one impression, they have their ends, and value not the curses they and their author meet with from the bubbled chapmen.

"Life of Lucian," '96. S-S XVIII 82

Borrowing (Verbal)

a. I wish we might at length leave to borrow words from other nations, which is now a wantonness in us, not a necessity; but so long as some affect to speak them, there will not want others, who will have the boldness to write them.

Ded. *Rival Ladies,* '64. K I 5

Cf. LANGUAGE

b. It is obvious that we have admitted many [new words and phrases], some of which we wanted, and therefore our language is richer for them . . . others are rather ornamental than necessary; yet, by their admission, the language is become more courtly, and our thoughts are better drest. . . . They, who have lately written with most care, have, I believe, taken the rule of Horace for their guide; that is, not to be too hasty in receiving of words, but rather to stay till custom has made them familiar to us:

Quem penes arbitrium est . . .

Defence of the Epilogue, '72. K I 170

GALLICIZING. HORACE, i. ACADEMY, b. Cf. DRYDEN, WORKS, bbb.

c. I will not excuse, but justify myself, for one pretended crime, with which I am liable to be charged by false critics, not only in this translation, but in many of my original poems; that I latinize too much. 'Tis true, that, when I find an English word significant and sounding, I neither borrow from the Latin, nor any other language; but, when I want at home, I must seek abroad.

If sounding words are not of our growth and manufacture, who shall hinder me to import them from a foreign country? I carry not out the treasure of the nation, which is never to return; but what I bring from Italy, I spend in England: here it remains, and here it circulates; for, if the coin be good, it will pass from one hand to another. I trade both with the living and the dead, for the enrichment of our native language. We have enough in England to supply our necessity; but, if we will have things of magnificence and splendour, we must get them by commerce. Poetry requires ornament; and that is not to be had from our old Teuton monosyllables: therefore, if I find any elegant word in a classic author, I propose it to be naturalized, by using it myself; and, if the public approves of it, the bill passes. But every man cannot distinguish between pedantry and poetry: every man, therefore, is not fit to innovate. Upon the whole matter, a poet must first be certain that the word he would introduce is beautiful in the Latin, and is to consider, in the next place, whether it will agree with the English idiom: after this, he ought to take the opinion of judicious friends, such as are learned in both languages: and, lastly, since no man is infallible, let him use this licence very sparingly; for if too many foreign words are poured in upon us, it/looks as if they were designed

not to assist the natives, but to conquer
them.

Ded. *Æneis,* '97. K II 234–35
COINAGE, c.

Bossu, René le

. . . Bossu, the best of modern critics
. . . [See RULES, c.] Pref. *Troilus,* '79.
K I 211

MORAL OF A WORK. PASSIONS, e. EPIC VS.
TRAGEDY, d. EPIC, c. UNITIES (DRA-
MATIC), GENERAL, e. STATIUS, c. EPIC
VS. TRAGEDY, j. ENGLISH VS. FRENCH, m.
["Spenser wanted only to have read the
rules of Bossu . . ."]

**Buckingham (George Villiers, Second
Duke of)**

Tis a strange quality in a man to love
idlenesse so well as to destroy his Estate by
it; and yet at the same time to pursue so
violently the most toilesome, and most unpleasant part of businesse. [See SAT-
IRE, q]

Letter to Rochester, '73. Ward No. 4, p. 9
DRYDEN, LITERARY LIFE, d, e. SATIRE, b.

Burlesque

a. . . . the images of the Burlesque,
which is contrary to this [i.e., heroic po-
etry] . . . beget laughter: for the one
shows nature beautified, as in the picture
of a fair woman, which we all admire; the
other shows her deformed, as in that of a
Lazar, or of a fool with distorted face and
antic gestures, at which we cannot forbear
to laugh, because it is a deviation from Nature.

Pref. *Annus Mirabilis,* '66. K I 18

b. Of the same manner [as that in the
Greek *silli*] are our songs, which are
turned into burlesque, and the serious
words of the author perverted into a ridiculous meaning.[1]

Discourse of Satire, '93. K II 52
BUTLER, b. PROSODY, m. BOILEAU, c.

Busby, Richard

Cf. PROSODY, n.

a. . . . I have no fault to find with my
sonns punishment; for that is and ought to
be reserv'd to any Master, much more to
you who have been his fathers. . . . My
first rash resolutions were to have brought
things past any composure, by immediately
sending for my sonns things/out of the
College: but upon recollection I find I
have a double tye upon me not to do it. one
my obligations to you for my Education:
another my great tendernesse of doeing
anything offensive to my Lord Bishop of
Rochester, as cheife Governour of the College.

Letter to the Reverend Mr. Busby, '82.
Ward No. 9, pp. 18–19.
DRYDEN, LIFE, a.

b. [¶] The judicious *Casaubon,* in his
Proem to this Satyr [Persius's Fifth]
tells us, that *Aristophanes* the Gramma-
rian, being ask'd, what Poem of *Archilochus* his Iambicks he preferr'd before the
rest, answer'd, the longest. His answer may
justly be apply'd to this Fifth Satyr; which,
being of greater length than any of the rest,
is also, by far, the most instructive. For
this Reason, I have selected it from all the
others; and inscrib'd it to my Learned
Master Doctor *Busby;* to whom I am not
only oblig'd my self, for the best part of my
own Education, and that of my two Sons;
but have also receiv'd from him the first
and truest Taste of *Persius.* May he be
pleas'd to find in this Translation, the
Gratitude, or at least some small Acknowledgment of his unworthy Scholar, at the
distance of 42 Years, from the time when I
departed from under his Tuition.

Argument of the Fifth Satyr [Per-
sius], '93. JK II 771
DRYDEN, WORKS, yyy.

Butler, Samuel

a. Tis enough for one Age to have neglected Mr Cowley, and sterv'd Mr Buttler . . .

Letter to Lawrence Hyde, 1683. Ward
No. 10, p. 21

b. The sort of verse which is called *burlesque,* consisting of eight syllables, or four
feet, is that which our excellent Hudibras
has chosen. . . . The worth of his poem is
too well known to need my commendation,
and he is above my censure. His satire is of
the Varronian kind, though unmixed with
prose. The choice of his numbers is suitable enough to his design, as he has managed it; but in any other hand, the shortness of his verse, and the quick returns of
rhyme, had debased the dignity of style.
And besides, the double rhyme, (a necessary companion of burlesque writing,) is
not so proper for manly satire; for it turns
earnest too much to jest, and gives us a boyish kind of pleasure. It tickles awkwardly
with a kind of pain . . . we are pleased
ungratefully, and . . . against our liking.
We thank him not for giving us that unseasonable delight, when we know he could
have given us a better, and more solid.
He/might have left that task to others,
who, not being able to put in thought, can
only make us grin with the excrescence of
a word of two or three syllables in the close.
'Tis, indeed, below so great a master to
make use of such a little instrument. But
his good sense is perpetually shining
through all he writes; it affords us not the
time of finding faults. We pass through the
levity of his rhyme, and are immediately
carried into some admirable useful thought.
After all, he has chosen this kind of verse,
and has written the best in it: and had he
taken another, he would always have excelled . . .

Discourse of Satire, '93. K II 105–6

Camoens, Luiz de

. . . Camoens, the author of the *Lusiads,*
ought to be censured by all his readers,
when he brings in Bacchus and Christ into
the same adventure of his fable. [See Poetic License, f]

Author's Apology, '77. K I 190

Caro, Hannibal

Hannibal Caro's [translation], in the
Italian, is the nearest, the most poetical,
and the most sonorous of any translation
of the *Æneids;* yet, though he takes the advantage of blank verse, he commonly allows two lines for one of Virgil, and does
not always hit his sense.

Pref. *Sylvæ,* '85. K I 256

DRYDEN, WORKS, oo. MILTON, c.
TRANSLATION, gg. PROSODY, hh. DRYDEN,
LITERARY LIFE, i.

Casaubon, Isaac

a. [Casaubon] is a vehement friend to
any author with whom he has taken any
pains; and his partiality to Persius, in opposition to Juvenal, is too fresh in my
memory to be forgotten.

"Character of Polybius," '93. S-S
XVIII 47

Satire, v, g, hh.

b. This passage of Diomedes has also drawn Dousa, the son, into the same error of Casaubon, which I say, not to expose the little failings of those judicious men, but only to make it appear, with how much diffidence and caution we are to read their works, when they treat a subject of so much obscurity, and so very ancient, as is this of Satire.

Discourse of Satire, '93. K II 64.

Persius, b. Scaliger, b. Persius, h. Satire, k. Persius, i.

c. [¶] The Commentatours before *Casaubon,* were ignorant of our Author's secret meaning [i.e., of Persius, the Fourth Satire]; and thought he had only written against Young Noblemen in General . . . But this Excellent Scholiast has unravell'd the whole Mystery: And made it apparent, that the Sting of this Satyr, was particularly aim'd at *Nero.*

Argument of the Fourth Satire [Persius], '93. JK II 766

Busby, b.

Catachresis

Poetaster[s], c. Cf. Cleveland, a.

(Eugenius) 'Tis true, no poet but may sometimes use a catachresis: Virgil does it —. . .¹ And Ovid . . .¹ But to do this always . . . though it may be admired by some few pedants, will not pass upon those who know that wit is best conveyed to us in the most easy language . . . but we cannot read a verse of Cleveland's without making a face at it, as if every word were a pill to swallow: he gives us many times a hard nut to break our teeth, without a kernel for our pains.

Dram. Poesy, '65. K I 52

Shakespeare, r.

Catastrophe [See also Deus ex Machina]

Play (Parts). Fletcher, e. Tragedy,

q. Dryden, Works, kkk. Aristotle, b. Cf. Character[s], c. Cf. Dryden, Works, gg.

Catullus, Caius Valerius

Dryden, Works, y. Obscenity, c. Chaucer, c. [Mistaken for Martial: see K II, note to p. 258] Poet, e.

Censorship

Dorset, d.

Chapelain, Jean

Prosody, gg. French Authors, b. Epic Poets, c.

Chapman, George

Prosody, gg.

a. I have sometimes wondered, in the reading, what was become of those glaring colours which amazed me in *Bussy D'Amboys* upon the theatre; but when I had taken up what I supposed a fallen star, I found I had been cozened with a jelly; nothing but a cold, dull mass, which glittered no longer than it was shooting; a dwarfish thought, dressed up in gigantic words, repetition in abundance, looseness of expression, and gross hyperboles; the sense of one line expanded prodigiously into ten; and, to sum up all, uncorrect English, and a hideous mingle of false poetry, and true nonsense; or, at best, a scantling of wit, which lay gasping for life, and groaning beneath a heap of rubbish. A famous modern poet used to sacrifice every year a Statius to Virgil's *Manes;* and I have indignation enough to burn a *D'Amboys* annually, to the memory of Johnson.

Ded. *Spanish Friar,* '81. K I 246

Translation, c. Prosody, ii.

b. The Earl of Mulgrave and Mr. Waller, two of the best judges of our age, have assured me, that they could never read over the translation of Chapman [Homer] without incredible pleasure and extreme transport. This admiration

. . . must needs proceed from the author himself; for the translator has thrown him down as low as harsh numbers, improper English, and a monstrous length of verse could carry him.

Ded. *Examen Poeticum,* '93. K II 14
PROSODY, jj.

Character[s] (Cf. DRAMATIS PERSONAE)
RHYME, e.   TRAGEDY, n.   COMEDY, e.
SETTLE, b. Cf. TRAGEDY, m. MANNERS, b.

a. [¶] From the manners, the characters of persons are derived; for, indeed, the characters are no other than the inclinations, as they appear in the several persons of the poem; a character being thus defined,—that which distinguishes one man from another.

Pref. *Troilus,* '79. K I 215

b. A character, or that which [by definition] distinguishes one man from all others, cannot be supposed to consist of one particular virtue, or vice, or passion only; but 'tis a composition of qualities which are not contrary to one another in the same person . . .[1] yet it is still to be observed, that one virtue, vice, and passion, ought to be shown in every man, as predominant over all the rest . . .[1]

Pref. *Troilus,* '79. K I 215

SHAKESPEARE, p, l, r. PASSIONS, f. SU-
PERNATURAL,   g.   SHAKESPEARE   AND
FLETCHER, b.

c. [¶] The business of his [Bellori's] preface is to prove that a learned painter should form to himself an idea of perfect nature. . . . and to draw from thence . . . the beauties which are to enter into his work; thereby correcting Nature from what she actually is in individuals, to what she ought to be, and what she was created. Now, as this idea of perfection is of little use in portraits . . . so neither is it in the characters of Comedy and Tragedy,

which are never to be made perfect, but always to be drawn with some specks of frailty and deficience; such as they have been described to us in history, if they were real characters, or such as the poet began to shew them at their first appearance, if they were only fictitious or imaginary. The perfection of such stage-characters consists chiefly in their likeness to the deficient faulty nature, which is their original; only . . . in such cases there will always be found a better likeness and a worse, and the better is constantly to be chosen; I mean in tragedy, which represents the figures of the highest form amongst mankind. Thus in portraits, the painter will not take that side of the face which has some notorious blemish in it; but either draw it in profile . . .[1] or else shadow the more imperfect side. For an ingenious flattery is to be allowed to the professors of both arts, so long as the likeness is not destroyed. 'Tis/ true, that all manner of imperfections must not be taken away from the characters . . . that there may be left some grounds of pity for their misfortunes. We can never be grieved for their miseries who are thoroughly wicked, and have thereby justly called their calamities on themselves. . . .[1] If, on the other side, their characters were wholly perfect (such as, for example, the character of a saint or martyr in a play), his or her misfortunes would produce impious thoughts in the beholders . . .[1] In this I have accused myself for my own *St. Catherine;* but let truth prevail. Sophocles has taken the just medium in his *Œdipus* . . .[1] In Comedy there is somewhat more of the worse likeness to be taken, because that is often to produce laughter, which is occasioned by the sight of some deformity; but for this I refer the reader to Aristotle. 'Tis a sharp manner of instruction for the vulgar, who are never well amended till they are more than sufficiently exposed.

Parallel, '95. K II 125–26

d. [¶] But besides the outlines of the posture, the design of the picture comprehends, in the next place, the forms of faces, which are to be different; and so in a poem or/a play must the several characters of the persons be distinguished from each other. I knew a poet, whom out of respect I will not name, who, being too witty himself, could draw nothing but wits in a comedy of his; even his fools were infected with the disease of their author. They overflowed with smart reparties, and were only distinguished from the intended wits by being called coxcombs, though they deserved not so scandalous a name. Another [Lee: Ker],[1] who had a great genius for Tragedy, following the fury of his natural temper, made every man, and woman too, in his plays, stark raging mad . . .[1]

Parallel, '95. K II 141–42

e. Du Fresnoy tells us, *That the figures of the groups must not be all on a side, that is, with their face and bodies all turned the same way; but must contrast each other by their several positions.* Thus in a play, some characters must be raised, to oppose others, and to set them off the better; according to the old maxim, *contraria juxta se posita magis elucescunt.* Thus, in *The Scornful Lady,* the usurer is set to confront the prodigal: thus, in my *Tyrannic Love,* the atheist Maximin is opposed to the character of St. Catherine.

Parallel, '95. K II 147

PRESENT AGE, p. Cf. EPIC HERO, f. Cf. CHAUCER, e.

Charles II

RESTORATION. EPIC, l. DRYDEN, WORKS, i. DECORUM, f. DRYDEN, LITERARY LIFE,

m. CONVERSATION, b. DRYDEN, LITERARY LIFE, k. DRYDEN, WORKS, s, x. Cf. TRANSLATION, w. DRYDEN, WORKS, xx-2. DRYDEN, LITERARY LIFE, l. Cf. CRITIC[s], f. PARONOMASIA, b.

Chaucer*

ACADEMY, b. Cf. ASTROLOGY. DRYDEN, LITERARY LIFE, b.

a. . . . Chaucer (our English Ennius) . . . [See ARCHAISMS, c] Postscript *Æneis,* '97. K II 241

Cf. PEPYS. MILTON, d.

b. . . . having done with Ovid for this time, it came into my mind, that our old English poet, Chaucer, in many things resembled him, and that with no disadvantage on the side of the modern author . . . and as I am, and always have been, studious to promote the honour of my native country, so I soon resolved/to put their merits to the trial, by turning some of the *Canterbury Tales* into our language, as it is now refined . . . [I]f I seem partial to my countryman, and predecessor in the laurel, the friends of antiquity are not few . . .

Pref. *Fables,* 1700. K II 247–48

BOCCACCIO. RYMER, g. TURNS, b.

c. It remains that I say somewhat of Chaucer in particular.

In the first place, as he is the father of English poetry, so I hold him in the same degree of veneration as the Grecians held Homer, or the Romans Virgil. He is a perpetual fountain of good sense; learn'd in all/sciences; and, therefore, speaks properly on all subjects. As he knew what to say, so he knows also when to leave off; a

---

* See Caroline F. E. Spurgeon, *Five Hundred Years of Chaucer Criticism and Allusion* (1375–1900) [Chaucer Society, 2nd ser., 48], London, 1914.

continence which is practised by few writers, and scarcely by any of the ancients, excepting Virgil and Horace. . . . [See Cowley]

Chaucer followed Nature everywhere, but was never so bold to go beyond her; and there is a great difference of being *poeta* and *nimis poeta,* if we may believe Catullus, as much as betwixt a modest behaviour and affectation. The verse of Chaucer, I confess, is not harmonious to us; but 'tis like the eloquence of one whom Tacitus commends, it was *auribus istius temporis accommodata:* they who lived with him, and some time after him, thought it musical; and it continues so even in our judgment, if compared with the numbers of Lidgate and Gower, his contemporaries: there is the rude sweetness of a Scotch tune in it, which is natural/and pleasing, though not perfect. 'Tis true, I cannot go so far as he [Speght] who published the last edition of him; for he would make us believe the fault is in our ears, and that there were really ten syllables in a verse where we find but nine: but this opinion is not worth confuting; 'tis so gross and obvious an error, that common sense (which is a rule in everything but matters of Faith and Revelation) must convince the reader, that equality of numbers, in every verse which we call *heroic,* was either not known, or not always practised, in Chaucer's age. It were an easy matter to produce some thousands of his verses, which are lame for want of half a foot, and sometimes a whole one, and which no pronunciation can make otherwise. We can only say, that he lived in the infancy of our poetry, and that nothing is brought to perfection at the first. We must be children before we grow men. There was an Ennius, and in process of

time a Lucilius, and a Lucretius, before Virgil and Horace; even after Chaucer there was a Spenser, a Harrington, a Fairfax, before Waller and Denham were in being; and our numbers were in their nonage till these last appeared.

Pref. *Fables,* 1700. K II 257–59

d. As for the religion of our poet, he seems to have some little bias towards the opinions of Wickliff, after John of Gaunt his patron; somewhat of which appears in the tale of *Piers Plowman* [i.e., The Ploughman's Tale: Ker]: yet I cannot blame him for inveighing so sharply against the vices of the clergy in his age: their pride, their ambition, their pomp, their avarice, their worldly interest, deserved the lashes which he gave them, both in that, and in most of his *Canterbury Tales.*

Pref. *Fables,* 1700. K II 260

e. [¶] He must have been a man of a most wonderful comprehensive nature, because, as it has been truly observed of him, he has taken into the compass of his *Canterbury Tales* the various manners and humours (as we now call them) of the whole English nation, in his age. Not a single character has escaped him. All his pilgrims are severally distinguished from each other; and not only in their inclinations, but in their very physiognomies and persons. Baptista Porta could not have described their natures better . . . The matter and manner of their tales, and of their telling, are so suited to their different educations, humours, and callings, that each of them would be improper in any other mouth. Even the grave and serious characters are distinguished by their several sorts of gravity: their discourses are such as belong to their age, their calling, and their breeding . . .[1] Even the ribaldry of the low characters is different: the Reeve, the Miller, and the Cook, are several men, and distinguished from each other as much as the mincing Lady-Prioress and the broad-speaking, gap-toothed Wife of Bath. But enough of this; there is such a variety of game springing up before me, that I am distracted in my choice, and know not which to follow. 'Tis sufficient to say according to the proverb, that here is God's plenty.

Pref. *Fables,* 1700. K II 262
DRYDEN, PERSONAL CHARACTER, e.

f. You have here [lines 725–742] a *Specimen* of Chaucer's language, which is so obsolete, that his sense is scarce to be understood; and you have likewise more than one example of his unequal numbers . . . Yet many of his verses consist of ten syllables, and the words not much behind our present English . . .[1]

Pref. *Fables,* 1700. K II 264

g. I find some people are offended that I have turned these tales into modern English; because they think them unworthy of my pains, and look on Chaucer as a dry, old-fashioned wit, not worth reviving. . ./.[1] [See COWLEY, j] Chaucer, I confess, is a rough diamond, and must first be polished ere he shines. I deny not likewise, that, living in our early days of poetry, he writes not always of a piece; but sometimes mingles trivial things with those of greater moment. Sometimes also, though not often, he runs riot, like Ovid, and knows not when he has said enough. But there are more great wits besides Chaucer, whose fault is their excess of conceits, and those ill sorted. An author is not to write all he can, but only all he ought. Having observed this redundancy in Chaucer, (as

it is an easy matter for a man of ordinary parts to find a fault in one of greater,) I have not tied myself to a literal translation . . .[1] [See TRANSLATION, p]

Pref. *Fables,* 1700. K II 264–65
MODERNIZING. OBSCENITY, f.

h. [¶] I prefer, in our countryman, far above all his other stories, the noble poem of Palamon and Arcite, which is/of the epic kind, and perhaps not much inferior to the *Ilias,* or the *Æneis.* The story is more pleasing than either of them, the manners as perfect, the diction as poetical, the learning as deep and various, and the disposition full as artful: only it includes a greater length of time, as taking up seven years at least; but Aristotle has left undecided the duration of the action; which yet is easily reduced into the compass of a year, by a narration of what preceded the return of Palamon to Athens. I had thought, for the honour of our narration, and more particularly for his, whose laurel, though unworthy, I have worn after him, that this story was of English growth, and Chaucer's own: but I was undeceived by Boccace . . .[1] [However] I question not but the poem has received many beauties, by passing through his [Chaucer's] noble hands.

Pref. *Fables,* 1700. K II 269–70
FLOWER AND THE LEAF.

Chaucer and Boccaccio

[¶] Boccace comes last to be considered, who, living in the same age with Chaucer, had the same genius, and followed the same studies. Both writ novels, and each of them cultivated his mother tongue. But the greatest resemblance . . . being in their familiar style, and pleasing way of relating comical adventures, I may pass it over, because I have translated nothing from Boccace of that nature. In the serious part of poetry, the advantage is wholly on Chaucer's side; for though the Englishman has borrowed many tales from the Italian, yet it appears, that those of Boccace were not generally of his own making . . . so that what there was of invention, in either/of them, may be judged equal. But Chaucer has refined on Boccace, and has mended the stories, which he has borrowed, in his way of telling; though prose allows more liberty of thought, and the expression is more easy when unconfined by numbers. Our countryman carries weight, and yet wins the race at disadvantage.

Pref. *Fables,* 1700. K II 268–69

Chaucer and Ovid

CHAUCER, b.

With Ovid ended the golden age of the Roman tongue; from Chaucer the purity of the English tongue began. The manners of the poets were not unlike. Both of them were well-bred, well-natured, amorous, and libertine, at least in their writings, it may be also in their lives. Their studies were the same, philosophy and philology. Both of them were knowing in astronomy . . .[1] But Chaucer was likewise an astrologer, as were Virgil, Horace, Persius, and Manilius. Both writ with wonderful facility and clearness; neither were great inventors . ./.[1] the genius of our countrymen in general being rather to improve an invention than to invent themselves . . . [See PREFACES, d]

Both of them built on the inventions of other men; yet since Chaucer had something of his own, as the Wife of Bath's Tale, the *Cock and the Fox* . . . and some others, I may justly give our countryman the precedence in that part . . . Both of

them understood the manners [*q.v.*] . . .[1]/Yet even there too the figures of Chaucer are much more lively, and set in a better light . . . The thoughts and words remain to be considered . . . and I have saved myself one-half of the labour, by owning that Ovid lived when the Roman tongue was at its meridian; Chaucer, in the dawning of our language: therefore that part of the comparison stands not on an equal foot, any more than the diction of Ennius and Ovid, or of Chaucer and our present English. . . . The thoughts remain . . . and they are to be measured only by their propriety; that is, as they flow more or less naturally from the persons described, on such and such occasions. The vulgar judges, which are nine parts in ten of all nations, who call conceits and jingles wit, who see Ovid full of them, and Chaucer altogether without them, will think me little less than mad for preferring the Englishman to the Roman. Yet, with their leave, I must presume to say, that the things they admire are only glittering trifles, and so far from being witty, that in a serious poem they are nauseous, because they are unnatural. . . .[1] On these occasions the poet should endeavour to raise pity; but, instead of/this, Ovid is tickling you to laugh. Virgil never made use of such machines when he was moving you to commiserate the death of Dido . . . Chaucer makes Arcite violent in his love, and unjust in the pursuit of it; yet, when he came to die, he made him think more reasonably . . .[1] What would Ovid have done on this occasion? He would certainly have made Arcite witty on his deathbed; he had complained he was further off from possession, by being so near, and a thousand such boyisms, which Chaucer rejected as below

27

the dignity of the subject. They who think otherwise, would, by the same reason, prefer Lucan and Ovid to Homer and Virgil, and Martial to all four of them. As for the turn of words, in which Ovid particularly excels all poets, they are sometimes a fault, and sometimes a beauty, as they are used properly or improperly; but in strong passions always to be shunned, because passions are serious, and will admit no playing. The French have a high value for them; and, I confess, they are often what they call delicate, when they are introduced with judgment; but Chaucer writ with more simplicity, and followed Nature more closely, than to use them.

Pref. *Fables,* 1700. K II 254–57

CHAUCER, g.

Chiaroscuro

RHYME (DEBATE), q. Cf. TRANSLATION, x. PROSODY, v. Cf. SATIRE, b. EXPRESSION, b.

[¶] The lights and shadows which belong to colouring put me in mind of that verse in Horace:

Hoc amat obscurum, vult hoc sub luce videri.

Some parts of a poem require to be amply written, and with all the force and elegance of words; others must be cast into shadows, that is, passed over in silence, or but faintly touched. This belongs wholly to the judgment of the poet and the painter. The most beautiful parts of the picture, and the poem, must be the most finished, the colours and words most chosen; many things in both, which are not deserving of this care, must be shifted off; content with vulgar expressions, and those very short, and left, as in a shadow, to the imagination of the reader.

Parallel, '95. K II 151

Chorus

ANCIENTS, w. RYMER, e.

a. For if we, or our greater fathers, have not yet brought the drama to an absolute perfection, yet at least we have carried it much further than those ancient Greeks; who, beginning from a Chorus, could never totally exclude it, as we have done; who find it an unprofitable encumbrance, without any necessity of entertaining it amongst us, and without the possibility of establishing it here, unless it were supported by a public charge.

Ded. *Examen Poeticum,* '93. K II 6

UNITIES (DRAMATIC), GENERAL, e. EPIC, b.

b. [¶] The Grecian Tragedy was at first nothing but a chorus of singers; afterwards one actor was introduced, which was the poet himself, who entertained the people with a discourse in verse, betwixt the pauses of the singing. This succeeding . . . more actors were added, to make the variety the greater; and, in process of time, the chorus only sung betwixt the acts, and the Coryphæus, or chief of them, spoke for the rest, as an actor concerned in the business of the play.

Parallel, '95. K II 143

c. But as a good picture may be without a group, so a good tragedy may subsist without a chorus, notwithstanding . . . Dacier to the contrary.

Parallel, '95. K II 144

RACINE, b.

d. . . . [a chorus] is impracticable on our stage. A new theatre, much more ample and much deeper, must be made for that purpose, besides the cost of sometimes forty or fifty habits, which is an expence too large to be supplied by a company of actors. 'Tis true, I should not be sorry to see a chorus on a theatre more than as large and as deep again as ours, built and adorned at a king's charges; and on that condition, and another, which is, that my hands were not bound behind me, as now they are, I should not despair of making such a tragedy as might be both instructive and delightful, according to the manner of the Grecians.

Parallel, '95. K II 144

Chudleigh, Lady Mary

[¶] You were no sooner gone, but I felt in my pocket, & found my Lady Chudleighs verses; which this Afternoon I gave Mr Walsh to read in the Coffee house. His opinion is the same with mine, that they are better than any wch are printed before the Book [Virgil]: so thinks also Mr Wycherley.

Letter to Tonson, December 1697. Ward No. 50, p. 98

Cicero

DIALOGUE (GENRE), a. Cf. DRYDEN, WORKS, d. SENECA, d. WALSH, b. PROSODY, x. POLYBIUS AND TACITUS. [Ciceronian style] FAME.

a. [¶] The Latin of this Couplet [verses 190–191 of the translation of the tenth Satire of Juvenal] is a Famous Verse of *Tully's,* in which he sets out the Happiness of his own Consulship; Famous for the Vanity, and the ill Poetry of it. For *Tully* as he had a good deal of the one, so he had no great share of the other.

Notes to the Tenth Satire [Juvenal], '93. JK II 735

FIGURES, c. Cf. COINAGE, c.

b. [Comparing Homer and Virgil, *q.v.*] One warms you by degrees; the other sets you on fire all at once, and never intermits his heat. 'Tis the same difference which Longinus makes betwixt the effects of eloquence/in Demosthenes and Tully;

one persuades, the other commands.

Pref. *Fables,* 1700. K II 253–54

Claudian

Cf. RHYME (DEBATE), e.

On the contrary [to Virgil], Ovid and Claudian, though they write in styles differing from each other, yet have each of them but one sort of music in their verses. All the versification and little variety of Claudian is included within the compass of four or five lines, and then he begins again in the same tenor; perpetually closing his sense at the end of a verse, and that verse commonly which they call golden, or two substantives and two adjectives, with a verb betwixt them to keep the peace.

Pref. *Sylvæ,* '85. K I 255

CRITIC[s], d. ["a faulty poet . . . living in a barbarous age"]

Clenches [Cf. PARONOMASIA]

POETASTERS, c. SHAKESPEARE, b.

Nay, he [Jonson] was not free from the lowest and most grovelling kind of wit, which we call clenches . . .

Defence of the Epilogue, '72. K I 173

WIT, k. PARONOMASIA, b.

Clergy*

POETASTERS, b. SPEECHES (DRAMATIC), a. ENDS OF POETRY, k. SUPERNATURAL, e. WIT, k. REFORMATION OF STAGE. PARONOMASIA, b. Cf. FARCE, f. Cf. DRYDEN, LITERARY LIFE, o. OBSCENITY, d, e. CHAUCER, d.

. . . the scandal which is given by particular priests reflects not on the sacred function.

Pref. *Fables,* 1700. K II 260

SATIRE, n. MILBOURNE. COLLIER.

Cleveland, John

a. (Eugenius) [¶] The not observing

---

* See E. S. de Beer, "Dryden's Anti-Clericalism," *N and Q,* CLXXIX (1940), 254–57.

this rule [custom as arbiter of language] is that which the world has blamed in our satyrist, Cleveland: to express a thing hard and unnaturally, is his new way of elocution.

Dram. Poesy, '65. K I 52

CATACHRESIS. Cf. WIT, c. DONNE, a.

b. (Eugenius) . . . 'tis true, in some places his wit is independent of his words, as in that of the *Rebel Scot* . . .[1]

Si sic omnia dixisset! This is wit in all languages: 'tis like Mercury, never to be lost or killed: —and so that other— . . .[1] You see, the last line is highly metaphorical, but it is so soft and gentle, that it does not shock us as we read it.

Dram. Poesy, '65. K I 52–53

Clevelandism

POETASTERS, c.

Coinage

PLAUTUS, a.

a. (Eugenius) For Horace himself was cautious to obtrude a new word on his readers, and makes custom and common use the best measure of receiving it into our writings . . .[q]

Dram. Poesy, '65. K I 51

b. Upon your [Howard's] first perusal of this poem, you have taken notice of some words, which I have innovated (if it be too bold for me to say refined) upon his [Virgil's] Latin; which, as I offer not to introduce into English prose, so I hope they are neither improper, nor altogether unelegant in verse; and in this Horace will again defend me—

> *Et nova, fictaque nuper, habebunt*
> *verba fidem . . .*

The inference is exceeding plain; for, if a Roman poet might have liberty to coin a word, supposing only/that it was derived

from the Greek, was put into a Latin termination, and that he used this liberty but seldom, and with modesty; how much more justly may I challenge that privilege to do it with the same prerequisites, from the best and most judicious of Latin writers?

Pref. *Annus Mirabilis,* '66. K I 17–18

Cf. CRITIC[s], b. SHAKESPEARE, r. OPERA, f. ARCHAISMS, b. Cf. ENGLISH LANGUAGE, e.

c. [Concerning line 1094 in the translation of *Æneid,* IX] When I read this *Æneid* to many of my friends in company together, most of them quarrel'd at the word *falsified,* as an innovation in our language. The fact is confess'd; for I remember not to have read it in any English author, tho' perhaps it may be found in Spenser's *Fairy Queen.* But suppose it be not there, why am I forbidden to borrow from the Italian (a polish'd language) the word which is wanting in my native tongue? Terence has often Greciz'd; Lucretius has follow'd his example, and pleaded for it: *Sic quia me cogit patrii sermonis egestas.* Virgil has confirm'd it by his frequent practice; and even Cicero in prose, wanting terms of philosophy in the Latin tongue, has taken them from Aristotle's Greek. Horace has given us a rule for coining words, *si Græco fonte cadunt:* especially when other words are join'd with them, which explain the sense. . . . They who will not admit a new word may take the old; the matter is not worth dispute.

Notes and Observations on Virgil's Works, '97. N 715

Collier, Jeremy

OBSCENITY, e.

[¶] I shall say the less of Mr. Collier,

because in many things he has taxed me justly; and I have pleaded guilty to all thoughts and expressions of mine, which can be truly argued of obscenity, profaneness, or immorality, and retract them. If he be my enemy, let him triumph; if he be my friend, as I have given him no personal occasion to be otherwise, he will be glad of my repentance. It becomes me not to draw my pen in the defence of a bad cause, when I have so often drawn it for a good one. Yet it were not difficult to prove, that in many places he has perverted my meaning . . . and interpreted my words into blasphemy and bawdry, of which they were not guilty. Besides that, he is too much given to horse-play in his raillery, and comes to battle like a dictator from the plough. I will not say, *The Zeal of God's House has eaten him up;* but I am sure it has devoured some part of his good manners and civility. It might also be doubted, whether it were altogether zeal which prompted him to this/rough manner of proceeding; perhaps it became not one of his function to rake into the rubbish of ancient and modern plays . . .[1] Neither has he judged impartially betwixt the former age and us. There is more bawdry in one play of Fletcher's, called *The Custom of the Country,* than in all ours together. . . . But I am not to prejudice the cause of my fellow-poets, though I abandon my own defence: they have some of them answered for themselves, and neither they nor I can think Mr. Collier so formidable an enemy that we should shun him. He has lost ground at the latter end of the day, by pursuing his point too far . . . from immoral plays to no plays, *ab abusu ad usum, non valet consequentia.*

Pref. *Fables,* 1700. K II 272–73

Comedy*

Comedy and Farce

a. Comedy consists, though of low persons, yet of natural actions and characters; I mean such humours, adventures, and designs, as are to be found and met/with in the world. Farce, on the other side, consists of forced humours, and unnatural events. Comedy presents us with the imperfections of human nature: Farce entertains us with what is monstrous and chimerical. The one causes laughter in those who can judge of men and manners, by the lively representation of their folly or corruption: the other produces the same effect in those who can judge of neither, and that only by its extravagances. The first works on the judgment and fancy; the latter on the fancy only: there is more of satisfaction in the former kind of laughter, and in the latter more of scorn . . . [See LAUGHTER, c] In short, there is the same difference betwixt Farce and Comedy, as betwixt an empiric and a true physician: both of them may attain their ends; but what the one performs by hazard, the other does by skill.

Pref. *Evening's Love,* '71. K I 135–36

Definition

b. (Neander) . . . Comedy . . . is the imitation of common persons and ordinary speaking . . .

Dram. Poesy, '65. K I 100

See below, h.

Difficulty

DRYDEN, WORKS, j.

Dryden's Personal View of

DRYDEN, PERSONAL CHARACTER, f, g.

---

* See Margaret Sherwood, *Dryden's Dramatic Theory and Practice* (Boston: Lamson, Wolffe & Co., 1898).

DRYDEN, WORKS, o. Cf. DRYDEN, LITER-
ARY LIFE, k.
Effect
POETIC JUSTICE, c. SATIRE, p.
Ends
GENRE, b. POETIC JUSTICE, c.

c. . . . Comedy/is both excellently in-
structive, and extremely pleasant . . .
Author's Apology, '77. K I 181–82
English vs. Ancient
SHAKESPEARE, i.
Figures in
FIGURES, e.
Humors (Depleted)
DRYDEN, LITERARY LIFE, v.
Imaging
IMITATION, j.
Inferiority

d. Neither, indeed, do I value a reputa-
tion gained/from Comedy, so far as to
concern myself about it, any more than I
needs must in my own defence; for I think
it, in its own nature, inferior to all sorts of
dramatic writing. Low comedy especially
requires . . . much of conversation with
the vulgar, and much of ill nature in the
observation of their follies.
Pref. *Evening's Love,* '71. K I 134–35
Cf. FARCE, a. Cf. TRAGEDY, o, p.
Love in
JONSON, d.
Low
JONSON, l. See below, h.
Manners of
MANNERS, h.
Mixed

e. I will not deny, but that I approve
most of the mixed way of Comedy; that
which is neither all wit, nor all humour,
but the result of both. Neither so little of
humour as Fletcher shows, nor so little of

love and wit as Johnson; neither all cheat,
with which the best plays of the one are
filled, nor all adventure, which is the common practice of the other. I would have the
characters well chosen, and kept distant
from interfering with each other; which is
more than Fletcher or Shakespeare did: but
I would have more of the *urbana, venusta,
salsa, faceta,* and the rest which Quintilian
reckons up as the ornaments of wit; and
these are extremely wanting in Ben Johnson. As for repartie, in particular; as it is
the very soul of conversation, so it is the
greatest grace of Comedy, where it is
proper to the characters.
Pref. *Evening's Love,* '71. K I 139
Poetic Justice in

f. It is charged upon me that I make
debauched persons (such as, they say, my
Astrologer and Gamester are) my pro-
tagonists, or the chief persons of the
drama; and that I make them happy in the
conclusion of my play; against the law of
Comedy, which is to reward virtue, and
punish vice. I answer, first, that I know no
such law to have been constantly observed
in Comedy, either by the ancient or modern poets. . . .[1] Ben Johnson himself,
after whom I may be proud to err, has
given me more than once the example of
it. . ./.[1] As for Beaumont and Fletcher, I
need not allege examples out of them; for
that were to quote almost all their comedies.
Pref. *Evening's Love,* '71. K I 141–42
POETIC JUSTICE, c.
Popular Taste for
ENGLISH VS. FRENCH, x. AUDIENCE, POPU-
LAR, b.
Repartee in

g. (Neander) As for Comedy, repartee is

one of its chiefest graces; the greatest pleasure of the audience is a chace of wit, kept up on both sides, and swiftly managed.

Dram. Poesy, '65. K I 72

REPARTEE, b.

Satire in

SATIRE, jj.

Satire, Relation to

SATIRE, k.

Subject

GENRE, b. TRAGEDY, o.

h. . . . as Comedy is a representation of human life in inferior persons, and low subjects, and by that means creeps into the nature of poetry, and is a kind of juniper, a shrub belonging to the species of cedar, so is the painting of clowns . . .¹ and a thousand other things of this mean invention; a kind of picture which belongs to nature, but of the lowest form. Such is a Lazar in comparison to a Venus . . . [See FARCE, f. LAUGHTER, d]

Parallel, '95. K II 132

Unity of Time

UNITIES (DRAMATIC), TIME, c.

Verse Form

PROSODY, h. RHYME (DEBATE), g, h.

Comines, Philippe de

a. . . . but above all men [i.e., historians], in my opinion, the plain, sincere, unaffected, and most instructive Philip de Comines [excels in history] . . . [See HISTORY, e]

"Life of Plutarch," '83. S-S XVII 59

b. [¶] I was so strongly persuaded of this myself [that "Truth is the foundation of all knowledge, and the cement of all societies . . ."], in the perusal of the present history [Polybius], that I confess, amongst all the ancients I never found

any who had the air of it so much; and amongst the moderns, none but Philip de Commines.

"Character of Polybius," '93. S-S XVIII 38

Commentators [See also under proper names]

EPIC VS. TRAGEDY, d. CASAUBON, b, c. CRITIC[s], f. TRANSLATION, l. CRITIC[s], d.

Commentators, Dutch

PREFACES, b. DRYDEN, WORKS, mm.

a. . . . not to follow the Dutch commentators always, may be forgiven to a man who thinks them, in the general, heavy gross-witted fellows, fit only to gloss on their own dull poets.

Ded. *Examen Poeticum,* '93. K II 10

b. I shall continue still to speak my thoughts like a free-born subject, as I am; though such things, perhaps, as no Dutch commentator could, and I am sure no Frenchman durst.

Ded. *Æneis,* '97. K II 174

Common Sense [See CONSENSUS GENTIUM. Cf. GOOD SENSE]

Commonwealth Period

ENGLISH VS. FRENCH, a. Cf. ENGLISH DRAMA, d. RESTORATION. ENDS OF POETRY, k. HEROIC PLAY, b. Cf. CONVERSATION, b. Cf. HORACE AND JUVENAL AND PERSIUS, f. Cf. COWLEY, g.

Conceit

(Crites) . . . some thin conceit, the ghost of a jest . . .

Dram. Poesy, '65. K I 32

WIT, g. PLUTARCH, f. VIRGIL, oo. TASSO, b. EPIC, j. CRITIC[s], a. ["prefer a quibble, a conceit . . . before solid sense"] CHAUCER AND OVID. ["The vulgar judges . . . who call conceits . . . wit"] COWLEY, i. CHAUCER, g.

Congreve, William

a. . . . there are two fragments of Homer translated in this *Miscellany;* one by Mr. Congreve, (whom I cannot mention without the honour which is due to his excellent parts, and that entire affection which I bear him,) and the other by myself. Both the subjects are pathetical; and I am sure my friend has added to the tenderness which he found in the original, and without flattery, surpassed his author.

Ded. *Examen Poeticum,* '93. K II 12

b. I wish Mr. Congreve had the leisure to translate him [Homer], and the world the good nature and justice to encourage him in that noble design, of which he is more capable than any man I know. . . . What . . . would he appear in the harmonious version of one of the best writers, living in a much better age than was the last?

Ded. *Examen Poeticum,* '93. K II 14

c. I am Mr Congreve's true Lover & desire you to tell him, how kindly I take his often Remembrances of me: I wish him all prosperity; & hope I shall never loose his Affection.

Letter to Tonson, 30 August 1693. Ward No. 26, p. 59

d. His [Congreve's] Double Dealer is much censur'd by the greater part of the Town: and is defended onely by the best Judges, who, you know, are commonly the fewest. Yet it gets ground daily, and has already been acted Eight times. The women thinke he has exposed their Bitchery too much; & the Gentlemen, are offended with him; for the discovery of their follyes: & the way of their Intrigues, under the notion of Friendship to their Ladyes Husbands. My verses, which you will find before it, were written before the play was acted. but I neither alter'd them nor do I alter my opinion of the play.

Letter to Walsh, 12 December 1693. Ward No. 28, p. 63.

DRYDEN, WORKS, lll.

e. . . . Mr. Congreve has done me the favour to review the *Æneis,* and compare my version with the original. I shall never be ashamed to own, that this excellent young man has shewed me many faults, which I have endeavoured to correct.

Ded. *Æneis,* '97. K II 235

f. Congreves New Play [*The Way of the World*] has had but moderate success; though it deserves much better.

Letter to Mrs. Steward, 12 March 1700. Ward No. 74, p. 134

Consensus Gentium

(Neander) . . . the universal consent of the most civilized parts of the world ought in this [rhyme], as it doth in other customs, to include the rest.

Dram. Poesy, '65. K I 98

AUTHORITY, d.   NATURE, c.   Cf. PLUTARCH, c.   Cf. CHAUCER, c.

Consonants

We are full of monosyllables, and those clogged with consonants . . .

Ded. *Troilus,* '79. S-S VI 252

Cf. FRENCH LANGUAGE, a.   ENGLISH LANGUAGE, a.   OPERA, f.   PROSODY, b, r, s. ENGLISH LANGUAGE, f.   DRYDEN, WORKS, sss.

Contraction [See GRAMMAR]

Contrast

TRAGICOMEDY, b.

For, as contraries, the nearer they are placed are brighter, and the Venus is illustrated by the neighbourhood of the lazar, so the unblemished loyalty of your Grace . . .

Ded. *Plutarch's Lives,* '83. S-S XVII 13

CHARACTER[s], e.

Conversation

a. (Neander) [Beaumont and Fletcher] understood and imitated the conversation of gentlemen . . .

Dram. Poesy, '65. K I 81

JONSON, p. Cf. DRYDEN, PERSONAL CHARACTER, f. WIT, j. Cf. RHYME (DEBATE), aa. LAST AGE, d, h, i. PRESENT AGE, l.

b. [¶] Now, if they ask me, whence it is that our conversation is so much refined? I must freely, and without flattery, ascribe it to the court; and, in it, particularly to the King, whose example gives a law to it. His own misfortunes, and the nation's, afforded him an opportunity . . . of travelling, and being conversant in the most polished courts of Europe; and, thereby, of cultivating a spirit which was formed by nature to receive the impressions of a gallant and generous education. . . . The desire of imitating so great a pattern first awakened the dull and heavy spirits of the English from their natural reservedness; loosened them from their stiff forms of conversation, and made them easy and pliant to each other in discourse. Thus, insensibly, our way of living became more free; and the fire of the English wit, which was before stifled under a constrained, melancholy way of breeding, began first to display its force, by mixing the solidity of our nation with the air and gaiety of our neighbours.

Defence of the Epilogue, '72. K I 176

Cf. SETTLE, c. POET, n. Cf. SETTLE, d. Cf. CRITIC[s], a.

c. [¶] Certainly the poets of that age [Augustan Rome] enjoyed much happiness in the conversation and friendship of one another. They imitated the best way of living, which was, to pursue an innocent and inoffensive pleasure, that which one of the ancients called *eruditam voluptatem.* We have, like them, our genial nights, where our discourse is neither too serious nor too light, but always pleasant, and, for the most part, instructive; the raillery, neither too sharp upon the present, nor too censorious on the absent; and the cups only such as will raise the conversation of the/ night, without disturbing the business of the morrow.

Ded. *Assignation, '73.* S-S IV 372–73

Conversion (Simple Change of Will, Dramatic) [Cf. COUNTERTURN]

(Lisideius) . . . you never see any of their [the French] plays end with a conversion or simple change of will, which is the ordinary way which our poets use to end theirs. It shows little art in the conclusion of a dramatic poem, when they who have hindered the felicity during the four acts, desist from it in the fifth, without some powerful cause to take them off; and though I deny not but such reasons may be found, yet it is a path that is cautiously to be trod, and the poet is to be sure he convinces the audience that the motive is strong enough.

Dram. Poesy, '65. K I 66

ARISTOTLE, b.

Corneille, Pierre*

UNITIES (DRAMATIC), ACTION, a.

a. (Lisideius) . . . Corneille, and some other Frenchmen, reformed their theatre . . .

Dram. Poesy, '65. K I 56 [See ENGLISH vs. FRENCH, b]

ENGLISH vs. FRENCH, t. NARRATIONS (DRAMATIC), c. LIAISON, b.

---

* See John M. Aden, "Dryden, Corneille, and the *Essay of Dramatic Poesy," RES,* n.s., VI (1955), 147–56.

a-2. (Neander) For objects of incredibility, I would be satisfied from Lisideius, whether we have any so removed from all appearance of truth, as are those of Corneille's *Andromede* . . .¹ Those indeed were objects of delight; yet the reason is the same as to the probability; for he makes it not a Ballette or masque, but a play, which is to resemble truth.

Dram. Poesy, '65. K I 74

SPEECHES (DRAMATIC), a. ENGLISH VS. FRENCH, r. JONSON, q. Cf. DRYDEN, WORKS, g. AUTHORITY, a, b. HEROIC PLAY, b.

b. . . . a judicious reader will easily observe how much the copy is inferior to the original . ./. The truth is, he [Corneille] miserably failed in the character of his hero: If he desired that Œdipus should be pitied, he should have made him a better man. . . .¹ [And] He introduced a greater hero than Œdipus himself; for when Theseus was once there, that companion of Hercules must yield to none. The poet was obliged . . .¹ to lose his other king of Brentford in the crowd.

Pref. *Œdipus*, '79. S-S VI 131–32

SENECA, b. ARISTOTLE, b. DRYDEN, WORKS, lll. UNITIES (DRAMATIC), TIME, e.

Corneille, Thomas

MOLIÈRE, a. UNITIES (DRAMATIC), PLACE, d.

Correctness

PRESENT AGE, d. ["nothing so majestic, so correct"] SHAKESPEARE AND JONSON. JONSON, i.

a. 'Tis enough for those who make one poem the business of their lives, to leave that correct: yet, excepting Virgil, I never met with any which was so in any language.

Defence of An Essay, '68. K I 110

DRYDEN, WORKS, k. DAVENANT, b. Cf. DRYDEN, WORKS, m. LAST AGE, f. [See *passim*, analysis of solecisms in "Catiline," *Defence of the Epilogue* K I 167–69] LAST AGE, g. FLETCHER, d. DONNE, c. OVID, a. MANUM DE TABULA, b. CRITICASTERS, j. DRYDEN, LIFE, d. Cf. DRYDEN, WORKS, yyy, zzz.

b. They who think too well of their own performances, are apt to boast in their prefaces how little time their works have cost them, and what other business of more importance interfered; but the reader will be as apt to ask the question, why they allowed not a longer time to make their works more perfect? and why they had so despicable an opinion of their judges as to thrust their indigested stuff upon them, as if they deserved no better?

Pref. *Fables*, 1700. K II 250

Counterturn [Cf. CONVERSION]

PLAY (PARTS). ENGLISH VS. FRENCH, r. ENGLISH DRAMA, c.

Couplet [See PROSODY]

Court

a. (Neander) [In defense of verse plays] . . . no serious plays written since the King's return have been more kindly received by them [the "noblesse"], than *The Siege of Rhodes*, the *Mustapha*, *The Indian Queen*, and *Indian Emperor*.

Dram. Poesy, '65. K I 100

b. The Court, which is the best and surest judge of writing, has generally allowed of verse . . .

Epistle Dedicatory, *Dram. Poesy*, '67. K I 24

HEROIC PLAY, a. Cf. BORROWING, b. LAST AGE, i. CONVERSATION, b. DRYDEN, WORKS, o. Cf. COWLEY, c. ACADEMY, b. Cf. OVID, j. Cf. THEOCRITUS, a.

c. But conversing in a manner wholly with the court, which is not always the truest judge, he [St. Évremond] has been unavoidably led into mistakes [regarding English comedy] . . .

"Character of St. Évremont," '92. S-S XVIII 16

d. It is necessary, for the polishing of manners, to have breathed that air [i.e., of the Court]; but it is infectious, even to the best morals, to live always in it.

Ded. *Georgics,* '97. S-S XIV 8

Court Poets [See DORSET; MULGRAVE; ORRERY; ROCHESTER; ROSCOMMON] POETASTERS, e.

Courtier without Wit

These are they, who, wanting wit, affect gravity, and go by the name of solid men; and a solid man is, in plain English, a solid, solemn fool. Another disguise they have . . . and that is, the title of honest fellows. . . . and if they speak not maliciously, or sharply, of witty men, it is only because God has not bestowed on them the gift of utterance. . ./.

This, my lord, is the character of a courtier without wit . . .

Ded. *Aureng-Zebe,* '76. S-S V 189–90

Cowley, Abraham*

a. (Eugenius) [The last age] can produce nothing . . ./so elevated, so copious and full of spirit, as Mr. Cowley . . .

Dram. Poesy, '65. K I 34–35

WIT, h.

b. Neither am I much concerned at Mr. Cowley's verses before *Gondibert* (though his authority is almost sacred to me): 'tis true, he has resembled the epic poetry to a fantastic fairy-land; but he has contradicted himself by his own example. For he has himself made use of angels and

---

* See Jean Loiseau, *Abraham Cowley's Reputation in England,* Paris, 1931; A. H. Nethercot, "The Reputation of Abraham Cowley (1660–1800)," *PMLA,* XXXVIII (1923), 588–641.

visions in his *Davideis,* as well as Tasso in his *Godfrey.*

Essay of Heroic Plays, '72. K I 154

c. I am sure his [Lucretius's] master Epicurus, and my better master Cowley, preferred the solitude of a garden, and the conversation of a friend, to any consideration . . . of those unhappy people. whom . . . we call the great.

Ded. *Aureng-Zebe,* '76. S-S V 194

d. [¶] What fustian, as they call it, have I heard these gentlemen find out in Mr. Cowley's *Odes!* I acknowledge myself unworthy to defend so excellent an author . . . only in general I will say, that nothing can appear more beautiful to me, than the strength of those images which they condemn.

Author's Apology, '77. K I 186

TRANSLATION, a, h.

e. To add and to diminish what we please [in a translation], which is the way avowed by him, ought only to be granted to Mr. Cowley, and that too only in his translation of Pindar; because he alone was able to make him amends, by giving him better of his own, whenever he refused his author's thoughts. Pindar is generally known to be a dark writer, to want connection, (I mean as to our understanding,) to soar out of sight, and leave his reader at a gaze. So wild and ungovernable a poet cannot be translated literally; his genius is too strong to bear a chain, and Samson-like he shakes it off. A genius so elevated and unconfined as Mr. Cowley's, was but necessary to make Pindar speak English, and that was to be performed by no other way than imitation.

Pref. *Ovid's Epistles,* '80. K I 240

f. [¶] Thus I have ventured to give my opinion on this subject [translation] against the authority of two great men

[Cowley and Denham], but I hope without offence to either of their memories; for I both loved them living, and reverence them now they are dead.

Pref. *Ovid's Epistles,* '80. K I 242

Cf. APHRA BEHN. PATRONAGE, c. OBSCENITY, b. PROSODY, u, w. AUTHORITY, e. DONNE, c. DRYDEN, LITERARY LIFE, b. ["the darling of my youth, the famous Cowley"] PROSODY, y, e. TRANSLATION, gg. PROSODY, jj.

g. On the other side, without being injurious to the memory of our English Pindar, I will presume to say, that his metaphors are sometimes too violent, and his language is not always pure. But at the same time I must excuse him; for through the iniquity of the times he was forced to travel, at an age when, instead of learning foreign languages, he should have studied the beauties of his mother-tongue, which, like all other speeches, is to be cultivated early, or we shall never write it with any kind of elegance.[1]

Ded. *Æneis,* '97. K II 229

PROSODY, k.

h. Mr. Cowley's *Praise of a Country Life* is excellent, but is rather an imitation of Virgil than a version.

Postscript *Æneis,* '97. K II 244

i. One of our late great poets is sunk in his reputation, because he could never forgive any conceit which came in his way; but swept like a drag-net, great and small. There was plenty enough, but the dishes were ill sorted; whole pyramids of sweetmeats, for boys and women; but little of solid meat, for men. All this proceeded not from any want of knowledge, but of judgment. Neither did he want that in discerning the beauties and faults of other poets, but only indulged himself in the luxury of

writing; and perhaps knew it was a fault, but hoped the reader would not find it. For this reason, though he must always be thought a great poet, he is no longer esteemed a good writer; and for ten impressions, which his works have had in so many successive years, yet at present a hundred books are scarcely purchased once a twelvemonth; for, as my last Lord Rochester said, though somewhat profanely, *Not being of God, he could not stand.*

Pref. *Fables,* 1700. K II 258

j. I have often heard the late Earl of Leicester say, that Mr. Cowley himself was of that opinion [that Chaucer was 'not worth reviving']; who, having read him over/at my Lord's request, declared he had no taste of him. I dare not advance my opinion against the judgment of so great an author; but I think it fair . . . to leave the decision to the public. Mr. Cowley was too modest to set up for a dictator; and being shocked perhaps with his old style, never examined into the depth of his good sense.

Pref. *Fables,* 1700. K II 264–65

Creech, Thomas

a. I have considered the verses [translated by Creech from Lucretius, *De rerum natura,* I, 225–28], & find the Authour of them [Creech] to have notoriously bungled: that he has plac'd the words as confus'dly, as if he had studied to do so.

Letter to an Unidentified Person, '82. Ward No. 7, p. 15

TRANSLATION, s.

b. This last consideration puts me in mind of what I owe to the ingenious and learned translator of Lucretius [Creech]. . . . The ways of our translation are very different. He follows him more closely than I have done, which became an interpreter of the whole poem: I take more liberty, because it best suited with my design, which was, to make him as pleasing as I could. . . . The preference, then, is justly his; and I join with Mr. Evelyn in the confession of it . . . If I have/been anywhere obscure, in following our common author, of if Lucretius himself is to be condemned, I refer myself to his excellent annotations, which I have often read, and always with some new pleasure.

Pref. *Sylvæ,* '85. K I 264–65

c. . . . I have given leave to my bookseller to print the life of Cleomenes, as it is elegantly and faithfully translated out of Plutarch, by my learned friend, Mr. Creech, to whom the world/has been indebted for his excellent version of Lucretius, and I particularly obliged in his translation of Horace.

Pref. *Cleomenes,* '92. S-S VIII 222–23
Prosody, s. Cf. Theocritus, c.

Crites [See Howard, Sir Robert]

[Narrator: Neander, Dryden] . . . Crites, a person of sharp judgment, and somewhat too delicate a taste in wit, which the world have mistaken in him for ill-nature . . .

Dram. Poesy, '65. K I 29
Moderns, e.

Critic[s]

Classes

a. Segrais has distinguished the readers of poetry, according to their capacity of judging, into three classes (he might have said the same of writers too, if he had pleased): in the lowest form he places those whom he calls *les petits esprits;* such things as are our upper-gallery audience in a playhouse, who like nothing but the husk and rind of wit; prefer a quibble, a con-

ceit, an epigram, before solid sense and elegant expression. These are mob readers: if Virgil and Martial stood for Parliament-men, we know already who would carry it. But, though they make the greatest appearance in the field, and cry the loudest, the best on't is, they are but a sort of French Huguenots, or Dutch boors, brought over in herds, but not naturalized; /who have not land of two pounds *per annum* in Parnassus, and therefore are not privileged to poll. Their authors are of the same level, fit to represent them on a mountebank's stage, or to be masters of the ceremonies in a bear-garden. Yet these are they who have the most admirers. But it often happens . . . that, as their readers improve their stock of sense (as they may by reading better books, and by conversation with men of judgment), they soon forsake them . . . There are a middle sort of readers . . . such as have a further insight than the former, yet have not the capacity of judging right . . . I mean a company of warm young men, who are not yet arrived so far as to discern the difference betwixt fustian, or ostentatious sentences, and the true sublime. These are above liking Martial, or Owen's Epigrams, but they would certainly set Virgil below Statius or Lucan. I need not say their poets are of the same taste with their admirers. They affect greatness in all they write; but 'tis a bladdered greatness . . . Even these too desert their authors, as their judgment ripens. The young gentlemen themselves are commonly misled by their pedagogue at school, their tutor at the university, or their governor in their travels: and many of those three sorts are the most positive blockheads in the world. How many of those flatulent writers have I known, who have sunk in their reputation, after seven or eight editions of their works!/for indeed they are poets only for young men. They had great success at their first appearance; but, not being of God (as a wit said formerly), they could not stand.

I have already named two sorts of judges; but Virgil wrote for neither of them: and, by his example, I am not ambitious of pleasing the lowest or the middle form of readers.

He chose to please the most judicious: souls of the highest rank, and truest understanding. These are few in number; but whoever is so happy as to gain their approbation can never lose it, because they never give it blindly.

Ded. *Æneis,* '97. K II 223–25
Distinguished from Laugher

b. [Speaking of Dryden's lines in *The State of Innocence* ending "And all dissolved in hallelujahs lie."] [¶] I have heard (says one of them [critics]) of anchovies dissolved in sauce; but never of an angel in hallelujahs. A mighty witticism! (if you will pardon a new word,) but there is some difference between a laugher and a critic. He might have burlesqued Virgil too, from whom I took the image: *Invadunt urbem, somno vinoque sepultam. . . .*[1] How easy 'tis to turn into ridicule the best descriptions, when once a man is in the humour of laughing, till he wheezes at his own dull jest!

Author's Apology, '77. K I 188
Fewness of Good

CONGREVE, d. CHAUCER AND OVID.
French and English
ENGLISH VS. FRENCH, l.
The Generality

c. . . . how I have acquitted myself . . . must be left to the opinion of the world, in spite of any protestation which I can enter against the present age, as incompetent or corrupt judges. For my comfort they are but Englishmen; and, as such, if they think ill of me to-day, they are inconstant enough to think well of me to-morrow.

Ded. *Eleonora,* '92. S-S XI 126
Generation of

d. Ill writers are usually the sharpest censors; for they, as the best poet and the best patron said,

> When in the full perfection of decay,
> Turn vinegar, and come again in play.

Thus the corruption of a poet is the generation of/a critic; I mean of a critic in the general acceptation of this age; for formerly they were quite another species of men. They were defenders of poets, and commentators on their works; to illustrate obscure beauties; to place some passages in a better light; to redeem others from malicious interpretations; to help out an author's modesty, who is not ostentatious of his wit; and, in short, to shield him from the ill-nature of those fellows, who were then called *Zoili* and *Momi,* and now take upon themselves the venerable name of censors. . . . Are our auxiliary forces turned our enemies? are they, who at best are but wits of the second order, and whose only credit amongst readers is what they obtained by being subservient to the fame of writers, are these become rebels, of slaves, and usurpers, of subjects? or, to speak in the most honourable terms of them, are they from our seconds become principals against us? . . . .What labour would it cost them to put in a better line, than the worst of those which they expunge in a true poet? Petronius, the greatest wit perhaps of all the Romans, yet when his envy prevailed upon his judgment to fall on Lucan, he fell himself in his attempt; he performed worse in his *Essay of the Civil War* than the author of the *Pharsalia* . . . Julius Scaliger would needs turn down Homer, and abdicate him after the possession of three thousand years: has he succeeded in his attempt? He has indeed shown us some of those imperfections in him, which are incident to humankind; but who had not rather be that/Homer than this Scaliger? You see the same hyper-critic, when he endeavours to mend the beginning of Claudian, (a faulty poet, and living in a barbarous age,) yet how short he comes of him, and substitutes such verses of his own as deserve the ferula. What a censure has he made of Lucan, that "he rather seems to bark than sing"! Would any but a dog have made so snarling a comparison? . . . We have two sorts of those gentlemen in our nation; some of them, proceeding with a seeming modera-tion and pretence of respect to the dra-matic writers of the last age, only scorn and vilify the present poets, to set up their predecessors. But this is only in appear-ance; for their real design is nothing less than to do honour to any man, besides themselves. Horace took notice of such men in his age—

Non ingeniis favet ille sepultis,
Nostra sed impugnat; nos nostraque lividus odit.

'Tis not with any ultimate intention to pay reverence to the *Manes* of Shakespeare, Fletcher, and Ben Johnson, that they com-mend their writings, but to throw dirt on the writers of this age . . . If they could compass their intent, what would wit and learning get by such a change? If we are bad poets, they are worse; and when any of

their woeful pieces come/abroad, the dif-ference is so great betwixt them and good writers, that there need no criticisms on our part to decide it. . . . But there is an-other sort of insects, more venomous than the former; those who manifestly aim at the destruction of our poetical church and state; who allow nothing to their country-men, either of this or of the former age. These attack the living by raking up the ashes of the dead; well knowing that if they can subvert their original title to the stage, we who claim under them must fall of course.

Ded. *Examen Poeticum,* '93. K II 2–5
Hasty critics

e. But, on the other side, my reason tells me, that, in probability, what I have se-riously and long considered may be as likely to be just and natural, as what an ordinary judge (if there be any such among those ladies [who complained of the last act of *Aureng-Zebe*]) will think fit, in a transient presentation, to be placed in the room/of that which they condemn. The most judicious writer is sometimes mis-taken, after all his care; but the hasty critic, who judges on a view, is full as liable to be deceived. Let him first consider all the ar-guments, which the author had, to write this, or to design the other, before he ar-raigns him of a fault; and then, perhaps, on second thoughts, he will find his reason oblige him to revoke his censure. Yet, after all, I will not be too positive. *Homo sum, humani à me nihil alienum puto.* As I am a man, I must be changeable: and some-times the gravest of us all are so, even upon ridiculous accidents. Our minds are per-petually wrought on by the temperament of our bodies . . .

Ded. *Aureng-Zebe,* '76. S-S V 198–99

Judices Natos
IMAGINATION, e.
Partial

f. It is observed by Rigaltius . . . that these three poets [Horace, Juvenal and Persius] have all their particular partisans, and favourers. Every commentator . . . thinks himself obliged to prefer his author to the other two; to find out their failings, and decry them, that he may make room for his own darling. Such is the partiality of mankind, to set up that interest which they have once espoused, though it be to the prejudice of truth, morality, and common justice; and especially in the productions of the brain. As authors generally think themselves the best poets, because they cannot go out of themselves to judge sincerely of their betters; so it is with critics, who, having first taken a liking to one of these poets, proceed to comment on him, and to illustrate him; after which, they fall in love with their own labours, to that degree of blind fondness, that at length they defend and exalt their author, not so much for his sake as for their own. . . .[1] I am now myself on/the brink of the same precipice; I have spent some time on the translation of Juvenal and Persius; and it behoves me to be wary, lest, for that reason, I should be partial to them, or take a prejudice against Horace. Yet, on the other side, I would not be like some of our judges, who would give the cause for a poor man, right or wrong; for, though that be an error on the better hand, yet it is still a partiality . . . [an anecdote of Charles II] It had been much fairer, if the modern critics, who have embarked in the quarrels of their favourite authors, had rather given to each his proper due; without taking from

another's heap, to raise their own. There is praise enough for each of them in particular, without encroaching on his fellows, and detracting from them, or enriching themselves with the spoils of others.[1]

Discourse of Satire, '93. K II 68–69
Qualifications [See *passim* under this topic. CRITIC(s)]

g. 'Tis true, there are limits to be set betwixt the boldness and rashness of a poet; but he must understand those limits who pretends to judge as well as he who undertakes to write: and he who has no liking to the whole, ought, in reason, to be excluded from censuring of the parts. He must be a lawyer before he mounts the tribunal; and the judicature of one court, too, does not qualify a man to preside in another. He may be an excellent pleader/in the Chancery, who is not fit to rule the Common Pleas.

Author's Apology, '77. K I 182–83

h. Poets themselves are the most proper, though I conclude not the only critics. But till some genius, as universal as Aristotle, shall arise, one who can penetrate into all arts and sciences, without the practice of them, I shall think it reasonable, that the judgment of an artificer in his own art should be preferable to the opinion of another man; at least where he is not bribed by interest, or prejudiced by malice. And this, I suppose, is manifest by plain induction: for, first, the crowd cannot be presumed to have more than a gross instinct, of what pleases or displeases them . . . ; but then, by a particular kindness to himself, he draws his own stake first, and will be distinguished from the multitude, of which other men may think him one. But, if I come closer to those who are allowed for witty men . . . and affirm that neither are they qualified to decide sovereignly concerning poetry, I shall yet have a strong party of my opinion; for most of them severally will exclude the rest, either from the number of witty men, or at least of able judges. But here again they are all indulgent to themselves; and every one who believes himself a wit, that is, every man, will pretend at the same time to a right of judging. But to press it yet further, there are many witty men, but few poets; neither/have all poets a taste of Tragedy. And this is the rock on which they are daily splitting. Poetry, which is a picture of Nature, must generally please; but 'tis not to be understood that all parts of it must please every man; therefore is not Tragedy to be judged by a witty man, whose taste is only confined to Comedy. Nor is every man, who loves Tragedy, a sufficient judge of it; he must understand the excellencies of it too, or he will only prove a blind admirer, not a critic.

Pref. *All for Love,* '78. K I 195–96

Cf. STYLE, a.

hh. [To Francis, Lord Radcliffe] . . . being yourself a critic of the genuine sort, who have read the best authors in their own language, who perfectly distinguish of their several merits . . .

Ded. *Examen Poeticum,* '93. K II 6

Cf. RULES, g.

Tolerance [See below, CRITICAL TOLERANCE]

PROSODY, x. DRYDEN, LIFE, e.

Value

i. They [poets of the Last Age] had many who admired them, and few who blamed them; and certainly a severe critic is the greatest help to a good wit: he does

the office of a friend, while he designs that of an enemy; and his malice keeps a poet within those bounds, which the luxuriancy of his fancy would tempt him to overleap.

Defence of the Epilogue, '72. K I 166

j. The commendation of adversaries is the greatest triumph of a writer, because it never comes unless extorted. But I can be satisfied on more easy terms; if I happen to please the more moderate sort, I shall be sure of an honest party, and, in all probability, of the best judges; for the least concerned are commonly the least corrupt. [See SATIRE, a]

Pref. *Absalom,* '81. S-S IX 212

Critical Tolerance [Cf. CRITICISM]

(Eugenius) . . . as to my own particular, I am so great a lover of poesy, that I could wish them all rewarded, who attempt but to do well . . .

Dram. Poesy, '65. K I 30

Criticasters

a. (Crites) [¶] But . . . since the rewards of honour [customary among the Ancients] are taken away, that virtuous emulation is turned into direct malice; yet so slothful, that it contents itself to condemn and cry down others, without attempting to do better: 'tis a reputation too unprofitable, to take the necessary pains for it; yet, wishing they had it is incitement enough to hinder others from it. And this . . . is the reason why you have now so/ few good poets, and so many severe judges.

Dram. Poesy, '65. K I 37–38

b. . . . I am as little apt to defend my own errors, as to find those of other poets. Only, I observe, that the great censors of wit and poetry, either produce nothing of their own, or what is more ridiculous than anything they reprehend. Much of ill nature, and a very little judgment, go far in finding the mistakes of writers.

Pref. *Tyrannic Love,* '70. S-S III 379

DRYDEN, LITERARY LIFE, e-2.

c. Not that there is anything here [*An Evening's Love*] which I would not defend to an ill-natured judge (for I despise their censures, who I am sure would write worse on the same subject) . . .

Pref. *Evening's Love,* '71. K I 137

c-2. And this [superiority of the comedy of the present age to that of the past age] will be denied by none, but some few old fellows who value themselves on their acquaintance with the *Black Friars;* who, because they saw their plays, would pretend a right to judge ours. . . . Learning I never saw in any of them; and wit no more than they could remember.

Defence of the Epilogue, '72. K I 175

d. Let Mævius and Bavius admire each other; I wish to be hated by them and their fellows, by the same reason for which I desire to be loved by you [Sedley].

Ded. *Assignation,* '73. S-S IV 376

e. And though I could not refuse the partiality [in Dryden's behalf before *The State of Innocence*] of my friend [Lee], who is pleased to commend me in his verses, I hope they will rather be esteemed the effect of his love to me, than of his deliberate and sober judgment. His genius is able to make beautiful what he pleases: yet, as he has been too favourable to me, I doubt not but he will hear of his kindness from many of our contemporaries; for we are fallen into an age of illiterate, censorious, and detracting people, who, thus qualified, set up for critics.

Author's Apology, '77. K I 179

CRITIC, b.

f. My comfort is, that by this opinion

[of Montaigne] my enemies are but sucking critics, who would fain be nibbling ere their teeth are come.

Pref. *All for Love,* '78. K I 193

ENGLISH vs. FRENCH, j. ["our *Chedreux* critics"] ROCHESTER (WILMOT), c. ["this rhyming judge of the twelvepenny gallery, this legitimate son of Sternhold"] DRYDEN, WORKS, ee.

g. They [attackers of *The Duke of Guise*] go on: "If I may be allowed to judge;" (as men that do not poetise may be judges of wit, human nature, and common decencies;) so then the sentence is begun with *I* . . . but presently it is *men;* two more in buckram would be judges too. Neither of them, it seems, poetise; that is true, but both of them are in at rhyme doggrel; witness the song against the bishops, and the Tunbridge ballad.

Vindication, '83. S-S VII 199

DRYDEN, WORKS, mm.

h. [Following the acknowledgment of a verbal slip in the translation of Lucretius] [¶] There are a sort of blundering, half-witted people who make a great deal of noise about a verbal slip;/though Horace would instruct them better in true criticism—

> . . . *non ego paucis*
> *Offendar maculis* . . .

True judgment in Poetry, like that in Painting, takes a view of the whole together . . . and where the beauties are more than the faults, concludes for the poet against the little judge; 'tis a sign that malice is hard driven, when 'tis forced to lay hold on a word or syllable; to arraign a man is one thing, and to cavil at him is another. In the midst of an ill-natured generation of scribblers, there is always justice enough left in mankind to protect good writers: and they too are obliged, both by humanity and interest, to espouse each other's cause against false critics, who are the common enemies.

Pref. *Sylvæ* '85. K I 263–64

i. [I should set forth the principles guiding my performance in *Albion and Albanius,* but that would only be] to set up some little judges, who, not understanding thoroughly, would be sure to fall upon the faults, and not to acknowledge any of the beauties; an hard measure, which I have often found from false critics.

Pref. *Albion and Albanius,* '85. K I 276
DRYDEN, LITERARY LIFE, v. CRITIC[s], d. Cf. PROSODY, y.

j. . . . criticism is now become mere hangman's work, and meddles only with the faults of authors; nay, the critic is disgusted less with their absurdities than excellence; and you cannot displease him more than in leaving him little room for his malice, in your correctness and perfection; though that indeed is what he never allows any man; for, like the bed of Procrustes, they stretch or cut off an author to its length. These spoilers of Parnassus are a just excuse for concealing the name, since most of their malice is levelled more at the person than the thing; and as a sure mark of their judgment, they will extol to the skies the anonymous work of a person they will not allow to write common sense.

"Life of Lucian," '96. S-S XVIII 80
CRITIC[s], a. CHAUCER AND OVID. COLLIER.

k. As for the rest of those who have written against me, they are such scoundrels, that they deserve not the least notice to be taken of them. B—— and M—— are only distinguished from the crowd by being remembered to their infamy:

> . . . *Demetri, teque Tigelli,*
> *Discipulorum inter jubeo plorare cathedras.*

Pref. *Fables,* 1700. K II 273

Criticism

a. (Neander) . . . if we can persuade ourselves to use the candour of that poet, who, though the most severe of critics, has left us this caution by which to moderate our censures—

> . . . *ubi plura nitent in carmine* . . .

if, in consideration of their many and great beauties, we can wink at some slight and little imperfections, if we, I say, can be thus equal to ourselves, I ask no favour from the French.

Dram. Poesy, '65. K I 89

b. (Neander) And if I do not venture upon any particular judgment of our late plays, 'tis out of the consideration which an ancient writer gives me: *vivorum, ut magna admiratio, ita censura difficilis:* betwixt the extremes of admiration and malice, 'tis hard to judge uprightly of the living.

Dram. Poesy, '65. K I 89

c. [¶] In the first place, I must take leave to tell them, that they wholly mistake the nature of criticism who think its business is principally to find fault. Criticism, as it was first instituted by Aristotle, was meant a standard of judging well; the chiefest part of which is, to observe those excellencies which should delight a reasonable reader. [See next entry]

Author's Apology, '77. K I 179

d. If the design, the conduct, the thoughts, and the expressions of a poem, be generally such as proceed from a true genius of Poetry, the critic ought to pass his judgment in favour of the author. 'Tis malicious and unmanly to snarl at the little

45

lapses of a pen, from which Virgil himself stands not exempted. Horace acknowledges, that honest Homer nods sometimes . . . And Longinus, who was undoubtedly, after Aristotle, the greatest critic amongst the Greeks, in his twenty-/seventh chapter ΠΕΡΙ ῾ΥΨΟΥΣ, has judiciously preferred the sublime genius that sometimes errs, to the middling or indifferent one, which makes few faults, but seldom or never rises to any excellence.

Author's Apology, '77. K I 179–80

FRENCH AUTHORS, a. ACTING AND ACTORS, b. Cf. STYLE, a. CRITICASTERS, h, i. Cf. ST. ÉVREMOND, d.

e. [¶] Good sense and good nature are never separated, though the ignorant world has thought otherwise. Good nature, by which I mean beneficence and candour, is the product of right reason; which of necessity will give allowance to the failings of others, by considering that there is nothing perfect in mankind; and by distinguishing that which comes nearest to excellency, though not absolutely free from faults, will certainly produce a candour in the judge.

Discourse of Satire, '93. K II 17

CRITIC[s], f. PERSIUS, f. CRITIC[s], d. CRITICASTERS, j. Cf. SEGRAIS, c. Cf. RULES, k.

Crowne, John

He used sometimes to own that Crown had some genius; but then added, 'that his father and Crown's mother were very well acquainted.' Old Jacob Tonson.

Spence, *Anecdotes* (1820), p. 45

Cultural Interchange

For great contem/poraries whet and cultivate each other; and mutual borrowing, and commerce, makes the common riches of learning, as it does of the civil government. [GOLDEN AGES, b]

Discourse of Satire, '93. K II 25–26

Curiosa Felicitas [See STYLE]

[Of a fine stroke in Virgil] Good Heavens!/how the plain sense is raised by the beauty of the words! But this was happiness, the former might be only judgment: this was the *curiosa felicitas,* which Petronius attributes to Horace; it is the pencil thrown luckily full upon the horse's mouth, to express the foam which the painter with all his skill could not perform without it. These hits of words a true poet often finds . . . without seeking; but he knows their value when he finds them, and is infinitely pleased. A bad poet may sometimes light on them, but he discerns not a diamond from a Bristol-stone; and would have been of the cock's mind in Æsop; a grain of barley would have pleased him better than the jewel.

Parallel, '95. K II 150–51

❧ D ❧

Dacier, André

. . . but Dacier knows no more of it than I do. [See Satire, ee]

Discourse of Satire, '93. K II 61

Satire, hh, t. Aristotle, b. Chorus, c. Cf. Racine, b.

Danish Language

English Langauge, a.

Dante Alighieri

Cf. Italian Language and Literature, b.

. . . Dante, in his *Inferno,* has put him [Brutus] and Cassius, and Judas Iscariot betwixt them, into the/great Devil's mouth . . .

Ded. Æneis, '97. K II 169–70

Boccaccio.

Davenant, Sir William

a. But if we owe the invention of it [rhymed verse] to Mr. Waller, we are acknowledging for the noblest use of it to Sir William D'Avenant, who at once brought it upon the stage, and made it perfect, in the *Siege of Rhodes.*

Ded. Rival Ladies, '64. K I 7

Rhyme (Debate), k. Cf. Court, a. Dryden, Works, l.

b. But Sir William Davenant, as he was a man of quick and piercing imagination, soon found that somewhat might be added to the design of Shakespeare [in the *Tempest*], of which neither Fletcher nor Suckling had ever thought: And, therefore . . . he designed the counterpart to Shakespeare's plot, namely, that of a man who had never seen a woman . . . This excellent contrivance he was pleased to communicate to me, and to desire my assistance

in it. I confess that from the very first moment it so pleased me, that I never writ anything with more delight. I must likewise do him that justice to acknowledge that my writing received daily his amendments; and/that is the reason why it is not so faulty, as the rest which I have done, without the help or correction of so judicious a friend. . . . In the time I writ with him, I had the opportunity to observe somewhat more nearly of him, than I had formerly done, when I had only a bare acquaintance with him: I found him then of so quick a fancy, that nothing was proposed to him, on which he could not suddenly produce a thought, extremely pleasant and surprising: and those first thoughts of his, contrary to the old Latin proverb, were not always the least happy. And as his fancy was quick, so likewise were the products of it remote and new. He borrowed not of any other; and his imaginations were such as could not easily enter into any other man. His corrections were sober and judicious: and he corrected his own writings much more severely than those of another man, bestowing twice the time and labour in polishing, which he used in invention.

Pref. Tempest, '69. S-S III 106–7

Heroic Play, b.

c. But as few men have the happiness to begin and finish any new project, so neither did he [Davenant] live to make his design [of a heroic play] perfect: there wanted the fulness of a plot, and the variety of characters . . . and, perhaps, something might have been added to the beauty of the style. . . . For myself and others . . . we are bound, with all veneration to his memory, to acknowledge what advantage we received from that excellent groundwork which he laid . . .

Essay of Heroic Plays, '72. K I 150
HEROIC PLAY, c, d.

d. Thus he [Davenant] takes the image of an heroic poem from the Drama, or stage poetry; and accordingly intended to divide it into five books, representing the same number of acts; and every book into several cantos, imitating the scenes which compose our acts.

But this, I think, is rather a play in narration . . . than an heroic poem . . .

Essay of Heroic Plays, '72. K I 151
Cf. OPERA, g. FARCE, g.

Decay (Natura effoeta) [See also NATURE; Cf. PROGRESS]
LAST AGE, b.

. . . not only the bodies, but the souls of men, have decreased from the vigour of the first ages . . . [See ANCIENTS, a.]

Ded. *Plutarch, '83.* S-S XVII 5
MODERNS, f. Cf. FONTENELLE, b.

Decorum [See also PROPRIETY]

a. (Eugenius) . . . in short, there is no indecorum in any of our modern plays, which if I would excuse, I could not shadow with some authority from the Ancients. [See ANCIENTS, r.]

Dram. Poesy, '65. K I 50
ENGLISH VS. FRENCH, p. TUMULT, a.

b. (Lisideius) [¶] I have observed that in all our tragedies, the audience cannot forbear laughing when the actors are to die; it is the most comic part of the whole play. All *passions* may be lively represented on the stage, if to the well-writing of them the actor supplies a good commanded voice, and

limbs that move easily, and without stiffness; but there are many *actions* which can never be imitated to a just height: dying especially is a thing which none but a Roman gladiator could naturally perform on the stage, when he did not imitate or represent, but naturally do it; and therefore it is better to omit the representation of it.

Dram. Poesy, '65. K I 63
NARRATIONS, c.

c. (Lisideius) [Having quoted Horace, . . . *Non tamen intus . . .* and *Nec pueros coram populo Medea trucidet . . .*]/That is, those actions which by reason of their cruelty will cause aversion in us, or by reason of their impossibility, unbelief, ought either wholly to be avoided . . . or only delivered by narration. To which we may have leave to add such as to avoid tumult . . . or to reduce the plot into a more reasonable compass of time, or for defect of beauty in them, are rather to be related than presented . . .

Dram. Poesy, '65. K I 64–65

d. (Neander) . . . I must acknowledge with him [Lisideius], that the French have reason when they hide that part of the action which would occasion too much tumult on the stage, and choose rather to have it made known by narration . . . Farther, I think it very convenient . . . that all incredible actions were removed; but, whether custom has so insinuated itself into our countrymen, or nature has so formed them to fierceness, I know not; but they will scarcely suffer combats and other objects of horror to be taken from them. And indeed, the indecency of tumults is all which can be objected against fighting: for why may not our imagination as well suffer itself to be deluded with the probability of it, as with any other thing in the play? For my part, I can with as great ease persuade myself that the blows which are struck, are given in good earnest, as I can, that they who strike them are kings or princes, or those persons which they represent.

Dram. Poesy, '65. K I 74
CORNEILLE (PIERRE), a-2.

e. (Neander) But for death, that it ought not to be represented, I have, besides the arguments alleged by Lisideius, the authority of/Ben Johnson, who has forborn it in his tragedies . . .[1]

Dram. Poesy, '65. K I 74–75
JONSON, h. NARRATIONS, d. Cf. STYLE, b.

f. That which with more reason was objected as an indecorum [in *Secret Love*], is the management of the last scene of the play, where Celadon and Florimel are treating too lightly of their marriage in the presence of the queen, who likewise seems to stand idle, while the great action of the drama is still depending. This I cannot otherwise defend, than by telling you, I so designed it on purpose, to make my play go off more smartly; that scene being, in the opinion of the best judges, the most divertising of the whole comedy. But though the artifice succeeded, I am willing to acknowledge it as a fault,/since it pleased his Majesty, the best judge, to think it so.

Pref. Secret Love, '67. S-S II 420–21
POINTS. Cf. ARCHAISMS, a. FLETCHER, b. Cf. SHAKESPEARE, u.

g. The French poets, I confess, are strict observers of these punctilios: they would not, for example, have suffered Cleopatra and Octavia to have met; or, if they had met, there must have only passed betwixt them some cold civilities, but no eagerness of repartee, for fear of offending against the greatness of their characters, and the modesty of their sex. This objection I foresaw/and at the same time contemned; for I judged it both natural and probable, that Octavia, proud of her new-gained conquest, would search out Cleopatra to triumph over her; and that Cleopatra, thus attacked, was not of a spirit to shun the encounter . . . 'Tis true, some actions, though natural, are not fit to be represented; and broad obscenities in words ought in good manners to be avoided . . . If I have kept myself within the bounds of modesty, all beyond it is but nicety and affectation; which is no more but modesty depraved into a vice.

Pref. All for Love, '78. K I 192–93
FRENCH AUTHORS, a. Cf. RACINE, a.

h. We [Lee and Dryden] were indeed obliged, by the laws of poetry, to cast into shadows the vices of this prince [Henry III of France]; for an excellent critic [Rymer, *Tragedies* . . .] has lately told us, that when a king is named, a hero is supposed . . .

Vindication, '83. S-S VII 159
Cf. TRAGICOMEDY, e. Cf. SATIRE, s, f.

i. [¶] In poetry Horace calls these things [mere ornaments] *versus inopes rerum, nugaeque canorae;* these are also the *lucus et ara Dianae,* which he mentions in the same *Art of Poetry.* But since there must be ornaments both in painting and poetry, if they are not necessary, they must at least be decent; that is, in their due place, and but moderately used. . . . [N]either is the poet, who is working up a passion, to make similes, which will certainly make it languish. My Montezuma dies with a fine one in his mouth; but it is ambitious, and out of season. . . . So I have seen in some modern plays above twenty actors, when the action has not required half the number. In the principal

49

figures of a picture, the painter is to employ the sinews of his art; for in them consists the principal beauty of his work. Our author saves me the comparison with Tragedy; for he says, that herein he is to imitate the tragic poet, who employs his utmost force in those places wherein consists the height and beauty of the action.

Parallel, '95. K II 140

Cf. TRAGICOMEDY, g. VIRGIL, v.

Demosthenes

. . . the/force and gravity of Demosthenes . . . [See POLYBIUS AND TACITUS]

"Character of Polybius," '93. S-S XVIII 51–52

PERSIUS, g. FIGURES, c. HOMER AND VIRGIL, d.

Denham, Sir John

a. This sweetness of Mr. Waller's lyric poesy was afterwards followed in the epic by Sir John Denham, in his *Cooper's Hill*, a poem which your Lordship knows for the majesty of the style, is, and ever will be, the exact standard of good writing.

Ded. *Rival Ladies*, '64. K I 7

PRESENT AGE, d. ["nothing so majestic, so correct, as Sir John Denham"] TRANSLATION, h.

b. Sir John Denham (who advised more liberty than he took/himself) gives his reason for his innovation [in translation: the imitative method], in his admirable Preface before the translation of the Second *Æneid: Poetry is of so subtile a spirit, that, in pouring out of one language into another, it will all evaporate; and, if a new spirit be not added in the transfusion, there will remain nothing but a* caput mortuum. I confess this argument holds good against a literal translation; but who defends it?

Pref. *Ovid's Epistles*, '80. K I 240–41

Cf. TRANSLATION, b. COWLEY, f. DRYDEN, LITERARY LIFE, b. PROSODY, d. Cf. TRANSLATION, gg. CHAUCER, c.

Dennis, John

Your own Poetry is a more Powerful Example, to prove that the Modern Writers may enter into comparison with the Ancients, than any which Perrault could produce in France; yet neither he, nor you who are a better Critick, can persuade me that there is any room left for a Solid Commendation at this time of day, at least for me. If I undertake the Translation of Virgil, the little which I can perform will shew at least, that no Man is fit to write after him, in a barbarous/Modern tongue.

Letter to Dennis, March 1694. Ward No. 31, pp. 70–71

PROSODY, y.

Description[s] [See also IMAGES; FIGURES]

TRAGEDY, n.

[The wit of an Heroic Poem] is some lively and apt description, dressed in such colours of speech, that it sets before your eyes the absent object, as perfectly, and more delightfully than nature.

Pref. *Annus Mirabilis*, '66. K I 15

EPIC, a. IMAGES, b. FABLE, c. PASSIONS, i. DESIGNING. FIGURES, e. MANNERS, l.

Design [Cf. ORDONNANCE]

PLAY (PARTS). FLETCHER, a.

(Neander) If . . . the parts are managed so regularly, that the beauty of the whole be kept entire, and that the variety become not a perplexed and confused mass of accidents, you will find it infinitely pleasing to be led in a labyrinth of design, where you see some of your way before you, yet discern not the end till you arrive at it.

Dram. Poesy, '65. K I 73

DAVENANT, b. FABLE, c. HEROIC PLAY, c. CRITICISM, d. DRYDEN, WORKS, X. ANCIENTS, u. DICTION, a. DRYDEN, WORKS, z. SHAKESPEARE, f. AUTHORITY, e. TRAGICOMEDY, d. DONNE, b. Cf. LUCAN, e. SPENSER, b. DRYDEN, LITERARY LIFE, l. SATIRE, c. ENGLISH VS. FRENCH, k. EPIC, c. EXPRESSION, b. VIRGIL, n. EXPRESSION, c. EPIC, d.

Designing

JONSON, g. ENGLISH DRAMA, c. OVID, e.

[The necessary cutting from the play *Don Sebastian* made it] impossible to prevent some part of the action from being precipitated, and coming on without that due preparation which is required to all great events: as, in particular, that of raising the mobile, in the beginning of the fourth act,/. . . On this consideration, I have replaced those lines through the whole poem, and thereby restored it to that clearness of conception, and (if I may dare to say it) that lustre and masculine vigour in which it was first written. It is obvious to every understanding reader, that the most poetical parts, which are descriptions, images, similitudes, and moral sentences, are those which of necessity were to be pared away, when the body was swollen into too large a bulk for the representation of the stage. [See DRAMA READ AND ACTED]

Pref. *Don Sebastian,* '90. S-S VII 307–08

FABLE, f. SATIRE, c. HOMER AND VIRGIL, d. INVENTION, e.

Deus ex Machina [Cf. EPIC MACHINERY; SUPERNATURAL]

a. (Eugenius) [Speaking of the pat discovery in Roman comedy] . . . one or other sees a little box or cabinet which was carried away with her [heroine], and so discovers her to her friends, if some god do not prevent it, by coming down in a machine, and take the thanks of it to himself.

Dram. Poesy, '65. K I 47

b. Neither is it so trivial an undertaking, to make a tragedy end happily; for 'tis more difficult to save than 'tis to kill. The dagger and the cup of poison are always in a readiness . . . [See TRAGEDY, q]

Ded. *Spanish Friar,* '81. K I 249

c. . . . as I have somewhere said [see above, b.], the poison and the dagger are still at hand to butcher a hero when a poet wants the brains to save him.

Pref. *Don Sebastian,* '90. S-S VII 311

d. Oh, how convenient is a machine sometimes in a heroic poem![1]

Dedication *Æneis,* '97. K II 189

e. As for what Horace says in his *Art of Poetry,* that no machines are to be used, unless on some extraordinary occasion,

Nec deus intersit, nisi dignus vindice nodus—

that rule is to be applied to the theatre, of which he is then speaking; and means no more than this, that, when the knot of the play is to be untied, and no other way is left for making the discovery; then, and not otherwise, let a God descend upon a rope, and clear the business to the audience: but this has no relation to the machines which are used in an epic poem.

Ded. *Æneis,* '97. K II 211

Dialogue (Dramatic)

RHYME (DEBATE), g, n.

This [ease of diction] is the proper wit of dialogue or discourse, and consequently of the Drama, where all that is said is supposed to be the effect of sudden thought; which, though it excludes not the quickness of wit in repartees, yet admits not a too curious election of words, too frequent allusions, or use of tropes, or, in fine, anything that shows remoteness of thought, or labour in the writer.

Pref. *Annus Mirabilis*, '66. K I 15

EPIC VS. TRAGEDY, j. FIGURES, e.

Dialogue (Genre)

a. And yet, my Lord, this war of opinions, you well know, has fallen out among the writers of all ages, and sometimes betwixt friends. Only it has been prosecuted by some like pedants, with violence of words, and managed by others like gentlemen, with candour and civility. Even Tully had a controversy with his dear Atticus; and in one of his Dialogues, makes him sustain the part of an enemy . . .

Epistle Dedicatory, *Dram. Poesy*, '67. K I 26

b. . . . he [Howard] gives me the compellation of 'The Author of *a Dramatic Essay*'; which is a little discourse in dialogue, for the most part borrowed from the observations of others . . .

Defence of An Essay, '68. K I 112

DRYDEN, WORKS, d.

c. In my Dialogue [*Dramatic Poesy*], as I before hinted, several persons maintained their several opinions . . .

Defence of An Essay, '68. K I 130

WALSH, b. Cf. DRYDEN, LITERARY LIFE, a.

d. [¶] The way which Lucian chose of delivering these profitable and pleasing truths, was that of dialogue: a choice worthy of the author; happily followed . . . by Erasmus, and Fontenelle particularly, to whom I may justly add a triumvir of our own—the reverend, ingenious, and learned Dr. Eachard, who, by using the same method, and the/same ingredients of raillery and reason, has more baffled the philosopher of Malmesbury, than those

who assaulted him with blunt heavy arguments, drawn from orthodox divinity; for Hobbes foresaw where those strokes would fall, and leaped aside before they could descend; but he could not avoid those nimble passes, which were made on him by a wit more active than his own . . . [See next entry.]

"Life of Lucian," '96. S-S XVIII 76–77

e. [¶] I will not here take notice of the several kinds of dialogue, and the whole art of it, which would ask an entire volume to perform. This has been a work long wanted, and much desired, of which the ancients have not sufficiently informed us; and I question whether any man now living can treat it accurately. Lucian, it seems, was very sensible of the difficult task, which he undertook in writing dialogues . . . He owns himself . . . to be the inventor of a new work, attempted in a new manner . . . For, to quit the beaten road of the ancients, and to take a path of his own choosing, he acknowledges to be a bold and ridiculous attempt, if it succeed not.[q]

"Life of Lucian," '96. S-S XVIII 77

Diction [See also EXPRESSION]

a. [¶] Rapin attributes more to the *dictio*, that is, to the words and discourse of a tragedy, than Aristotle . . . who places them in the last rank of beauties; perhaps, only last in order, because they are the last product of the design . . . Rapin's words are remarkable: It is not the admirable intrigue, the surprising events, and extraordinary incidents, that make the beauty of a tragedy; it is the discourses, when they are natural and passionate.—So are Shakespeare's.

Heads of an Answer, '77. S-S XV 392

Choice of
ENGLISH LANGUAGE, i. Cf. THOMAS, ELIZABETH, c.
Coloring, compared to
EXPRESSION, b, c. EPIC, d.
Dialogue, diction proper to
OVID AND VIRGIL, a. DIALOGUE (DRA-MATIC).
Dictio Virgiliani
VIRGIL, l, m, n. Cf. TRANSLATION, n. ENGLISH VS. FRENCH, w. ENGLISH LANGUAGE, e.
Donne's
DONNE, c, d.
"Easy [Sounding] and Significant"
PRESENT AGE, f. ENGLISH LANGUAGE, i. IMAGINATION, c. LANGUAGE. DRYDEN, WORKS, bbb. BORROWING (VERBAL), c. MODERNIZING.
Epic and Tragedy
TRAGEDY, r.
Homer, Virgil, and Shakespeare

b. In the last of these [words, or diction, the fifth part of a tragedy or epic], Homer excels Virgil; Virgil excels all other ancient poets; and Shakespeare all modern poets.

Heads of an Answer, '77. S-S XV 389

Horatian
HORACE, j.
Onomatopoeic
VIRGIL, l. DRYDEN, WORKS, sss.
Panegyrical
PROSODY, x.
Persius's
PERSIUS, b.
Poverty of English
BORROWING (VERBAL), c.
Rank among Parts of Epic
EPIC, d.
Shakespearean [See above, b]
TRAGEDY, e. See SHAKESPEARE entry

Technical
TECHNICAL TERMS, a, b.
"Village Words"
ENGLISH LANGUAGE, f.

Dictionary
ACADEMY, b. PROSODY, z.

Digressions

Then he [Plutarch] was more happy in his digressions than any we have named. I have always been pleased to see him, and his imitator, Montaigne, when they strike a little out of the common road; for we are sure to be the better for their wandering. The best quarry lies not always in the open field; and who would not be content to follow a good huntsman over hedges and ditches, when he knows the game will reward his pains?

"Life of Plutarch," '83. S-S XVII 64

POLYBIUS, c. DRYDEN, WORKS, ttt. PROSODY, hh. PREFACES, d.

Dion Cassius
ENGLISH LANGUAGE, c. PLUTARCH, g. POLYBIUS, a. LUCIAN, g.

Disposition [Cf. DESIGN]

[¶] Under this head of *Invention* is placed the disposition of the work; to put all things in a beautiful order and harmony, that the whole may be of a piece.

Parallel, '95. K II 139

INVENTION, d. VIRGIL, cc. EPIC, d.

Donne, John

a. So that there is this difference betwixt his *Satires* [i.e., Cleveland's] and doctor Donne's; that the one gives us deep thoughts in common language, though rough cadence; the other gives as common thoughts in abstruse words . . .

Dram. Poesy, '65. K I 52

b. [¶] Doctor Donne, the greatest wit, though not the best poet of our nation, acknowledges, that/he had never seen Mrs.

Drury, whom he has made immortal in his admirable "Anniversaries." I have had the same fortune, though I have not succeeded to the same genius. However, I have followed his footsteps in the design of his panegyric; which was to raise an emulation in the living, to copy out the example of the dead. And therefore it was, that I once intended to have called this poem "The Pattern". . . .

Ded. *Eleonora,* '92. S-S XI 123–24

c. Donne alone, of all our countrymen, had your [Dorset's] talent; but was not happy enough to arrive at your versification; and were he translated into numbers, and English, he would yet be wanting in the dignity of expression. . . . You equal Donne in the variety, multiplicity, and choice of thoughts; you excel him in the manner and the words. I read you both with the same admiration, but not with the same delight. He affects the metaphysics, not only in his satires, but in his amorous verses, where nature only should reign; and perplexes the minds of the fair sex with nice speculations of philosophy, when he should engage their hearts, and entertain them with the softnesses of love. In this (if I may be pardoned for so bold a truth) Mr. Cowley has copied him to a fault; so great a one, in my opinion, that it throws his *Mistress* infinitely below his Pindarics and his latter compositions, which are undoubtedly the best of his poems, and the most correct.

Discourse of Satire, '93. K II 19

d. Would not Donne's *Satires,* which abound with so much wit, appear more charming, if he had taken care of his words, and of his numbers? But he followed Horace so very close, that of necessity he must fall with him; and I may safely say it of this present age, that if we are not so great wits as Donne, yet certainly we are better poets.

Discourse of Satire, '93. K II 102

Dorset (Charles Sackville, Earl of)

See The Epistle Dedicatory of *An Essay of Dramatic Poesy,* Ker I.

a. . . . the accurate judgment of my Lord Buckhurst . . . [DRYDEN, WORKS, d]

Defence of An Essay, '68. K I 124

SHAKESPEARE, h.

b. [¶] There is not an English writer this day living, who is not perfectly convinced that your Lordship excels all others in all the several parts of poetry which you have undertaken to adorn. . . .

I will not attempt, in this place, to say anything particular of your lyric poems, though they are the delight and wonder of this age, and will be the envy of the next. The subject of this book confines me to Satire; and in that, an author of your own quality [Rochester], (whose ashes I will not disturb,) has given you all the commendation which his self-sufficiency could afford to any man: *The best good man, with the worst natur'd Muse.* In that character, methinks, I am reading Johnson's verses to the memory of Shakespeare; an insolent, sparing, and invidious panegyric: where good nature, the most godlike commendation . . . is only attributed to your/ person, and denied to your writings; for they are everywhere so full of candour, that, like Horace, you only expose the follies of men, without arraigning their vices; and in this excel him, that you add the pointedness of thought, which is visibly wanting in our great Roman. There is more of salt in all your verses, than I have seen . . . but you have been sparing of the gall . . . [See DONNE, c]

Discourse of Satire, '93. K II 18–19

c. For my part, I must avow it freely to the world, that I never attempted anything in satire, wherein I have not studied your [Dorset's] writings as the most perfect model.

Discourse of Satire, '93. K II 19

POETASTERS, g.

d. [Dryden will presume to tell Dorset] how lawfully you may/exercise it [power], over the petulant scribblers of this age. As Lord Chamberlain . . . you are absolute by your office, in all that belongs to the decency and good manners of the stage. You can banish from thence scurrility and profaneness, and restrain the licentious insolence of poets, and their actors, in all things that shock the public quiet, or the reputation of private persons . . . But I mean not the authority, which is annexed to your office; I speak of that only which is inborn and inherent to your person . . . an excellent wit, a masterly and commanding genius over all writers . . .

Discourse of Satire, '93. K II 22–23

MODERNS, f. POETRY, a, g. SATIRE, b. HORACE, e. HORACE AND JUVENAL AND PERSIUS, k. CRITIC[s], d. CHAPMAN, b. TRANSLATION, f.

Double Plot

See UNDERPLOT; cf. UNITY OF ACTION (DRAMATIC)

Drama: Epic Origins

For the original of the stage was from the Epic Poem. Narration, doubtless, preceded acting, and gave laws to it . ./. Those episodes of Homer, which were proper for the stage, the poets amplified each into an action . . . Nor were they only animated by him, but their measure and symmetry was owing to him. His one, entire, and great action was copied by them according to the proportions of the drama. If he finished his orb within the year, it sufficed to teach them, that their action being less . . . their orb, of consequence, must be . . . less . . . , which they reduced within the limits either of a natural or an artificial day . . . Tragedy is the miniature of human life; an epic poem is the draught at length.

Ded. *Æneis,* '97. K II 156–57

EPIC VS. TRAGEDY, f.

Drama Read and Acted

a. . . . more proper for the study than the stage . . . [See SENECA, b]

FLETCHER, e.

a-2. . . . a judicious reader will discover, in his closet, that trashy stuff, whose glittering deceived him in the action. [See JUDGMENT (RESPONSIVE)]

Ded. *Spanish Friar,* '81. K I 245

CHAPMAN, a. DESIGNING.

b. But there is a vast difference betwixt a public entertainment on the theatre, and a private reading in the closet: in the first, we are confined to time; and though we talk not by the hour-glass, yet the watch often drawn out of the pocket warns that the audience is weary: in the last, every reader is judge of his own convenience; he can take up the book and lay it down at his pleasure, and find out those beauties of propriety in thought and writing which escaped him in the tumult and hurry of representing.

Pref. *Don Sebastian,* '90. S-S VII 308

EPIC VS. TRAGEDY, f. ACTING AND ACTORS, c. EPIC VS. TRAGEDY, g, j.

Dramatis Personae

a. (Neander) But this [Lisideius's point that a drama naturally has one main character] hinders not that there may be more shining characters in the play: many persons of a second magnitude, nay, some so very near, so almost equal to the first, that greatness may be opposed to greatness,

55

and all the persons be made considerable, not only by their quality, but their action. 'Tis evident that the more the persons are, the greater will be the variety of the plot.

Dram. Poesy, '65. K I 73

Cf. JONSON, l. FABLE, c. ANCIENTS, v, e.

b. . . . every critic understands the reason, *ne quarta loqui persona laboret.* I am never willing to cumber the stage with many speakers, when I can reasonably avoid it, as here [in a scene of the *Duke of Guise*] I might.

Vindication, '83. S-S VII 162

ENGLISH VS. FRENCH, k. DECORUM, i. EPIC VS. TRAGEDY, f.

Dryden, Life

Boyhood and School

PROSODY, n. SYLVESTER'S *Du Bartas.* POLYBIUS, a.

a. [¶] I remember I translated this Satyr [Persius's Third], when I was a *Kings-Scholar* at *Westminster* School, for a *Thursday* Nights *Exercise;* and believe that it, and many other of my *Exercises* of this nature, in *English Verse,* are still in the Hands of my *Learned Master,* the Reverend Doctor *Busby.*

Argument of the Third Satire [Persius], '93. JK II 758

BUSBY, b. TRANSLATION, c.

University

UNIVERSITY, c.

Family [See below, *Financial Embarrassment*]

Cf. DRYDEN, LITERARY LIFE, p.

b. What I had forgotten before, in its due place, I must here tell the Reader; That the first half of this Satyr [Persius's Second] was translated by one of my Sons, now in *Italy:* But I thought so well of it, that I let it pass without any Alteration.

Notes to the Second Satire [Persius], '93. JK II 757

THOMAS, ELIZABETH, a.

Financial Embarrassment

DRYDEN, LITERARY LIFE, k, s, l.

b-2. I have never been an Impudent Beggar at the Doors of Noblemen: My Visits have indeed been too rare to be unacceptable; and but just enough to testifie my Gratitude for their Bounty, which I have frequently received, but always unask'd, as themselves will Witness.

Letter to Dennis, March 1694. Ward No. 31, p. 73

See below, d-2.

Political Embarrassment

DRYDEN, LITERARY LIFE, s, l. CHORUS, d. SATIRE, j.

c. If they [the Court] will consider me as a Man, who have done my best to improve the Language, & Expecially the Poetry, & will be content with my acquiescence under the present Government, & forbearing satire on it, that I can promise, because I can perform it: but I can neither take the Oaths, nor forsake my Religion . . .

Letter to Mrs. Steward, 7 November 1699. Ward No. 67, p. 123

Social Life

HORACE, k. DRYDEN, WORKS, ccc. MULGRAVE, b. DRYDEN, WORKS, qqq, rrr.

Status

PRESENT AGE, m. DRYDEN, LITERARY LIFE, t.

Age and Health

DRYDEN, LITERARY LIFE, s, l.

d. [¶] Virgil employed eleven years upon his *Æneis;* yet he left it, as he thought himself, imperfect; which when I seriously consider, I wish that, instead of three years, which I have spent in the translation of his works, I had four years more allowed me to correct my errors, that I might make my version somewhat more tolerable than it is.

For a poet cannot have too great a reverence for his readers, if he expects his labours should survive him. Yet I will neither plead my age nor sickness, in excuse of the faults which I have made: that I wanted time, is all that I have to say; for some of my subscribers grew so clamorous, that I could no longer defer the publication.

Ded. *Æneis,* '97. K II 216

d-2. [¶] What Virgil wrote in the vigour of his age, in plenty and at ease, I have undertaken to translate in my declining years; struggling with wants, oppressed with sickness, curbed in my genius, liable to be misconstrued in all I write; and my judges, if they are not very equitable, already prejudiced against me, by the lying character which has been given them of my morals. Yet steady to my principles, and not dispirited with my afflictions, I have, by the blessing of God on my endeavours, overcome all the difficulties, and, in some/measure, acquitted myself of the debt which I owed the public when I undertook this work.

Postscript *Æneis,* '97. K II 240–41

DRYDEN, WORKS, ooo. DRYDEN, LITERARY LIFE, c.

e. By the mercy of God, I am already come within twenty years of his number [88 years], a cripple in my limbs, but what decays are in my mind, the reader must determine. I think myself as vigorous as ever in the faculties of my soul, excepting only my memory, which is not impaired to any great degree; and if I lose not more of it, I have no great reason to complain. What judgment I had, increases rather than diminishes; and thoughts, such as they are, come crowding in so fast upon me, that my only difficulty is to choose or to reject, to run them into verse, or to give them the other harmony of prose: I have so long

studied and practised both, that they are grown into a habit, and become familiar to me. In short, though I may lawfully plead some part of the old gentleman's excuse,/ yet I will reserve it till I think I have greater need, and ask no grains of allowance for the faults of this my present work, but those which are given of course to human frailty.

Pref. *Fables,* 1700. K II 249–50

Dryden, Personal Character

Christian Conscience

SATIRE, s. DRYDEN, LITERARY LIFE, t.

Self-Esteem

DRYDEN, LITERARY LIFE, m. PRESENT AGE, k. SATIRE, q.

a. [In connection with his disavowal of designing a parallel between the Duke of Guise and Monmouth] And yet I fancy, that where I make it my business to draw likeness, it will be no hard matter to judge who sate for the picture.

Vindication, '83. S-S VII 154

SHADWELL, e, f.

b. [Of his performance in *Albion and Albanius*] . . . I may, without vanity, own some advantages, which are not common to every writer; such as are the knowledge of the Italian and French language, and the being conversant with some of their best performances in this kind . . .

Pref. *Albion and Albanius,* '85. K I 275

TRANSLATION, gg. DRYDEN, WORKS, ooo. Cf. DRYDEN, LIFE, c. MILBOURNE.

Modesty

DRYDEN, LITERARY LIFE, k, g. HORACE, k. DRYDEN, WORKS, fff. WYCHERLEY, c, d. INVENTION, e, f. VIRGIL, mm. PROSODY, b, d. ENGLISH LANGUAGE, e.

c. [¶] Lay by Virgil, I beseech your Lordship, and all my better sort of judges, when you take up my version; and it will appear a passable beauty when the original/Muse is absent.

Ded. *Æneis,* '97. K II 233–34

ADDISON. DRYDEN, LITERARY LIFE, c. THOMAS (ELIZABETH), b. CHAUCER, g. MODERNIZING, a. DRYDEN, WORKS, www.
Morality
POETIC JUSTICE, c. DRYDEN, LITERARY LIFE, e. DRYDEN, LIFE, d-2.

d. More libels have been written against me, than almost any man now living; and I had reason on my side, to have defended my own innocence. I speak not of my poetry, which I have wholly given up to the critics: let them use it as they please: posterity, perhaps, may be more favourable to me; for interest and passion will lie buried in another age, and partiality and prejudice be forgotten. I speak of my morals, which have been sufficiently aspersed: that only sort of reputation ought to be dear to every honest man, and is to me. But let the world witness for me, that I have been often wanting to myself in that particular; I have seldom answered any scurrilous lampoon, when it was in my power to have exposed my enemies: and, being naturally vindicative, have suffered in silence, and possessed my soul in quiet.

Discourse of Satire, '93. K II 80
DRYDEN, LITERARY LIFE, t.

d-2. For my Morals, betwixt Man and Man, I am not to be my own Judge. I appeal to the World if I have Deceiv'd or defrauded any Man: And for my private Conversation, they who see me every day can be the best Witnesses, whether or no it be Blameless and Inoffensive. Hitherto I have no reason to complain that Men of either Party shun my Company.

Letter to Dennis, March 1694. Ward No. 31, p. 73

LUCIAN, c. OBSCENITY, e.

e. May I have leave to do myself the justice, (since my enemies will do me none, and are so far from granting me to be a good poet, that they will not allow me so much as to be a Christian, or a moral man), may I have leave, I say, to inform my reader, that I have confined my choice to such tales of Chaucer as savour nothing of immodesty. If I had desired more to please than to instruct, the Reeve, the Miller, the Shipman, the Merchant, the Sumner, and, above all, the Wife of Bath, in the *Prologue* to her *Tale,* would have procured me as many friends and readers, as there are *beaux* and ladies of pleasure in the town. But I will no more offend against good manners: I am sensible as I ought to be of the scandal I have given by my loose writings; and make what reparation I am able, by this public acknowledgment. If anything of this nature, or of profaneness, be crept into these poems, I am so far from defending it, that I disown it. *Totum hoc indictum volo.* Chaucer makes another manner of apology for his broad speaking, and Boccace makes the like; but I will follow neither of them.

Pref. *Fables,* 1700. K II 263
COLLIER

Personality [See below, *Philosophical Temper*]

f. If the humour of this [age] be for low comedy, small accidents, and raillery, I will force my genius to obey it, though with more reputation I could write in verse. I know I am not so fitted by nature to write comedy: I want that gaiety of humour which is required to it. My conversation is slow and dull; my humour saturnine and reserved; in short, I am none of those who endeavour to break jests in company, or make reparties. So that those, who decry my comedies, do me no injury, except it be in point of profit: reputation in them is the last thing to which I shall pretend.

Defence of An Essay, '68. K I 116

g. . . . I am sometimes ready to imagine, that my disgust of low comedy proceeds not so much from my judgment as from my temper; which is the reason why I so seldom write it; and that when I succeed in it (I mean so far as to please the audience), yet I am nothing satisfied with what I have done; but am often vexed to hear the people laugh, and clap, as they perpetually do, where I intended 'em no jest; while they let pass the better things, without taking notice of them.

Pref. *Evening's Love*, '71. K I 135
FARCE, a.

h. The merry philosopher is more to my humour than the melancholic; and I find no disposition in myself to cry, while the mad world is daily supplying me with such occasions of laughter.

Ded. *Amphitryon*, '90. S-S VIII 8
DRYDEN, PERSONAL CHARACTER, d. DRYDEN, LITERARY LIFE, d, e.

Philosophical Temper [See *Personality*]
CRITIC, e.

i. Being naturally inclined to scepticism in philosophy, I have no reason to impose my opinions in a subject which is above it . . .

Pref. *Religio Laici,* '82. S-S X 11
DRYDEN, WORKS, qq. OPINION.

Physical Temper
DRYDEN, WORKS, ss.

Poetical Temper
DRYDEN, LITERARY LIFE, l. DRYDEN, WORKS, ccc. HOMER, a. HOMER AND VIRGIL, c, d. TRANSLATION, p.

Pose (of Insolence)
UNIVERSITY, b.

Dryden, Literary Life

Apprenticeship and Art
TECHNICAL TERMS, a. DRYDEN, WORKS, b. DRYDEN, PERSONAL CHARACTER, f. AUDIENCE, b. DAVENANT, b. See below, m. ACADEMY, b. DRYDEN, WORKS, vv.

a. When I was myself in the rudiments of my poetry, without name or reputation in the world, having rather the ambition of a writer, than the skill; when I was drawing the outlines of an art, without any living/master to instruct me in it; an art which had been better praised than studied here in England, wherein Shakespeare, who created the stage among us, had rather written happily, than knowingly and justly, and Johnson, who, by studying Horace, had been acquainted with the rules, yet seemed to envy to posterity that knowledge, and, like an inventor of some useful art, to make a monopoly of his learning; when thus, as I may say, before the use of the loadstone, or knowledge of the compass, I was sailing in a vast ocean, without other help than the pole-star of the Ancients, and the rules of the French stage amongst the Moderns, which are extremely different from ours, by reason of their opposite taste; yet even then, I had the presumption to dedicate to your Lordship [Dorset]: a very unfinished piece, I must confess, and which only can be excused by the little experience of the author, and the modesty of the title *An Essay*.

Discourse of Satire, '93. K II 16–17
DORSET, c.

b. With these beautiful turns [of words and thoughts in poetry], I confess myself to have been unacquainted, till about twenty years ago, in a conversation which

I had with that noble wit of Scotland, Sir George Mackenzie, he asked me why I did not imitate in my verses the turns of Mr. Waller and Sir John Denham, of which he repeated many to me. I had often read with pleasure, and with some profit, those two fathers of our English poetry, but had not seriously enough considered those beauties which gave the last perfection to their works. Some sprinklings of this kind I had also formerly in my plays; but they were casual, and not designed. But this hint . . . first made me sensible of my own wants, and brought me afterwards to seek for the supply of them in other English authors. I looked over the darling of my youth, the famous Cowley; there I found, instead of them, the points of/wit, and quirks of epigram, even in the *Davideis,* an heroic poem, which is of an opposite nature to those puerilities; but no elegant turns either on the word or on the thought. Then I consulted a greater genius, (without offence to the *Manes* of that noble author,) I mean Milton. But as he endeavours everywhere to express Homer, whose age had not arrived to that fineness, I found in him a true sublimity, lofty thoughts, which were clothed with admirable Grecisms, and ancient words, which he had been digging from the mines of Chaucer and Spenser, and which, with all their rusticity, had somewhat of venerable in them; but I found not there neither that for which I looked. At last I had recourse to his master, Spenser, the author of that immortal poem called the *Fairy Queen;* and there I met with that which I had been looking for so long in vain. Spenser had studied Virgil to as much advantage as Milton had done Homer; and amongst the rest of his excellencies had copied that. Looking farther into the Ital-

ian, I found Tasso had done the same; nay more, that all the sonnets in that language are on the turn of the first thought; which Mr. Walsh, in his late ingenious preface to his poems, has observed. In short, Virgil and Ovid are the two principal fountains of them in Latin poetry. And the French at this day are so fond of them, that they judge them to be the first beauties: *délicat et bien tourné,* are the highest commendations which they bestow on somewhat which they think a master piece.[1]

Discourse of Satire, '93. K II 108–9
See below, t. ENGLISH LANGUAGE, e. BORROWING, c.

c. In the mean time, betwixt my intervalls of physique and other remedies . . . for my gravell, I am still drudging on: always a Poet, and never a good one. I pass my time sometimes with Ovid, and sometimes with our old English poet, Chaucer; translating such stories as best please my fancy; and intend besides them to add somewhat of my own: so that it is not impossible, but ere the summer be pass'd, I may come down to you with a volume in my hand, like a dog out of the water, with a duck in his mouth.

Letter to Mrs. Steward, February 1699.
Ward No. 57, p. 109
PEPYS. HOMER, a.
Bayes

d. [¶] Much less am I concerned at the noble name of Bayes; that is a brat so like his own father, that he cannot be mistaken for any other body./They might as reasonably have called Tom Sternhold, Virgil, and the resemblance would have held as well.

Vindication, '83. S-S VII 175–76
e. [Speaking of the 'multitude of scriblers, who daily pester the world with their

insufferable stuff'] I complain not of their lampoons and libels, though I have been the public mark for many years. I am vindictive enough to have repelled force by force, if I could imagine that any of them had ever reached me; but they either shot at rovers, and therefore missed, or their powder was so weak, that I might safely stand them, at the nearest distance. I answered not *The Rehearsal,* because I knew the author sat to himself when he drew the picture, and was the very Bayes of his own farce: because also I knew, that my betters were more concerned than I was in that satire: and, lastly, because Mr. Smith and Mr. Johnson, the main pillars of it, were two such languishing gentlemen in their conversation, that I could liken them to nothing but to their own relations, those noble characters of/men of wit and pleasure about the town. The like considerations have hindered me from dealing with the lamentable companions of their prose and doggerel. I am so far from defending my poetry against them, that I will not so much as expose theirs. And for my morals, if they are not proof against their attacks, let me be thought by posterity, what those authors would be thought, if any memory of them, or of their writings, could endure so long as to another age.

Discourse of Satire, '93. K II 21–22
SATIRE, b.
Critical Candor [See DRYDEN, WORKS, *passim*]
DECORUM, f. CRITICASTERS, b.

e-2. [¶] For the little critics, who pleased themselves with thinking they have found a flaw in that line of the prologue,

> And he, who servilely creeps after sense,
> Is safe, etc.,

as if I patronised my own nonsense, I may reasonably suppose they have never read Horace. *Serpit humi tutus,* etc., are his words: He, who creeps after plain, dull, common sense, is safe from committing absurdities; but can never reach any height, or excellence of wit; and sure I could not mean, that any excellence were to be found in nonsense.

Pref. Tyrannic Love, '70. S-S III 381
f. . . . I love to deal clearly and plainly, and to speak of my own faults with more criticism, than I would of another poet's.

Pref. Evening's Love, '71. K I 137
HUMORS, c. See below, m, k.

g. But, it may be, I am partial to my own writings; yet I have laboured as much as any man, to divest myself of the self-opinion of an author; and am too well satisfied of my own weakness, to be pleased with anything I have written.

Ded. Aureng-Zebe, '76. S-S V 198
CRITIC[s], e. MILTON, a. SHAKESPEARE, d, g.

h. [¶] For my own part, I am ready to acknowledge that I have transgressed [in the translation of Ovid's Epistles] the rules which I have given; and taken more liberty than a just translation will allow.

Pref. Ovid's Epistles, '80. K I 243
DRYDEN, WORKS, dd. CREECH, b. WALSH, c. DONNE, b. CRITIC[s], f. PERSIUS, a. EPIC VS. TRAGEDY, h. TURNS, a.

i. [Referring to Caro's translation of the *Æneid*] Doctor Morelli, who is no mean critic in our poetry, and therefore may be presumed to be a better in his own language . . . thinks, withal, that he [Caro] has often mistaken his master's sense. I would say so, if I durst, but am afraid I have committed the same fault more often, and more grossly; for I have forsaken Ruæus (whom generally I follow) in many places, and made expositions of my own in some, quite contrary to him . . .[1]

Ded. *Æneis*, '97. K II 221.

PROSODY, s. CHAUCER, h.

Critical Guides

j. Aristotle with his interpreters, and Horace, and Longinus, are the authors to whom [in the Grounds of Criticism in Tragedy] I owe my lights . . .

Pref. *Troilus*, '79. K I 207.

ROSCOMMON, b. See above, a. DORSET, c. See above, b.

Digressive Impulse

DRYDEN, WORKS, ttt. PROSODY, hh. PREFACES, d.

Epic Aspirations

k. The truth is, the consideration of so vain a creature as man, is not worth our pains. I have fool enough at home, without looking for it abroad; and am a sufficient theatre to myself of ridiculous actions, without expecting company, either in a court, a town, or a playhouse. It is on this account that I am weary with drawing the deformities of life, and lazars of the people, where every figure of imperfection more resembles me than it can do others. If I must be condemned to rhyme, I should find some ease in my change of punishment. I desire to be no longer the Sisyphus of the stage; to roll up a stone with endless labour (which, to follow the proverb, gathers no moss), and which is perpetually falling down again. I never thought myself very fit for an employment, where many of my predecessors have excelled me in all kinds; and some of my contemporaries, even in my own/partial judgment, have outdone me in Comedy. Some little hopes I have yet remaining, and those too, considering my abilities, may be vain, that I may make the

world some part of amends, for many ill plays, by an heroic poem. Your lordship [Mulgrave] has been long acquainted with my design; the subject of which you know is great, the story English, and neither too far distant from the present age, nor too near approaching it. Such it is in my opinion, that I could not have wished a nobler occasion to do honour by it to my king, my country, and my friends; most of our ancient nobility being concerned in the action. And your lordship has one particular reason to promote this undertaking, because you were the first who gave me the opportunity of discoursing it to his Majesty, and his Royal Highness: They were then pleased, both to commend the design, and to encourage it by their commands. But the unsettledness of my condition has hitherto put a stop to my thoughts concerning it. As I am no successor to Homer in his wit, so neither do I desire to be in his poverty. I can make no rhapsodies, nor go a-begging at the Grecian doors, while I sing the praises of their ancestors. The times of Virgil pleased me better, because he had an Augustus for his patron; and, to draw the allegory nearer you, I am sure I shall not want a Mæcenas with him. It is for your lordship to stir up that remembrance in his Majesty . . ./For my own part, I am satisfied to have offered the design, and it may be to the advantage of my reputation to have it refused me.

Ded. *Aureng-Zebe*, '76. S-S V 195–97

EPIC, CHRISTIAN, b. EPIC POET, a.

l. [¶] Thus, my Lord, I have . . . given . . . a rude draught of what I have been long labouring in my imagination, and what I had intended to have put in practice, (though far unable for the attempt of such a poem,) and to have left the stage, (to which my genius never much inclined/me,) for a work which would have taken up my life in the performance of it. This, too, I had intended chiefly for the honour of my native country, to which a poet is particularly obliged. Of two subjects, both relating to it, I was doubtful whether I should choose that of King Arthur conquering the Saxons, which, being farther distant in time, gives the greater scope to my invention; or that of Edward, the Black Prince, in subduing Spain, and restoring it to the lawful prince, though a great tyrant, Don Pedro the Cruel: which, for the compass of time, including only the expedition of one year; for the greatness of the action, and its answerable event; for the magnanimity of the English hero, opposed to the ingratitude of the person whom he restored; and for the many beautiful episodes, which I had interwoven with the principal design, together with the characters of the chiefest English persons; wherein, after Virgil and Spenser, I would have taken occasion to represent my living friends and patrons . . . and also shadowed the events of future ages, in the succession of our imperial line; with these helps, and those of the machines, which I have mentioned, I might perhaps have done as well as some of my predecessors . . . But being encouraged only with fair words by King Charles II, my little salary ill paid, and no prospect of a future subsistence, I was then discouraged in the beginning of my attempt; and now age has overtaken me, and want, a more insufferable evil, through the change of the times, has wholly disenabled me.

Discourse of Satire, '93. K II 37–38

Epic, Christian, c.

Literary Models

Last Age, k. See above, a, b. Prosody, b, e. Virgil, ll.

Plagiarism, Charges of

m. [Concerning the charge of stealing his plots] There is one answer which I will not make; but it has been made for me, by him to whose grace and patronage I owe all things—

Et spes et ratio studiorum in Cæsare tantum—

and without whose command they should no longer be troubled with anything of mine:—that he only desired, that they, who accused me of theft, would always steal him plays like mine. But though I have reason to be proud of this defence, yet I should waive it, because I have a worse opinion of my own comedies than any of my enemies can have. 'Tis true, that wherever I have liked any story in a romance, novel, or foreign play, I have made no difficulty, nor ever shall, to take the foundation of it, to build it up, and to make it proper for the English stage. And I will be so vain to say, it has lost nothing in my hands: but it always cost me so much trouble to heighten it for our theatre (which is incomparably more curious in all the ornaments of dramatic poesy than the French or Spanish), that when I had finished my play, it was like the hulk of Sir Francis Drake, so strangely altered, that there/scarcely remained any plank of the timber which first built it.[1]

Pref. *Evening's Love,* '71. K I 144–45

n. [¶] The next accusation is particular to me,—"that I, the said Bayes, would falsely and/feloniously have robbed Nat. Lee of his share in the representation of "Œdipus." Now I am culprit; I writ the first and third acts of "Œdipus," and

63

drew the scenery of the whole play: whenever I have owned a further proportion, let my accusers speak . . . When my friends help my barren fancy, I am thankful for it: I do not use to receive assistance, and afterwards ungratefully disown it.

Vindication, '83. S-S VII 202–03

o. As for the particular exceptions against this or that passage [in the *Æneis*], Macrobius and Pontanus have answered them already. If I desired to appear more learned than I am, it had been as easy for me to have taken their objections and solutions, as it is for a country parson to take the expositions of the fathers out of Junius and Tremellius, or not to have named the authors from whence I had them; for so Ruæus, otherwise a most judicious commentator on Virgil's works, has used Pontanus, his greatest benefactor; of whom he is very silent; and I do not remember that he once cites him.

Ded. *Æneis*, '97. K II 204

Public Office, Sense of [See also *Epic Aspirations,* above]
PRESENT AGE, n. SATIRE, i, j. CHAUCER, b, h.

Quarrel to Detractors
CRITICASTERS, d. RYMER, f. SHAKESPEARE, i.

o-2. [¶] As a corollary to this preface [Fables], in which I have done justice to others, I owe somewhat to myself: not that I think it worth my time to enter the lists with one M—, or one B—, but barely to take notice, that such men there are, who have written scurrilously against me, without any provocation.

Pref. *Fables*, 1700. K II 270

BLACKMORE, b. CRITICASTERS, k.

Reading Habits
HISTORY, a.

Reputation
p. [¶] I am so many ways obliged to you [Howard], and so little able to return your favours, that, like those who owe too much, I can only live by getting farther into your debt. You have not only been careful of my fortune . . . but you have been solicitous of my reputation . . . It is not long since I gave you the trouble of perusing a play for me, and now, instead of an acknowledgment, I have given you a greater, in the correction of a poem.

Pref. *Annus Mirabilis*, '66. K I 10

q. . . . I repose upon your [Howard's] management what is dearest to me, my fame and reputation . . .

Pref. *Annus Mirabilis*, '66. K I 19

See DRYDEN, PERSONAL CHARACTER, f. COMEDY, d.

r. [¶] There is another crime with which I am charged, at which I am yet much less concerned, because it does not relate to my manners . . . but only to my reputation as a poet: a name of which I assure the reader I am nothing proud; and therefore cannot be very solicitous to defend it.

Pref. *Evening's Love*, '71. K I 144

See DRYDEN, LITERARY LIFE, k. DRYDEN, WORKS, n.

s. Nobody can imagine that, in my declining age, I write willingly, or that I am desirous of exposing, at this time of day, the/small reputation which I have gotten on the theatre. The subsistence which I had from the former Government is lost; and the reward I have from the stage is so little, that it is not worth my labour.

Pref. *Cleomenes*, '92. S-S VIII 221–22

See DRYDEN, PERSONAL CHARACTER, d.

t. 'Tis a vanity common to all writers, to overvalue their own productions; and 'tis better for me to own this failing in myself, than the world to do it for me. For what other reason have I spent my life in so unprofitable a study? why am I grown old, in seeking so barren a reward as fame?/The same parts and application which have made me a poet might have raised me to any honours of the gown, which are often given to men of as little learning and less honesty than myself. No Government has ever been, or ever can be, wherein time-servers and blockheads will not be uppermost. . . . These considerations have given me a kind of contempt for those who have risen by unworthy ways. I am not ashamed to be little, when I see them so infamously great; neither do I know why the name of poet should be dishonourable to me, if I am truly one, as I hope I am; for I will never do anything that shall dishonour it. The notions of morality are known to all men . . . and if I see one thing, and practise the contrary, I must disingenuous not to acknowledge a clear truth, and base to act against the light of my own conscience. For the reputation of my honesty, no man can question it, who has any of his own; for that of my poetry, it shall either stand by its own merit, or fall for want of it.

Ded. *Examen Poeticum,* '93. K II 1–2
DENNIS. IMITATION OF MODELS, d. IMAGINATION, e.

u. . . . I found I had a soul congenial to his [Chaucer's], and that I had been conversant in the same studies. Another poet, in another age, may take the same liberty with my writings; if at least they live long enough to deserve correction.

Pref. *Fables,* 1700. K II 265
Self-Indulgence, Literary
RHYME (DEBATE), y. TRAGICOMEDY, c.

DRYDEN, WORKS, ll, ff, ss. UNITIES (DRAMATIC), GENERAL, d.
Stage

v. Having been longer acquainted with the stage than any poet now living, and having observed how difficult it was to please; that the humours of comedy were almost spent; that love and honour (the mistaken topics of tragedy) were quite worn out; that the theatres could not support their charges; that the audience forsook them; that young men, without learning, set up for judges, and that they talked loudest who understood the least; all these discouragements had not only weaned me from the stage, but had also given me a loathing of it.

Pref. *Don Sebastian,* '90. S-S VII 307
Virgil's Effect
VIRGIL, s.

Dryden, Works

Preface to The Rival Ladies
RHYME (DEBATE), i.
Verses to Her Highness the Duchess (1665)
STYLE, b.
An Essay of Dramatic Poesy

a. I confess I find many things in this discourse which I do not now approve; my judgment being a little altered since the writing of it; but whether for the better or the worse, I know not: neither indeed is it much material, in an Essay where all I have said is problematical.

Ded. *Dram. Poesy,* '67. K I 23

b. For my own part, if, in treating of this subject, I sometimes dissent from the opinion of better wits, I declare it is not so much to combat their opinions, as to defend my own, which were first made public. Sometimes, like a scholar in a fencing-school, I put forth myself, and show my own ill play, on purpose to be better taught. Sometimes I stand desperately to my arms, like the foot when deserted by their horse; not in hope to overcome, but only to yield on more honourable terms.

Ded. *Dram. Poesy*, '67. K I 26
ENGLISH VS. FRENCH, i.

c. [¶] To begin with me, he [Howard] gives me the compellation of 'The Author of *a Dramatic Essay'*; which is a little discourse in dialogue, for the most part borrowed from the observations of others . . .

Defence of An Essay, '68. K I 112

d. . . . I must crave leave to say, that my whole discourse was sceptical, according to that way of reasoning which was used by Socrates, Plato, and all the Academics of old, which Tully and the best of the Ancients followed, and which is imitated by the modest inquisitions of the Royal Society. That it is so, not only the name will show, which is *an Essay,* but the frame and composition of the work. You see it is a dialogue sustained by persons of several opinions, all of them left doubtful, to be determined by the readers in general; and more particularly deferred to the accurate judgment of my Lord Buckhurst . . .

Defence of An Essay, '68. K I 124
AUTHORITY, b.

e. In my Dialogue, as I before hinted, several persons maintained their several opinions: one of them, indeed, who supported the cause of the French Poesy, said how strict they were in that particular [unity of time]; but he who answered, in behalf of our nation, was willing to give more latitude . . . and cites the words of Corneille himself, complaining against the severity of it, and observing, what beau-

ties it banished from the stage, *pag.* 44 of my *Essay.*

Defence of An Essay, '68. K I 130
The Indian Queen; The Indian Emperor
COURT, a. See below, i.

f. His story [Montezuma's, in *The Indian Emperor*] is, perhaps, the greatest which was ever represented in a poem of this nature; the action of it including the discovery and conquest of a new world.

Ded. *Indian Emperor*, '67. S-S II 288

g. It [*The Indian Emperor*] is an irregular piece, if compared with many of Corneille's, and, if I may make a judgment of it, written with more flame than art . . .

Ded. *Indian Emperor*, '67. S-S II 288

h. I the rather name this fault ['pointed wit, and sentences affected out of season'], that it may serve to mind me of my former errors; neither will I spare myself, but give an/example of this kind from my *Indian Emperor*. Montezuma, pursued by his enemies, and seeking sanctuary, stands parleying without the fort, and describing his danger to Cydaria, in a simile of six lines—

As on the sands the frighted traveller
Sees the high seas come rolling from afar, &c.

My Indian potentate was well skilled in the sea for an inland prince, and well improved since the first act, when he sent his son to discover it. The image had not been amiss from another man, at another time: *sed nunc non erat hisce locus*: he destroyed the concernment which the audience might otherwise have had for him; for they could not think the danger near when he had the leisure to invent a simile.

Pref. *Troilus,* '79. K I 223–24

DECORUM, i.

Secret Love; or, The Maiden Queen

HERO (DRAMATIC), a. DECORUM, f.

i. . . . this play [*Secret Love*] . . . I have ever valued above the rest of my follies of this kind; yet not thereby in the least dissenting from their judgment, who have concluded the writing of this to be much inferior to my "Indian Emperor." But the argument of that was much more noble, not having the allay of comedy to depress it; yet if this be more perfect, either in its kind, or in the general notion of a play, it is as much as I desire to have granted for the vindication of my opinion, and what as nearly touches me, the sentence of a royal judge.

Pref. *Secret Love*, '67. S-S II 419

REGULARITY, b.

The Wild Gallant

j. It [*The Wild Gallant*] was the first attempt I made in dramatic poetry; and, I find since, a very bold one, to begin with comedy, which is the most difficult part of it.

Pref. *Wild Gallant*, '69. S-S II 27

k. I doubt not but you will see in it [*The Wild Gallant*] the uncorrectness of a young writer; which is yet but a small excuse for him, who is so little amended since.

Pref. *Wild Gallant*, '69. S-S II 28

The Tempest; or, The Enchanted Island

l. Give me leave, therefore, to tell you, reader, that I do not set a value on anything I have written in this play, but out of gratitude to the memory of/Sir William Davenant, who did me the honour to join me with him in the alteration of it.

Pref. *Tempest*, '69. S-S III 105–6

DAVENANT, b. OPERA, g.

Tyrannic Love; or, The Royal Martyr

IMITATION, c. POETIC JUSTICE, b.

m. [¶] I pretend not that anything of mine can be correct . . .

Yet the scenes [in *Tyrannic Love*] are everywhere unbroken, and the unities of place and time more exactly kept, than perhaps is requisite in a tragedy; or, at least, than I have since preserved them in "The Conquest of Granada."

Pref. *Tyrannic Love*, '70. S-S III 379

PROSODY, q. HISTORICAL TRUTH, b.

n. But now, My Lord, I am sensible, perhaps too late, that I have gone too far: for, I remember some verses of my own *Maximin* and *Almanzor,* which cry vengeance upon me for their extravagance, and which I wish heartily in the same fire with Statius and Chapman. All I can say for those passages, which are, I hope, not many, is, that I knew they were bad enough to please, even when I writ them; but I repent of them amongst my sins; and if any of their fellows intrude by chance into my present writings, I draw a stroke over all those Delilahs of the theatre; and am resolved I will settle myself no reputation by the applause of fools. 'Tis not that I am mortified to all ambition, but I scorn as much to take it from half-witted judges, as I should to raise an estate by cheating of bubbles.

Ded. *Spanish Friar*, '81. K I 246

CHARACTERS, c, e.

An Evening's Love; or, The Mock-Astrologer

AUDIENCE, POPULAR, d. CRITICASTERS, c. POETIC JUSTICE, c. COMEDY, f.

The Conquest of Granada by the Spaniards

See above, m. EPIC HERO, b. See above, n.

Marriage à la Mode

o. I am sure, if there be anything in this play, wherein I have raised myself beyond the ordinary lowness of my comedies, I ought wholly to acknowledge it to the favour of being admitted into your Lordship's conversation. And not only I, who pretend not to this way, but the best comic writers of our age, will join with me to acknowledge, that they have copied the gallantries of/courts, the delicacy of expression, and the decencies of behaviour, from your Lordship [Rochester], with more success, than if they had taken their models from the court of France.

Ded. *Marriage à la Mode,* '73. S-S IV 253–54

p. . . . though perhaps it be the best of my comedies, is yet so faulty, that I should have/feared you [Rochester] for my critic . . .

Ded. *Marriage à la Mode,* '73. S-S IV 256–57

q. As, to avoid a satire upon others, I will make bold with my own *Marriage à la Mode,* where there are manifestly two actions, not depending on one another . . .

Pref. *Troilus,* '79. K I 208

Amboyna

r. . . . this play [*Amboyna*]; which, though it succeeded on the stage, will scarcely bear a serious perusal; it being contrived and written in a month, the subject barren, the persons low, and the writing not heightened with many laboured scenes.

Ded. *Amboyna,* '73. S-S V 8

Aureng-Zebe

s. . . . I take the confidence to present you with a tragedy, the characters of which are the nearest to those of an heroic poem. . . . It may be some vanity in me to add his [the King's] testimony then, and

which he graciously confirmed afterwards, that it was the best of all my tragedies; in which he has made authentic my private opinion of it; at least, he has given it a value by his commendation, which it had not by my writing.

Ded. *Aureng-Zebe,* '76. S-S V 197

The State of Innocence and Fall of Man

t. [¶] I wish I could produce any one example of excellent imaging in all this poem [*State of Innocence*]. Perhaps I cannot; but that/which comes nearest it, is in these four lines, which have been sufficiently canvassed by my well-natured censors—

Seraph and cherub . . .
. . . .
And all dissolved in hallelujahs lie.

[See CRITIC(s), b]

Author's Apology, '77. K I 187–88

All for Love; or, The World Well Lost

u. The fabric of the play is regular enough, as to the inferior parts of it; and, the Unities of Time, Place, and Action, more exactly observed, than perhaps the English theatre requires. Particularly, the action is so much one, that it is the only of the kind without episode, or underplot; every scene in the tragedy conducing to the main design, and every act concluding with a turn of it. The greatest error in the contrivance seems to be in the person of Octavia; for, though I might use the privilege of a poet, to introduce her into Alexandria, yet I had not enough considered, that the compassion she moved to herself and to her children was destructive to that which I reserved for Anthony and Cleopatra . . .

Pref. *All for Love,* '78. K I 192

DECORUM, g.

v. In my style [in *All for Love,*] I

have professed to imitate the divine Shakespeare; which that I might perform more freely, I have disencumbered myself from rhyme. Not that I condemn my former way, but that this is more proper to my present purpose.

Pref. *All for Love*, '78. K I 200

w. I hope/I need not to explain myself, that I have not copied my author [Shakespeare] servilely . . . Yet, I hope, I may affirm, and without vanity, that, by imitating him, I have excelled myself throughout the play; and particularly, that I prefer the scene betwixt Antony and Ventidius in the first act, to anything which I have written in this kind.

Pref. *All for Love*, '78. K I 200–201

IMITATION, d. See below, gg.

The Kind Keeper; or, Mr. Limberham

x. But the Kings Comedy lyes in the Sudds till you please to send me into Northamptonshyre: it will be almost such another piece of businesse as the fond Husband, for such the King will have it, who is parcell poet with me/in the plott; one of the designes being a story he was pleasd formerly to tell me; and therefore I hope he will keep the jeast in countenance by laughing at it.

Letter to Edward Osborne, Lord Latimer, July 1677. Ward No. 5, pp. 11–12

y. It was intended for an honest satire against our crying sin of *keeping;* how it would have succeeded, I can but guess, for it was permitted to be acted only thrice. The crime, for which it suffered, was that which is objected against the satires of Juvenal, and the epigrams of Catullus, that it expressed too much of the vice which it decried. Your lordship knows what answer was returned by the elder of those poets, whom I last mentioned, to his accusers—

Ipsum. . . .
    —castum esse decet pium poetam

But I dare not make that apology for myself; and therefore have taken a becoming care, that those things which offended . . . might be either altered, or omitted in the press . ./. I will be bold enough to say, that this comedy is of the first rank of those which I have written, and that posterity will be of my opinion. It has nothing of particular satire in it . . .

Ded. *Limberham,* '80. S-S VI 9–10

Œdipus

y-2. . . . in *Œdipus* there cannot properly be said to be two actions, because the love of Adrastus and Eurydice has a necessary dependence on the principal design into which it is woven.

Pref. *Troilus,* '79. K I 208

IMITATION, d.

Troilus and Cressida; or, Truth Found Too Late

z. [Of his revision of Shakespeare's *Troilus and Cressida*] . . . I new-modelled the plot, threw out many unnecessary persons, improved those characters which were begun and left unfinished . . .[1] After this, I made, with no small trouble, an order and connexion of all the scenes . . . and, though it was impossible to keep them all unbroken . . . yet I have so ordered them, that there is a coherence of them with one another, and a dependence on the main design; no leaping from Troy to the Grecian tents, and thence back again, in the same act, but a due proportion of time allowed for every motion. [See next entry]

Pref. *Troilus,* '79. K I 204

aa. I need not say that I have refined his language, which before was obsolete; but I am willing to acknowledge, that as I have often drawn his English nearer to our times, so I have sometimes conformed my own to his; and consequently, the language is not altogether so pure as it is significant.

Pref. *Troilus, '79*. K I 204

SHAKESPEARE, d.

Preface to Troilus and Cressida

bb. It [the Preface to *Troilus and Cressida*] is, I confess, but cursorily written; yet the judgment, which is given here, is generally founded upon experience . . . [See RULES, d]

Pref. *Troilus, '79*. K I 228

cc. It is upon this encouragement [See ACADEMY, b] that I have adventured on the following critique ["The Grounds of Criticism in Tragedy"] . . . in which, though I have not had the leisure, nor indeed the encouragement, to proceed to the principal subject of it, which is the words and thoughts that are suitable to tragedy; yet the whole discourse has a tendency that way, and is preliminary to it. In what I have already done, I doubt not but I have contradicted some of my former opinions, in my loose essays of the like nature; but of this, I dare affirm, that it is the fruit of my riper age and experience, and that self-love, or envy have no part in it. The application to English authors is my own, and therein, perhaps, I may have erred unknowingly; but the foundation of the rules is reason, and the authority of those living critics who have had the honour to be known to you abroad, as well as of the ancients, who are not less of your acquaintance.

Ded. *Troilus, '79*. S-S VI 253

See above, bb.

The Spanish Friar; or, The Double Discovery

dd. [¶] When I first designed this play, I found, or thought I found, somewhat so moving in the serious part of it, and so pleasant in the comic, as might de-serve a more than ordinary care in both; accordingly, I used the best of my endeavour, in the management of two plots, so very different from each other, that it was not perhaps the talent of every writer to have made them of a piece. Neither have I attempted other plays of the same nature, in my opinion, with the same judgment, though with like success. And though many poets may suspect themselves for the fondness and partiality of parents to their youngest children, yet I hope I may stand exempted from this rule, because I know myself too well to be ever satisfied with my own conceptions, which have seldom reached to those ideas that I had within me; and consequently, I presume/I may have liberty to judge when I write more or less pardonably . . . For my own part, I have both so just a diffidence of myself, and so great a reverence for my audience, that I dare venture nothing without a strict examination; and am as much ashamed to put a loose indigested play upon the public, as I should be to offer brass money in a payment . . .

Ded. *Spanish Friar, '81*. K I 244–45

ee. I had not said thus much, if some young gallants, who pretend to criticism,/ had not told me that this tragi-comedy wanted the dignity of style; but as a man . . . is apt to be too eager in his own defence, so perhaps I have vindicated my play with more partiality than I ought, or than such a trifle can deserve. Yet, whatever beauties it may want, 'tis free at least from the grossness of those faults I mentioned: what credit it has gained upon the stage, I value no further than in reference to my profit, and the satisfaction I had in seeing it represented with all the justness and gracefulness of action.

Ded. *Spanish Friar, '81*. K I 247–48

ff. I am not vain enough to think I have left no faults in this, which that touchstone [Time and Truth] will not discover; neither indeed is it possible to avoid them in a play of this nature. [See TRAGICOMEDY, c]

Ded. *Spanish Friar,* '81. K I 249

TRAGICOMEDY, g.

gg. This rule [of *manum de tabula*] I had before my eyes in the conclusion of the *Spanish Friar,* when the discovery was made that the king was living, which was the knot of the play untied; the rest is shut up in the compass of some few lines, because nothing then hindered the happiness of Torrismond and Leonora. The faults of that drama are in the kind of it, which is tragi-comedy. But it was given to the people: and I never writ anything for myself but *Antony and Cleopatra.*

Parallel, '95. K II 152

Absalom and Achitophel

SATIRE, a. Cf. POET, d.

hh. The conclusion of the story I purposely forbore to prosecute, because I could not obtain from myself to show Absalom unfortunate. The frame of it was cut out but for a picture to the waist; and if the draught be so far true, it is as much as I designed.

Were I the inventor, who am only the historian, I should certainly conclude the piece with the reconcilement of Absalom to David.

Pref. *Absalom and Achitophel,* '81. S-S IX 213

SATIRICASTER, b. SATIRE, pp, b.

The Medal; a Satire against Sedition

ii. I must confess I am no great artist; but sign-post painting will serve the turn to remember a friend by, especially when better is not to be had. Yet, for your comfort, the lineaments are true; and, though

he sat not five times to me, as he did to B. [George Bower], yet I have consulted history . . .

"Epistle to the Whigs," prefixed to *The Medal,* '82. S-S IX 422

SATIRICASTER, b.

MacFlecknoe; or, a Satire upon the True-Blue Protestant Poet

SATIRE, pp. [See Spence, *Anecdotes* (1820), p. 60]

Religio Laici; or, a Layman's Faith

STYLE, c. See below, ll.

The Duke of Guise

HISTORICAL TRUTH, c. ASTROLOGY.

Life of Plutarch

jj. [¶] I pretend not to an exactness of method in this Life, which I am forced to collect by patches from several authors, and therefore without much regard to the connection of times which are so uncertain.

"Life of Plutarch," '83. S-S XVII 40

History of the League, Translation of Maimbourg's

kk. You have written diverse things which gave me great satisfaction; particularly that the History of the League is commended: & I hope the onely thing I feard in it, is not found out. Take it all together, & I dare say without vanity 'tis the best translation of any History in English, though I cannot say 'tis the best History; but that is no fault of mine.

Letter to Tonson, 1684. Ward No. 11, p. 22

TRANSLATION, j.

Sylvæ; or, The second Part of Poetical Miscellanies

ll. Your opinion of the Miscellanyes [*Sylvæ,* 1685: Ward] is likewise mine: I will for once lay by the Religio Laici, till another time. But I must also add, that since we are to have nothing but new, I am resolvd we will have nothing but good, whomever we disoblige. You will have of mine four Odes of Horace . . . forty lines from Lucretius: the whole story of Nisus & Eurialus, both in the fifth, & the ninth of Virgils Eneids; & I care not who translates them beside me, for let him be friend or foe, I will please my self, & not give off in consideration of any man. there [*sic*] will be forty lines more of Virgil in another place; to answer those of Lucretius; I meane those very lines which Montaign has compar'd in those two poets: & Homer shall sleep on for me: I will not now meddle with him. and [*sic*] for the Act wch remaines of the opera [*Albion and Albanius*], I believe I shall have no leysure to mind it after I have done what I proposd: for my business heere is to unweary my selfe, after my studyes, not to drudge . . .

Letter to Tonson, 1684. Ward No. 11, p. 23

Translation, j.

mm. Yet withal, I must acknowledge, that I have many times exceeded my commission; for I have both added and omitted, and even sometimes very boldly made such expositions of my authors, as no Dutch commentator will forgive me. Perhaps . . . I have thought that I discovered some beauty yet undiscovered by those pedants, which none but a poet could have found. Where I have taken away some of their expressions, and cut them shorter, it may possibly be on this consideration, that what was beautiful in the Greek or Latin, would not appear so shining in the English: and where I have enlarged them, I desire the false critics would not always think, that those thoughts are wholly mine, but that either they are secretly in the poet, or

may be fairly deduced from him; or at least . . . that my own is of a piece with his, and that if he were living, and an Englishman, they are such as he would probably have written.

Pref. *Sylvæ,* '85. K I 252

nn. . . . [I] must confess, to my shame, that I have not been able to translate any part of him [Virgil] so well, as to make him appear wholly like himself. For where the original is close, no version can reach it in the same compass.[1]

Pref. *Sylvæ,* '85. K I 256

oo. I own that, endeavouring to turn his *Nisus and Euryalus* as close as I was able, I have performed that episode too literally; that, giving more scope to *Mezentius and Lausus,* that version, which has more of the majesty of Virgil, has less of his conciseness; and all that I can promise for myself, is only that I have done both better than Ogleby, and perhaps as well as Caro; so that, methinks, I come like a malefactor, to make a speech upon the gallows, and to warn all other poets, by my sad example, from the sacrilege of translating Virgil. Yet . . . I have made some faint resemblance of him; and had I taken more time, might possibly have succeeded better; but never so well as to have satisfied myself.

Pref. *Sylvæ,* '85. K I 257

pp. The turns of his [Virgil's] verse, his breakings, his propriety, his numbers, and his gravity, I have as far imitated, as the poverty of our language, and the hastiness of my performance, would allow. I may seem sometimes to have varied from his sense; but I think the greatest variations may be fairly deduced from him; and where I leave his commentators, it may be I understand him better: at least I writ without consulting them in many places. But two particular lines in *Mezentius and Lausus,* I cannot so easily excuse. . . . The first of them I have forgotten . . . The second is this:

> When Lausus died, I was already slain.

This appears pretty enough at first sight; but I am convinced . . . that the expression is too bold; that Virgil would not have said it, though Ovid would.

Pref. *Sylvæ,* '85. K I 258

qq. And accordingly [in evaluating the character of Lucretius, preparatory to translating him] I laid by my natural diffidence and scepticism for a while, to take up that dogmatical way of his . . .

Pref. *Sylvæ,* '85. K I 260

rr. . . . I must take the liberty to own that/I was pleased with my own endeavours [in translating Lucretius], which but rarely happens to me; and that I am not dissatisfied upon the review of anything I have done in this author. [See next entry]

Pref. *Sylvæ,* '85. K I 261–62

ss. [¶] It is true, there is something, and that of some moment, to be objected against my Englishing the *Nature of Love,* from the fourth book of Lucretius; and I can less easily answer why I translated it, than why I thus translated it. The objection arises from the obscenity of the subject; which is aggravated by the too lively and alluring delicacy of the verses. In the first place, without the least formality of an excuse, I own it pleased me; and let my enemies make the worst they can of this confession. I am not yet so secure from that passion, but that I want my author's antidotes against it. He has given the truest and most philosophical account, both of

the disease and remedy, which I ever found in any author . . . But it will be asked, why I turned him into this luscious English, for I will not give it a worse word. Instead of an answer, I would ask again of my supercilious adversaries, whether I am not bound, when I translate an author, to do him all the right I can . . . ? If, to mince his meaning, which I am satisfied was honest and instructive, I had either omitted some part . . . or taken from the strength of his expression . . . he had no longer been Lucretius. If nothing of this kind to be read, physicians must not study nature, anatomies must not be seen, and somewhat I could say of particular passages in books which, to avoid profaneness, I do not name. But the intention qualifies the act; and both mine and my/author's were to instruct, as well as to please. [Obscenity, b]

Pref. *Sylvæ,* '85. K I 262–63

tt. One Ode [29, Book III, Horace] which infinitely pleased me in the reading, I have attempted to translate in Pindaric verse: 'tis that which is inscribed to the present Earl of Rochester [Lawrence Hyde] . . . 'Tis his darling in the Latin, and I have taken some pains to make it my master-piece in English: for which reason I took this kind of verse, which allows more latitude than any other. [Prosody, u]

Pref. *Sylvæ,* '85. K I 267

Preface to Sylvæ

uu. [¶] To conclude, I am sensible that I have written this [i.e., the Preface to *Sylvæ*] too hastily and too loosely; I fear I have been tedious, and, which is worse, it comes out from the first draught, and uncorrected. This I grant is no excuse . . . but, in part of recompense, let me assure the reader, that, in hasty productions, he is sure to meet with an author's present sense, which cooler thoughts would possible have disguised. There is undoubtedly more of spirit, though not of judgment, in these uncorrect essays; and consequently, though my hazard be the greater, yet the reader's pleasure is not the less.

Pref. *Sylvæ*, '85. K I 269

Albion and Albanius

vv. [Complaining of the difficulties of writing poetry for the opera *Albion and Albanius*] . . . as if I had not served out my time in poetry, but was bound apprentice to some doggrel rhymer, who makes songs to tunes, and sings them for a livelihood. It is true, I have not been often put to this drudgery; but where I have, the words will sufficiently show that I was then a slave to the composition, which I will never be again: it is my part to invent, and the musician's to humour that invention. I may be counselled, and will always follow my friend's advice where I find it reasonable, but will never part with the power of the militia.

Pref. *Albion and Albanius*, '85. K I 278

ww. [Speaking of the original design for which *Albion and Albanius* was prepared as a mere prologue] It cannot properly be called a play, because the action of it is supposed to be conducted sometimes by supernatural means, or magic; nor an opera, because the story of it is not sung.

Pref. *Albion and Albanius*, '85. K I 278

xx. It is divided, according to the plain and natural method of every action, into three parts. For even Aristotle himself is contented to say simply, that in all actions there is a beginning, a middle, and an end;

after which model all the Spanish plays are built.

Pref. *Albion and Albanius*, '85. K I 279

xx-1. [¶] He [Charles II] had been pleased twice or thrice to command that it [*Albion and Albanius*] should be practised before him, especially the first and third acts of it; and publicly declared, more than once, that the composition and choruses were more just and more beautiful than any he had heard/in England. How nice an ear he had in music is sufficiently known; his praise therefore has established the reputation of it above censure, and made it in a manner sacred. 'Tis therefore humbly and religiously dedicated to his memory.

Postscript *Albion and Albanius*, '85. K I 280–81

Preface to Albion and Albanius

xx-2. [¶] This Preface being wholly written before the death of my late Royal Master (*quem semper acerbum, semper honoratum, sic di voluistis habebo*) I have now lately reviewed it, as supposing I should find many notions . . . that would require correction . . . After four months lying by me, I looked on it as no longer mine, because I had wholly forgotten it; but I confess with some satisfaction, and perhaps a little vanity, that I found myself entertained by it . . . [See OPERA, h]

Postscript *Albion and Albanius*, '85. K I 280

The Hind and the Panther

yy. [¶] I have but one word more to say concerning the poem as such . . . The First Part, consisting most in general characters and narration, I have endeavoured to raise, and give it the majestic turn of heroic poesy. The Second, being matter of dispute, and chiefly concerning

Church authority, I was obliged to make as plain and perspicuous as possibly I could; yet not wholly neglecting the numbers, though I had not frequent occasions for the magnificence of verse. The Third, which has more of the nature of domestic conversation, is, or ought to be, more free and familiar than the two former.

Pref. *Hind and the Panther*, '87. S-S X 117

zz. [¶] There are in it [*Hind and the Panther*] two episodes, or fables, which are interwoven with the main design; so that/they are properly parts of it, though they are also distinct stories of themselves. In both of these I have made use of the common-places of satire, whether true or false, which are urged by the members of the one Church against the other: at which I hope no reader of either party will be scandalised, because they are not of my invention, but as old, to my knowledge, as the times of Boccace and Chaucer on the one side, and as those of the Reformation on the other.

Pref. *Hind and the Panther*, '87. S-S X 117–18

Don Sebastian, King of Portugal

aaa. [¶] Whether it happened through a long disuse of writing, that I forgot the usual compass of a play, or that, by crowding it with characters and incidents, I put a necessity upon myself of lengthening the main action, I know not; but the first day's audience sufficiently convinced me of my error, and that the poem was insupportably too long. It is an ill ambition of us poets, to please an audience with more than they can bear . . .

Pref. *Don Sebastian*, '90. S-S VII 306
Designing.

bbb. And I dare boldly promise for this play, that in the roughness of the numbers and cadences, (which I assure was not casual, but so designed) you will see somewhat more masterly arising to your view, than in most, if not any, of my former tragedies. There is a more noble daring in the figures, and more suitable to the loftiness of the subject; and, besides this, some newnesses of English, translated from the beauties of modern tongues, as well as from the elegancies of the Latin; and here and there some old words are sprinkled, which, for their significance and sound,/ deserved not to be antiquated; such as we often find in Sallust amongst the Roman authors, and in Milton's "Paradise" amongst ours; though perhaps the latter, instead of sprinkling, has dealt them with too free a hand, even sometimes to the obscuring of his sense.

Pref. *Don Sebastian*, '90. S-S VII 308–9
Unities (Dramatic), General, c.
Tragicomedy, d.
Eleonora: a Panegyrical Poem . . .
Panegyric, c. Donne, b. Critic[s], c.
King Arthur; or, The British Worthy
Opera, i.
Cleomenes, the Spartan Hero
Farce, c. Tragicomedy, e. Unities (Dramatic), General, d. Unities (Dramatic), Action, f.
Examen Poeticum [Third Miscellany]

ccc. Your/Lady and you [Lord Radcliffe] have done me the favour to hear me read my translations of Ovid; and you both seemed not to be displeased with them. Whether it be the partiality of an old man to his youngest child, I know not; but they appear to me the best of all my endeavours in this kind. Perhaps this poet is more easy to be translated than some others whom I have lately attempted; perhaps, too, he was more according to my genius. [See OVID, a]

Ded. *Examen Poeticum*, '93. K II 8–9

[ddd. Cancel]

eee. . . . I have given my author's [Ovid's] sense for the most part truly; for, to mistake sometimes is incident to all men; and not to follow the Dutch commentators always, may be forgiven to a man who thinks them, in the general, heavy gross-witted fellows, fit only to gloss on their own dull poets. But I leave a further satire on their wit, till I have a better opportunity to show how much I love and honour them. I have likewise attempted to restore Ovid to his native sweetness, easiness, and smoothness; and to give my poetry a kind of cadence, and, as we call it, a run of verse, as like the original, as the English can . . . As he seldom uses any synaloephas, so I have endeavoured to avoid them . . . I have likewise given him his own turns, both on the words and on the thought . . .

Ded. *Examen Poeticum*, '93. K II 10

PROSODY, ii.

fff. This *Miscellany* is, without dispute, one of the best of the kind which has hitherto been extant in our tongue. At least, as Sir Samuel Tuke has said before me, a modest man may praise what is not his own.

Ded. *Examen Poeticum*, '93. K II 14

To My Dear Friend Mr. Congreve, On . . . The Double-Dealer (1694)

CONGREVE, d.

The Satires of Decimus Junius Juvenalis . . . A. Persius Flaccus.

TRANSLATION, k.

ggg. [¶] This must be said for our translation [of Juvenal], that, if we give not the whole sense of Juvenal, yet we give the most considerable part of it: we give it, in general, so clearly, that few notes are sufficient to make us intelligible. We make our author at least appear in a poetic dress. We have actually made him more sounding, and more elegant, than he was before in English; and have endeavoured to make him speak that kind of English, which he would have spoken had he lived in England,/and had written to this age. If sometimes any of us (and 'tis but seldom) make him express the customs and manners of our native country rather than of Rome, 'tis either when there was some kind of analogy . . . or when, to make him more easy to vulgar understandings, we give him those manners which are familiar to us. But I defend not this innovation, 'tis enough if I can excuse it. For . . . the manners of nations and ages are not to be confounded . . .

Discourse of Satire, '93. K II 113–14

TRANSLATION, l. JUVENAL, c.

hhh. [Of line 50 in the translation of Persius's Fourth Satire] The Name of *Vectidius* is here us'd Appellatively to signifie any Rich Covetous Man . . . I have Translated this passage Paraphrastically, and loosely: And leave it for those to look on, who are not unlike the Picture.

Notes to the Fourth Satire [Persius], '93. JK II 770

iii. [Of lines 98, 102 of the translation of the Sixth Satire of Persius] . . . the Empress *Cæsonia*, whom I here call Queen; though I know that name was not us'd amongst the *Romans*: But the word Empress wou'd not stand in that verse: For which Reason I Adjourn'd it to another.

Notes to the Sixth Satire [Persius], '93. JK II 788

Love Triumphant; or, Nature will prevail

jjj. I call it [my Play] Love Triumphant; or Nature will prevaile: Unless instead of the second Title, you like this other Neither Side to blame: which is very proper, to the two chief Characters of the Heroe & Heroine: who notwithstanding the Extravange [*sic*] of their passion, are neither of them faulty, either in duty, or in Honour.

Letter to Walsh, 12 December 1693. Ward No. 28, p. 62

kkk. A man may be just to himself, though he ought not to be partial; and I dare affirm, that the several manners which I have given to the persons of this drama are truly drawn from nature, all perfectly distinguished from each other; that the fable is not injudiciously contrived; that the turns of fortune are not managed unartfully; and that the last revolution is happily enough invented. [See ARISTOTLE, b]

Ded. *Love Triumphant*, '94. S-S VIII 374
PROGRESS, f.

lll. As for the mechanic unities;—that of time is much within the compass of an astrological day, which begins at twelve, and ends at the same hour the day following: that of place is not observed so justly by me, as by the ancients; for their scene was always one, and almost constantly in some public place. Some of the late French poets, and, amongst the English, my most ingenious friend, Mr. Congreve, have observed this rule strictly; though the place was not altogether so public as a street. I have followed the example of Corneille, and stretched the latitude to a street and palace, not far distant from each other in the same city. They, who will not allow this liberty to a poet, make it a very ridiculous thing for an audience to suppose themselves sometimes to be in a field, sometimes in a garden, and at other times in a chamber. There are not, indeed, so many absurdities in their supposition as in ours; but it is an original absurdity for the audience to suppose themselves to be in any other place than in the very theatre in which they sit, which is neither chamber, nor garden, nor yet a public place of any business, but that of the representation. For my action, it is evidently double . . .

Ded. *Love Triumphant*, '94. S-S VIII 375
UNITIES (DRAMATIC), ACTION, g.

De Arte Graphica. The Art of Painting . . .

mmm. [Speaking of his translation of *De Arte Graphica*] . . . a tolerable translation. Not elegant, for I proposed not that to myself, but familiar, clear, and instructive. . . . The prose translation of this poem is not free from poetical expressions, and I dare not promise that some of them are not fustian, or at least highly metaphorical; but this being a fault in the first digestion (that is, the original Latin), was not to be remedied in the second . . .

Parallel, '95. K II 116

The Works of Virgil . . . Pastorals, Georgics and Æneis

VIRGIL, d, q, y, t. TRANSLATION, n.

nnn. . . . but I have done great wrong to Virgil in the whole translation: want of time, the inferiority of our language, the inconvenience of rhyme, and all the other excuses I have made, may alleviate my fault, but cannot justify the boldness of my undertaking. . . . To which no other answer can be made, than that I have done him less injury than any of his former libellers.

Ded. *Æneis*, '97. K II 238

ooo. For, what I have done [in the translation of the *Æneis,* etc.], imperfect as it is for want of health and leisure to correct it, will be judged in after-ages, and possibly in the present, to be no dishonour to my native country, whose language and poetry would be more esteemed abroad, if they were better understood. Somewhat (give me leave to say) I have added to both of them in the choice of words, and harmony of numbers, which were wanting, especially the last, in all our poets, even in those who, being endued with genius, yet have not cultivated their mother-tongue with sufficient care; or, relying on the beauty of their thoughts, have judged the ornament of words, and sweetness of sound, unnecessary. . . . Others have no ear for verse, nor choice of words, nor distinction of thoughts; but mingle farthings with their gold, to make up the sum.

Postscript *Æneis,* '97. K II 241

ppp. I must also add, that, if the last *Æneid* shine amongst its fellows, 'tis owing to the commands of Sir William Trumball, one of the principal Secretaries of State, who/recommended it, as his favourite, to my care; and for his sake particularly, I have made it mine.

Postscript *Æneis,* '97. K II 242–43

qqq. [¶] Being invited by that worthy gentleman, Sir William Bowyer, to Denham Court, I translated the First *Georgic* at his house, and the greatest part of the last *Æneid.* . . . No wonder, therefore, if both those versions surpass the rest . . .

Postscript *Æneis,* '97. K II 243

rrr. The Seventh Æneid was made English at Burleigh, the magnificent abode of the Earl of Exeter. In a village belonging to his family I was born; and under his roof

I endeavoured to make that *Æneid* appear in English with as much lustre as I could; though my author has not given the finishing strokes either to it, or to the Eleventh, as I perhaps could prove in both, if I durst presume to criticise my master.

Postscript *Æneis,* '97. K II 243

sss. [Of *Æneid* IX, line 853] The first of these lines is all of monosyllables, and both verses [853–54] are very rough, but of choice; for it had been easy for me to have smooth'd them. But either my ear deceives me, or they express the thing which I intended in their sound; for the stress of a bow which is drawn to the full extent is express'd in the harshness of the first verse, clogg'd not only with monosyllables, but with consonants; and these words, *the tough yew,* which conclude the second line, seem as forceful as they are unharmonious. Homer and Virgil are both frequent in their adapting sounds to the thing they signify. . . .[1]

Our language is not often capable of these/beauties, tho' sometimes I have copied them . . .[1]

Notes and Observations on Virgil's Works in English, '97. N 714–15

Dedication of the Æneis

ttt. . . . in this address to your Lordship, I design not a Treatise of Heroic Poetry, but write in a loose epistolary way, somewhat tending to that subject, after the example of Horace, in his *First Epistle* of the Second Book *to Augustus Caesar,* and in that to the Piso's [*sic*], which we call his *Art of Poetry;* in both of which he observes no method that I can trace, whatever Scaliger . . . or Heinsius, may have seen . . . I have taken up, laid down, and resumed as often as I pleased, the same subject; and this loose proceeding I shall use through all this prefatory Dedication.

Ded. *Æneis*, '97. K II 164

POET, l. SEGRAIS, c.

Alexander's Feast; or, The Power of Musique

uuu. I am glad to heare from all Hands, that my Ode is esteemed the best of all my poetry, by all the Town: I thought so my self when I writ it but being old, I mistrusted my own Judgment.

Letter to Tonson, December 1697. Ward No. 50, p. 98

Fables, Ancient and Modern

TRANSLATION, o.

vvv. . . . I have added some original papers of my own, which whether they are equal or inferior to my other poems, an author is the most improper judge . . .

Pref. *Fables*, 1700. K II 249

TRANSLATION, p.

www. About that time [a week prior], my new Poems were publish'd . . . They are a debt to you I must Confess, and I am glad, because they are so Unworthy to be made a Present. . . . The Town encourages them with more Applause than any thing of mine deserves; And particularly My Cousin Driden accepted One from me so very Indulgently, that it makes me more & more in Love with him.

Letter to Mrs. Steward, 12 March 1700. Ward No. 74, p. 134

xxx. [¶] The Ladies of the Town have infected you at a distance: they are all of your Opinion; & like my last Book of Poems, better than any thing they have formerly seen of mine. I always thought my Verses to my Cousin Driden were the best of the whole; & to my comfort the Town thinks them so; & He, which pleases me most is of the same Judgment

as appears by a noble present he has sent me, which surprisd me, because I did not in the least expect it.

Letter to Mrs. Steward, 11 April 1700. Ward No. 75, p. 135

To my Honour'd Kinsman, John Driden, of Chesterton [in *Fables*]

yyy. [¶] These verses had waited on you with the former [to the Duchess of Ormond]; but they then wanted that Correction, which I have since given them, that they may the better endure the Sight of so great a Judge & Poet. I am now in feare that I have purgd them out of their Spirit; as our Master Busby, usd to whip a Boy so long, till he made him a Confirmed Blockhead.

Letter to Charles Montague, October 1699. Ward No. 65, p. 120

zzz. . . . the Earl of Dorsett, & your Cousin Montague have both seen the two Poems, to the Duchess of Ormond, & my worthy Cousin Driden: And are of opinion that I never writt better. My other friends, are divided in their Judgments . . . but the greater part are for those to my dear Kinsman; which I have Corrected with so much care, that they/will now be worthy of his Sight: & do neither of any dishonour after our death.

Letter to Mrs. Steward, 7 November 1699. Ward No. 67, pp. 123–24

See above, www, xxx.

Dryden, Miscellaneous

Francophobia

EPIC HERO, d. DECORUM, g.

Obiter Dicta

. . . it is madness to be sober alone, while the nation continues drunk . . .

Pref. *Religio Laici*, '82. S-S X 21

COMMENTATORS, DUTCH, b.

Dullness

Ends of Poetry, k.

    a. . . . He, who creeps after plain, dull common sense, is safe from . . . absurdities; but can never reach any height, or excellence of wit . . . [See Dryden, Literary Life, e-2]

    Pref. *Tyrannic Love,* '70. S-S III 381

Shakespeare, u. French Authors, a. Shadwell, b, c, d. Satire, s. Cf. Epic, Christian, c. Fancy, j.

D'Urfey, Thomas

    Durfey has brought another farce [*The Richmond Heiress*] upon/the Stage: but his luck has left him: it was sufferd but foure dayes; and then kickd off for ever. Yet his Second Act, was wonderfully diverting; where the scene was in Bedlam: & Mrs. Bracegirdle and Solon were both mad: the Singing was wonderfully good, And the two whom I nam'd, sung better than Redding and Mrs Ayloff, whose trade it was: at least our partiality carryed it for them. The rest was woefull stuff, & concluded with Catcalls . . .

    Letter to Walsh, May 1693. Ward No. 24, pp. 52–53

Dutch Commentators

    See Commentators, Dutch

Dutch Poetry and Song

    Italian Language and Literature, b.

Dutch Poets

    . . . as insipid as a Dutch poet . . . [See Lucian, e]

    "Life of Lucian," '96. S-S XVIII 73

Dying on the Stage

    Decorum, b, e.

E

Eclectic. School

    Persius, i. Lucian, a.

Elegy

    Prosody, y. English vs. French, n.

Elocution [See Expression]

    Imagination, c. Ovid and Virgil, a. Cf. Settle, c. Plutarch, h.

Emulation

    a. (Crites) *Alit æmulatio ingenia,* (says Paterculus) *et nunc invidia, nunc admiratio incitationem accendit:* Emulation is the spur of wit; and sometimes envy, sometimes admiration, quickens our endeavours.

    Dram. Poesy, '66. K I 37

    b. For 'tis most certain, as our author [Du Fresnoy], amongst others, has observed, that reward is the spur of virtue, as well in all good arts, as in all laudable attempts; and emulation, which is the other spur, will never be wanting, either amongst poets or painters, when particular rewards and prizes are proposed to the best deservers.

    Parallel, '95. K II 136

    Cf. Cultural Interchange, Ambition, and like topics.

Ends of Poetry [Cf. Ethical Function]

Comedy: Satire or Correction

Genre, b. Character[s], c.

Comedy: Delight

Poetic Justice, c.

Comedy: Pleasure and Profit
COMEDY, c.
Drama: Correction

a. The business of the theatre is to expose vice and folly; to dissuade men by examples from one, and to shame them out of the other.

Vindication, '83. S-S VII 166
Drama: Delight
RHYME (DEBATE), v.

b. . . . for delight is the chief, if not the only, end of poesy: instruction can be admitted but in the second place, for poesy instructs as it delights.

Defence of An Essay, '68. K I 113

c. For I confess my chief endeavours are to delight the age in which I live.

Defence of An Essay, '68. K I 116
AUDIENCE, POPULAR, b.

d. . . . the poet's business is certainly to please the audience.

Heads of an Answer, '77. S-S XV 386
CRITIC[s], h.   AUDIENCE, POPULAR, j.
See below, e-2.
Drama: Pleasure and Profit
PLAY (DEFINITION), a.

e. (Eugenius) . . . one main end of Dramatic Poesy in its definition . . . was to cause delight . . .

Dram. Poesy, '65. K I 47

e-2. (Eugenius) . . . one intention of a play, which was delight . . .

Dram. Poesy, '65. K I 50
See above, b.   See below, k.
Epic: Admiration
EPIC, a.   FIGURES, e.
Epic: Correction
EPIC vs. TRAGEDY, f.
Epic: Pleasure and Profit
EPIC vs. TRAGEDY, b, d.   EPIC, f, g.
Epic: Profit
EPIC, e.   EPIC HERO, i, k.

Lampoon: Revenge, Public Service
SATIRE, s.
Poetry: Admiration and Pleasure
IMITATION, h.
Poetry: Imitation of Moral Truth
ETHICAL FUNCTION, a.
Poetry: Pleasure
RULES, g.
Poetry: Pleasure and Profit
POET, i.   EPIC, f.

f. [¶] To instruct delightfully is the general end of all poetry. Philosophy instructs, but it performs its work by precept; which is not delightful, or not so delightful as example.

Pref. *Troilus,* '79. K I 209
LUCRETIUS, b.   Cf. DRYDEN, WORKS, ss.

g. . . . profit and delight . . . are the two ends of poetry in general.

Discourse of Satire, '93. K II 81

h. Let profit have the pre-eminence of honour, in the end of poetry. Pleasure, though but the second in degree, is the first in favour. And who would not choose to be loved better, rather than to be more esteemed?

Discourse of Satire, '93. K II 87

i. [¶] They who will not grant me, that pleasure is one of the ends of poetry, but that it is only a means of compassing the only end, which is instruction, must yet allow, that, without the means of pleasure, the instruction is but a bare and dry philosophy: a crude preparation of morals, which we may have from Aristotle and Epictetus, with more profit than from any poet.

Discourse of Satire, '93. K II 112

j. [¶] He [Du Fresnoy] tells you . . . that 'the chief end of Painting is, to please the eyes; and 'tis one great end of Poetry to please the mind.' Thus far the parallel of the arts holds true; with this difference, that the principal end of Painting is to please, and the chief design of Poetry is to instruct. In this the latter seems to have the advantage of the former; but if we consider the artists themselves on both sides, certainly their aims are the very same; they would both make sure of pleasing, and that in preference to instruction. Next, the means of this pleasure is by deceit; one imposes on the sight, and the other on the understanding.

　Parallel, '95. K II 128

TRANSLATION, cc. DRYDEN, PERSONAL CHARACTER, e.

Poetry: Pleasure, Profit, Piety

　k. [In writing *Tyrannic Love*] I considered that pleasure was not the only end of poesy; and that even the instructions of morality were not so wholly the business of a poet, as that the precepts and examples of piety were to be omitted. For, to leave that employment altogether to the clergy, were to forget that religion was first taught in verse, which the laziness, or dulness, of succeeding priesthood, turned afterwards into prose; and it were also to grant (which I never shall) that representations of this kind may not as well be conducing to holiness, as to good manners. Yet far be it from me to compare the use of dramatic poesy with that of divinity: I only maintain, against the enemies of the stage, that patterns of piety, decently represented, and equally removed from the extremes of superstition and profaneness, may be of excellent use to second the precepts of our/religion. By the harmony of words we elevate the mind to a sense of devotion, as our solemn music, which is inarticulate poesy, does in churches: and by the lively images of piety, adorned by action, through the

senses allure the soul . . . into the practice of that which it admires. Now if, instead of this, we sometimes see on our theatres the examples of vice rewarded, or, at least, unpunished; yet it ought not to be an argument against the art, any more than the extravagances and impieties of the pulpit, in the late times of rebellion, can be against the office and dignity of the clergy.

　Pref. *Tyrannic Love,* '70. S-S III 376–77

Satire: Correction

SATIRE, m. PRESENT AGE, n. PERSIUS, i. HORACE, h, e.

Satire: Instruction

SATIRE, c.

Satire: Pleasure and Profit

HORACE AND JUVENAL AND PERSIUS, c. See above, h.

Satire: Purging Vice, Ignorance, Error

SATIRE, f, j.

Tragedy: Admiration and Compassion

TRAGICOMEDY, a. GENRE, b.

Tragedy: Correction

EPIC VS. TRAGEDY, f.

Tragedy: Joy, Indignation

TRAGEDY, f.

Tragedy: Love

TRAGEDY, e, f.

Tragedy: Pity and Terror [See HERO (DRAMATIC), *passim*]

TRAGEDY, b, m, c, d, e, f, g, h, a, i, k. HERO (DRAMATIC), b, d, e. RULES, c. FLETCHER, e. PASSIONS, c. CHARACTER[s], c.

Tragedy: Pleasure and Profit

EPIC VS. TRAGEDY, b. TRAGEDY, h, p.

Tragedy: Profit

POETIC JUSTICE, c. TRAGEDY, j.

Tragedy: Purge and Reform

UNITIES (DRAMATIC), TIME, e.

Tragedy: Reform

TRAGEDY, c, d, f, g.

English Composition and Speech
  ACADEMY, b.

English Drama
  Characteristics
  ANCIENTS, w.
  Conformity to Ancient
  ANCIENTS, m.
  Defence against Rymer [See Heads of an Answer to Rymer, *passim*] ANCIENTS, u. TRAGEDY, b. ARISTOTLE, e.

a. [¶] Then make a judgment on what the English have added to their [*i.e.,* the Greeks'] beauties; as, for example, not only more plot, but also new passions, as, namely, that/of love, scarce touched on by the ancients, except in this one example of Phædra, cited by Mr. Rymer; and in that how short they were of Fletcher.

Heads of an Answer, '77. S-S XV 382–83
TRAGEDY, d. See below, g, c, h. POETIC JUSTICE, f. TRAGEDY, e, g.

b. [¶] He [Rymer] therefore unjustly blames us for not building on what the ancients left us; for it seems, upon consideration of the premises, that we have wholly finished what they began.

Heads of an Answer, '77. S-S XV 390
RYMER, c. SHAKESPEARE, i.
Fable

c. [¶] For the fable itself: it is in the English more adorned with episodes, and larger than in the Greek poets; consequently more diverting. For/if the action be but one, and that plain, without any counter-turn of design or episode, *i.e.* underplot, how can it be so pleasing as the English, which have both underplot and a turned design, which keeps the audience in expectation of the catastrophe? whereas in the Greek poets we see through the whole design at first.

Heads of an Answer, '77. S-S XV 387–88

Genius of
FRENCH AUTHORS, a.
Immediacy
POETRY AND PAINTING, b.
Inferiority to Ancient
ANCIENTS, k.
Of the Last Age

d. (Lisideius) Beaumont, Fletcher, and Johnson (who were only capable of bringing us to that degree of perfection which we have) were just then leaving the world; as if (in an age of so much horror) wit, and those milder studies of humanity, had no farther business among us.

Dram. Poesy, '65. K I 56
LAST AGE, c.

e. . . . the Greek writers only gave us the rudiments of a stage which they never finished . . . [and] many of the tragedies in the former age amongst us were without comparison beyond those of Sophocles and Euripides.

Ded. *Examen Poeticum*, '93. K II 5
Present Inferiority to Last Age
PRESENT AGE, c, o.
Shakespeare's Place in
SHAKESPEARE, c.
Superiority to Ancient

f. (Eugenius) . . . I never judged the plays of the Greek or Roman poets comparable to ours . . .

Dram. Poesy, '65. K I 34

g. [¶] To conclude, therefore; if the plays of the ancients are more correctly plotted, ours are more beautifully written. And if we can raise passions as high on worse foundations, it shows our genius in tragedy is greater; for, in all other parts of it, the English have manifestly excelled them.

Heads of an Answer, '77. S-S XV 387

h. [¶] The thoughts and words,

which are the fourth and fifth beauties of tragedy, are certainly more noble and more poetical in the English than in the Greek . . .

Heads of an Answer, '77. S-S XV 388

RADCLIFFE, a.

i. Indeed, there is a vast difference betwixt arguing like Perrault, in behalf of the French poets, against Homer and Virgil, and betwixt giving the English poets their undoubted due, of excelling Æschylus, Euripides, and Sophocles. For if we, or our greater fathers, have not yet brought the drama to an absolute perfection, yet at least we have carried it much further than those ancient Greeks . . .

Ded. *Examen Poeticum,* '93. K II 6

SHAKESPEARE, i.
Superiority to European
PRESENT AGE, e.
Variety of
UNITIES (DRAMATIC), TIME, e.

English Language
Barbarity
HORACE, k.   PROSODY, z.   HOLYDAY, c.
See below, j.   DENNIS.   See below, b.
Coarseness
VIRGIL, mm.
Defects
ACADEMY, b.   PROSODY, r.
Disadvantages

a. The English [language] has yet more natural disadvantages than the French; our original Teutonic, consisting most in monosyllables, and/those encumbered with consonants, cannot possibly be freed from those inconveniences. The rest of our words, which are derived from the Latin chiefly, and the French, with some small sprinklings of Greek, Italian, and Spanish, are some relief in Poetry, and help us to soften our uncouth numbers; which,

together with our English genius, incomparably beyond the trifling of the French, in all the nobler parts of verse, will justly give us the pre-eminence. But, on the other hand, the effeminacy of our pronunciation (a defect common to us and to the Danes), and our scarcity of female rhymes, have left the advantage of musical composition for songs, though not for recitative, to our neighbours [the Italians].

Pref. *Albion and Albanius,* '85. K I 274–75

OPERA, f.   PROSODY, b.

b. He [Virgil] studies brevity more than any other poet: but he had the advantage of a language wherein much may be comprehended in a little space. We, and all the modern tongues, have more articles and pronouns, besides signs of tenses and cases, and other barbarities on which our speech is built by the faults of our forefathers. The Romans founded theirs upon the Greek: and the Greeks, we know, were labouring many hundred years upon their language, before they brought it to perfection. They rejected all those signs, and cut off as many articles as they could spare; comprehending in one word what we are constrained to express in two; which is one reason why we cannot write so concisely as they have done. . . .[1]

This inconvenience is common to all modern tongues; and this alone constrains us to employ more words than the ancients needed.

Ded. *Æneis,* '97. K II 227

Compared with French
See above, a.
ENGLISH VS. FRENCH, n.
French Contempt of

c. [Dion Cassius, Herodian, Appian, Polybius] by writing the Roman History

84

in the Greek language, had shewn as manifest a contempt of Latin, in respect of the other, as Frenchmen now do of English . . . This is to arrogate a superiority in nature over us, as undoubtedly the Grecians did over their conquerors, by establishing their language for a standard . . . /This, though it be a digression, yet deserves to be considered at more leisure; for the honour of our wit and writings, which are of a more solid make than that of our neighbours, is concerned in it.

"The Life of Plutarch," '83. S-S XVII 27–28

French, superiority over

d. [The translation of Lucian for which Dryden wrote the Life] has indeed the advantage [over that of d'Ablancourt] of appearing in a language more strong and expressive than French . . .

"Life of Lucian," '96. S-S XVIII 81

Latin Superiority [See above, b, and *passim* under ENGLISH LANGUAGE] See below, e, f. DRYDEN, WORKS, nnn.

Latinizing of [See LATINITY]

GRAMMAR, c. JONSON, a.

Limitations

POETIC LICENSE, e. LATIN, b. DRYDEN, WORKS, pp. Cf. THEOCRITUS, a. TRANSLATION, bb.

e. . . . from the beginning of the First *Georgic* to the end of the last *Æneid*, I found the difficulty of translation growing on me in every succeeding book. For Virgil, above all poets, had a stock, which I may call almost inexhaustible, of figurative, elegant, and sounding words: I, who inherit but a small portion of his genius, and write in a language so much inferior to the Latin, have found it very painful to vary phrases, when the same sense returns upon me. Even he him/self, whether out

of necessity or choice, has often expressed the same thing in the same words, and often repeated two or three whole verses which he had used before. Words are not so easily coined as money . . .

Ded. *Æneis,* '97. K II 231–32

f. There is a beauty of sound, as Segrais has observed, in some Latin words, which is wholly lost in any modern language. He instances in that *mollis amaracus,* on which Venus lays Cupid, in the First Æneid. If I should translate it *sweet marjoram,* as the word signifies, the reader would think I had mistaken Virgil: for those village words, as I may call them, give us a mean idea of the thing; but the sound of the Latin is so much more pleasing, by the just mixture of the vowels with the consonants, that it raises our fancies to conceive somewhat more noble than a common herb . . .

Ded. *Æneis,* '97. K II 233

Cf. DRYDEN, WORKS, sss. TRANSLATION, p.

Obsolescence in

SPENSER, b. CHAUCER AND OVID. MODERNIZING.

Perfecting of

BEAUMONT AND FLETCHER. JONSON, g.

f-2. [¶] To begin with Language. That an alteration is lately made in ours, or since the writers of the last age (in which I comprehend Shakespeare, Fletcher, and Johnson), is manifest. . . . but that this is an improvement . . . or an alteration for the better, will not so easily be granted. For many are of a contrary opinion, that the English tongue was then in the height of its perfection; that from Johnson's time to ours it has been in a continual declination, like that of the Romans from the age of Virgil to Statius, and so downward to

85

Claudian; of which, not only Petronius, but Quintilian himself so much complains, under the person of Secundus, in his famous dialogue *de Causis corruptæ Eloquentiæ.*

Defence of the Epilogue, '72. K I 164

GALLICIZING. SHAKESPEARE, n. NORTH'S PLUTARCH. DRYDEN, WORKS, ooo. CHAUCER, b. BOCCACCIO. RYMER, g. CHAUCER AND OVID.

Prose Rhythm

PROSODY, f. Cf. DRYDEN, LIFE, e.

Quantity

OPERA, e.

Regulation

ACADEMY, a.

g. In the age of that poet [Æschylus], the Greek tongue was arrived to its full perfection; they had then amongst them an exact standard of writing and of speaking: the English language is not capable/of such a certainty; and we are at present so far from it, that we are wanting in the very foundation of it, a perfect grammar.

Pref. *Troilus,* '79. K I 202–3

ACADEMY, b. PROSODY, z. See below, j.

Use, difficulty of

h. . . . I have endeavoured to write English, as near as I could distinguish it from the tongue of pedants, and that of affected travellers.

Ded. *Rival Ladies,* '64. K I 5

STYLE, a.

Virtues

i. (Neander) Our language is noble, full, and significant; and I know not why he who is master of it may not clothe ordinary things in it as decently as the Latin, if he use the same diligence in his choice of words.

Dram. Poesy, '65. K I 104

Cf. WALSH, c.

j. For after all, our language is both copious, significant, and majestical, and

might be reduced into a more harmonious sound. But for want of public encouragement, in this Iron Age, we are so far from making any progress in the improvement of our tongue, that in few years we shall speak and write as barbarously as our neighbours.

Ded. *Examen Poeticum,* '93. K II 12

English Poets: Inventive Genius

. . . the genius of our countrymen in general [is] rather to improve an invention than to invent themselves . . .

Pref. *Fables,* 1700. K II 255

English Stage

DRYDEN, LITERARY LIFE, m. Cf. FABLE, c. FRENCH AUTHORS, a. CHORUS, d.

English vs. French

a. (Lisideius) [¶] If the question had been stated . . . who had writ best, the French or English, forty years ago, I should have been of your opinion, and adjudged the honour to our own nation; but since that time . . . we have been so long together bad Englishmen, that we had not leisure to be good poets.

Dram. Poesy, '65. K I 56

b. (Lisideius) . . . it was then that the great Cardinal of Richelieu began to take them [the Muses] into his protection; and that, by his encouragement, Corneille, and some other Frenchmen, reformed their theatre, which before was as much below ours, as it now surpasses it and the rest of Europe.

Dram. Poesy, '65. K I 56

c. (Lisideius) . . . I shall only . . . demand of you, whether you are not convinced that of all the nations the French have best observed them [the rules of the stage]?

Dram. Poesy, '65. K I 57

d. (Neander) [¶] I shall grant Lisideius, without much dispute, a great part of what he has urged against us; for I acknowledge that the French contrive their plots more regularly, and observe the laws of comedy, and decorum of the stage (to speak generally), with more exactness than the English. Farther, I deny not but he has taxed us justly in some irregularities of ours . . . yet, after all, I am of opinion that neither our faults/nor their virtues are considerable enough to place them above us.

Dram. Poesy, '65. K I 67–68

e. (Neander) 'Tis true, those beauties of the French poesy are such as will raise perfection higher where it is, but are not sufficient to give it where it is not: they are indeed the beauties of a statue, but not of a man, because not animated with the soul of Poesy, which is imitation of humour and passions . . .

Dram. Poesy, '65. K I 68

f. (Neander) [¶] I hope I have already proved in this discourse, that though we are not altogether so punctual as the French, in observing the laws of Comedy, yet our errors are so few, and little, and those things wherein we excel them so considerable, that we ought of right to be preferred before them.

Dram. Poesy, '65. K I 75

g. (Neander) Now what, I beseech you, is more easy than to write a regular French play, or more difficult than write an irregular English one, like those of Fletcher, or of Shakespeare?

Dram. Poesy, '65. K I 77

h. (Neander) . . . be it spoken to the honour of the English, our nation can never want in any age such who are able to dispute the empire of wit with any people in the universe.

Dram. Poesy, '65. K I 88

CRITICISM, a.

i. [¶] The drift of the ensuing Discourse was chiefly to vindicate the honour of our English writers, from the censure of those who unjustly prefer the French before them.

To the Reader, *Dram. Poesy,* '67. K I 27

Cf. FARCE, b. Cf. DRYDEN, LITERARY LIFE, m.

j. I should not have troubled myself thus far with the French poets, but that I find our *Chedreux* critics wholly form their judgments by them. But for my part, I desire to be tried by the laws of my own country; for it seems unjust to me, that the French should prescribe here, till they have conquered.

Pref. *All for Love,* '78. K I 195

ENGLISH DRAMA, i.

k. As little can I grant, that the French dramatic writers excel the English. Our authors as far surpass them in genius, as our soldiers excel theirs in courage. 'Tis true, in conduct they surpass us either way; yet that proceeds not so much from their greater knowledge, as from the difference of tastes in the two nations. They content themselves with a thin design, without episodes, and managed by few persons. Our audience will not be pleased, but with variety of accidents, an underplot, and many actors. They follow the ancients too servilely in the mechanic rules, and we assume too much licence to ourselves, in keeping them only in view at too great a distance. But if our audience had their tastes, our poets could more easily comply with them, than the French writers could come up to the sublimity of our thoughts, or to the difficult variety of our designs.

Ded. *Examen Poeticum,* '93. K II 7

l. For, impartially speaking, the French are as much better critics than the English, as they are worse poets. . . . I shall say perhaps as much of other nations, and their poets, excepting only Tasso; and hope to make my assertion good, which is but doing justice to my country . . .

Ded. *Æneis,* '97. K II 178

m. [¶] But Heroic Poetry is not of the growth of France, as it might be of England, if it were cultivated. Spenser wanted only to have read the rules of Bossu; for no man was ever born with a greater genius, or had more knowledge to support it. But the performance of the French is not equal to their skill; and hitherto we have wanted skill to perform better.

Ded. *Æneis,* '97. K II 220

Boileau
BOILEAU, b.
Conversion (Dramatic)
CONVERSION.
Heroes (Literary)
EPIC HERO, d.
Humors
HUMORS, b.
Languages
ENGLISH LANGUAGE, c, a, d.

n. Formerly the French, like us, and the Italians, had but five feet, or ten syllables, in their heroic verse; but, since Ronsard's time as I suppose, they found their tongue too weak to support their epic poetry, without the addition of another foot. That indeed has given it somewhat of the run and measure of a trimeter; but it runs with more activity than strength: their language is not strung with sinews, like our English; it has the nimbleness of a greyhound, but not the bulk and body of a mastiff. Our men and our verses overbear them by their weight; and *Pondere,/non numero,* is the British motto. The French have set up purity for the standard of their language; and a masculine vigour is that of

ours. Like their tongue is the genius of their poets, light and trifling in comparison of the English; more proper for sonnets, madrigals, and elegies, than heroic poetry. The turn on thoughts and words is their chief talent; but the Epic Poem is too stately to receive those little ornaments.[1]

Ded. *Æneis,* '97. K II 218–19

Music
OPERA, g.
Narrations (Dramatic)

o. (Lisideius) [¶] There are indeed some protatick persons in the Ancients, whom they make use of in their plays, either/to hear or give the relation: but the French avoid this with great address, making their narrations only to, or by such, who are some way interested in the main design.

Dram. *Poesy,* '65. K I 61–62

p. (Lisideius) . . . the French . . . often use them [narrations] with better judgment and more *à propos* than the English do. Not that I commend narrations in general,—but there are two sorts of them. One, of those things which are antecedent to the play, and are related to make the conduct of it more clear to us. But 'tis a fault to choose such subjects . . . as will force us on that rock . . .

But there is another sort of relations, that is, of things happening in the action of the play, and supposed to be done behind the scenes; and this is many times both convenient and beautiful; for by it the French avoid the tumult which we are subject to in England, by representing duels, battles, and the like; which renders our stage too like the theatres where they fight prizes.[1] [See TUMULT, a]

Dram. *Poesy,* '65. K I 62
NARRATIONS (DRAMATIC), d.

Plots [*See below, Unities*]

q. (Neander) [¶ And this [the English achievement in tragicomedy] leads me to wonder why Lisideius and many others should cry up the barrenness of the French plots, above the variety and copiousness of the English.

Dram. Poesy, '65. K I 70

r. (Neander) [¶ If they [the French] content themselves, as Corneille did, with some flat design, which, like an ill riddle, is found out ere it be half proposed, such plots we can make every way regular, as easily as they; but whene'er they endeavour to rise to any quick turns and counterturns of plot, as some of them have attempted, since Corneille's plays have been less in vogue, you see they write as irregularly as we, though they cover it more speciously. [See next entry]

Dram. Poesy, '65. K I 77

s. (Neander) Hence the reason is perspicuous, why no French plays, when translated, have, or ever can succeed on the/English stage. For, if you consider the plots, our own are fuller of variety; if the writing, ours are more quick and fuller of spirit; and therefore 'tis a strange mistake in those who decry the way of writing plays in verse, as if the English therein imitated the French. We have borrowed nothing from them; our plots are weaved in English looms: we endeavour therein to follow the variety and greatness of characters which are derived to us from Shakespeare and Fletcher; the copiousness and well-knitting of the intrigues we have from Johnson; and for the verse itself we have English precedents of elder date than any of Corneille's plays.

Dram. Poesy, '65. K I 77–78

Principal Character (*in Drama*)

t. (Lisideius) [To the objection that the French "make but one person considerable in a play"] If he intends this by it, that there is one person in the play who is of greater dignity than the rest, he must tax, not only theirs, but those of the Ancients, and . . . the best of ours; for it is impossible but that one person must be more conspicuous in it than any other, and consequently the greatest share in the action must devolve on him. . . .

But, if he would have us to imagine, that in exalting one character the rest of them are neglected, and that all of them have not some share or other in the action . . . I desire him to produce any of Corneille's tragedies, wherein every person, like so many servants in a well-governed family, has not some employment . . .

Dram. Poesy, '65. K I 61

Regularity

u. (Neander) . . . I dare boldly affirm these two things of the English drama;—First, that we have many plays of ours as regular as any of theirs [the French], and which, besides, have more variety of plot and characters; and secondly, that in most of the/irregular plays of Shakespeare or Fletcher (for Ben Johnson's are for the most part regular) there is a more masculine fancy and greater spirit in the writing, than there is in any of the French.

Dram. Poesy, '65. K I 78–79

JONSON, i.

v. If heerafter the Audience, will come to tast the confinement of the French (which I believe the English never will,) then it will be easy for their Poets, to follow the strictness of the Mechanique rules, in the three Unities.

Letter to Walsh, 12 December 1693. Ward No. 28, p. 61

w. Let the French and Italians value themselves on their regularity; strength and elevation are our standard. I said before, and I repeat it, that the affected purity of the French has unsinewed their heroic verse. The language of an epic poem is almost wholly figurative: yet they are so fearful of a metaphor, that no example of Virgil can encourage them to be bold with safety. . . . Not that I would discourage that purity of diction in which he [Virgil] excels all other poets. But he knows how far to extend his franchises, and advances to the verge, without venturing a foot beyond it.

Ded. Æneis, '97. K II 229

Speeches (Dramatic) [See main heading, a]

x. (Neander) I deny not but this [long, solemn speeches] may suit well enough with the French; for as we, who are a more sullen people, come to be diverted at our plays, so they, who are of an airy and gay temper, come thither to make themselves more serious: and this I conceive to be one reason why comedy is more pleasing to us, and tragedies to them.

Dram. Poesy, '65. K I 72

Translation. [See main heading, t, gg]

Unities (General)

y. (Neander) . . . by their servile observations of the Unities of Time and Place, and integrity of scenes, they have brought on themselves that dearth of plot, and narrowness of imagination, which may be observed in all their plays. How many beautiful accidents might naturally happen in two or three days, which cannot arrive with any probability in the compass of twenty-four hours? There is time to be allowed also for maturity of design, which, amongst great and prudent persons, such

as are often represented in Tragedy, cannot, with any likelihood of truth, be brought to pass at so short a warning. Farther; by tying themselves strictly to the Unity of Place, and unbroken scenes, they are forced many times to omit some beauties which cannot be shown where the act began; but might, if the scene were interrupted . . . and therefore the French poets are often forced upon absurdities . . .[1]

Dram. Poesy, '65. K I 76

Unity of Action

z. (Lisideius) The Unity of Action in all [French] plays is yet more conspicuous; for they do not burden them with underplots, as the English do: which is the reason why many scenes of our tragicomedies carry on a design that is nothing of kin to the main plot; and that we see two distinct webs in a play, like those in ill-wrought stuffs; and two actions, that is, two plays, carried on together, to the confounding of the audience . . . From hence likewise it arises, that the one half of our actors are not known to the other. They keep their distances, as if they were Montagues and Capulets, and seldom begin an acquaintance till the last scene of the fifth act, when they are all to meet upon the stage.

Dram. Poesy, '65. K I 57

Tragicomedy, a.

aa. (Lisideius) [The French] do not embarrass, or cumber themselves with too much plot; they only represent so much of a story as will constitute one whole and great action sufficient for a play; we . . . do but multiply adventures; which, not being produced from one another, as effects from causes, but barely following, constitute many actions . . . and consequently make it many plays.

Dram. Poesy, '65. K I 60

bb. (Lisideius) . . . by pursuing close one argument . . . the French have gained more liberty for verse . . . ; they have leisure to dwell on a subject which deserves it; and to represent the passions (which we have acknowledged to be the poet's work), without being hurried . . .

Dram. Poesy, '65. K I 60

TRAGICOMEDY, b. UNITIES (DRAMATIC), ACTION, b.

Unity of Place

cc. (Lisideius) . . . in the Unity of Place they are full as scrupulous; for many of their critics limit it to that very spot of ground where the play is supposed to begin; none of them exceed the compass of the same town or city.

Dram. Poesy, '65. K I 57

Unity of Time

dd. (Lisideius) In the Unity of Time you find them [the French] so scrupulous, that it yet remains a dispute among their poets, whether the artificial day of twelve hours, more or less, be not meant by Aristotle, rather than the natural one of twenty-four . . .

Dram. Poesy, '65. K I 57

UNITIES (DRAMATIC), TIME, e.

Englishmen

ENGLISH VS. FRENCH, a, x. DECORUM, d. FLETCHER, c. CONVERSATION, b. CRITIC[s], c. PROSODY, jj.

Enthusiast in Poetry

Cf. SUPERNATURAL, b. SETTLE, d.

[In a context on "sectaries"] Truth is never to be expected from authors whose understandings are warped with enthusiasm . . .

Ded. *Plutarch's Lives, '83.* S-S XVII 16

Epic*

Authority of Ancients

AUTHORITY, e. MODERNS, f. AUTHORITY, f.

Dryden's Projected Epic

DRYDEN, LITERARY LIFE, k, l.

Ends [See also ETHICAL FUNCTION]

a. Such descriptions or images, well wrought . . . are . . . the adequate delight of Heroic Poesy; for they beget admiration, which is its proper object; as the images of the Burlesque, which is contrary to this, by the same reason beget laughter: for the one shows nature beautified, as in the picture of a fair woman, which we all admire; the other shows her deformed, as in that of a Lazar, or of a fool with distorted face and antic gestures, at which we cannot forbear to laugh, because it is a deviation from Nature.

Pref. *Annus Mirabilis, '66.* K I 18

See below, f. HOMER, c. See below, g.

Episodes

b. [¶] As in a picture, besides the principal figures . . . in the midst of it, there are less groups . . . disposed at proper distances, which . . . seem to carry on the same design in a more inferior manner; so, in epic poetry there are episodes, and a chorus in tragedy, which are members of the action, as growing out of it, not inserted into it.[1]

Parallel, '95. K II 143

Heroic Play, Relation to

HEROIC PLAY, c, d, e. DAVENANT, d.

History, distinguished from

LUCAN, a, b.

---

* See H. T. Swedenburg Jr., *The Theory of the Epic in England 1650–1800* ("University of California Publications in English," Vol. XV [Berkeley: University of California Press, 1944]).

Images in
IMAGES, c.
Magna Charta of
PROSODY, jj.
Moral Basis
MORAL (OF A WORK).

c. For the moral (as Bossu observes) is the first business/of the poet, as being the groundwork of his instruction. This being formed, he contrives such a design, or fable, as may be most suitable to the moral; after this he begins to think of the persons whom he is to employ in carrying on his design; and gives them the manners which are most proper to their several characters. The thoughts and words are the last parts, which give beauty and coloring to the piece.

Parallel, '95. K II 127–28

Parts
TRAGEDY, r. See above, c.

d. . . . Mr. Hobbes, I say, begins the praise of Homer where he should have ended it. He tells us, that the first beauty of an epic poem consists in diction; that is, in the choice of words, and harmony of numbers. Now the words are the colouring of the work, which, in the order of nature, is last to be considered. The design, the disposition, the manners, and the thoughts, are all before it: where any of those are wanting or imperfect, so much wants or is imperfect in the imitation of human/life, which is in the very definition of a poem. Words, indeed, like glaring colours, are the first beauties that arise and strike the sight; but, if the draught be false or lame, the figures ill disposed, the manners obscure or inconsistent, or the thoughts unnatural, then the finest colours are but daubing, and the piece is a beautiful monster at best.

Pref. *Fables,* 1700. K II 252–53

92

Pre-eminence
e. [¶] Heroic poesy has always been sacred to princes, and to heroes. Thus Virgil inscribed his Æneids to Augustus Cæsar; and of latter ages, Tasso and Ariosto dedicated their poems to the house of Este. It is indeed but justice, that the most excellent and most profitable kind of writing should be addressed by poets to such persons, whose characters have, for the most part, been the guides and patterns of their imitation; and poets, while they imitate, instruct. The feigned hero inflames the true; and the dead virtue animates the living. Since, therefore, the world is governed by precept and example, and both these can only have influence from those persons who are above us; that kind of poesy, which excites to virtue the greatest men, is of the greatest use to humankind.

Ded. *Conquest of Granada,* '72. S-S IV 11

HEROIC PLAY, e.

f. Heroic Poetry, which they [hypercritics of English poetry] condemn, has ever been esteemed, and ever will be, the greatest work of human nature: in that rank has Aristotle placed it; and Longinus is so full of the like expressions, that he abundantly confirms the other's testimony. Horace as plainly delivers his opinion. . . . Quotations are superfluous in an established truth; otherwise I could reckon up, amongst the moderns, all the Italian commentators on Aristotle's book of poetry; and, amongst the French, the greatest of this age, Boileau and Rapin; the latter of which is alone sufficient, were all other critics lost, to teach anew the rules of writing. Any man, who will seriously consider the nature of an Epic Poem, how it agrees with that of Poetry in general, which is to instruct and to delight, what actions it describes, and what persons they are chiefly whom it informs, will find it a work which indeed is full of difficulty in the attempt, but admirable when it is well performed.

Author's Apology, '77. K I 181

g. [¶] A HEROIC POEM, truly such, is undoubtedly the greatest work which the soul of man is capable to perform. The design of it is to form the mind to heroic virtue by example; 'tis conveyed in verse, that it may delight, while it instructs. The action of it is always one, entire, and great. The least and most trivial episodes, or under-actions, which are interwoven in it, are parts either necessary or convenient to carry on the main design . . . /Even the least portions . . . must be of the epic kind; all things must be grave, majestical, and sublime; nothing of a foreign nature, like the trifling novels, which Ariosto, and others, have inserted in their poems; by which the reader is misled into another sort of pleasure, opposite to that which is designed in an epic poem. One raises the soul, and hardens it to virtue; the other softens it again, and unbends it into vice.

Ded. *Æneis, '97.* K II 154–55

Prosperous Conclusion

Milton, c.

Source of Drama

Drama, Epic Origins.

Style

h. Are all the flights of Heroic Poetry to be concluded bombast, unnatural, and mere madness, because [some] are not affected with their excellencies?

Author's Apology, '77. K I 182

i. No man will disagree from another's judgment concerning the dignity of style in Heroic Poetry; but all reasonable men will conclude it necessary, that sublime subjects ought to be adorned with the sublimest, and consequently often with the most figurative expressions.

Author's Apology, '77. K I 190

Tasso, b.

j. And those who are guilty of so boyish an ambition [as conceit, epigram, witticism] in so grave a subject, are so far from being considered as heroic poets, that they ought to be turned down from Homer to the *Anthologia,* from Virgil to Martial and Owen's Epigrams, and from Spenser to Fleckno; that is, from the top to the bottom of all poetry.

Discourse of Satire, '93. K II 27

Cf. Satire, o. Cf. Dryden, Literary Life, b. See above, g. Figures, e. Turns, a. English vs. French, w.

Sub-Classes

k. . . . the epic poesy, and . . . the historic and panegyric, which are branches of it . . .

Pref. Annus Mirabilis, '66. K I 18

Subject

l. For I have chosen the most heroic subject, which any poet could desire . . . a most just and necessary war . . . the care, management, and prudence of our King; the conduct and valour of a Royal Admiral, and of two incomparable Generals; the invincible courage of our captains and seamen, and three glorious victories, the result of all. After this, I have/in the Fire, the most deplorable, but withal the greatest argument that can be imagined . . . I have called my poem *historical,* not *epic,* though both the actions and actors are as much heroic as any poem can contain. But since the action is not properly one, nor that accomplished in the last successes, I have judged it too bold a title for a few stanzas.

Pref. *Annus Mirabilis*, '66. K I 10–11

POETRY, f-3. DRYDEN, LITERARY LIFE, k.

m. The honour and gallantry of the Earl of Lindsey [General of the Royalist forces under Charles I, killed in the first battle] is so illustrious a subject, that it is fit to adorn an heroic poem; for he was the proto-martyr of the cause, and the type of his unfortunate royal master.

Ded. *All for Love*, '78. S-S V 324

MILTON, c. DRYDEN, LITERARY LIFE, l.

OBSCENITY, c. POETRY, SUBJECT OF, b.

Verse

PROSODY, d. ENGLISH vs. FRENCH, w.

PROSODY, k.

Wit of

WIT, e.

Epic, Christian

POETIC LICENSE, f.

a. [Among the reasons why it is alleged the Moderns can not succeed equally with the Ancients in Epic:] The fault is laid on our religion; they say, that Christianity is not capable of those embellishments which are afforded in the belief of those ancient heathens.

And 'tis true, that, in the severe notions of our faith, the fortitude of a Christian consists in patience, and suffering, for the love of God, whatever hardships can/befall him in the world; not in any great attempt, or in performance of those enterprises which the poets call heroic, and which are commonly the effects of interest, ostentation, pride, and worldly honour: that humility and resignation are our prime virtues; and that these include no action, but that of the soul; when as . . . an heroic poem requires . . . some great action of war, the accomplishment of some extraor-

dinary undertaking; which requires . . . as much, or more, of the active virtue, than the suffering. But to this the answer is very obvious. God has placed us in our several stations; the virtues of a private Christian are patience . . . and the like, but those of a magistrate, or general, or a king, are prudence, counsel, active fortitude, coercive power, awful command, and the exercise of magnanimity, as well as justice. So that this objection hinders not, but that an Epic poem, or the heroic action of some great commander, enterprised for the common good, and honour of the Christian cause, and executed happily, may be as well written now, as it was of old by the heathens; provided the poet be endued with the same talents; and the language, though not of equal dignity, yet as near approaching to it, as our modern barbarism will allow . . . [See next entry]

Discourse of Satire, '93. K II 30–31

b. [¶] I wish I could as easily remove that other difficulty which yet remains. 'Tis objected by a great French critic, as well as admirable poet, yet living, and whom I have mentioned with that honour which his merit/exacts from me, I mean Boileau, that the machines of our Christian religion, in heroic poetry, are much more feeble to support that weight than those of heathenism. . . .[1] Now, our religion (says he) is deprived of the greatest part of those machines . . . [Instancing from Boileau accounts of Christian machinery in Ariosto and Tasso, and of the latter, thus]/This, says Boileau, is a very unequal match for the poor devils, who are sure to come by the worst of it in the combat; for nothing is more easy, than for an Almighty Power to bring his old rebels to reason when he pleases. Consequently, what pleasure . . .

can be raised from so pitiful a machine, where we see the success of the battle from the very beginning of it; unless that, as we are Christians, we are glad that we have gotten God on our side, to maul our enemies, when we cannot do the work ourselves? . . .

This, my Lord, I confess, is such an argument against our modern poetry, as cannot be answered by those mediums which have been used. . . .

But what if I venture to advance an invention of my own, to supply the manifest defect of our new writers? . . ./

It is this, in short, that Christian poets have not hitherto been acquainted with their own strength. If they had searched the Old Testament as they ought, they might there have found the machines which are proper for their work . . . The perusing of one chapter in . . . Daniel, and accommodating what there they find with the principles of Platonic philosophy, as it is now Christianized, would have made the ministry of angels as strong an engine, for the working up heroic poetry, in our religion, as that of the Ancients has been to raise theirs by all the fables of their gods, which were only received for truths by the most ignorant and weakest of the people.

'Tis a doctrine almost universally received by Christians . . . that there are guardian angels, appointed by God Almighty, as his vicegerents, for the protection and government of cities, provinces, kingdoms, and monarchies . . ./[1] But 'tis an undoubted truth, that, for ends best known to the Almighty Majesty of Heaven, his providential designs for the benefit of his creatures, for the debasing and punishing of some nations, and the exaltation . . . of others,

were not wholly known to these his ministers . . .[1]/ But how far these controversies and appearing enmities of those glorious creatures [thus sometimes contesting in their ignorance of Providential design] may be carried; how these oppositions may best be managed, and by what means conducted, is not my business to show or determine . . . [See Epic Poet, a]

There is another part of these machines yet wanting; but . . . easily supplied by a judicious writer. He could not have failed to add the opposition of ill spirits to the good; they have also their design, ever opposite to that of Heaven; and this alone has hitherto been the practice of the Moderns: but this imperfect system . . . which I have given, will infinitely advance and carry further that hypothesis of the evil spirits contending with the good . . .[1]

Discourse of Satire, '93. K II 31–36

Epic Poet, a.

c. Neither will his [Virgil's] Machines be of any service to a Christian Poet. We see how ineffectually they have been try'd by Tasso, and by Ariosto. 'Tis using them too dully if we only make Devils of his Gods: As if, for Example, I would raise a Storm, and make use of Æolus, with this only difference of calling him Prince of the Air. What invention of mine would there be in this; or who would not see Virgil through me; only the same trick play'd over again by a Bungling Juggler? Boileau has well observed, that it is an easie matter in a Christian Poem, for God to bring the Devil to reason. I think I have given a better hint for New Machines in my Preface to Juvenal; where I have particularly recommended two Subjects, one of King Arthur's Conquest of the Saxons, and the other of the Black Prince in his Conquest of Spain. But the Guardian Angels of Monarchys and Kingdoms, are not to be touch'd by every hand. A man must be deeply conversant in the Platonick Philosophy, to deal with them: and therefore I may reasonably expect that no poet of our Age will presume to handle those Machines for fear of discovering his own Ignorance; or if he should, he might perhaps be Ingrateful enough not to own me for his Benefactour.

Letter to Dennis, March 1694. Ward No. 31, p. 71.

Epic Hero

a. (Crites) Homer described his heroes men of great appetites, lovers of beef broiled upon the coals, and good fellows . . .

Dram. Poesy, '65. K I 55

b. I have formed a hero [in the *Conquest of Granada*], I confess, not absolutely perfect, but of an excessive and overboiling courage; but Homer and Tasso are my precedents. Both the Greek and the Italian poet had well considered, that a tame hero, who never transgresses the bounds of moral virtue, would shine but dimly in an epic poem; the strictness of those rules might well give precepts to the reader, but would administer little of occasion to the writer. But a character of an eccentric virtue is the more exact image of human life, because he is not wholly exempted from its frailties; such a person is Almanzor . . . I designed in him a roughness of character, impatient of injuries, and a confidence of himself, almost approaching to an arrogance. But these errors are incident only to great spirits; they are moles and dimples, which hinder not a face from being beautiful, though that beauty be not regular . . .

Ded. *Conquest of Granada,* '72. S-S IV 16

c. Heroes should only be judged by heroes; because they only are capable of measuring great and heroic actions by the rule and standard of their own.

Ded. *Conquest of Granada,* '72. S-S IV 17

d. [¶][1] You see how little these great authors [Homer, Tasso] did esteem the *point of honour,* so much magnified by the French, and so ridiculously aped by us. They made their/heroes men of honour; but so as not to divest them quite of human passions and frailties: they contented themselves to show you, what men of **great** spirits would certainly do when they were provoked, not what they were obliged to do by the strict rules of moral virtue. For my own part, I declare myself for Homer and Tasso, and am more in love with Achilles and Rinaldo, than with Cyrus and Oroondates. I shall never subject my characters **to** the French standard, where love and honour are to be weighed by drachms and scruples.

Essay of Heroic Plays, '72. K I 156–57

VIRGIL, a.

e. . . . concerning perfect ideas [as expressed by Bellori], I have only this to say, —that the parallel is often true in Epic Poetry. The heroes of the poets are to be drawn according to this rule. There is scarce a frailty to be left in the best of them, any more than is to be found in a divine nature; and if Æneas sometimes weeps, it is not in bemoaning his own miseries, but those which his people undergo.

Parallel, '95. K II 127

f. Though it must be an idea of perfection, from which both the epic poet and the history painter draws, yet all perfections are not suitable to all subjects; but **every** one must be designed according to that perfect beauty which is proper to him. . . .[1] and so, in poetry, an Æneas [must be distinguished] from any other hero; for piety is his chief perfection. [See next entry]

Parallel, '95. K II 127

g. Homer's Achilles is a kind of exception to this rule [of perfection in the epic hero]; but then he is not a perfect hero, nor so intended by the poet. All his gods had somewhat of human imperfection, for which he has been taxed by Plato, as an imitator of what was bad; but Virgil observed his fault, and mended it. Yet, Achilles was perfect in the strength of his body, and the vigour of his mind. Had he been less passionate, or less revengeful, the poet well foresaw that Hector had been killed, and Troy taken, at the first assault . . .

Parallel, '95. K II 127

h. [¶] When I say that the manners of the hero ought to be good in perfection, I contradict not the Marquis of Normanby's opinion, in that admirable verse, where, speaking of a perfect character, he calls it *A faultless monster, which the world ne'er knew.* For that excellent critic intended only to speak of dramatic characters, and not of epic.

Parallel, '95. K II 128

VIRGIL, kk. HERO (DRAMATIC), f. IMITATION, d.

i. The shining quality of an epic hero, his magnanimity, his constancy, his patience, his piety, or whatever characteristical virtue his poet gives him, raises first our admiration; we are naturally prone to imitate what we admire; and frequent acts produce a habit. If the hero's chief quality be vicious, as, for example, the choler and obstinate desire of vengence in Achilles, yet the moral is instructive: and, besides, we are informed in the very proposition of the *Iliads,* that this anger was pernicious . . . The courage of Achilles is proposed to imi-

tation, not his pride and disobedience . . . nor his brutal cruelty to his dead enemy, nor the selling of his body to his father. We abhor these actions . . . and what we abhor we never imitate. The poet only shows them, like rocks or quicksands, to be shunned. [See next entry]

Ded. Æneis, '97. K II 159

j. [¶] By this example [i.e., Achilles], the critics have concluded that it is not necessary the manners of the hero should be virtuous. They are poetically good, if they are of a piece: though where a character of perfect virtue is set before us, it is more lovely; for there the whole hero is to be imitated. This is the Æneas of our author; this is that idea of perfection in an epic poem which painters and statuaries have only in their minds, and which no hands are able to express.

Ded. Æneis, '97. K II 159

k. I have said already from Bossu, that a poet is not obliged to make his hero a virtuous man; therefore, neither Homer nor Tasso are to be blamed for giving what predominant quality they pleased to their first character. But Virgil, who designed to form a perfect prince, and would insinuate that Augustus, whom he calls Æneas in his poem, was truly such, found himself obliged to make him without blemish, thoroughly virtuous; and a thorough virtue begins and ends in piety. Tasso, without question, observed this before me, and therefore split his hero in two: he gave Godfrey piety, and Rinaldo fortitude, for their chief qualities or manners. **Homer,** who had chosen another moral, makes both Agamemnon and Achilles vicious; for his design was to instruct in virtue, by showing the deformity of vice.

Ded. Æneis, '97. K II 179

l. But, in defence of Virgil, I dare positively say, that he has been more cautious in this particular [the supernatural immunity of the hero] than either his predecessor, or his descendants: for Æneas was actually wounded, in the Twelfth of the *Æneis;* though he had the same God-smith to forge his arms as had Achilles. It seems he was no warluck, as the Scots commonly call such men . . .

Ded. *Æneis,* '97. K II 182

m. [¶] In the first place, if tears are arguments of cowardice, what shall I say of Homer's hero? Shall Achilles pass for timorous because he wept, and wept on less occasions than Æneas? Herein Virgil must be granted to have excelled his master. For once both heroes are described lamenting their lost loves . . .[1] But Achilles went roaring along the salt sea-shore, and, like a booby, was complaining to his mother, when he should have revenged his injury by arms. Æneas took a nobler course; for, having secured his father and his son, he repeated all his former dangers, to have found his wife, if she had been above ground. And . . . it was not for nothing that this passage was related with all these tender circumstances. Æneas told it; Dido heard it. That he had been so affectionate a husband was no ill argument to the coming dowager, that he might prove as kind to her. Virgil has a thousand secret beauties . . .

Ded. *Æneis,* '97. K II 183

n. Science distinguishes a man of honour from one of those athletic brutes whom, undeservedly, we call heroes. Cursed be the poet, who first honoured with that name a mere Ajax, a man-killing idiot! The Ulysses of Ovid upbraids his ignorance, that he understood not the shield for which he pleaded; there was engraven on it plans of cities, and maps of countries, which Ajax could not comprehend, but looked on them as stupidly as his fellow-beast, the lion.

Ded. *Fables,* 1700. S-S XI 203

Homer and Virgil, d.

Epic Machines

Cf. Milton, c. Epic, Christian, b, e. Epic Poet, c. Deus ex Machina, d.

a. [¶] I have yet a word or two to say of Virgil's machines . . . He has imitated those of Homer, but not copied them. . . .[1]/It was not . . . for Virgil to create new ministers: he must take what he found in his religion. It cannot therefore be said, that he borrowed them from Homer . . . but he invents the occasions for which he uses them. . . .[1] Virgil, generally speaking, employed his machines in performing those things which might possibly have been done without them . . .[1]

But machines sometimes are specious things to amuse the reader, and give a colour of probability to things otherwise incredible. And besides it soothed the vanity of the Romans, to find the Gods so visibly/ concerned in all the actions of their predecessors. We, who are better taught by our religion, yet own every wonderful accident, which befalls us for the best, to be brought to pass by some special providence of Almighty God, and by the care of guardian Angels: and from hence I might infer, that no heroic poem can be writ on the Epicurean principles.

Ded. *Æneis,* '97. K II 208–10

b. The most crude machine which Virgil uses is in the episode of Camilla, where Opis, by the command of her mistress, kills Aruns. The next is in the Twelfth Æneid, where Venus cures her son Æneas. But in the last of these the poet was driven to a necessity; for Turnus was to be slain that very day; and Æneas, wounded as he was, could not have engaged him . . . unless his hurt had been miraculously healed. . . . After all, that his machine might not seem too violent, we see the hero limping after Turnus . . . But what reason had our author to wound Æneas at so critical a time? and how came the cuisses to be worse tempered than the rest of his armour. . . ? These difficulties are not easily/to be solved without confessing that Virgil had not life enough to correct his work . . .

Ded. *Æneis,* '97. K II 210–11

DEUS EX MACHINA, e.

c. In answer to which, I say, that this machine [the *Dira* fluttering about Turnus in the duel] is one of those which the poet uses only for ornament, and not out of necessity. Nothing can be more beautiful or more poetical than his description of the three *Diræ,* or the setting of the balance, which our Milton has borrowed from him, but employed to a different end: for, first, he makes God Almighty set the scales for St. Michael and Satan, when he knew no combat was to follow; then he makes the good angel's scale descend, and the Devil's mount, quite contrary to Virgil . . .[1] Yet I dare not condemn so great a genius as Milton: for I am much mistaken if he alludes not to the text/in Daniel, where Belshazzar was put into the balance and found too light.

Ded. *Æneis,* '97. K II 212–13

d. [¶] The *episode* of Orpheus and Eurydice begins here [line 656 of the translation of *Georgics,* IV], and contains the only machine which Virgil uses in the *Georgics.* I have observed, in the epistle before the *Æneis,* that our author seldom employs machines but to adorn his poem, and that the action which they seemingly per-

form is really produc'd without them. Of this nature is the legend of the bees restor'd . . . The only beautiful machine which I remember in the modern poets is in Ariosto, where God commands St. Michael to take care that Paris, then besieg'd by the Saracens, should be succor'd by Rinaldo.

Notes and Observations on Virgil's Works '97. N 710

e. [Translation of Aeneid X, line 312. *A choir of Nereids*] This is almost as violent a machine as the death of Aruns by a goddess in the *episode* of Camilla. But the poet makes use of it with greater art; for here it carries on the main design. . . . so that this *episodical* machine is properly a part of the great poem . . . Whereas the machine relating to Camilla is only ornamental; for it has no effect which I can find, but to please the reader . . .

Notes and Observations on Virgil's Works '97. N 715

Epic Poet

AUTHORITY, e.   SUPERNATURAL, c.

a. [The poet of the Christian epic] . . . if any of so happy genius be now living, or any future age can produce a man, who, being conversant in the philosophy of Plato, as it is now accommodated to Christian use, (for, as Virgil gives us to understand by his example, that is the only proper, of all others, for an epic poem,) who, to his natural endowments, of a large invention, a ripe judgment, and a strong memory, has joined the knowledge of the liberal arts and sciences, and particularly moral philosophy, the mathematics, geography, and history, and with all these qualifications is born a poet; knows, and can practise the variety of numbers, and is master of the language in which he writes;—if such a man, I say, be now arisen, or shall

99

arise, I am vain enough to think, that I have proposed a model to him, by which he may build a nobler, a more beautiful and more perfect poem, than any yet extant since the Ancients.

Discourse of Satire, '93. K II 36

EPIC VS. TRAGEDY, d.

b. . . . what soul, though sent into the world with great advantages of Nature, cultivated with the liberal arts and sciences, conversant with histories of the dead, and enriched with observations on the living, can be sufficient to inform the whole body of so great a work [as an epic]?

Ded. *Æneis,* '97. K II 156

c. . . . the file of heroic poets is very short; all are not such who have assumed that lofty title in ancient or modern ages, or have been so esteemed by their partial and ignorant admirers.

There have been but one great *Ilias* and one *Æneis* in so many ages. The next, but . . . with a long interval betwixt, was the *Jerusalem:* I mean not so much in distance of time, as in excellency. After these three are entered, some Lord Chamberlain should be appointed . . . to keep out a crowd of little poets, who press for admission, and are not of quality. Mævius would be deafening your Lordship's ears with his/ . . . mere fustian . . . Pulci, Boiardo, and Ariosto, would cry out, 'make room for the Italian poets, the descendants of Virgil in a right line:' Father Le Moine, with his *Saint Louis,* and Scudery with his *Alaric* . . . and Chapelain would take it ill that his *Maid* should be refused a place . . . Spenser has a better plea for his *Fairy Queen,* had his action been finished, or had been one. And Milton, if the Devil had not been his hero, instead of Adam . . . and if

there had not been more machining persons than human in his poem. After these, the rest of our English poets shall not be mentioned. I have that honour for them which I ought to have; but, if they are worthies, they are not to be ranked amongst the three whom I have named . . .

Ded. *Æneis,* '97. K II 164–65

Epic Unities

General

Cf. ARIOSTO, a. Cf. TASSO, b. Cf. DRYDEN, LITERARY LIFE, l. EPIC VS. TRAGEDY, d. UNITIES (DRAMATIC), GENERAL, e.

Action

EPIC, l. LUCAN, a. SPENSER, b. EPIC, g. DRAMA: EPIC ORIGINS.

Time

UNITIES (DRAMATIC), GENERAL, e. DRAMA: EPIC ORIGINS. UNITIES (DRAMATIC), TIME, e.

[¶] What follows next is no objection; for that implies a fault: and it had been none in Virgil, if he had extended the time of his action beyond a year. At least Aristotle has set no precise limits to it. Homer's, we know, was within two months: Tasso, I am sure, exceeds not a summer . . . Bossu leaves it doubtful whether Virgil's action were within the year, or took up some months beyond it. Indeed, the whole dispute is of no more concernment to the common reader, than it is to a ploughman, whether February this year had 28 or 29 days in it.

Ded. *Æneis,* '97. K II 204

CHAUCER, h.

Epic vs. Tragedy

a. (Neander) [Blank verse is too low] for Tragedy, which is by Aristotle, in the dispute betwixt the epic poesy and the dramatic, for many reasons he there alleges, ranked above it. [Question mark, in the original, omitted]

Dram. Poesy, '65. K I 101

b. (Neander) For though Tragedy be justly preferred above the other, yet there is a great affinity between them [tragedy and epic] . . . The *genus* of them is the same, a just and lively image of human nature, in its actions, passions, and traverses of fortune: so is the end, namely, for the delight and benefit of mankind. The characters and persons are still the same, viz. the greatest of both sorts; only the manner of acquainting us with those actions, passions, and fortunes, is different. Tragedy performs it *viva voce,* or by action, in dialogue; wherein it excels the Epic Poem, which does it chiefly/by narration, and therefore is not so lively an image of human nature.

Dram. Poesy, '65. K I 101–2

Epic, e. Heroic Play, d, e. Epic, f.

c. I do not dispute the preference of Tragedy; let every man enjoy his taste: but 'tis unjust, that they, who have not the least notion of heroic writing, should therefore condemn the pleasure which others receive from it . . .

Author's Apology, '77. K I 182

d. [¶] The most perfect work of Poetry, says our master Aristotle, is Tragedy. His reason is, because it is the most united; being more severely confined within the rules of action, time, and place . . .[I] Being exactly proportioned thus, and uniform in all its parts, the mind/is more capable of comprehending the whole beauty of it without distraction.

But after all these advantages, an Heroic Poem is certainly the greatest work of human nature. The beauties and perfections of the other are but mechanical; those of the Epic are more noble: though Homer has limited his place to Troy, and the fields about it; his actions to forty-eight natural days, whereof twelve are holidays, or cessation from business, during the funeral of Patroclus. To proceed; the action of the Epic is greater; the extension of time enlarges the pleasure of the reader, and the episodes give it more ornament, and more variety. The instruction is equal; but the first is only instructive, the latter forms a hero, and a prince.

If it signifies anything which of them is of the more ancient family, the best and most absolute Heroic Poem was written by Homer long before Tragedy was invented. But if we consider the natural endowments and acquired parts which are necessary to make an accomplished writer in either kind, Tragedy requires a less and more confined knowledge; moderate learning, and observation of the rules, is sufficient, if a genius be not wanting. But in an epic poet, one who is worthy of that name, besides an universal genius, is required universal learning, together with all those qualities and acquisitions which I have named above, and as many more as I have, through haste or negligence, omitted. And, after all, he must have exactly studied Homer and Virgil as his patterns; Aristotle and Horace as his guides; and Vida and Bossu as their commentators; with many others, both Italian and French critics, which I want leisure here to recommend.

. . . /the greatness of an heroic poem, beyond that of a tragedy, may easily be discovered, by observing how few have attempted that work in comparison to those who have written dramas; and, of those few, how small a number have succeeded.

Discourse of Satire, '93. K II 42–44

Unities (Dramatic), General, e. Cf. Epic, g. Drama: Epic Origins. Unities (Dramatic), Time, e.

e. Tragedy is the miniature of human life; an epic poem is the draught at length. . . ./An epic poem is not in such haste [as the tragedy, in its time of action]: it works leisurely; the changes which it makes are slow; but the cure is likely to be more perfect. The effects of tragedy, as I said, are too violent to be lasting. If it be answered that, for this reason, tragedies are often to be seen, and the dose to be repeated, this is tacitly to confess that there is more virtue in one heroic poem than in many tragedies. . . .[1] It is one reason of Aristotle's to prove that Tragedy is the more noble, because it turns in a shorter compass . . . He might prove as well that a mushroom is to be preferred before a peach, because it shoots up in the compass of a night . . ./[1] And, besides, what virtue is there in a tragedy which is not contained in an epic poem, where pride is humbled, virtue rewarded, and vice punished; and those more amply treated than the narrowness of the drama can admit? [See Epic Hero, i.]

Ded. *Æneis,* '97. K II 157–59

f. After all, on the whole merits of the cause, it must be acknowledged that the Epic Poem is more for the manners, and Tragedy for the passions. The passions, as I have said, are violent; and acute distempers require medicines of a strong and speedy operation. Ill habits of the mind are like chronical diseases, to be corrected by degrees . . . The matter being thus stated,

it will appear that both sorts of poetry are of use for their proper ends. The stage is more active; the Epic Poem works at greater leisure, yet is active too, when need requires; for dialogue is imitated by the drama from the more active parts of it. One puts off a fit, like the quinquina, and relieves us only for a time; the other roots out the distemper, and gives a healthful habit. . . . I proceed, from the greatness of the action, to the dignity of the actors . . . There likewise Tragedy will be seen to borrow from the Epopee; and that which borrows is always of less dignity, because it has not of its own. . . ./ And suppose the persons of the drama wholly fabulous, or of the poet's invention, yet Heroic Poetry gave him the examples of that invention, because it was first, and Homer the common father of the stage. I know not of any one advantage which Tragedy can boast above Heroic Poetry, but that it is represented to the view, as well as read, and instructs in the closet, as well as on the theatre yet . . . herein the actors share the poet's praise.

Ded. *Æneis,* '97. K II 160–61

g. [¶] I might also add that many things, which not only please, but are real beauties in the reading, would appear absurd upon the stage; and those not only the *speciosa miracula,* as Horace calls them, of transformations . . .[1] but the prowess of Achilles or Æneas would appear ridiculous in our dwarf heroes of the theatre. We can believe they routed armies, in Homer or in Virgil; but *ne Hercules contra duos* in the drama. [See next entry]

Ded. *Æneis,* '97. K II 161

h. I forbear to instance in many things, which the stage cannot, or ought not to repre/sent; for . . . it might be turned against me, that I plead for the pre-eminence of Epic Poetry because I have taken some pains in translating Virgil, if this were the first time that I had delivered my opinion in this dispute. But I have more than once already maintained the rights of my two masters against their rivals of the scene, even while I wrote tragedies myself, and had no thoughts of this present undertaking.

Ded. *Æneis,* '97. K II 161–62

i. The comparison, therefore, which I made betwixt the Epopee and the Tragedy was not altogether a digression; for 'tis concluded on all hands that they are both the master-pieces of human wit.

Ded. *Æneis,* '97. K II 164

j. [¶] Before I quitted the comparison betwixt Epic Poetry and Tragedy, I should have acquainted my judge with one advantage of the former over the latter, which I now casually remember out of the preface of Segrais . . . or out of Bossu, no matter which: *the style of the Heroic Poem is, and ought to be, more lofty than that of the drama.* The critic is certainly in the right, for the reason already urged; the work of Tragedy is on the passions, and in dialogue; both of them abhor strong metaphors, in which the Epopee delights. A poet cannot speak too plainly on the stage: for *volat irrevocabile verbum;* the sense is lost, if it be not taken flying. But what we read alone, we have leisure to digest; there an author may beautify his/sense by the boldness of his expression, which if we understand not fully at the first, we may dwell upon it till we find the secret force and excellence.

Ded. *Æneis,* '97. K II 165–66

Epicureanism

Cowley, c.   Plutarch, c.   Cf. The-

ocritus, a.   Fame.   Cf. Persius, i.   Epic Machines, a.

Epigram [See also Martial; Owen]

. . . the jerk or sting of an epigram . . . [See Wit, e]

Pref. *Annus Mirabilis,* '66. K I 14

Lucan, b.   Virgil, oo.   Tasso, b.   Epic, j. Dryden, Literary Life, b.   Critic[s], a. a.

Episodes

. . . adorned with episodes . . . [See English Drama, c]

Heads of an Answer, '77. S-S XV 387

Dryden, Literary Life, l.   Epic vs. Tragedy, d.   Epic, b, g.   Drama: Epic Origin.   Epic Machines, e.

Erasmus, Desiderius

Satire, pp.

. . . he, who has best imitated him [Lucian] in Latin, is Erasmus . . .

"Life of Lucian," '96. S-S XVIII 76

Dialogue (Genre), d.

Etherege, Sir George

Satire, q.

. . . I will never enter the lists in Prose with the undoubted best Author of it wch our nation has produc'd [*i.e.,* Etherege].

Letter to Etherege, 16 February 1686/87. Ward No. 13, p. 26.

Ethical Function [See also Ends of Poetry]

a. . . . for moral truth is the mistress of the poet as much as of the philosopher; Poesy must resemble natural truth, but it must *be* ethical. Indeed, the poet dresses truth, and adorns nature, but does not alter them:

Ficta voluptatis causâ sint proxima veris.

Therefore that is not the best poesy which resembles notions of things that are not, to things that are: though the fancy may be

103

great and flowing, yet the soul is but half satisfied when there is not truth in the foundation. This is that which makes Virgil be/preferred before the rest of poets. In variety of fancy, and sweetness of expression, you see Ovid far above him; for Virgil rejected many of those things which Ovid wrote. *A great wit's great work is to refuse,* as my worthy friend Sir John Berkenhead has ingeniously expressed it: you rarely meet with anything in Virgil but truth, which therefore leaves the strongest impression of pleasure in the soul. This I thought myself obliged to say in behalf of Poesy; and to declare . . . that when poets do not argue well, the defect is in the workman, not in the art.

Defence of An Essay, '68. K I 121–22

ENDS OF POETRY, k. EPIC, e. POET, i. TRAGEDY, f. POET, q. ANTONY AND CLEOPATRA. TRAGEDY, k. POET, o. HISTORY, a. EPIC vs. TRAGEDY, d. Cf. HORACE AND JUVENAL AND PERSIUS, c. SATIRE, c. TRAGEDY, p. EPIC, g. EPIC vs. TRAGEDY, e. EPIC HERO, i. EPIC vs. TRAGEDY, f.

b. [Speaking of the ethical function of the epic hero] The shining quality of an epic hero . . . [See EPIC HERO, i] raises first our admiration; we are naturally prone to imitate what we admire; and frequent acts produce a habit. . . . [EPIC HERO, i] We abhor these actions [of Achilles's viciousness] . . . and what we abhor we never imitate. The poet only shows them, like rocks or quicksands, to be shunned.

Ded. *Æneis,* '97. K II 159

HOMER AND VIRGIL, a.

Euripides

(Eugenius) . . . Euripides, in tying himself to one day, has committed an absurdity never to be forgiven him; for in one

of his tragedies he has made Theseus go from Athens to Thebes, which was about forty English miles, under the walls of it to give battle, and appear victorious in the next act; and yet, from the time of his departure to the return of the Nuntius, who gives the relation of his victory, Æthra and the Chorus have but thirty-six verses; that is not for every mile a verse.

Dram. Poesy, '65. K I 48

ANCIENTS, e. SHAKESPEARE, e. MANNERS, i. ANCIENTS, a. AUTHORITY, f. IMITATION, d.

Expression Cf. also MEANNESS and (under PROSODY) *Sweetness*

IMAGINATION, c. POET, c. FIGURES, b.

a. . . . expressions therefore are a modest clothing of our thoughts, as breeches and petticoats are of our bodies.

Pref. *All for Love,* '78. K I 193

MANNERS, c. WIT, m.

b. Expression, and all that belongs to words, is that in a poem which colouring is in a picture. The colours well chosen in their proper places, together with the lights and shadows which belong to them, lighten the design, and make it pleasing to the eye. The words, the expressions, the tropes and figures, the versification, and all the other elegancies of sound, as cadences, turns of words upon the thought, and many other things, which are all parts of expression, perform exactly the same office both in dramatic and epic poetry. Our author calls Colouring, *lena sororis;* in plain English, the bawd of her sister, the design or drawing: she clothes, she dresses her up, she paints/her, she makes her appear more lovely than naturally she is; she procures for the design . . . for the design of itself is only so many naked lines. Thus in poetry, the expression is that which charms

the reader, and beautifies the design, which is only the outlines of the fable. 'Tis true, the design must of itself be good; if it be vicious, or . . . unpleasing, the cost of colouring is thrown away upon it . . . but granting the design to be moderately good, it is like an excellent complexion with indifferent features . . . *Operum colores* is the very word which Horace uses to signify words and elegant expressions, of which he himself was so great a master in his Odes.
Parallel, '95. K II 147–48

FIGURES, c. CURIOSA FELICITAS. CHIAROSCURO.

c. As the words, &c., are evidently shown to be the clothing of the thought, in the same sense as colours are the clothing of the design, so the painter and the poet ought to judge exactly, when the colouring and expressions are perfect, and then to think their work is truly finished.
Parallel, '95. K II 152
VIRGIL, ee.

F

Fable

a. . . . the feigned action, or fable . . .
Dram. Poesy, '65. K I 39
ANCIENTS, s, t.

b. (Lisideius) I have noted one great advantage they [the French] have had in the plotting of their tragedies; that is, they are always grounded upon some known history: according to that of Horace, *Ex noto fictum carmen sequar;* and in that they have so imitated the Ancients, that they have surpassed them. For the Ancients, as was observed before, took for the foundation of their plays some poetical fiction, such as under that consideration could move but little concernment in the audience, because they already knew the event of it. But the French goes farther:

Atque ita mentitur . . .

He so interweaves truth with probable fiction, that he/puts a pleasing fallacy upon us; mends the intrigues of fate, and dis-

penses with the severity of history, to reward that virtue which has been rendered to us there unfortunate. Sometimes the story has left the success so doubtful, that the writer is free, by the privilege of a poet, to take that which of two or more relations will best suit with his design . . .[1] Nay more, when the event is past dispute, even then we are willing to be deceived, and the poet, if he contrives it with appearance of truth, has all the audience of his party . . .
Dram. Poesy, '65. K I 58–59
FLETCHER, a. ENGLISH vs. FRENCH, y, s. TRAGEDY, n.

c. [¶] But these little critics do not well consider what is the work of a poet, and what the graces of a poem: the story is the least part of either: I mean the foundation of it, before it is modelled by the art of him who writes it . . . On this foundation . . . the characters are raised: and, since no story can afford characters enough for the variety of the English stage, it fol-

105

lows, that it is to be altered and enlarged with new persons, accidents, and designs, which will almost make it new. When this is done, the forming it into acts and scenes, disposing of actions and passions into their proper places, and beautifying both with descriptions, similitudes, and propriety of language, is the principal employment of the poet; as being the largest field of fancy, which is the principal quality required in him: for so much the word ποιητής implies. Judgment, indeed, is necessary in him; but 'tis fancy that gives the life-touches, and the secret graces to it;/especially in serious plays, which depend not much on observation.

Pref. *Evening's Love*, '71. K I 146–47
LAST AGE, c. Cf. POET, i. ANCIENTS, u. TRAGEDY, l, m. ANCIENTS, v. ENGLISH DRAMA, c.

d. [¶] For the second of these [parts of a poem], the order: the meaning is, that a fable ought to have a beginning, middle, and an end, all just and natural; so that that part, *e.g.* which is the middle, could not naturally be the beginning or end, and so of the rest: all depend on one another, like the links of a curious chain.

Heads of an Answer, '77. S-S XV 389
MANNERS, c. MORAL (OF A WORK).

e. [¶] This ground-work the history afforded me, and I desire no better to build a play upon; for where the event of a great action is left doubtful, there the poet is left master. He may raise what he pleases on that foundation, provided he makes it of a piece, and according to the rule of probability.[1]

Pref. *Don Sebastian*, '90. S-S VII 311
f. Though, if I had taken the whole story [from the French novel "Don Sebas-

tian"], and wrought it up into a play, I might have done it exactly according to the practice of almost all the ancients, who were never accused of being plagiaries for building their tragedies on known fables. . . .[1] It is the contrivance, the new turn, and new characters, which alter the property, and make it ours. The *materia/poetica* is as common to all writers as the *materia medica* to all physicians.[1]

Pref. *Don Sebastian*, '90. S-S VII 312–13
ENGLISH VS. FRENCH, k. EXPRESSION, b.
Fairfax, Edward
. . . Spenser and Fairfax . . . great masters in our language . . .

Pref. *Fables*, 1700. K II 247
MILTON, d. CHAUCER, c.
Fame
DRYDEN, LITERARY LIFE, q. Cf. DRYDEN, PERSONAL CHARACTER, f. POET, a. Cf. AUDIENCE, f.

[¶] Fame is in itself a real good, if we may believe Cicero, who was perhaps too fond of it. But even fame, as Virgil tells us, acquires strength by going forward. Let Epicurus give indolency as an attribute to his gods, and place in it the happiness of the blest; the Divinity which we worship has given us not only a precept against it, but his own example to the contrary.

Discourse of Satire, '93. K II 20
Cf. TRANSLATION, k. DRYDEN, LITERARY LIFE, t. Cf. IMAGINATION, e.
Fancy [See also IMAGINATION]
a. [¶] This worthless present was designed you [Orrery], long before it was a play; when it was only a confused mass of thoughts, tumbling over one another in the dark; when the fancy was yet in its first work, moving the sleeping images of things towards the light, there to be dis-

tinguished, and then either chosen or rejected by the judgment . . .

Ded. *Rival Ladies,* '64. K I 1

Cf. IMAGINATION, a. PLAY WRITING. RHYME (DEBATE), d.

b. But certainly, that which most regulates the fancy, and gives the judgment its busiest employment, is like to bring forth the richest and clearest thoughts.

Ded. *Rival Ladies,* '64. K I 8

WIT, a. RHYME (DEBATE), g, r. IMAGINATION, c. OVID AND VIRGIL, a. POET, c. ETHICAL FUNCTION, a. DAVENANT, b. COMEDY, a. LAUGHTER, c.

c. [The various modification of basic story, or plot, is] the largest field of fancy, which is the principal quality required in him [the poet]: for so much the word ποιητής implies. Judgment, indeed, is necessary in him; but 'tis fancy that gives the life-touches, and the secret graces to it;/ especially in serious plays, which depend not much on observation. [See next entry]

Pref. *Evening's Love,* '71. K I 146–47

d. For, to write humour in comedy (which is the theft of poets from mankind), little of fancy is required; the poet observes only what is ridiculous and pleasant folly, and by judging exactly what is so, he pleases in the representation of it.

Pref. *Evening's Love,* '71. K I 147

HEROIC PLAY, d. SUPERNATURAL, e. CRITIC[s], i. JONSON, u. FLETCHER, d. Cf. SETTLE, c. POETIC LICENSE, b.

e. [¶] Men that are given over to fancy only, are little better than madmen. What people say of fire, viz. that it is a good servant, but an ill master, may not unaptly be applied to fancy; which, when it is too active, rages, but when cooled and allayed/by the judgment, produces admirable effects

. . . [remarks on Settle's "rage of fancy"]

. . . I hope the reader will excuse some digression upon the extravagant use of fancy and poetical licence.

Fanciful poetry and music, used with moderation, are good; but men who are wholly given over to either of them, are commonly as full of whimsies as diseased and splenetic men can be. Their heads are continually hot, and they have the same elevation of fancy sober, which men of sense have when they drink. . . . so, mere poets and mere musicians are as sottish as mere drunkards are, who live in a continual mist, without seeing or judging any thing clearly.

Postscript *N and O,* '74. S-S XV 405–6

f. Nothing is more frequent in a fanciful writer, than to foil himself by not managing his strength; therefore, as in a wrestler, there is first required some measure of force . . . /without which all instruction would be vain; yet, these being granted, if he want the skill . . . he shall make but small advantage of his natural robustuousness: so, in a poet, his inborn vehemence and force of spirit will only run him out of breath the sooner, if it be not supported by the help of Art.

Pref. *Troilus,* '79. K I 220–21

g. No man should pretend to write, who cannot temper his fancy with his judgment: nothing is more dangerous to a raw horseman, than a hot-mouthed jade without a curb.

Pref. *Troilus,* '79. K I 222

SHAKESPEARE, r. RULES, d. OVID, h.

h. Few good pictures have been finished at one sitting; neither can a true just play, which is to bear the test of ages, be produced at a heat, or by the force of fancy, without the maturity of judgment.

Ded. *Spanish Friar,* '81. K I 245

LUCRETIUS, b. PROSODY, u. WIT, m. FIGURES, d. EPIC POET, a. OVID, a. Cf. VIRGIL, aa.

i. It is observed both/of him [Virgil] and Horace (and I believe it will hold in all great poets), that, though they wrote before [*i.e.,* earlier in their careers] with a certain heat of genius which inspired them, yet that heat was not perfectly digested. There is required a continuance of warmth, to ripen the best and noblest fruits. Thus Horace, in his First and Second Book of Odes, was still rising, but came not to his meridian till the Third; after which his judgment was an overpoise to his imagination: he grew too cautious to be bold enough . . . and, in his Satires and Epistles, was more a philosopher and a critic than a poet. In the beginning of summer the days are almost at a stand, with little variation of length or shortness, because at that time the diurnal motion of the sun partakes more of a right line than of a spiral. The same is the method of nature in the frame of man. He seems at forty to be fully in his summer tropic; somewhat before, and somewhat after, he finds in his soul but small increases or decays. From fifty to three-score, the balance generally holds even, in our colder climates: for he loses not much in fancy; and judgment, which is the effect of observation, still increases. His succeeding years afford him little more than the stubble of his own harvest: yet, if his constitution be healthful, his mind may still retain a decent vigour; and the gleanings of that Ephraim, in comparison with others, will surpass the vintage of Abiezer. I have called this some-

where, by a bold metaphor, a green old age; but Virgil has given me his authority for the figure—

Jam senior; sed cruda Deo, viridisque senectus.

Ded. *Georgics,* '97. S-S XIV 2–3

j. . . . too much of heat is required at first, that there may/not be too little left at last. A prodigal fire is only capable of large remains . . . In my small observations of mankind, I have ever found, that such as are not rather too full of spirit when they are young, degenerate to dulness in their age.

Ded. *Georgics,* '97. S-S XIV 4–5

Fancy (Responsive)

. . . the fancy, which in these cases [stage production] will contribute to its own deceit . . . [See UNITIES (DRAMATIC), PLACE, b]

Dram. Poesy, '65. K I 40

IMAGINATION (RESPONSIVE), b. LAUGHTER, c. IMAGINATION (RESPONSIVE), c. VIRGIL, ff.

Farce

TRAGICOMEDY, a. FLETCHER, a. COMEDY, d. Cf. DRYDEN, PERSONAL CHARACTER, g.

a. [¶] But I have descended . . . from Comedy to Farce; which consists principally of grimaces. That I admire not any comedy equally with tragedy, is, perhaps, from the sullenness of my humour; but that I detest those farces, which are now the most frequent entertainments of the stage, I am sure I have reason on my side.

Pref. *Evening's Love,* '71. K I 135

COMEDY, a.

b. [¶] After all, it is to be acknowledged, that most of those comedies, which have been lately written, have been allied too much to Farce: and this must of necessity/fall out, till we forbear the translation of French plays: for their poets, wanting judgment to make or to maintain true characters, strive to cover their defects with ridiculous figures and grimaces.

Pref. *Evening's Love*, '71. K I 136–37

UNITIES (DRAMATIC), ACTION, d. Cf. FLETCHER, e.

c. The success [of *Cleomenes*] has justified my opinion; and that at a time when the world is running mad after Farce, the extremity of bad poetry, or rather the judgment that is fallen upon dramatic writing. Were I in the humour, I have sufficient cause to expose it in its true colours; but, having for once escaped, I will forbear my satire, and only be thankful/ for my deliverance.

Pref. *Cleomenes*, '92. S-S VIII 219–220

d. The character of them [Satyr dances in the earliest Greek tragedy] was also kept, which was mirth and wantonness; and this was given, I suppose, to the folly of the common audience, who soon grow weary of good sense, and, as we daily see in our own age and country, are apt to forsake poetry, and still ready to return to buffoonry and farce.

Discourse of Satire, '93. K II 50

SATIRE, w, aa, cc. D'URFEY.

e. There is yet a lower sort of poetry and painting, which is out of nature; for a farce is that in poetry, which *grotesque* is in a picture. The persons and action of a farce are all unnatural, and the manners false, that is, inconsisting with the characters of mankind. Grotesque painting is the just resemblance of this; and Horace begins his *Art of Poetry* by describing such a figure . . . [See also LAUGHTER, d]

Parallel, '95. K II 132

f. [Of farce] 'Tis a kind of bastard-

pleasure too, taken in at the eyes of the vulgar gazers, and at the ears of the beastly audience. Church-painters use it to divert the honest countryman at public prayers, and keep his eyes open at a heavy sermon; and farce-scribblers make use of the same noble invention, to entertain citizens, country-gentlemen, and Covent Garden fops. If they are merry, all goes well on the poet's side. The better sort go thither too, but in despair of sense and the just images of Nature, which are the adequate pleasures of the mind.

Parallel, '95. K II 133

g. And as Sir William D'Avenant observes in his Preface to *Gondibert*, ' 'Tis the wisdom of a government to permit plays' (he might have added—farces), 'as 'tis the prudence of a carter to put bells upon his horses, to make them carry their burthens cheerfully.'

Parallel, '95. K II 133

PRESENT AGE, p.

Fiction

FABLE, b. IMAGINATION (RESPONSIVE), a, b. VERISIMILITY, b. POETIC LICENSE, c. POET, i. IMAGINATION (RESPONSIVE), d. IMITATION, j. POETIC LICENSE, d. Cf. RULES, d. OPERA, a. Cf. ENDS OF POETRY, j.

Fiction is of the essence of Poetry, as well as of painting; there is a resemblance in one, of human bodies,/things, and actions, which are not real; and in the other, of a true story by a fiction . . .

Parallel, '95. K II 128–29

INVENTION, c.

Figures

ARISTOTLE, d.

a. [¶] 'Tis true, the boldness of the figures is to be hidden sometimes by the address of the poet; that they may work their effect upon the mind, without discovering the art which caused it. And therefore they are principally to be used in passion; when we speak more warmly, and with more precipitation than at other times . . .

Author's Apology, '77. K I 185

b. The sum of all depends on what before I hinted, that this boldness of expression [i.e., of figures] is not to be blamed, if it be managed by the coolness and discretion which is necessary to a poet.

Author's Apology, '77. K I 186

POETIC LICENSE, d. EPIC, i. AESCHYLUS. SHAKESPEARE, n. Cf. BOMBAST, a. HEIGHTENING, d. STYLE, c. HISTORY, d. VIRGIL, oo. PROSODY, u. DRYDEN, WORKS, bbb. PERSIUS, b. SATIRE, f. EXPRESSION, b. Cf. TRANSLATION, n. ENGLISH VS. FRENCH, w.

Hyperbole

LUCAN, c. CHAPMAN, a.

Metaphor

PLAUTUS, a. PASSIONS, i. Cf. OBSCENITY, b. PERSIUS, b, g. HORACE AND JUVENAL AND PERSIUS, a. Cf. DRYDEN, WORKS, mmm.

c. Strong and glowing colours are the just resemblances of bold metaphors: but both must be judiciously applied; for there is a difference betwixt daring and foolhardiness. Lucan and Statius often ventured them too far; our Virgil never. But the great defect of the *Pharsalia* and the *Thebais* was in the design: if that had been more perfect, we might have forgiven many of their bold strokes in the colouring, or at least excused them: yet some of them are such as Demosthenes or Cicero could not have defended. Virgil, if he could have seen the first verses of the *Sylvæ,* would

have thought Statius mad, in his fustian description of the statue on the brazen horse. But that poet was always in a foam at his setting out . . .[1]/But Virgil knew how to rise by degrees in his expressions: Statius was in his towering heights at the first stretch of his pinions.[1]

Parallel, '95. K II 149–50

EPIC VS. TRAGEDY, j. See below, e. ENGLISH VS. FRENCH, w. COWLEY, g.

Paronomasia [see main heading]

Prosopopoeia

LUCRETIUS, c.

Similitudes

FABLE, c. PASSIONS, h. DRYDEN, WORKS, h. PASSIONS, i. PLUTARCH, g. DESIGNING.

d. The reader will easily observe, that I was transported by the multitude and variety of my similitudes; which are generally the product of a luxuriant fancy, and the wantonness of wit. Had I called in my judgment to my assistance, I had certainly retrenched many of them.

Ded. *Eleonora,* '92. S-S XI 122

DECORUM, i.

e. [¶] This accusation [of unseasonable similitudes] is general against all who would be thought heroic poets; but I think it touches Virgil less than any. He is too great a master of his art, to make a blot which may so easily be hit. Similitudes, as I have said, are not for tragedy, which is all violent, and where the passions are in a perpetual ferment; for there they deaden where they should animate; they are not of the nature of dialogue, unless in comedy: a metaphor is almost all the stage can suffer, which is a kind of similitude comprehended in a word. But this figure has a contrary effect in heroic poetry; there it is employed to raise the admiration, which is its proper business; and admiration is not of so violent a nature as fear or hope, compassion or horror, or any concernment we can have for such or such a person on the stage. Not but I confess that similitudes and descriptions, when drawn into an unreasonable length, must needs nauseate the reader. . . . This I have observed of his [Virgil's] similitudes in general, that they are not placed, as our unobserving critics tell us, in the heat of any action, but commonly in its declining. When he has warmed/us in his description as much as possibly he can, then, lest that warmth should languish, he renews it by some apt similitude, which illustrates his subject, and yet palls not his audience.[1]

Ded. *Æneis,* '97. K II 202–3

Miscellaneous

Cf. IMAGING, b. PASSIONS, h, i. DESIGNING. See above, e. Cf. *Irony,* under SATIRE, p.

Flecknoe, Richard

. . . you may please to take notice by the way how natural the connection of thought is betwixt a bad poet and Flecknoe . . .

Ded. *Limberham,* '80. S-S VI 6

EPIC, j.

Fletcher, John [See also BEAUMONT AND FLETCHER; SHAKESPEARE AND FLETCHER] Cf. SENECA, a. ENGLISH DRAMA, d.

a. (Lisideius) I have taken notice but of one tragedy of ours, whose plot has that uniformity and unity of design in it . . . and that is *Rollo* . . . : there indeed the plot is neither large nor intricate, but just enough to fill the minds of the audience . . . Besides, you see it founded upon the truth of history, only the time of the action is not reduceable to the strictness of the

rules; and you see in some places a little farce mingled . . .

Dram. Poesy, '65. K I 60

ENGLISH VS. FRENCH, s.

a-2. (Neander) You find him [Jonson] likewise commending Fletcher's pastoral of *The Faithful Shepherdess,* which is for the most part rhyme, though not refined to that purity to which it hath since been brought.

Dram. Poesy, '65. K I 78

ENGLISH VS. FRENCH, u. RHYME (DEBATE), l. COMEDY, e. WIT, h. SHAKESPEARE, m.

b. . . . I could easily demonstrate, that our admired Fletcher . . . neither understood correct plotting, nor that which they/call *the decorum of the stage.*[1]

Defence of the Epilogue, '72. K I 165–66

GRAFFING, b.

c. Neither is the luxuriance of Fletcher . . . a less fault than the carelessness of Shakespeare. He does not well always; and, when he does, he is a true Englishman; he knows not when to give over. If he wakes in one scene, he commonly slumbers in another . . .

Defence of the Epilogue, '72. K I 172

d. Let us imitate, as we are able, the quickness and easiness of Fletcher, without proposing him as a pattern to us, either in the redundancy of his matter, or the incorrectness of his language. Let us/admire his wit and sharpness of conceit; but let us at the same time acknowledge, that it was seldom so fixed, and made proper to his character, as that the same things might not be spoken by any person in the play. Let us applaud his scenes of love; but let us confess, that he understood not either greatness or perfect honour in the parts of any of his

111

women. In fine, let us allow, that he had so much fancy, as when he pleased he could write wit; but that he wanted so much judgment, as seldom to have written humour, or described a pleasant folly.

Defence of the Epilogue, '72. K I 176–77
ENGLISH DRAMA, a.   AGE, GENIUS OF, c.
POETIC JUSTICE, e.   ANCIENTS, e.   SHAKE-
SPEARE, f, s.

e. The best of their [poets of the Last Age] designs, the most approaching to antiquity, and the most conducing to move pity, is the *King and no King;* which, if the farce of Bessus were thrown away, is of that inferior sort of tragedies, which end with a prosperous event. . . . The taking of this play, amongst many others, I cannot wholly ascribe to the excellency of the action; for I find it moving when it is read . . . The beauties of it must therefore lie either in the lively touches of the passion; or we must conclude . . . that even in imperfect plots there are less degrees of Nature, by which some faint emotions of pity and terror are raised in us . . .

Pref. Troilus, '79. K I 212
SHAKESPEARE AND FLETCHER AND JONSON.

f. Fletcher, on the other side, gives neither to Arbaces, nor to his king, in the *Maid's Tragedy,* the qualities [manners] which are suitable to a monarch . . .

Pref. Troilus, '79. K I 218

f-2. . . . when Philaster wounds Arethusa and the boy; and Perigot his mistress, in the *Faithful Shepherdess,* both these are contrary to the character of manhood. Nor is *Valentinian* managed much better . . .

Pref. Troilus, '79. K I 218

g. The characters of Fletcher are poor and narrow, in comparison of Shake-

speare's; I remember not one which is not borrowed from him; unless you will accept that strange mixture of a man in the *King and no King;* so that in this part Shakespeare is generally worth our imitation; and to imitate Fletcher is but to copy after him who was a copyer.

Pref. Troilus, '79. K I 220
COLLIER.

Flower and the Leaf, The

Besides this tale [*Palamon and Arcite*], there is another of his [Chaucer's] own invention, after the manner of the Provençals, called *The Flower and the Leaf,* with which I was so particularly pleased, both for the invention and the moral, that I cannot hinder myself from recommending it to the reader.

Pref. Fables, 1700. K II 270

Fontenelle, Bernard le Bovier de
WALSH, b.

a. . . . Fontenelle . . . his "Dialogues of the Dead," which I never read but with a new pleasure. [See LUCIAN, h]

"Life of Lucian," S-S XVIII 76
DIALOGUE (GENRE), d.

b. [In a discussion of pastoral literature] Neither will I mention Monsieur Fontenelle, the living glory of the French. It is enough for him to have excelled his master Lucian, without attempting to compare our miserable age with that of Virgil, or Theocritus. Let me only add, for his reputation,

—Si Pergama dextrâ
Defendi possint, etiam hâc defensa fuissent

Ded. *Pastorals,* '97. S-S XIII 325

Fools and Fops

GALLICIZING.   AUDIENCE, e.   POETIC LICENSE, b.   COURTIER WITHOUT WIT.
SHADWELL, b.   HORACE AND JUVENAL AND

PERSIUS, c. SATIRE, b. FARCE, f. Cf. TRANSLATION, ee.

French Authors [Cf. ENGLISH VS. FRENCH, *passim*]

PROSODY, gg. FARCE, b. EPIC HERO, d. DECORUM, g.

a. [¶] Yet in this nicety of manners does the excellency of French poetry consist: their heroes are the most civil people breathing; but their good breeding seldom/extends to a word of sense; all their wit is in their ceremony; they want the genius which animates our stage; and therefore 'tis but necessary, when they cannot please, that they should take care not to offend. But as the civilest man in the company is commonly the dullest, so these authors, while they are afraid to make you laugh or cry, out of pure good manners make you sleep. They are so careful not to exasperate a critic, that they never leave him any work; so busy with the broom, and make so clean a riddance, that there is little left either for censure or for praise: for no part of a poem is worth our discommending, where the whole is insipid . . .[1]

Pref. *All for Love,* '78. K I 193–94

ENGLISH VS. FRENCH, j. MANNERS, j. TRAGICOMEDY, e.

b. The French have performed nothing in this kind which is not far below those two Italians [Ariosto and Tasso], and subject to a thousand more reflections, without examining their *St. Lewis,* their *Pucelle,* or their *Alaric.*

Discourse of Satire, '93. K II 28

DRYDEN, LITERARY LIFE, b. ENGLISH DRAMA, i. PROSODY, ii, c, d. ENGLISH VS. FRENCH, n. TURNS, a.

c. The want of genius, of which I have accused the French, is laid to their charge by one of their own great authors, though I have forgotten his name, and where I read it. [Ker suggests St. Évremond]

Ded. *Æneis,* '97. K II 219

ENGLISH VS. FRENCH, w. CHAUCER AND OVID. TURNS, b.

French Critics [See individual critics, by name]

ENGLISH VS. FRENCH, cc. DRYDEN, WORKS, cc. DRYDEN, LITERARY LIFE, a. EPIC VS. TRAGEDY, d. RULES, g. COMMENTATORS, DUTCH, b. ENGLISH VS. FRENCH, l.

French Drama [See also ENGLISH VS. FRENCH; SPANISH CRITICS]

Cf. RHYME (DEBATE), b.

(Eugenius) . . . as for the . . . French . . . plays, I can make it evident, that those [in English] who now write surpass them . . .

Dram. Poesy, '65. K I 35

UNITIES (DRAMATIC), PLACE, c. ANCIENTS, x. ENGLISH VS. FRENCH, b. FABLE, b. TUKE, a. SPANISH PLAYS, c. TRAGICOMEDY, a. ACTION (DEFINED). TRAGICOMEDY, b. SPEECHES (DRAMATIC), a. FARCE, b. TRAGEDY, e.

French Language

ACADEMY, b.

a. . . . the French . . . are not less ambitious to possess their [the Italians'] elegance in Poetry and Music; in both which they labour at impossibilities. 'Tis true, indeed, they have reformed their tongue, and brought both their prose and poetry to a standard; the sweetness, as well as the purity, is much improved, by throwing off the unnecessary consonants, which made their spelling tedious, and their pronunciation harsh: but . . . neither can the natural harshness of the French, or their perpetual ill accent, be ever refined into perfect harmony like the Italian.

Pref. *Albion and Albanius*, '85. K I 274 ENGLISH VS. FRENCH, n.

b. [The women in Juvenal's Sixth Satire] Love to speak Greek (which was then the Fashionable Tongue, as *French* is now with us.)

Argument of the Sixth Satire [Juvenal], '97. JK II 695

French Nation

For the French [in respect to rhymed drama], I do not name them, because it is the fate of our countrymen to admit little of theirs among us, but the basest of their men, the extravagancies of their fashions, and the frippery of their merchandise.

Ded. *Rival Ladies*, '64. K I 6

French Romances

(Crites) . . . the French Romances, whose heroes neither eat, nor drink, nor sleep, for love.

Dram. Poesy, '65. K I 55

Fustian [See BOMBAST]

G

Gallicizing

For I cannot approve of their way of refining, who corrupt our English idiom by mixing it too much with French: that is a sophistication of language, not an improvement of it . . . We meet daily with those fops, who value themselves on their travelling, and pretend they cannot express their meaning in English, because they would put off to us some French phrase of the last edition; without considering, that, for aught they know, we have a better of our own.

Defence of the Epilogue, '72. K I 170

Genius

Cf. RHYME (DEBATE), w.

a. . . . Longinus . . ./has judiciously preferred the sublime genius that sometimes errs, to the middling or indifferent one, which makes few faults, but seldom or never rises to any excellence.

Author's Apology, '77. K I 179–80 SHAKESPEARE, c, t. Cf. RULES, c. SHAKESPEARE AND FLETCHER, a. PASSIONS, d. Cf. TRANSLATION, u. Cf. TRAGICOMEDY, c. SUCCESS. Cf. UNITIES (DRAMATIC), GENERAL, c. GOLDEN AGES, b. SATIRE, b. HORACE, e. SHAKESPEARE, i.

b. A happy genius is the gift of nature: it depends on the influence of the stars, say the astrologers; on the organs of the body, say the naturalists; it is the particular gift of Heaven, say the divines, both Christians and heathens. How to improve it, many books can teach us; how to obtain it, none; that nothing can be done without it, all agree:

Tu nihil invita dices faciesve Minerva.

Parallel, '95. K II 138 FANCY, i. Cf. MULGRAVE, b. INVENTION, c. ENGLISH VS. FRENCH, n.

Genre [See also DIALOGUE (GENRE)]

a. (Eugenius) . . . the sock and the buskin were not worn by the same poet. [See ANCIENTS, i]

Dram. Poesy, '65. K I 50

EPIC VS. TRAGEDY, b. IMAGES, c. Cf. STYLE, b.

b. If he [Howard] means that there is no essential difference betwixt Comedy, Tragedy, and Farce, but what is only made by the people's taste . . . that is so manifest an error, that I need not lose time to contradict it. Were there neither judge, taste, nor opinion in the world, yet they would differ in their natures; for the action, character, and language of Tragedy, would still be great and high; that of Comedy, lower and more familiar; admiration would be the delight of one, and satire of the other.

Defence of An Essay, '68. K I 120

AUDIENCE, POPULAR, b. STYLE, c. THEOCRITUS, a. Cf. DRYDEN, WORKS, yy. VIRGIL, mm. Cf. ENGLISH VS. FRENCH, n.

German Verse

PROSODY, h.

Golden Ages [See also DECAY]

LAST AGE, e.

a. That age was most famous amongst the Greeks which ended with the death of Alexander; amongst the Romans, learning seemed again to revive and flourish in the century which produced Cicero, Varro, Sallust, Livy, Lucretius, and Virgil: and after a short interval of years, wherein nature seemed to take a breathing time for a second birth, there sprung up under the Vespasians, and those . . . who succeeded . . . a race of memorable wits, such as were the two Plinies, Tacitus, and Suetonius; and, as if Greece was emulous of

the Roman learning, under the same favourable constellation was born the famous philosopher and historian, Plutarch; than whom antiquity has never produced a man more generally knowing, or more virtuous; and no succeeding age has equalled him.

Ded. *Plutarch's Lives,* '83. S-S XVII 6

Cf. OPERA, d.

b. [¶] It is manifest, that some particular ages have been more happy than others in the production of great men, in all sorts of arts and sciences; as that of Euripides, Sophocles, Aristophanes . . . for stage poetry . . . that of Augustus, for heroic, lyric, dramatic, elegiac . . . in the persons of Virgil, Horace, Varius, Ovid . . . A famous age in modern times, for learning in every kind, was that of Lorenzo de Medici, and his son Leo the Tenth . . .

Examples in all these are obvious: but what I would infer is this; that in such an age, it is possible some great genius may arise, to equal any of the ancients; abating only for the language. For great contem/poraries whet and cultivate each other; and mutual borrowing, and commerce, makes the common riches of learning, as it does of the civil government.

Discourse of Satire, '93. K II 25–26

CHAUCER AND OVID.

Good Nature

[¶] Good sense and good nature are never separated . . . [See CRITICISM, e]

Discourse of Satire, '93. K II 17

DORSET, b.

Good Sense

Cf. DRYDEN, LITERARY LIFE, e-2. RULES, d. SATIRE, jj. Cf. PLUTARCH, c. CRITICISM, e.

For good sense is the same in all or most ages; and course of time rather improves

Nature, than impairs her. What has been, may be again: another Homer, and another Virgil, may possibly arise from those very causes which produced the first; though it would be impudence to affirm, that any such have yet appeared.

Discourse of Satire, '93. K II 25

FARCE, d. SATIRE, s. BUTLER, b. TRANSLATION, k. REFORMATION OF THE STAGE. CRITIC[s], a. HOPKINS. OBSCENITY, e. CHAUCER, c. COWLEY, j. MODERNIZING.

Gorboduc

RHYME (DEBATE), a.

Gower, John

CHAUCER, c.

Graffing

a. [¶] There is yet another way of improving language, which poets especially have practised in all ages; that is, by applying received words to a new signification; and this, I believe, is meant by Horace, in that precept which is so variously construed by expositors:

Dixeris egregie, notum si callida verbum Reddiderit junctura novum.

And, in this way, he himself had a particular happiness . . .

Defence of the Epilogue, '72. K I 171

b. By this graffing, as I may call it, on old words, has our tongue been beautified by . . . Shakespeare, Fletcher, and Johnson, whose excellencies I can never enough admire; and in this they have been followed, especially by Sir John Suckling and Mr. Waller, who refined upon them. Neither have they, who succeeded them, been wanting in their endeavours to adorn our mother tongue . . .

Defence of the Epilogue, '72. K I 171

ARCHAISMS, b. TRANSLATION, n.

116

Grammar [See *Defence of the Epilogue,* Ker, I, 162 ff., *passim*]

SHAKESPEARE, m.

a. [With reference to a Jonson example] The preposition in the end of the sentence; a common fault with him, and which I have but lately observed in my own writings.

Defence of the Epilogue, '72. K I 168

b. [Complains of Jonson's use of] *Ones,* in the plural number . . . frequent with him . . .

Defence of the Epilogue, '72. K I 168

c. He [Jonson] perpetually uses ports for gates; which is an affected error in him, to introduce Latin by the loss of the English idiom . . .

Defence of the Epilogue, '72. K I 169

d. . . . that gross way of two comparatives was then [the Last Age] ordinary . . .

Defence of the Epilogue, '72. K I 170

Cf. SETTLE, b. ENGLISH LANGUAGE, g. SHAKESPEARE, n. ACADEMY, b. WALSH, b, c. PROSODY, z.

Greek Language

SIDNEY, a. ENGLISH LANGUAGE, g, b.

[Discussion of Plutarch's style] Add to this, that in Plutarch's time, and long before it, the purity of the Greek tongue was corrupted, and the native splendour of it had taken the tarnish of barbarism, and contracted the filth and spots of degenerating ages: for the fall of empires always draws after it/the language and eloquence of the people . . .

"The Life of Plutarch," '83. S-S XVII 66–67

Cf. FRENCH LANGUAGE, b. PROSODY, ii.

Grotesque

a. . . . he who purposely avoids nature,

must fall into grotesque,/and make no likeness. [See PORTRAIT PAINTING]

Ded. *Plutarch's Lives,* '83. S-S XVII 16–17

b. When they [detractors of the present age] describe the writers of this age, they draw such monstrous figures of them, as resemble none of us; our pretended pictures are so unlike, that 'tis evident we never sat to them: they are all grotesque; the products of their wild imaginations, things out

of nature; so far from being copied from us, that they resemble nothing that ever was, or ever can be.

Ded. *Examen Poeticum,* '93. K II 5

FARCE, e. NATURE, f.

Guarini, Giovanni Battista

. . . Guarini's [shepherds] seem to have been bred in courts . . . [See THEOCRITUS, a]

Pref. *Sylvæ,* '85. K I 265

SATIRE, c. TRAGICOMEDY, f, g. SPENSER, c.

H

Halifax, First Earl of [See CHARLES MONTAGUE]

Harrington, Sir John

CHAUCER, c.

Heightening [See also IMITATION]

Cf. RHYME (DEBATE), e.

a. . . . a serious play . . . is indeed the representation of Nature, but 'tis Nature wrought up to an higher pitch. [See TRAGEDY, n]

Dram. Poesy, '65. K I 100

b. (Neander) A play, as I have said, to be like Nature, is to be set above it; as statues which are placed on high are made greater than the life, that they may descend to the sight in their just proportion.

Dram. Poesy, '65. K I 102

RHYME (DEBATE), q. IMITATION, f. Cf. PROSE, a. IMITATION, g. JONSON, l. Cf. DRYDEN, LITERARY LIFE, m. RHYME (DEBATE), aa. HEROIC PLAY, d. POETRY AND PAINTING, b.

c. 'Tis true, there are limits to be betwixt the boldness and rashness of a poet

. . ./But I will presume for once to tell them, that the boldest strokes of poetry, when they are managed artfully, are those which most delight the reader.

Author's Apology, '77. K I 182–83

d. But as in a room contrived for state, the height of the roof should bear a proportion to the area; so, in the heightenings of Poetry, the strength and vehemence of figures should be suited to the occasion, the subject, and the persons. All beyond this is monstrous: 'tis out of Nature, 'tis an excrescence, and not a living part of Poetry.

Ded. *Spanish Friar,* '81. K I 247

STYLE, c. IMITATION, h. Cf. EXPRESSION, b.

Heinsius, Daniel

POETIC JUSTICE, c. HORACE AND JUVENAL AND PERSIUS, g. SATIRE, f. DRYDEN, WORKS, ttt.

Hemistich [See PROSODY]

Hero (Dramatic)

Cf. ENGLISH VS. FRENCH, t.

a. . . . I would inquire of my overwise censors, who told them I intended him [Philocles, in *Secret Love*] a perfect character, or, indeed, what necessity was there he should be so, the variety of images being one great beauty of a play? It was as much as I designed, to show one great and absolute pattern of honour in my poem, which I did in the person of the queen: all the defects of the other parts being set to show, the more to recommend that one character of virtue . . .

Pref. *Secret Love,* '67. S-S II 420

Epic Hero, b, d.   Tragedy, c.

b. [¶] That the criminal [he has been speaking of *Rollo*] should neither be wholly guilty, nor wholly innocent, but so participating of both as to move both pity and terror, is certainly a good rule, but not perpetually to be observed; for that were to make all tragedies too much alike . . .

Heads of an Answer, '77. S-S XV 387

Tragedy, h.

c. All reasonable men have long since concluded, that the hero of the poem ought not to be a character of perfect virtue, for then he could not, without injustice, be made unhappy; nor yet altogether wicked, because he could not then be pitied.

Pref. *All for Love,* '78. K I 191.

Corneille, b.

d. Here it is observable, that it is absolutely necessary to make a man virtuous, if we desire he should be pitied: we lament not, but detest, a wicked man; we are glad when we behold his crimes are punished, and that poetical justice is done upon him. . . . Shall we therefore banish all characters of villainy? I confess I am not of that opinion; but it is necessary that the hero of the play be not a villain; that is, the characters, which should move our pity, ought to have virtuous inclinations, and degrees of moral goodness in them. As for a perfect character of virtue, it never was in Nature, and therefore there can be no imitation of it; but there are alloys of frailty to be allowed for the chief persons, yet so that the/good which is in them shall outweigh the bad, and consequently leave room for punishment on the one side, and pity on the other.

Pref. *Troilus,* '79. K I 210–11

e. [¶] The chief character or hero in a tragedy, as I have already shown, ought in prudence to be such a man who has so much more of virtue in him than of vice, that he may be left amiable to the audience, which otherwise cannot have any concernment for his sufferings; and it is on this one character, that the pity and terror must be principally, if not wholly, founded: a rule which is extremely necessary, and which none of the critics, that I know, have fully enough discovered to us. For terror and compassion work but weakly when they are divided into many persons.[1]

Pref. *Troilus,* '79. K I 216

Character[s], c.   Epic Hero, h.

f. [As in picture] Thus, in/a tragedy, or an epic poem, the hero of the piece must be advanced foremost to the view of the reader, or spectator: he must outshine the rest of all the characters . . . because the hero is the centre of the main action . . . the chief object of pity in the drama, and of admiration in the epic poem.

Parallel, '95. K II 142–43

Imitation, d.

Heroic Play

a. [¶] The favour which heroic plays have lately found upon our theatres has been wholly derived to them from the countenance and approbation they have received at court. The most eminent persons for wit and honour in the royal circle having so far owned them, that they have judged no way so fit as verse to entertain a noble audience, or to express a noble passion; and among the rest/which have been written in this kind, they have been so indulgent to this poem, as to allow it no inconsiderable place.

Ded. *Indian Emperor,* '67. S-S II 285–86

b. [¶] For Heroic Plays . . . the first light we had of them, on the English theatre, was from the late Sir William D'Avenant. It being forbidden him in the rebellious times to act tragedies and comedies, because they contained some matter of scandal to those good people, who could more easily dispossess their lawful sovereign than endure a wanton jest, he was forced to . . . introduce the examples of moral virtue, writ in verse, and performed in recitative music. The original of his music, and of the scenes which adorned his work, he had from the Italian operas; but he heightened his characters (as I may probably imagine) from the example of Corneille and some French poets.

Essay of Heroic Plays, '72. K I 149

DAVENANT, C.

c. I observed . . . what was wanting to the perfection of [the] *Siege of Rhodes;* which was design, and variety of characters. And in the midst of this consideration, by mere accident, I opened the next book that lay by me, which was an Ariosto in Italian; and the very first two lines of that poem gave me light to all I could desire:

Le donne, i cavalier, l'arme, gli amori,
Le cortesie, l'audaci imprese io canto, etc.

For the very next reflexion which I made was this, that an heroic play ought to be an imitation, in little, of an heroic poem; and, consequently, that Love and Valour ought to be the subject of it.

Essay of Heroic Plays, '72. K I 150

d. The laws of an heroic poem did not dispense with those of the other [the drama, i.e., tragedy], but raised them to a greater height, and indulged him [Davenant] a further liberty of fancy, and of drawing all things as far above the ordinary proportion of the stage, as that is beyond the common words and actions of human life; and, therefore, in the scanting of his images and design, he complied not enough with the greatness and majesty of an heroic poem.

Essay of Heroic Plays, '72. K I 151

e. . . . I have modelled my heroic plays by the rules of an heroic poem. And if that be the most noble, the most pleasant, and the most instructive way of writing in verse, and withal the highest pattern of human life, as all poets have agreed, I shall need no other argument to justify my choice in this imitation. One advantage the drama has above the other, namely, that it represents to view what the poem only does relate; and, *Segnius irritant animum demissa per aures* . . . as Horace tells us.

Essay of Heroic Plays, '72. K I 154

TUMULT, b. AUDIENCE, POPULAR, e.

Highlighting

Cf. ENGLISH VS. FRENCH, t. DECORUM, i.

Thus, in/a tragedy, or an epic poem, the hero . . . must be advanced foremost to the view . . . [See HERO (DRAMATIC), f]

Parallel, '95. K II 142–43

CHARACTER[s], e. CHIAROSCURO.

Historian [See also BIOGRAPHY, and individual authors]

IMAGING, a. LUCAN, a. POET, q. Cf. DRYDEN, WORKS, hh.

a. [Historians] teach us wisdom by the surest ways (setting before us what we ought to shun or to pursue, by the examples of the most famous men whom they record, and by the experience of their faults and virtues) . . .

"Life of Plutarch," '83. S-S XVII 19

b. [¶] We find but few historians of all ages, who have been diligent enough in their search for truth: it is their common method to take on trust what they distribute to the public; by which means a falsehood once received from a famed writer becomes traditional to posterity. But Polybius weighed the authors from whom he was forced to borrow/. . . and oftentimes corrected them . . .

"Character of Polybius," '93. S-S XVIII 38–39

POLYBIUS AND TACITUS.

Historical Poem

I have called my poem [*Annus Mirabilis*] *historical,* not *epic,* though both the actions and actors are as much heroic as any poem can contain. But since the action is not properly one, nor that accomplished in the last successes, I have judged it too bold a title for a few stanzas . . .

Pref. *Annus Mirabilis,* '66. K I 11

WIT, e. IMAGES, c. EPIC, k.

Historical Truth (in Literature)

FABLE, b. FLETCHER, a.

a. In it [*The Indian Emperor*] I have neither wholly followed the truth of the history, nor altogether left it; but have taken all the liberty of a poet, to add, alter, or diminish, as I thought might best conduce to the beautifying of my work; it being not the business of a poet to represent historical truth, but probability.

Ded. *Indian Emperor,* '67. S-S II 288

b. [¶] It is easy to discover, that I have

been very bold in the alteration of the story [*Tyrannic Love*], which of itself was too barren for a play . . .

Pref. *Tyrannic Love,* '70. S-S III 379

LUCAN, b. IMAGINATION (RESPONSIVE), d. PROBABILITY, a, b.

c. Am I tied in poetry to the strict rules of history? I have followed it in this play [*Duke of Guise*] more closely than suited with the laws of the drama, and a great victory they will have who shall discover to the world this wonderful secret, that I have not observed the unities of place and time; but are they better kept in the farce of "The Libertine Destroyed"? It was our common business here to draw the parallel of the times, and not to make an exact tragedy. For this once we/were resolved to err with honest Shakespeare; neither can "Cataline" or "Sejanus," (written by the great master of our art,) stand excused, any more than we, from this exception . . .

Vindication, '83. S-S VII 162–63

FABLE, e. IMITATION, d. POET, f. VIRGIL, gg.

d. 'Tis not lawful, indeed, to contradict a point of history which is known to all the world . . ./.[1] but, in the dark recesses of antiquity, a great poet may and ought to feign such things as he finds not there, if they can be brought to embellish that subject which he treats.

Ded. *Æneis,* '97. K II 194–95

History [See also BIOGRAPHY]

POET, o.

a. . . . I think to commend it [history] is unnecessary, for the profit and pleasure of that study are both so very obvious . . . For my own part, who must confess it to my shame, that I never read anything but for pleasure, it has always been the most delightful entertainment of my life; but they who have employed the study of it as they ought, for their instruction, for the regulation of their private manners, and the management of public affairs, must agree with me, that it is the most pleasant school of wisdom. . . . It informs the understanding by the memory . . . For mankind being the same in all ages . . . nothing can come to pass, but some precedent of the like nature has already been produced; so that having the causes before our eyes, we cannot easily be deceived in the effects, if we have judgment enough but to draw the parallel.

"Life of Plutarch," '83. S-S XVII 56

b. [¶] The laws of history, in general, are truth of matter, method, and clearness of expression. The first propriety is necessary, to keep our understanding from the impositions of falsehood; for history is an argument framed from many particular examples or inductions . . . The second is grounded on the former; for if the method be confused, if the words or expressions of thought are any way obscure, then the ideas which we receive must be imperfect . . . Truth, therefore, is required as the foundation of history, to inform us; disposition and perspicuity, as the manner to inform us plainly; one is the being, the other the well-being of it.

"Life of Plutarch," '83. S-S XVII 57

c. [¶] History is principally divided into these three species: Commentaries, or Annals; History, properly so called; and Biographia, or the Lives of particular men.

"Life of Plutarch," '83. S-S XVII 57

d. [¶] Commentaries, or Annals, are (as [we] may so call them) naked history, or the plain relation of matter of fact, according to the succession of time, di-

vested of all other ornaments. The springs and motives of actions are not here sought . . ./The method is the most natural . . . depending only on the observation of months and years . . . The style is easy, simple, unforced, and unadorned with the pomp of figures . . . in a few words, a bare narration is its business. Of this kind the "Commentaries of Cæsar" are certainly the most admirable, and after him the "Annals of Tacitus" may have place; nay, even the prince of Greek historians, Thucydides, may almost be adopted into the number. For, though he instructs everywhere by sentences, though he gives the causes of actions, the councils of both parties, and makes orations where they are necessary, yet it is certain that he first designed his work a Commentary . . .

"Life of Plutarch," '83. S-S XVII 57–58

e. [¶] History, properly so called, may be described by the addition of those parts which are not required to Annals; and therefore there is little farther to be said concerning it; only, that the dignity and gravity of style is here necessary. That the guesses of secret causes inducing to the actions, be drawn at least from the most probable circumstances, not perverted by the malignity of the author to sinister interpretations (of which Tacitus is accused), but candidly laid down, and left to the judgment of the reader: That nothing/ of concernment be omitted; but things of trivial moment are still to be neglected, as debasing the majesty of the work: That neither partiality or prejudice appear, but that truth may everywhere be sacred: *Ne quid falsi dicere* . . . That he neither incline to superstition . . . nor to irreligion . . . but where general opinion has prevailed of any miraculous accident or portent, he ought to relate it as such, without imposing his opinion on our belief. Next to Thucydides, in this kind, may be accounted Polybius . . . Livy . . . Tacitus . . . [and] amongst the modern Italians, Guicciardini, and Davila . . . but above all men, in my opinion, the plain, sincere, unaffected, and most instructive Philip de Comines . . . I am sorry I cannot find in our own nation . . . any proper to be ranked with these. Buchanan, indeed, for the purity of his Latin, and for his learning . . . might be placed amongst the greatest, if he had not too much leaned to prejudice . . .

"Life of Plutarch," '83. S-S XVII 58–59

f. All history is only the precepts of moral philosophy reduced into examples. [See MORAL PHILOSOPHY]

"Life of Plutarch," '83. S-S XVII 61

POLYBIUS, b. POETRY, f-3. Cf. POET, f.

Hobbes, Thomas

Cf. SUPERNATURAL, e.

a. But I heard it first observed by an ingenious and learned old gentleman, lately deceased, that many of Mr. Hobbes his seeming new opinions, are gathered from those which Sextus Empiricus exposed.

"Life of Plutarch," '83. S-S XVII 42

b. From his [Lucretius's] time to ours, I know none so like him, as our poet and philosopher of Malmesbury. This is that perpetual dictatorship, which is exercised by Lucretius; who, though often in the wrong, yet seems to deal *bonâ fide* with his reader, and tells him nothing but what he thinks; in which plain sincerity, I believe, he differs from our Hobbes, who could not but be convinced, or at least doubt, of some eternal truths, which he had opposed.

Pref. *Sylvæ*, '85. K I 259

DIALOGUE (GENRE), d.

c. Mr. Hobbes, in the preface to his own bald translation of the *Ilias*, (studying poetry as he did mathematics, when it was too late,) Mr. Hobbes, I say, begins the praise of Homer where he should have ended it.

Pref. *Fables*, 1700. K II 252

Hoi Polloi [See also AUDIENCE, POPULAR; VOX POPULI]

(Neander) If by the people you understand the multitude, the οἱ πολλοί, 'tis no matter what they think; they are sometimes in the right, sometimes in the wrong: their judgment is a mere lottery.

Dram. Poesy, '65. K I 100

SATIRE, ll.

Holyday, Barten

a. . . . that learned critic, Barten Holyday, whose interpretation and illustrations of Juvenal are as excellent, as the verse of his translation and his English are lame and pitiful.

Discourse of Satire, '93. K II 92

TRANSLATION, bb. SATIRE, b. HORACE, e. HORACE AND JUVENAL AND PERSIUS, i. PROGRESS, e. TRANSLATION, k, e.

b. Neither Holyday nor Stapylton have imitated Juvenal in the poetical part of him, his diction and his elocution. Nor had they been poets, as neither of them were, yet, in the way they took, it was impossible for them to have succeeded in the poetic part.

Discourse of Satire, '93. K II 112

c. [¶] The English verse, which we call heroic, consists of no more than ten syllables; the Latin hexameter sometimes rises to seventeen . . .¹ Here is the difference of no less than seven syllables in a line, betwixt the English and the Latin. Now the medium of these is about fourteen syllables; because/the dactyl is a more frequent foot in hexameters than the spondee. But Holy-

day, without considering that he wrote
with the disadvantage of four syllables less
in every verse, endeavours to make one of
his lines to comprehend the sense of one of
Juvenal's. According to the falsity of the
proposition was the success. He was forced
to crowd his verse with ill-sounding monosyllables, of which our barbarous language
affords him a wild plenty; and by that
means he arrived at his pedantic end,
which was to make a literal translation.
His verses have nothing of verse in them,
but only the worst part of it, the rhyme;
and that . . . is far from good. But, which
is more intolerable, by cramming his ill-
chosen, and worse-sounding monosyllables
so close together, the very sense which he
endeavours to explain is become more obscure than that of his author . . .

Discourse of Satire, '93. K II 112–13

d. The Learned *Holiday,* (who has
made us amends for his bad Poetry in this
[Persius's Fourth Satire] and the rest of
these Satyrs, with his excellent Illustrations,) here tells us . . .

Notes to the Fourth Satire [Persius], '93.
JK II 770

Homer [See also HOMER AND VIRGIL]

Diction

DICTION, b.

Digressiveness

See below, c.

Dryden's Affinity

a. My thoughts at present are fixd on
Homer: And by my translation of the first
Iliad; I find him a poet more according to
my Genius than Virgil: and consequently
hope I may do him more justice, in his
fiery way of writeing; which, as it is liable
to more faults, so it is capable of more beauties, than the exactness, & sobriety of Virgil. ['T]is for my Country's honour as

well as for my own, that I am willing to undertake this task . . .

Letter to Charles Montague, '99. Ward
No. 65, p. 121

HOMER AND VIRGIL, c, d.

Father of Poetry

SHAKESPEARE AND JONSON. EPIC VS.
TRAGEDY, f.

Homeric Gods

IMITATION, j.

Homeric Hero

ANCIENTS, q. EPIC HERO, b, d.

b. Homer was ambitious enough of moving pity, for he has attempted twice on the
same subject of Hector's death . . . But if
[the] last excite compassion in you . . .
you are more obliged to the translator than
to the poet; for Homer . . . can move rage
better than he can pity. He stirs up the
irascible appetite, as our philosophers call
it; he provokes to murder, and the destruction of God's images; he forms and equips
those ungodly man-killers, whom we poets,
when we flatter them, call heroes; a race of
men who can never enjoy quiet in themselves, till they have taken it from all the
world. This is Homer's commendation
. . ./But let Homer and Virgil contend for
the prize of honour betwixt themselves; I
am satisfied they will never have a third
concurrent.

Ded. *Examen Poeticum,* '93. K II 13–14

EPIC HERO, g, i, j, k. POET, f.

Invention

VIRGIL, dd.

Judgment

MANUM DE TABULA, a.

Margites

SATIRE, dd.

Model

OGILBY. VIRGIL, kk. AUTHORITY, f. Cf.
STATIUS, c. Cf. DRAMA, EPIC ORIGINS.

Native Genius
SHAKESPEARE, h.
Passions

c. Yet I must needs say this in reference to Homer, that he is much more capable of exciting the manly passions than those of grief and pity. To cause admiration is, indeed, the proper and adequate design of an Epic Poem; and in that he has excelled even Virgil. Yet, without presuming to arraign our master, I may venture to affirm, that he is somewhat too talkative, and more than somewhat too digressive.[1]

Ded. *Examen Poeticum,* '93. K II 12
See above, b.
Pre-Eminence
MODERNS, f.

d. [Of epic poetry] . . . no man hitherto has reached, or so much as approached, to the excellencies of Homer, or of Virgil . . .

Discourse of Satire, '93. K II 26
EPIC POET, c.
Primitive Age
PROGRESS, e.   DRYDEN, LITERARY LIFE, b.
Scaliger compared
CRITIC, d.
Style
BELLORI. See above, a.
Superiority to Virgil
See above, c.
Supernatural
SUPERNATURAL, b.   POETIC LICENSE, f.
Talkativeness
See above, c.
Unities
EPIC VS. TRAGEDY, d.   UNITIES (DRAMATIC), GENERAL, e.
Versification

e. Perhaps a time may come when I may treat of this ['propriety of sound'] more largely, out of some observations which I have made from Homer and Virgil, who,

amongst all the poets, only understood the art of numbers, and of that which was properly called *rhythmus* by the ancients.

Pref. *Albion and Albanius,* '85. K I 277
DRYDEN, WORKS, sss.
Miscellaneous
DRYDEN, LITERARY LIFE, k.   DRYDEN, WORKS, ll.

Homer and Virgil
PROGRESS, e.   HOMER, c, b.   VIRGIL, n.
STATIUS, c.

a. They [critics of Virgil] begin with the moral of his poem, which I have elsewhere confessed, and still must own, not to be so noble as that of Homer. But . . ./I can show that Virgil's was as useful to the Romans . . . as Homer's was to the Grecians . . . Homer's moral was to urge the necessity of union, and of good understanding betwixt confederate states and princes . . . as also of discipline in an army, and obedience . . . to the supreme commander . . . To inculcate this, he sets forth the ruinous effects of discord . . ./[1] Had Virgil flourished in the age of Ennius, and addressed to Scipio, he had probably taken the same moral . . .[1] But we are to consider him as writing his poem in a time when the old form of government was subverted, and a new one just established by Octavius Cæsar, in effect by force of arms, but seemingly by the consent of the Roman people. . . .[1]

. . . . [Two pages]
I say, that Virgil having maturely weighed the condition of the times in which he lived; that an entire liberty was not to be retrieved; that the present settlement had the prospect of a long continuance . . . that he held his paternal estate from the bounty of the conqueror . . . that this conqueror, though of a bad kind, was the very best of it; that the arts of peace flour-

ished under him; that all men might be happy, if they would be quiet . . .[1] the poet . . . concluded it to be the interest of his/country to be so governed; to infuse an awful respect into the people towards such a prince; by that respect to confirm their obedience to him, and by that obedience to make them happy. This was the moral of his divine poem; honest in the poet; honourable to the Emperor . . . and reflecting . . . honour on the Roman people, whom he derives . . . from the Trojans; and not only profitable, but necessary, to the present age, and likely to be such to their posterity.

Ded. *Æneis,* '97. K II 166–72

EPIC HERO, m. INVENTION, e.

b. If it be urged, that I have granted a resemblance in some parts [between Homer and Virgil], yet therein Virgil has excelled him. For what are the tears of Calypso for being left, to the fury and death of Dido? Where is there the whole process of her passion and all its violent effects to be found, in the languishing episode of the *Odysseis?* If this be to copy, let the critics shew us the same disposition, features, or colouring, in their original. The like may/be said of the Descent to Hell . . .

Ded. *Æneis,* '97. K II 200–201

INVENTION, f. EPIC MACHINES, a. VIRGIL, j, k. HOMER, a.

c. And this I dare assure the world beforehand, that I have found, by trial, Homer a more pleasing task than Virgil, though I say not the translation will be less laborious; for the Grecian is more according to my genius than the Latin poet. [See next entry]

Pref. *Fables,* 1700. K II 251

d. Virgil was of a quiet, sedate temper; Homer was violent, impetuous, and full of fire. The chief talent of Virgil was propriety of thoughts, and ornament of words: Homer was rapid in his thoughts, and took all the liberties, both of numbers and of expressions, which his language, and the age in which he lived, allowed him. Homer's invention was more copious, Virgil's more confined; so that if Homer had not led the way, it was not in Virgil to have begun heroic/poetry; for nothing can be more evident, than that the Roman poem is but the second part of the *Ilias* . . .[1] I say not this in derogation to Virgil, neither do I contradict anything which I have formerly said in his just praise . . .[1] But this proves . . . that Homer taught Virgil to design; and if invention be the first virtue of an epic poet, then the Latin poem can only be allowed the second place. . . . [See HOBBES, c]/Neither Virgil nor Homer were deficient in any of the former beauties [design, disposition, manners, thoughts]; but in this last, which is expression, the Roman poet is at least equal to the Grecian . . . supplying the poverty of his language by his musical ear, and by his diligence.

But to return: our two great poets being so different in their tempers, one choleric and sanguine, the other phlegmatic and melancholic; that which makes them excel in their several ways is, that each of them has followed his own natural inclination, as well in forming the design, as in the execution of it. The very heroes shew their authors . . .[1] From all I have said, I will only draw this inference, that the action of Homer, being more full of vigour than that of Virgil . . . is of consequence more pleasing to the reader. One warms you by degrees; the other sets you on fire all at once, and never intermits his heat. 'Tis the same difference which Longinus makes betwixt the effects of eloquence/in Demosthenes and Tully; one persuades, the other commands. You never cool while you read Homer . . .[1] This vehemence of his, I confess, is more suitable to my temper; and therefore I have translated his First Book with greater pleasure than any part of Virgil . . .

Pref. *Fables,* 1700. K II 251–54

Hopkins, Charles

Vox Populi

There is this day to be acted a New tragedy, made by Mr. Hopkins [*Friendship Improv'd*]; & as I believe in rhime. He has formerly written a play in verse calld Boadicea, which you fair Ladyes likd: & is a poet who writes good verses without knowing how, or why; I mean he writes naturally well, without art or learning, or good sence.

Letter to Mrs. Steward, 7 November 1699. Ward No. 67, p. 124

Horace [See also HORACE AND JUVENAL AND PERSIUS]*

on *Ancients as Models*

ANCIENTS, m.

Art of Poetry

ARISTOTLE, c.

Authority

AUTHORITY, a, b. NATURE, c. DRYDEN, LITERARY LIFE, j. AUTHORITY, e. DRYDEN, LITERARY LIFE, a. EPIC VS. TRAGEDY, d. RULES, g.

Candor

DORSET, b.

on *Coinage*

COINAGE, a, b. BORROWING, b. GRAFFING, a. COINAGE, c.

Criticism

a. . . . his Criticisms . . . are the most

_____

* See Amanda M. Ellis, "Horace's Influence on Dryden," *PQ,* IV (1925), 39–60.

instructive of any that are written in this art . . .

Pref. *Sylvæ,* '85. K I 266

Eminence as Poet and Critic

LAST AGE, k. SATIRE, z.

Epistles

See below, l. FANCY, i. DRYDEN, WORKS, ttt.

Father, Character of his

b. [¶] 'Tis granted [Casaubon] that the father of Horace was *libertinus* . . . But Horace, speaking of him, gives him the best character of a father which I ever read in history; and I wish a witty friend of mine [Wycherley: Ker], now/living, had such another.

Discourse of Satire, '93. K II 77–78

Judgment

CHAUCER, c.

on *Manners*

MANNERS, g.

Odes

c. [Pindar is Horace's master in the odes] But Horace is of the more bounded fancy . . .

Pref. *Sylvæ,* '85. K I 266

DRYDEN, WORKS, tt. HYDE. HORACE AND JUVENAL AND PERSIUS, b. See below, k. EXPRESSION, b. FANCY, i.

Personal Satire

SATIRE, kk. See below, h.

Poetic Character

d. But the most distinguishing part of all his [Horace's] character seems to me to be his briskness, his jollity, and his good humour; and those I have chiefly endeavoured to copy [in his translations] . . .

Pref. *Sylvæ,* '85. K I 267

on *Poetic License*

POETIC LICENSE, e, f.

Pointedness, Lack of

DORSET, b.

Propriety
OVID, a. VIRGIL, mm.
Punning
PARONOMASIA.
Raillery
SATIRE, b.

e. [¶] And thus, my Lord, you see I have preferred the manner of Horace, and of your Lordship, in this kind of satire [the raillery of Horace's 'low satire', K II 92], to that of Juvenal . . . Holyday ought not to have arraigned so great an author, for that which was his excellency and his merit . . . And let the *Manes* of Juvenal forgive me if I say, that this way of Horace was the best for amending manners, as it is the most difficult. His was an *ense rescindendum;* but that of Horace was a pleasant cure, with all the limbs preserved entire . . . yet I contradict not the proposition which I formerly advanced. Juvenal's times required a more painful kind of operation; but if he had lived in the age of Horace, I must needs affirm, that he had it not about him. He took the method which was prescribed him by his own genius, which was sharp and eager; he could not rally, but he could declaim; and as his provocations were great, he has revenged them tragically.
Discourse of Satire, '93. K II 94
LUCIAN, d.
Satire—Design

f. *Lucilius* wrote long before *Horace;* who imitates his manner of Satyr, but far excels him, in the design.
Notes to the First Satire [Persius], '93. JK II 751
Satire, Unity of Theme
SATIRE, c.
Satires

g. . . . his Satires . . . are incompa-

rably beyond Juvenal's, (if to laugh and rally is to be preferred to railing and declaiming) . . .
Pref. *Sylvæ,* '85. K I 266

h. But the contention betwixt these two great masters is for the prize of Satire; in which controversy all the Odes and Epodes of Horace are to stand excluded. I say this, because Horace has written many of them satirically, against his private enemies; yet these, if justly considered, are somewhat of the nature of the Greek *Silli,* which were invectives against particular sects and persons. But Horace had purged himself of this choler before he entered on those discourses which are more properly called the Roman Satire. He has . . . now . . . to correct the vices and the follies of his time, and to give the rules of a happy and virtuous life.
Discourse of Satire, '93. K II 79
FANCY, i.
Style

i. [¶] And therefore, though he [Horace] innovated little, he may justly be called a great refiner of the Roman tongue. This choice of words, and heightening of their natural signification, was observed in him by the writers of the following ages; for Petronius says of him, *et Horatii curiosa felicitas.*
Defence of the Epilogue, '72. K I 171
AUTHORITY, d.

j. That which will distinguish his style from all other poets, is the elegance of his words, and the numerousness of his verse; there is nothing so delicately turned in all the Roman language. There appears in every part of his diction, or (to speak English) in all his expressions, a kind of noble and bold purity. His words are chosen/ with as much exactness as Virgil's; but there seems to be a greater spirit in them. There is a secret happiness attends his choice, which in Petronius is called *curiosa felicitas,* and which I suppose he had from the *feliciter audere* of Horace himself.

Pref. *Sylvæ,* '85. K I 266–67

k. You [Lawrence Hyde, Earl of Rochester] may please to remember that, in the late happy conversation which I had with your lordship . . . you took me aside, and pleased yourself with repeating to me one of the most beautiful pieces in that author [Horace]. It was the Ode to Barine, wherein you were so particularly affected with that elegant expression, *Juvenumque prodis publica cura.* There is indeed the virtue of a whole poem in those words; that *curiosa felicitas,* which Petronius so justly ascribes to our author. The barbarity of our language is not able to reach it; yet, when I have leisure, I mean to try how near I can raise my English to his Latin; though in the meantime, I cannot but imagine to myself, with what scorn his sacred *manes* would look on so lame a translation as I could make. His *recalcitrat undique tutus* might more easily be applied to me than he himself applied it to Augustus/Cæsar.

Ded. *Cleomenes,* '92. S-S VIII 215–16

Horace and Juvenal and Persius, a.

l. The low style of Horace is according to his subject, that is, generally grovelling. I question not but he could have raised it; for the First Epistle of the Second Book, which he writes to Augustus, (a most instructive satire concerning poetry,) is of so much dignity in the words, and of so much elegancy in the numbers, that the author plainly shows the *sermo pedestris,* in his other Satires, was rather his choice than his necessity. He was a rival to Lucilius, his predecessor, and was resolved to surpass him in his own manner. Lucilius . . .

minded neither his style, nor his numbers, nor his purity of words, nor his run of verse. Horace therefore copes with him in that humble way of satire . . . This, I imagine, was the chief reason why he minded only the clearness of his satire, and the cleanness of expression, without ascending to those heights to which his own vigour might have carried him.

Discourse of Satire, '93. K II 85

Donne, d. Expression, b. Curiosa Felicitas. Virgil, ll.

on *Unities*

Unities (Dramatic), General, a.

Verse

See above, j. Satire, dd. See above, l.

Virgil, Compared with

Virgil, ii.

Miscellaneous

m. Horace was certainly/in the right, when he said *that no man is satisfied with his own condition.*

Pref. *All for Love,* '78. K I 196–97

Horace and Juvenal and Persius

Horace, g. Critic[s], f. Persius, a, b, d, c, i.

a. If the advantage [of station, as affecting literary art] be anywhere, 'tis on the side of Horace; as much as the court of Augustus Cæsar was superior to that of Nero. As for the subjects which they treated, it will appear hereafter that Horace writ not vulgarly on vulgar subjects, nor always chose them. His style is constantly accommodated to his subject, either high or low. If his fault be too much lowness, that of Persius is the fault of the hardness of his metaphors, and obscurity: and so they are equal in the failings of their style; where Juvenal manifestly triumphs over both of them.

Discourse of Satire, '93. K II 78

b. [¶] The comparison betwixt Horace and Juvenal is more difficult; because their forces were more equal. A dispute has always been, and ever will continue, betwixt the favourers of the two poets. *Non nostrum est tantas componere lites.* I shall only venture to give my own/opinion, and leave it for better judges to determine. If it be only argued in general, which of them was the better poet, the victory is already gained on the side of Horace. Virgil himself must yield to him in the delicacy of his turns, his choice of words, and perhaps the purity of his Latin. He who says that Pindar is inimitable, is himself inimitable in his Odes.

Discourse of Satire, '93. K II 78–79

c. [¶] I would willingly divide the palm betwixt them, upon the two heads of profit and delight, which are the two ends of poetry in general. It must be granted . . . that Horace is the more copious and profitable in his instructions of human life; but, in my particular opinion . . ./Juvenal is the more delightful author. I am profited by both, I am pleased with both; but I owe more to Horace for my instruction, and more to Juvenal for my pleasure . . .

That Horace is somewhat the better instructor of the two, is proved from hence, that his instructions are more general, Juvenal's more limited. . . . *Bonum quo communius, eo melius.* Juvenal, excepting only his First Satire, is in all the rest confined to the exposing of some particular vice; that he lashes, and there he sticks. His sentences are truly shining and instructive; but they are sprinkled here and there. /Horace is teaching us in every line, and is perpetually moral: he had found out the skill of Virgil, to hide his sentences; to give you the virtue of them, without showing them in their full extent; which is the ostentation of a poet, and not his art . . .

Folly was the proper quarry of Horace, and not vice; and as there are but few notoriously wicked men, in comparison with a shoal of fools and fops, so 'tis a harder thing to make a man wise than to make him honest . . . There are blind sides and follies, even in the professors of moral philosophy; and there is not any one sect of them that Horace has not exposed: which, as it was not the design of Juvenal, who was wholly employed in lashing vices, some of them the most enormous that can be imagined, so, perhaps, it was not so much his talent. . . .[1] But . . . the divine wit of Horace left nothing untouched; . . . he entered into the inmost recesses of nature; found out the imperfections even of the most wise and grave, as well as of the common people . ./.[1] The exhortations of Persius are confined to noblemen; and the Stoic philosophy is that alone which he recommends to them; Juvenal exhorts to particular virtues, as they are opposed to those vices against which he declaims; but Horace laughs to shame all follies, and insinuates virtue rather by familiar examples than by the severity of precepts.

Discourse of Satire, '93. K II 81–84

d. [¶] This last consideration [Horace's raillery as compared to Juvenal's exhortation] seems to incline the balance on the side of Horace, and to give him the preference to Juvenal, not only in profit, but in pleasure. But, after all, I must confess, that the delight which Horace gives me is but languishing. Be pleased . . . to understand, that I speak of my own taste only: he may ravish other men; but I am too stupid and insensible to be tickled. Where he barely grins himself, and, as Scaliger says, only shows his white teeth, he cannot provoke me to any laughter. His urbanity, that is, his good manners, are to be commended, but his wit is faint; and his salt, if I may dare to say so, almost insipid.

Discourse of Satire, '93. K II 84

JUVENAL, a.

e. Horace is always on the amble, Juvenal on the gallop; but his way is perpetually on carpet-ground. He goes with more impetuosity than Horace, but as securely; and the swiftness adds a more lively agitation to the spirits.

Discourse of Satire, '93. K II 85

f. And, besides this [Juvenal's superiority in versification], the sauce of Juvenal is more poignant, to create in us an appetite of reading him. The meat of Horace is more nourishing; but the cookery of Juvenal more exquisite: so that, granting Horace to be the more general philosopher, we cannot deny that Juvenal was the greater poet, I mean in satire. His thoughts are sharper; his indignation against vice is more vehement; his spirit has more of the commonwealth genius; he treats tyranny, and all/the vices attending it, as they deserve, with the utmost rigour: and consequently, a noble soul is better pleased with a zealous vindicator of Roman liberty, than with a temporising poet, a well-mannered court-slave, and a man who is often afraid of laughing in the right place; who is ever decent, because he is naturally servile . . . [I]f we make Horace our minister of state in Satire, and Juvenal of our private pleasures, I think the latter has no ill bargain of it.

Discourse of Satire, '93. K II 86–87

g. Persius was grave, and particularly opposed his gravity to lewdness, which was the predominant vice in Nero's court . . . Horace was a mild admoniser, a court-satirist, fit for the gentle times of Augus-

tus . . . Juvenal was as proper for his times, as they for theirs; his was an age that deserved a more severe chastisement . . . Heinsius urges in praise of Horace, that, according to the ancient art and law of satire, it should be nearer to comedy than tragedy; not declaiming against vice, but only laughing at it. Neither Persius nor Juvenal were ignorant of this, for they had both studied Horace. And the thing itself is plainly true. But as they had read Horace, they had likewise read Lucilius . . ./[and] they thought the imitation of Lucilius was more proper to their purpose than that of Horace.

Discourse of Satire, '93. K II 91–92

HORACE, e.

h. [¶] This manner of Horace is indeed the best [i.e., raillery]; but Horace has not executed it altogether so happily, at least not often. The manner of Juvenal [declaiming] is confessed to be inferior . . . but Juvenal has excelled him/in his performance. Juvenal has railed more wittily than Horace has rallied. Horace means to make his readers laugh, but he is not sure of his experiment. Juvenal always intends to move your indignation, and he always brings about his purpose. Horace, for aught I know, might have tickled the people of his age; but amongst the moderns he is not so successful.[1]

Discourse of Satire, '93. K II 94–95

i. [¶] Barten Holyday, who translated both Juvenal and Persius, has made this distinction betwixt them, which is no less true than witty; that in Persius the difficulty is to find a meaning, in Juvenal to choose a meaning: so crabbed is Persius, and so copious is Juvenal; so much the understanding is employed in one, and so

much the judgment in the other; so difficult it is to find any sense in the former,
and the best sense of the latter.
Discourse of Satire, '93. K II 96

j. [¶] If . . . any one suppose I have
commended Horace below his merit, when
I have allowed him but the second place, I
desire him to consider, if Juvenal, a man of
excellent natural endowments, besides the
advantages of diligence and study, and
coming after him, and building upon his
foundations, might not probably, with all
these helps, surpass him; and whether it be
any dishonour to Horace to be thus surpassed, since no art or science is at once begun and perfected, but that it must pass
first through many hands, and even
through several ages. If Lucilius could add
to Ennius, and Horace to Lucilius, why,
without any diminution to the fame of
Horace, might not Juvenal give the last
perfection to that work? Or rather, what
disreputation is it to Horace, that Juvenal
excels in the tragical satire, as Horace does
in the comical?
Discourse of Satire, '93. K II 96

k. Let these three ancients be preferred
to all the moderns, as first arriving at the
goal; let them all be crowned, as victors,
with the wreath that properly belongs to
satire; but, after that, with this distinction
amongst themselves— . . .º let Juvenal
ride first in triumph . . .º/let Horace,
who is the second, and but just the second,
carry off the quivers and the arrows, as the
badges of his satire, and the golden belt,
and the diamond button . . .º and let Persius, the last of the first three worthies, be
contented with this Grecian shield, and
with victory, not only over all the Grecians,
who were ignorant of the Roman satire,

but over all the moderns in succeeding
ages, excepting Boileau and your Lordship.
Discourse of Satire, '93. K II 98–99
SATIRE, f.

Howard, Sir Robert [See also CRITES; see De-
fence of An Essay, passim]
COURT, a.   DRYDEN, LITERARY LIFE, p.
PLINY THE YOUNGER.   DRYDEN, WORKS, c.

a. . . . a noble and most ingenious per-
son . . .
Defence of An Essay, '68. K I 110
RHYME (DEBATE), u, y.

b. Of his [Jupiter's] power to defer
the blow, I once occasionally discoursed
with that excellent person Sir Robert Howard, who is better conversant, than any man
that I know, in the doctrine of the Sto-
ics . . .
Ded. Æneis, '97. K II 186

c. Sir Robert Howard, in his translation
of this *Æneid* [VI], which was printed
with his poems in the year 1660, has given
us the most learned and the most judicious
observations on this book which are extant
in our language.
Notes and Observations on Virgil's
Works, '97. N 712

Human Nature
HISTORY, a. [For mankind (is) the same
in all ages . . .]   PERSIUS, f.   Cf. VIRGIL,
aa.   FANCY, i, j.   NATURE, b.

Humors
BEAUMONT AND FLETCHER.   JONSON, a.

a. (Neander) Others say, it is not
enough to find one man of such an humour: it must be common to more, and the
more common the more natural. To prove
this, they instance in the best of comical
characters, Falstaff: there are many men
resembling him; old, fat, merry, cowardly,
drunken, amorous, vain, and lying. But to

convince these people, I need but tell them, that humour is the ridiculous extravagance of conversation, wherein one man differs from all others. If then it be common . . . how differs it . . . ? As for Falstaff, he is not properly one humour, but a miscellany of humours or images, drawn from so many several men: that wherein he is singular is his wit, or those things he says *præter expectatum* . . . his quick evasions . . .

Dram. Poesy, '65. K I 84

b. (Neander) The ancients had little of it [humor] in their comedies; for the τὸ γελοῖον of the/Old Comedy . . . was not so much to imitate a man, as to make the people laugh at some odd conceit, which had commonly somewhat of unnatural or obscene in it. . . . In their New Comedy . . . the poets sought indeed to express the ἦθος, as in their tragedies the πάθος of mankind. But this ἦθος contained only the general characters of men and manners . . . As for the French, though they have the word *humeur* among them, yet they have small use of it in their comedies or farces; they being but ill imitations of the *ridiculum,* or that which stirred up laughter in the Old Comedy. But among the English 'tis otherwise: where by humour is meant some extravagant habit, passion, or affection, particular . . . to some one person, by the oddness of which, he is immediately distinguished from the rest of men; which, being lively and naturally represented, most frequently begets that malicious pleasure in the audience which is testified by laughter; as all things which are deviations from common customs are ever the aptest to produce it:/though by the way this laughter is only accidental, as

the person represented is fantastic or bizarre; but pleasure is essential to it, as the imitation of what is natural.

Dram. Poesy, '65. K I 84–86
COMEDY, a.

c. As I pretend not that I can write humour, so none of them [his contemporaries] can reasonably pretend to have written it as they ought. Johnson was the only man, of all ages and nations, who has performed it well, and that but in three or four of his comedies: the rest are but a *crambe bis cocta;* the same humours a little varied and written worse.

Pref. *Evening's Love,* '71. K I 137
JUDGMENT, c.   COMEDY, e.   Cf. WIT, i.
WIT, j.   FANCY, d.   FLETCHER, d.   JONSON, d.

d. . . . humour represents folly so as to render it ridiculous.

Author's Apology, '77. K I 182
SHAKESPEARE, j.   DRYDEN, LITERARY LIFE, v. CHAUCER, e.

Hyde (Lawrence, Earl of Rochester)

PATRONAGE, c.   DRYDEN, WORKS, tt.

. . . to your experience in State affairs, you have also joined no vulgar erudition . . . for, to understand critically the delicacies of Horace is a height to which few of our noblemen have arrived; and that this is your deserved commendation, I am a living evidence, as far, at least, as I can be allowed a competent judge on that subject. Your affection to that admirable Ode, which Horace writes to his Mæcenas [29th Ode, 1st Book: Scott], and which I had the honor to inscribe to you, is not the only proof of this assertion.

Ded. *Cleomenes,* '92. S-S VIII 215
HORACE, k.

Idiom

JONSON, a. TECHNICAL TERMS, a. GRAMMAR, c. GALLICIZING. SHAKESPEARE, f. Cf. TRANSLATION, d. TRANSLATION, u. PLUTARCH, f. TRANSLATION, f. BORROWING, c.

Images [See also DESCRIPTIONS]

a. . . . the sleeping images of things . . . [See FANCY, a]

Ded. *Rival Ladies,* '64. K I 1

PLAY WRITING. NATURE, d. PLAY (DEFINITION), a. Cf. SHAKESPEARE, b. Cf. HUMORS, a. EPIC, a.

b. Such descriptions or images, well wrought . . . are, as I have said, the adequate delight of Heroic Poesy; for they beget admiration, which is its proper object . . .

Pref. *Annus Mirabilis,* '66. K I 18

c. But though the same images serve equally for the epic poesy, and for the historic and panegyric, which are branches of it, yet a several sort of sculpture is to be used in them: if some of them are to be like those of Juvenal, *stantes in curribus Aemiliani,* heroes drawn in their triumphal chariots, and in their full proportion; others are to be like that of Virgil, *spirantia mollius aera:* there is somewhat more of softness and tenderness to be shown in them.

Pref. *Annus Mirabilis,* '66. K I 18

HERO (DRAMATIC), a. RHYME (DEBATE), aa. HEROIC PLAY, d. COWLEY, d. IMITATION, j. PASSIONS, i. Cf. OVID, f.

DESIGNING. FARCE, f.

Imagination [See also FANCY; WIT]*

a. . . . I was then in that eagerness of imagination, which, by overpleasing fanciful men, flatters them into the danger of writing . . .

Ded. *Rival Ladies,* '64. K I 1

RHYME (DEBATE), d.

b. For imagination in a poet is a faculty so wild and lawless, that like an high-ranging spaniel, it must have clogs tied to it, lest it outrun the judgment.

Ded. *Rival Ladies,* '64. K I 8

WIT, a. TRAGEDY, n. JUDGMENT, b. WIT, d.

c. So then the first happiness of the poet's imagination is properly invention, or finding of the thought; the second is fancy, or the variation, deriving, or moulding, of that thought, as the judgment represents it proper to the subject; the third is elocution, or the art of clothing and adorning that thought, so found and varied, in apt, significant, and sounding words: the quickness of the imagination is seen in the invention, the fertility in the fancy, and the accuracy in the expression.

Pref. *Annus Mirabilis,* '66. K I 15

OVID AND VIRGIL, a. Cf. DAVENANT, b. WIT, j. SUPERNATURAL, c. POET, a. LUCAN, c. POETIC LICENSE, d. SHAKESPEARE, l. PROSODY, u.

---

* See John M. Aden, "Dryden and the Imagination: the First Phase," *PMLA,* LXXIV (1959), 28–40.

d. . . . the parts of the airy and earthy spirits, and that fairy kind of writing which depends only upon the force of imagination . . .

Ded. *King Arthur,* '91. S-S VIII 136

Cf. PROSODY, m. FANCY, i.

e. For this reason, a well-weighed judicious poem, which at its first appearance gains no more upon the world than to be just received, and rather not blamed than much applauded, insinuates itself by insensible degrees into the liking of the reader . . . And whereas poems which are produced by the vigour of imagination only have a gloss upon them at the first which time wears off, the works of judgment are like the diamond; the more they are polished, the more lustre they receive. Such is the difference betwixt Virgil's *Æneis* and Marini's *Adone.* And, if I may be allowed to change the metaphor, I would say, that Virgil is like the Fame which he describes—

Mobilitate viget, viresque acquirit eundo.

Such a sort of reputation is my aim, though in a far inferior degree, according to my motto in the title-page: *Sequiturque patrem non passibus æquis:* and therefore I appeal to the highest court of judicature . . ./

Without this ambition, which I own, of desiring to please the *judices natos,* I could never have been able to have done anything at this age, when the fire of poetry is commonly extinguished in other men.

Ded. *Æneis,* '97. K II 225–26

Imagination (Responsive) [See FANCY (RESPONSIVE)]

Cf. FABLE, b. Cf. DECORUM, b. ART AND LIFE, a.

a. (Lisideius) [In connection with narrations and decorum] When we see death represented, we are convinced it is but fiction; but when we hear it related, our eyes, the strongest witnesses, are wanting, which might have undeceived us; and we are all willing to favour the sleight, when the poet does not too grossly impose on us.

Dram. Poesy, '65. K I 63

NARRATIONS, b. TRAGICOMEDY, b. DECORUM, d. Cf. RHYME (DEBATE), g, o. UNITIES (DRAMATIC), PLACE, f.

b. Imagination in a man, or reasonable creature, is supposed to participate of Reason, and when that governs, as it does in the belief of fiction,/Reason is not destroyed, but misled, or blinded; that can prescribe to the Reason, during the time of the representation, somewhat like a weak belief of what it sees and hears; and Reason suffers itself to be so hoodwinked, that it may better enjoy the pleasures of the fiction: but it is never so wholly made a captive, as to be drawn headlong into a persuasion of those things which are most remote from probability: 'tis in that case a free-born subject, not a slave; it will contribute willingly its assent, as far as it sees convenient, but will not be forced. . . . Fancy and Reason go hand in hand; the first cannot leave the last behind: and though Fancy, when it sees the wide gulf, would venture over, as the nimbler, yet it is withheld by Reason, which will refuse to take the leap, when the distance over it appears too large.

Defence of An Essay, '68. K I 127–28

UNITIES (DRAMATIC), TIME, b. TUMULT, b.

c. The poet is then to endeavour an absolute dominion over the minds of the spectators; for, though our fancy will contribute to its own deceit, yet a writer ought to help its operation . . .

Essay of Heroic Plays, '72. K I 155

d. [¶] You are not obliged, as in History, to a literal belief of what the poet says; but you are pleased with the image, without being cozened by the fiction.

Author's Apology, '77. K I 185

Cf. FIGURES, a. Cf. PLUTARCH AND SENECA. DRYDEN, WORKS, lll. CHIAROSCURO. Cf. VIRGIL, ff.

Imaging

a. (Eugenius) But there are a thousand other concernments [besides 'extasy of love'] of lovers, as jealousies, complaints, contrivances, and the like, where not to open their minds at large to each other, were to be wanting to their own love, and to the expectation of the audience; who watch the movements of their minds, as much as the changes of their fortunes. For the imaging of the first is properly the work of a poet; the latter he borrows of the historian.

Dram. Poesy, '65. K I 54

WIT, e.

b. [¶] Imaging is, in itself, the very height and life of Poetry. It is, as Longinus describes it, a discourse, which, by a kind of enthusiasm, or extraordinary emotion of the soul, makes it seem to us that we behold those things which the poet paints, so as to be pleased with them, and to admire them.

Author's Apology, '77. K I 186

IMITATION, j. DRYDEN, WORKS, t.

Imitation

PLAY (DEFINITION), a.

a. (Lisideius) . . . *A just and lively image of human nature* . . .

Dram. Poesy, '65. K I 36

RHYME (DEBATE), g. PLAY (DEFINI-

TION), c. NATURE, c. CRITIC[s], h. SENECA, b. OVID, i, h. RULES, g.

b. But if the story which we treat be modern, we are to vary the customs, according to the time and the country where the scene of action lies; for this is still to imitate Nature, which is always the same, though in a different dress.

Parallel, '95. K II 139

Advantage of Modern

MODERNS, c.

Better and Worse Likeness

EPIC, a. Cf. BURLESQUE, a.

c. [Speaking of the character of his Maximin, in *Tyrannic Love*] If, with much pains, and some success, I have drawn a deformed piece of art, there is as much of art, and as near an imitation of nature, in a lazar, as in a Venus.

Pref. *Tyrannic Love,* '70. S-S III 377

PORTRAIT PAINTING.

d. In the character of an hero, as well as in an inferior figure, there is a better or worse likeness to be taken: the better is a panegyric, if it be not false, and the worse is a libel. Sophocles, says Aristotle, always drew men as they ought to be, that is, better than they were; another . . . drew them worse than naturally they were: Euripides altered nothing in the character, but made them such as they were represented by history, epic poetry, or tradition. Of the three, the draught of Sophocles is most commended by Aristotle. I have followed it in that part of *Œdipus* which I writ, though perhaps I have made him too good a man. But my characters of Antony and Cleopatra, though they are favourable to them, have nothing of outrageous panegyric. Their passions were their own, and such as were given them by history; only the deformities of them were cast into shadows, that they might be objects of compassion . . .

Parallel, '95. K II 146

Copy

Cf. PROSE, a. IMITATION OF MODELS, d. INVENTION, d, e.

Difficulty

THEATER. JONSON, u.

Ethical Effect [See ETHICAL FUNCTION]

EPIC, e. EPIC HERO, i, j.

Examples

PASSIONS, a, b. OVID, f. ARIOSTO, a. CHAUCER AND OVID, a.

Faulty

ANCIENTS, t. SHAKESPEARE, k. ETHICAL FUNCTION, a. NATURE, f.

Foundation of Dramatic Poetry

RHYME (DEBATE), i.

e. I never heard of any other foundation of Dramatic Poesy than the imitation of Nature; neither was there ever pretended any other by the Ancients or Moderns, or me, who endeavour to follow them in that rule.

Defence of An Essay, '68. K I 123

TRAGEDY, a. EPIC, d.

Heightened [See HEIGHTENING]

POETIC LICENSE, a.

f. 'Tis true, that to imitate well is a poet's work; but to affect the soul, and excite the passions, and, above all, to move admiration (which is the delight of serious plays), a bare imitation will not serve. The converse, therefore, which a poet is to imitate, must be heightened with all the arts and ornaments of poesy . . .

Defence of An Essay, '68. K I 113

PROSE, a. JONSON, l. ETHICAL FUNCTION, a. See below, h.

of Humors

HUMORS, b.

Idealized [See also HEIGHTENING]

g. . . . there may be too great a likeness;

as the most skillful painters affirm, that there may be too near a resemblance in a picture: to take every lineament and feature is not to make an excellent piece, but to take so much only as will make a beautiful resemblance of the whole: and, with an ingenious flattery of nature, to heighten the beauties of some parts, and hide the deformities of the rest. For so says Horace,

Ut pictura poesis . . .

Defence of An Essay, '68. K I 114

See below, h.

Limits

DECORUM, b.

Mathematical Properties in

Cf. POET, n. POETRY AND PAINTING, b. Cf. EPIC POET, a.

Natural (Unheightened)

WIT, g. Cf. JONSON, u.

as *Norm* [See NATURE as *Norm*]

UNITIES (DRAMATIC), TIME, a. RHYME (DEBATE), i.

of Perfection

HERO (DRAMATIC), d. CHARACTER[s], c. EPIC HERO, g.

Pleasing, Reasons for

h. Aristotle tells us, that imitation pleases, because it affords matter for a reasoner to inquire into the truth or falsehood of imitation, by comparing its likeness, or unlikeness, with the original; but by this rule every speculation in nature, whose truth falls under the inquiry of a philosopher, must produce the same delight; which is not true. I should rather assign another reason. Truth is the object of our understanding, as good is of our will; and the understanding can no more be delighted with a lie, than the will can choose an apparent evil. As truth is the end of all our speculations, so the discovery of it is the pleasure of them; and since a true knowledge of Nature gives us pleasure, a lively imitation of it . . . must of necessity produce a much greater: for both these arts [poetry and painting] . . . are not only true imitations of Nature, but of the best Nature, of that which is wrought up to a nobler pitch. . . . and we have the pleasure to see all the scattered beauties of Nature united by a happy chemistry, without its deformities or faults. They are imitations of the passions, which always move, and therefore consequently please; for without motion there can be no delight, which cannot be considered but as an active passion. When we view these elevated ideas of/nature, the result of that view is admiration, which is always the cause of pleasure.

This foregoing remark, which gives the reason why imitation pleases, was sent me by Mr. Walter Moyle, a most ingenious young gentleman . . .

Parallel, '95. K II 137–38
Proper Object
Cf. ACTION DEFINED.
Prose as Medium [See also PROSE]
RHYME (DEBATE), 1.
Rules for
RULES, b. Cf. AUTHORITY, b.

i. [¶] To imitate Nature well in whatsoever subject, is the perfection of both arts [poetry and painting]; and that picture, and that poem, which comes nearest to the resemblance of Nature, is the best. But it follows not, that what pleases most in either kind is good, but what ought to please. Our depraved appetites, and ignorance of the arts, mislead our judgments, and cause us often to take/that for true imitation of Nature which has no resemblance of Nature in it. To inform our judgments, and to reform our tastes, rules were invented, that by them we might discern when Nature was imitated, and how nearly. . . . The imitation of Nature is therefore justly constituted as the general, and indeed the only, rule of pleasing, both in Poetry and Painting.

Parallel, '95. K II 136–37
RULES, i.
of the *Supernatural*
SUPERNATURAL, c.

j. [¶] If poetry be imitation, that part of it must needs be best which describes most lively our actions and passions; our virtues and our vices; our follies and our humours: for neither is Comedy without its part of imaging . . . But how are poetical fictions, how are/hippocentaurs and chimeras, or how are angels and immaterial substances to be imaged; which, some of them, are things quite out of nature; others, such whereof we can have no notion? . . . The answer is easy to the first part of it: the fiction of some beings which are not in nature (second notions, as the logicians call them) has been founded on the conjunction of two natures, which have a real separate being. So hippocentaurs were imaged, by joining the natures of a man and horse together; as Lucretius tells us, who has used this word of *image* oftener than any of the poets—

Nam certe ex vivo centauri non fit imago . . .

The same reason may also be alleged for chimeras and the rest. And poets may be allowed the like liberty for describing things which really exist not, if they are founded on popular belief. Of this nature are fairies, pigmies, and the extraordinary effects of magic; for 'tis still an imitation, though of other men's fancies: and thus are Shakespeare's *Tempest,* his *Midsummer Night's Dream,* and Ben Johnson's *Masque of Witches* to be defended. For immaterial substances, we are authorized by Scripture in their description: and herein the text accommodates itself to vulgar apprehension, in giving angels the likeness of beautiful young men. Thus, after the pagan divinity, has Homer drawn his gods with human faces: and thus we have notions of things above us, by describing them like other beings more within our knowledge.

Author's Apology, '77. K I 186–87

Cf. Shakespeare, l.

Verse Proper to

Rhyme (Debate), i, l, m.

Imitation of Models

a. (Crites) . . . to imitate the Ancients well, much labour and long study is required . . .

Dram. Poesy, '65. K I 38

Ancients, k. Moderns, c. Poet, c. Cf. Jonson, d. Cf. Last Age, j. Cf. Rymer, c. Ancients, m.

b. I will conclude my reflections on it [the source from which he imitated his Troilus-Hector scene in *Troilus and Cressida*], with a passage of Longinus, concerning Plato's imitation of Homer: 'We ought not to regard a good imitation as a theft, but as a beautiful idea of him who undertakes to imitate, by forming himself on the invention and the work of another man . . .

Pref. *Troilus,* '79. K I 206

Shakespeare, f. Fletcher, g.

c. [Having spoken of Cowley's shortcomings in the pindaric form] Imitation is a nice point, and there are few poets who deserve to be models in all they write.

Pref. *Sylvæ,* '85. K I 268

Authority, e. Dorset, c. Cf. Tasso, b. Spenser, b. Satire, b. Boileau, c. Ancients, n. Virgil, kk. Rules, g.

d. Without invention, a painter is but a copier, and a poet but a plagiary of others.

Both are allowed sometimes to copy, and translate; but, as our author tells you, that is not the best part of their reputation. *Imitators are but a servile kind of cattle,* says the poet; or at best, the keepers of cattle for other men: they have nothing which is properly their own: that is a sufficient morti/fication for me, while I am translating Virgil. But to copy the best author is a kind of praise, if I perform it as I ought; as a copy after Raphael is more to be commended than an original of any indifferent painter.

Parallel, '95. K II 138–39

Cf. Lucian, h. Dialogue (Genre), e. Virgil, gg. Invention, e, f.

Immorality [See Obscenity]

Inspiration

Lucan, b.

a. [From Petronius] . . . *per ambages, deorumque ministeria, præcipitandus est liber spiritus, ut potius furentis animi vaticinatio appareat* . . .

Essay of Heroic Plays, '72. K I 152

Cf. Supernatural, b. Settle, d. Aeschylus, b.

b. We, who are priests of Apollo, have not the inspiration when we please; but must wait till the God comes rushing on us, and invades us with a fury which we are not able to resist; which gives us double strength while the fit continues, and leaves us languishing and spent, at its departure.

Ded. *Eleonora,* '92. S-S XI, 122

Cf. Genius, b. Passions, j.

Invention

a. So then the first happiness of the poet's imagination is properly invention, or finding of the thought . . .

Pref. *Annus Mirabilis,* '66. K I 15

Imagination, c. Ovid and Virgil, a. Davenant, b. Cf. Poetic License, b. Cf.

SHAKESPEARE, 1. EPIC POET, a. DRYDEN, LITERARY LIFE, l. Cf. VIRGIL, dd.

b. Invention is the first part, and absolutely necessary to them both [poetry and painting; yet no rule ever was or ever can be given, how to compass it. [See GENIUS, b]

Parallel, '95. K II 138

IMITATION OF MODELS, d. DISPOSITION. Cf. EPIC VS. TRAGEDY, f. VIRGIL, gg. Cf. HISTORICAL TRUTH, d.

c. On the other side, the pains and diligence of ill poets is but thrown away, when they want the genius to invent and feign agreeably. But, if the fictions be delightful (which they always are, if they are natural), if they be of a piece; if the beginning, the middle, and the end be in their due places, and artfully united to each other, such works can never fail of their deserved success. And such is Virgil's episode of Dido and Æneas . . .

Ded. *Æneis,* '97. K II 195

POET, k.

d. . . . if invention is to be taken in so strict a sense that the matter of a poem must be wholly new, and that in all its parts, then Scaliger has made out, says Segrais, that the history of Troy was no more the invention of Homer than of Virgil. . ./. At this rate, as Solomon hath told us, there is nothing new beneath the sun. Who then can pass for an inventor, if Homer, as well as Virgil, must be deprived of that glory? Is Versailles the less a new building, because the architect . . . hath imitated others . . . built before it? Walls, doors, and windows . . . are in all great houses. So descriptions, figures, fables, and the rest, must be in all heroic poems; they are the common materials of poetry, furnished from the magazine of nature; every poet hath as much right to them, as every man hath to air or water . . .? But the argument of the work, that is to say, its principal action, the oeconomy and disposition of it; these are the things which distinguish copies from originals. The poet who borrows nothing from others is yet to be born; he and the Jews' Messias will come together.

Ded. *Æneis,* '97. K II 197–98

VIRGIL, cc.

e. 'Tis one thing to copy, and another thing to imitate from Nature. The copier is that servile imitator, to whom Horace gives no better a name than that of animal; he will not so much as allow him to be a man. Raphael imitated Nature; they who copy one of Raphael's pieces imitate but him; for his work is their original. They translate him, as I do Virgil; and fall as short of him, as I of Virgil. There is a kind of invention in the imitation of Raphael; for, though the thing was in Nature, yet the idea of it was his own. . . /.[1] To return to my first similitude: suppose Apelles and Raphael had each of them painted a burning Troy, might not the modern painter have succeeded as well as the ancient, though neither of them had seen the town on fire? For the draughts of both were taken from the ideas which they had of Nature. . . . But . . . they would not have designed after the same manner. . . .[1] This, I think, is a just comparison betwixt the two poets . . . Virgil cannot be said to copy Homer; the Grecian had only the advantage of writing first.

Ded. *Æneis,* '97. K II 199–200

f. [¶] In the last place, I may safely grant that, by reading Homer, Virgil was taught to imitate his invention; that is, to imitate like him; which is no more than if a painter studied Raphael, that he might learn to design after his manner. And thus I might imitate Virgil, if I were capable of writing an heroic poem, and yet the invention be my own: but I should endeavour to avoid a servile copying.

    Ded. *Æneis,* '97. K II 201

TRANSLATION, ff. HOMER AND VIRGIL, d. CHAUCER AND OVID, a. Cf. MODERNIZING.

Inventors of Arts

TRAGEDY, k. RULES, c. SHAKESPEARE, f. AUTHORITY, e. DRYDEN, LITERARY LIFE, a. Cf. HORACE AND JUVENAL AND PERSIUS, j. AUTHORITY, f. Cf. DIALOGUE (GENRE), e. Cf. THEOCRITUS, b. Cf. CHAUCER, c.

Ipse Dixit [Cf. AUTHORITY]

[In connection with the respect due Jonson] Or why should there be any *Ipse dixit* in our poetry, any more than there is in our philosophy?

    Pref. *Evening's Love,* '71 K I 138

PROGRESS, e. Cf. PROSODY, d.

Irony [See SATIRE]

Italian Critics [See authors; see also SPANISH CRITICS]

Quotations are superfluous in an established truth; otherwise I could reckon up, amongst the moderns, all the Italian commentators on Aristotle's book of poetry . . .

    Author's Apology, '77. K I 181

EPIC VS. TRAGEDY, d.

Italian Drama

PRESENT AGE, e. ANCIENTS, t.

Italian Language and Literature

RHYME (DEBATE), b.

a. (Neander) . . . when, by the inundation of the Goths and Vandals into Italy, new languages were brought in . ./. a new way of poesy was practised . . . [See RHYME (DEBATE), j]

    Dram. Poesy, '65. K I 96–97

PROSODY, h, gg. ACADEMY, b. ASTROLOGY. OPERA, c.

b. All who are conversant in the Italian cannot but observe that it is the softest, the sweetest, the most harmonious, not only of any modern tongue, but even beyond any of the learned. It seems indeed to have been invented for the sake of Poetry and Music;/the vowels are so abounding . . . Then the pronunciation is so manly, and so sonorous, that their very speaking has more of music in it than Dutch poetry and song. It has withal derived so much copiousness and eloquence from the Greek and Latin . . . that if, after all, we must call it barbarous, 'tis the most beautiful and most learned of any barbarism in modern tongues . . . This language has in a manner been refined and purified from the Gothic ever since the time of Dante . . .

    Pref. *Albion and Albanius,* '85. K I 273–74

FRENCH LANGUAGE, a. ENGLISH LANGUAGE, a. OPERA, h. SATIRE, aa. DRYDEN, LITERARY LIFE, b. PROSODY, ii. BELLORI. PROSODY, b, c, d. ENGLISH VS. FRENCH, n. TRANSLATION, gg. ENGLISH VS. FRENCH, w. COINAGE, c. BOCCACCIO.

Italian Renaissance

GOLDEN AGES, b.

❧ J ❧

Jonson, Ben [See also combinations with Shakespeare]*

Small-caps ENGLISH DRAMA, d.

a. (Neander) [¶] As for Johnson . . . if we look upon him while he was himself (for his last plays were but his dotages), I think him the most learned and judicious writer which any theatre ever had. He was a most severe judge of himself, as well as others. One cannot say he wanted wit, but rather that he was frugal of it. In his works you find little to retrench or alter. Wit, and language, and humour/also in some measure, we had before him; but something of art was wanting to the Drama, till he came. He managed his strength to more advantage than any who preceded him. You seldom find him making love in any of his scenes, or endeavouring to move the passions; his genius was too sullen and saturnine to do it gracefully, especially when he knew he came after those who had performed both to such an height. Humour was his proper sphere; and in that he delighted most to represent mechanic people. He was deeply conversant in the Ancients . . . and he borrowed boldly from them . . . But he has done his robberies so openly, that one may see he fears not to be taxed by any law. He invades authors like a monarch; and what would

be theft in other poets, is only victory in him. . . . If there was any fault in his language, 'twas that he weaved it too closely and laboriously, in his serious plays: perhaps too, he did a little too much Romanize our tongue . . . wherein, though he learnedly followed the idiom of their language, he did not enough comply with the idiom of ours.

Dram. Poesy, '65. K I 81–82

b. [¶] But Ben Johnson is to be admired for many excellencies; and can be taxed with fewer failings than any English poet. I know I have been accused as an enemy of his writings; but without any other reason, than that I do not admire him blindly. . . . For why should he only be exempted from those frailties, from which Homer and Virgil are not free? [See IPSE DIXIT]

Pref. *Evening's Love, '71.* K I 138

c. As for Ben Johnson, I am loath to name him, because he is a most judicious writer; yet he very often falls into these errors [of nonsense and impropriety of language] . . .[1]

Defence of the Epilogue, '72. K I 167

d. Let us ascribe to Johnson, the height and accuracy of judgment in the ordering of his plots, his choice of characters, and maintaining what he had chosen to the end. But let us not think him a perfect pattern of imitation, except it be in humour; for love, which is the foundation of all comedies in other languages, is scarcely men-

---

* See J. F. Bradley and J. Q. Adams, *The Jonson Allusion-Book: A Collection of Allusions to Ben Jonson from 1597 to 1700* (New Haven: Yale University Press, 1922).

tioned in any of his plays; and for humour itself, the poets of this age will be more wary than to imitate the meanness of his persons.

Defence of the Epilogue, '72. K I 177
LAST AGE, k. DRYDEN, LITERARY LIFE, a. LAST AGE, l. PRESENT AGE, o.

Alchemist
See below, l. UNITIES (DRAMATIC), GENERAL, b-2.

Ancients, Imitator of

e. (Crites) . . . the greatest man of the last/age (Ben Johnson) was willing to give place to them in all things: he was not only a professed imitator of Horace, but a learned plagiary of all the others; you track him every where in their snow: if Horace, Lucan, Petronius Arbiter, Seneca, and Juvenal, had their own from him, there are few serious thoughts which are new in him: you will pardon me, therefore, if I presume he loved their fashion, when he wore their clothes.

Dram. Poesy, '65. K I 42–43

f. (Crites) . . . I will produce Father Ben to you, dressed in all the ornaments and colours of the Ancients; you will need no other guide to our party, if you follow him . . .

Dram. Poesy, '65. K I 43

g. Ben Johnson, indeed, has designed his plots himself; but no man has borrowed so much from the Ancients as he has done: and he did well in it, for he has thereby beautified our language.

Pref. *Evening's Love,* '71. K I 146

Authority
AUTHORITY, a, b. COMEDY, f.

Bartholomew Fair
See below, l. ART AND LIFE, b.

Borrowing (Linguistic)
GRAFFING, b.

Catiline
See below, t. RHYME (DEBATE), w. TUMULT, b. GRAMMAR, a, b, c. HISTORICAL TRUTH, c.

Correctness
See below, i.

Court, Acquaintance with
LAST AGE, i.

Decorum
DECORUM, e.

h. (Neander) . . . I should not animadvert on him, who was otherwise a painful observer of τὸ πρέπον, or the *decorum* of the stage, if he had not used extreme severity in his judgment on the incomparable Shakespeare for the same fault.

Dram. Poesy, '65. K I 75

Discoveries
UNITIES (DRAMATIC), ACTION, a.

i. (Neander) To conclude of him [Jonson]; as he has given us the most correct plays, so in the precepts which he has laid down in his *Discoveries,* we have as many and profitable rules for perfecting the stage, as any wherewith the French can furnish us.

Dram. Poesy, '65. K I 83

Dramatic Quality
ENGLISH VS. FRENCH, u. COMEDY, e.

Every Man in His Humour
See below, v.

Expression
TRAGEDY, s.

Grammar

j. [See analysis of solecisms in "Catiline," *Defence of the Epilogue*]
GRAMMAR, a, b, c.

Humors
BEAUMONT AND FLETCHER. HUMORS, c.

Imagination

k. (Neander) . . . his was not [a luxuriant fancy]: as he did not want imagination, so none ever said he had much to spare.

Dram. Poesy, '65. K I 107
Imitation
1. [¶] In *Bartholomew Fair,* or the lowest kind of comedy, that degree of heightening is used, which is proper to set off that subject: it is true the author was not there to go out of prose, as he does in his higher arguments of Comedy, *The Fox* and *Alchymist;* yet he does so raise his matter in that prose, as to render it delightful; which he could never have performed, had he only/said or done those very things, that are daily spoken or practised at the fair . . .

Defence of An Essay, '68. K I 114–15
Judgment
See below, s-2. JUDGMENT, c. CHAPMAN, a.
Manners
SHAKESPEARE AND FLETCHER AND JONSON. SHAKESPEARE, p.
Masque of Witches
IMITATION, j.
Personal Satire in
SATIRE, ii.
Plots
ENGLISH VS. FRENCH, s. UNITIES (DRAMATIC), TIME, d.
Regularity
SHAKESPEARE AND FLETCHER, a.
Sad Shepherd, The
RHYME (DEBATE), f, l.
Sejanus
See below, t. RHYME (DEBATE), w. HISTORICAL TRUTH, c.
Shakespeare [See combinations with Shakespeare]
See above, h. DORSET, b. [Cf. Spence, *Anecdotes,* 1820, p. 5]
Silent Woman, The [See Examen of, in *An Essay of Dramatic Poesy*]

m. (Neander) 'Tis all included in the limits of three hours and an half, which is no more than is required for the presentment on the stage. A beauty perhaps not much observed; if it had, we should not have looked on the Spanish translation of *Five Hours* [*Adventures of . . .*] with so much wonder.

Dram. Poesy, '65. K I 83
n. (Neander) The intrigue of it [*Silent Woman*] is the greatest and most noble of any pure unmixed comedy in any language; you see in it many persons of various characters and humours, and all delightful . . .

Dram. Poesy, '65. K I 83
o. (Neander) Some . . . say this humour of his [Morose, 'to whom all noise but his own talking is offensive'] is forced: but . . ./we may consider him first to be naturally of a delicate hearing . . . and secondly, we may attribute much of it to the peevishness of his age, or the wayward authority of an old man in his own house . . .

Dram. Poesy, '65. K I 83–84
p. (Neander) I shall not waste time in commending the writing of this play; but I will give you my opinion, that there is more wit and acuteness of fancy in it than in any of Ben Johnson's. Besides, that he has here described the conversation of gentlemen . . . with more gaiety, air, and freedom, than in the rest of his comedies. For the contrivance of the plot, 'tis extreme elaborate, and yet withal easy; for the λύσις, or untying of it, 'tis so admirable, that when it is done, no one of the audience would think the poet could have missed it; and yet it was concealed so much before the last scene, that any other way

would sooner have entered into your thoughts.

Dram. Poesy, '65. K I 86

q. (Neander) One of these advantages [taken by Jonson] is that which Corneille has laid down as the greatest which can arrive to any poem . . . viz. the making choice of some signal and long-expected day, whereon the action of the play is to depend.

Dram. Poesy, '65. K I 87

r. (Neander) [¶] There is another artifice of the poet, which I cannot here omit . . . that is, when he has any character or humour wherein he would show a *coup de Maistre* . . . he recommends it to your observation by a pleasant description of it before the person first appears. . . .[1] So that before they [Morose and others] come upon the stage, you have a longing expectation of them, which prepares you to receive them favourably . . .

Dram. Poesy, '65. K I 87

s. (Neander) [¶] I will observe yet one thing further of this admirable plot; the business of it rises in every act . . .[1] But that the poet might entertain you with more variety all this while, he reserves some new characters to show you, which he opens not till the second and third act. . . .[1] Thus, like a skillful chess-player, by little and little he draws out his men, and makes his pawns of use to his greater persons.

Dram. Poesy, '65. K I 88

s-2. . . . few Englishmen, except Ben Johnson, have ever made a plot, with variety of design in it, included in twenty-four hours, which was altogether natural. For this reason, I prefer the *Silent Woman* before all other plays, I think justly, as I do

its author, in judgment, above all other poets.

Defence of An Essay, '68. K I 131

Present Age, k.

Tragicomedy

t. (Lisideius) . . . even Ben Johnson himself, in *Sejanus* and *Catiline,* has given us this oleo of a play, this unnatural mixture of comedy and tragedy; which to me sounds just as ridiculously as the history of David with the merry humours of Golias.

Dram. Poesy, '65. K I 60

Translation

Translation, a.

Tumult

Tumult, b.

Volpone

Unities (Dramatic), General, b-2. See above, l.

Wit

Beaumont and Fletcher. Wit, g. Cf. Comedy, e. Wit, h.

u. [¶] For Ben Johnson, the most judicious of poets, he always writ properly, and as the character required; and I will not contest further with my friends who call that wit: it being very certain, that even folly itself, well represented, is wit in a larger signification; and that there is fancy, as well as judgment, in it, though not so much or noble: because all poetry being imitation, that of folly is a lower exercise of fancy, though perhaps as difficult as the other; for 'tis a kind of looking downward in the poet, and representing that part of mankind which is below him.

Defence of the Epilogue, '72. K I 172

v. [¶] In these low characters of vice and folly, lay the excellency of that inimitable writer; who, when at any time he aimed at wit in the stricter sense, that is, sharpness of conceit, was forced either to borrow from the Ancients,/ . . . or, when he trusted himself alone, often fell into meanness of expression. Nay, he was not free from the lowest and most grovelling kind of wit, which we call clenches, of which *Every Man in his Humour* is infinitely full . . .[1]

Defence of the Epilogue, '72. K I 172–73
PRESENT AGE, k.

Judgment [Cf. MANUM DE TABULA]

a. . . . the fancy was yet in its first work, moving the sleeping images of things towards the light, there to be distinguished, and then either chosen or rejected by the judgment . . .

Ded. *Rival Ladies, '64.* K I 1
PLAY WRITING. RHYME (DEBATE), d, g. IMAGINATION, b. FANCY, b. RHYME (DEBATE), g.

b. (Neander) Judgment is indeed the master-workman in a play; but he requires many subordinate hands, many tools to his assistance. And verse I affirm to be one of these; 'tis a rule and line by which he keeps his building compact and even, while otherwise lawless imagination would raise either irregularly or loosely.

Dram. Poesy, '65. K I 107
RHYME (DEBATE), r. IMAGINATION, c. POET, c. COMEDY, a.

c. To make men appear pleasantly ridiculous on the stage, was . . . his [Jonson's] talent; and in this he needed not the acumen of wit but that of judgment. For the characters and representations of folly are only the effects of observation; and observation is an effect of judgment.

Pref. *Evening's Love, '71.* K I 138
FABLE, c. Cf. FANCY, d. JONSON, s. FLETCHER, d. Cf. SETTLE, c. POETIC LICENSE, b. FANCY, e. LUCAN, c. FIGURES, b. PASSIONS, d. FANCY, f, g.

SHAKESPEARE, r. Cf. RULES, d. OVID, h. FANCY, h. Cf. PLUTARCH, b. FIGURES, d. PERSIUS, f. Cf. VIRGIL, dd. CHIAROSCURO. Cf. VIRGIL, ee, aa. FANCY, i. Cf. STATIUS, c. Cf. VIRGIL, gg. IMAGINATION, e. DRYDEN, LIFE, e. COWLEY, i.

d. An author is not to write all he can, but only all he ought.

Pref. *Fables,* 1700. K II 265

Judgment (Responsive) [Cf. DRAMA READ AND ACTED]

In a play-house, everything contributes to impose upon the judgment; the lights, the scenes, the habits, and, above all, the grace of action, which is commonly the best where there is the most need of it, surprise the audience, and cast a mist upon their understandings . . . But these false beauties of the stage are no more lasting than a rainbow; when the actor ceases to shine upon them . . . they/vanish in a twinkling.[1]

Ded. *Spanish Friar, '81.* K I 245–46
IMITATION, i.

Juvenal [See also HORACE AND JUVENAL AND PERSIUS]

a. Juvenal is of a more vigorous and masculine wit [than Horace]; he gives me as much pleasure as I can bear; he fully satisfies my expectation; he treats his subject home: his spleen is raised, and he raises mine: I have the pleasure of concernment in all he says; he drives his reader along with him; and when he is at the end of his way I willingly stop with him. If he went another stage, it would be too far . . . When he gives over, it is a sign the subject is exhausted, and the wit of man can carry it no further. If a fault can be justly/found in him, 'tis that he is sometimes too luxuriant, too redundant; says more than he needs, like my friend the *Plain-Dealer,* but never more than pleases. Add to this, that his thoughts are as just as those of Horace, and much more elevated. His expressions are sonorous and more noble; his verse more numerous, and his words are suitable to his thoughts, sublime and lofty. All these contribute to the pleasure of the reader; and the greater the soul of him who reads, his transports are the greater.

Discourse of Satire, '93. K II 84–85

Bite

Lucian, d.

Diction and Elocution

See above, a. Holyday, b.

Limitations

Virgil, ii.

Satires: First

Satire, d.

Satires: Second

Satire, e.

Satires: Sixth

b. But this [Juvenal's *Sixth Satire*], though the wittiest of all his satires, has yet the least of truth or instruction in it. He has run himself into his old declamatory way, and almost forgotten that he was now setting up for a moral poet.

Discourse of Satire, '93. K II 104

c. [¶] This Satyr [Juvenal's *Sixth*] . . . is a bitter invective against the fair Sex. Tis, indeed, a Common-place, from whence all the Moderns have notoriously stollen their sharpest Raileries . . . How they had offended him I know not: But upon the whole matter he is not to be excus'd for imputing to all, the Vices of some few amongst them. . . . Neither do I know what Moral he cou'd reasonably draw from it. . . . If he intended only to exercise his Wit, he has forfeited his Judgment, by making the one half of his Readers his mortal Enemies . . . The whole

World must allow this to be the wittiest of his Satyrs; and truly he had need of all his parts, to maintain with so much violence, so unjust a Charge. I am satisfied he will bring but few over to his Opinion: And on that Consideration chiefly I ventur'd to translate him./Though there wanted not another Reason, which was, that no one else would undertake it: at least, Sir C[harles]. S[edley]., who cou'd have done more right to the Author, after a long delay, at length absolutely refus'd so ungrateful an employment: And every one will grant, that the Work must have been imperfect and lame, if it had appear'd without one of the Principal Members belonging to it. Let the Poet therefore bear the blame of his own Invention; and let me satisfy the World, that I am not of his Opinion.

Argument of the Sixth Satire [Juvenal], '93. JK II 694–95

Satires: Tenth

d. . . . this Divine Satyr . . .

Argument of the Tenth Satire [Juvenal], '93. JK II 720

Satires: Sixteenth

e. This Satyr was written by *Juvenal,* when he was a Commander in *Egypt:* 'Tis certainly his, tho I think it not finish'd. And if it be well observ'd, you will find he intended an Invective against a standing Army.

Argument of the Sixteenth Satire [Juvenal], '93. JK II 737

Satires: Morality of

Dryden, Works, y.

Satires: Unity in

Satire, c.

Style

Progress, e.

Miscellaneous

Images, c.

❧ K ❧

Ketch, Jack
  SHADWELL, f. SATIRE, b.
Knowledge [See also PROGRESS]
  OPINION.

... knowledge, which is none of the worst preservatives against slavery.
  "Life of Lucian," '96. S-S XVIII 82

❧ L ❧

Lampoon [See SATIRE]
Language [See also following entries and BORROWING (VERBAL)]
  ... the refinement of a language principally consists ... *either in rejecting such old words, or phrases, which are ill-sounding, or improper; or in admitting new, which are more proper, more sounding, and more significant.*
  Defence of the Epilogue, '72. K I 164
  PRESENT AGE, j. GRAFFING, a. ACADEMY, b. GREEK LANGUAGE. BOCCACCIO.

Language Mastery
  Cf. LATIN, a. STYLE, a. COWLEY, g. DRYDEN, WORKS, ooo.

Languages, Modern [See also specific languages]
  ... the barbarity ... of modern tongues ...
  Pref. *Ovid's Epistles,* '80. K I 238
  TRANSLATION, d. Cf. VIRGIL, pp. LATIN, b. ITALIAN LANGUAGE, b. GOLDEN AGES, b. EPIC, CHRISTIAN, a. DENNIS. ENGLISH LANGUAGE, b, f. LATIN, c. PROSODY, d. VIRGIL, s.

Last Age [Cf. PRESENT AGE]
  a. (Narrator: Dryden) [¶] All of them were thus far of Eugenius his opinion, that the sweetness of English verse was never understood or practised by our fathers ...
  Dram. Poesy, '65. K I 35
  JONSON, e. ENGLISH VS. FRENCH, a.
  b. (Neander) But it is to raise envy to the living, to compare them with the dead. They are honoured, and almost adored by us, as they deserve; neither do I know any so presumptuous of themselves as to contend with them. Yet give me leave to say thus much, without injury to their ashes; that not only we shall never equal them, but they could never equal themselves, were they to rise and write again. We acknowledge them our fathers in wit; but they have ruined their estates themselves, before they came to their children's hands. There is scarce an humour, a character, or any kind of plot, which they have not blown upon. All comes sullied or wasted to us: and were they to entertain this age, they could not make so plenteous treatments out of such

decayed fortunes. This therefore will be a good argument to us, either not to write at all, or to attempt some other way [i.e., rhyme]. There is no bays to be expected in their walks . . .

Dram. Poesy, '65. K I 99

RHYME (DEBATE), l, w. WIT, h. ENGLISH LANGUAGE, f-2. PRESENT AGE, h, j.

c. That their [that of Last Age] wit is great, and many times their expressions noble, envy itself cannot deny . . . But the times were ignorant in which they lived. Poetry was then, if not in its infancy among us, at least not arrived to its vigour and maturity: witness the lameness of their plots; many of which, especially those which they writ first (for even that age refined itself in some measure), were made up of some ridiculous incoherent story, which in one play many times took up the business of an age. I suppose I need not name *Pericles* . . . nor the historical plays of Shakespeare: besides many of the rest, as the *Winter's Tale, Love's Labour Lost, Measure for Measure,* which were either grounded on impossibilities, or at least so meanly written, that the comedy neither caused your mirth, nor the serious part your concernment. [See FLETCHER, b]

Defence of the Epilogue, '72. K I 165

d. But these absurdities, which those poets [Shakespeare and Fletcher] committed, may more properly be called the age's fault than theirs: for, besides the want of education and learning (which was their particular unhappiness), they wanted the benefit of converse . . .

Defence of the Epilogue, '72. K I 166

e. Those, who call theirs [Last Age] *the Golden Age of Poetry,* have only this reason for it, that they were then content with acorns before they knew the use of bread,

or that ἅλις δρυὸς was become a proverb.

Defence of the Epilogue, '72. K I 166

f. . . . I dare almost challenge any man to show me a page [of the Last Age] which is correct in both [sense and language].

Defence of the Epilogue, '72. K I 167
Cf. GRAMMAR, d.

g. I will therefore only/observe to you, that the wit of the last age was yet more incorrect than their language.[1]

Defence of the Epilogue, '72. K I 171–72
WIT, k.

h. I have always acknowledged the wit of our predecessors, with all the veneration which becomes me; but, I am sure, their wit was not that of gentlemen; there was ever somewhat/that was ill-bred and clownish in it, and which confessed the conversation of the authors.

Defence of the Epilogue, '72. K I 174–75

i. In the age wherein those poets lived, there was less of gallantry than in ours; neither did they keep the best company of theirs. . . . I cannot find that any of them had been conversant in courts, except Ben Johnson . . . Greatness was not then so easy of access, nor conversation so free, as now it is.

Defence of the Epilogue, '72. K I 175

j. [¶] To conclude all, let us render to our predecessors what is their due, without confining ourselves to a servile imitation of all they writ; and, without assuming to ourselves the title of better poets, let us ascribe to the gallantry and civility of our age the advantage which we have above them, and to our knowledge of the customs and manner of it the happiness we have to please beyond them.

Defence of the Epilogue, '72. K I 177

k. . . . I am made a detractor from my

predecessors, whom I confess to have been my masters in the art. But this latter was the accusation of the best judge, and almost the best poet, in the Latin tongue. You find Horace complaining, that, for taxing some verses in Lucilius, he himself was blamed by others, though his design was no other than mine now, to improve the knowledge of poetry; and it was no defence to him, amongst his enemies, any more than it is for me, that he praised Lucilius where he deserved it; *paginâ laudatur eâdem*. It is for this reason I will be no more mistaken for my good meaning: I know I honour Ben Johnson more than my little critics, because, without vanity I may own, I understand him better.

Ded. *Assignation,* '73. S-S IV 375

NORTH's *Plutarch.* CRITIC[s], d.

l. Peace be to the venerable shades of Shakespeare and Ben Johnson! none of the living will presume to have any competition with them; as they were our predecessors, so they were our masters. We trail our plays under them; but as at the funerals of a Turkish emperor, our ensigns are furled or dragged upon the ground, in honour to the dead, so we may lawfully advance our own afterwards, to show that we succeed; if less in dignity, yet on the same foot and title, which we think too we can maintain against the insolence of our own Janizaries.

Examen Poeticum, '93. K II 5

ENGLISH DRAMA, e.   TRANSLATION, c. PRESENT AGE, o.   TRANSLATION, o.   COLLIER.

Latin

Cf. ENGLISH LANGUAGE, i, f-2. HORACE, i. ACADEMY, b. TRANSLATION, d.

a. But for the delicacies of the tongue [Latin], the turns of the expressions, the figures and connections of words, in which

consist the beauty of that language, he [Plutarch] plainly tells us . . . they required too great a labour for a man in age . . . to attain perfectly . . .

"Life of Plutarch," '83. S-S XVII 27

b. . . . Latin is naturally a more succinct/language than either the Italian, Spanish, French, or even than the English, which, by reason of its monosyllables, is far the most compendious of them.

Pref. *Sylvæ,* '85. K I 256–57

THEOCRITUS, a.   DRYDEN, WORKS, bbb. PERSIUS, b.   THEOCRITUS, b.

c. [In a discussion of pastoral literature] I will say nothing of the *Piscatory Eclogues* [of Sannazarius: *Piscatoria*], because no modern Latin can bear criticism. It is no wonder that, rolling down, through so many barbarous ages, from the spring of Virgil, it bears along with it the filth and ordures of the Goths/and Vandals.

Ded. *Pastorals,* '97. S-S XIII 324–25

VIRGIL, mm.   PROSODY, b.   ENGLISH LANGUAGE, b, e, f.   HOMER AND VIRGIL, d. CHAUCER AND OVID.

Latinity

(Neander) . . . perhaps . . . [Jonson] did a little too much Romanize our tongue . . . [See JONSON, a]

Dram. Poesy, '65. K I 82

GRAMMAR, c.   BORROWING (VERBAL), c.

Laughter

a. (Neander) . . . that malicious pleasure in the audience which is testified by laughter . . . [See HUMORS, b]

Dram. Poesy, '65. K I 85

b. (Neander) . . . all things which are deviations from common customs are ever the aptest to product it [laughter] . . . [HUMORS, b]

Dram. Poesy, '65. K I 85

EPIC, a. BURLESQUE, a. AUDIENCE, POPU-
LAR, c. COMEDY, a.

c. But, how it happens, that an impossible adventure should cause our mirth, I
cannot so easily imagine. Something there
may be in the oddness of it, because on the
stage it is the common effect of things unexpected to surprise us into a delight: and
that is to be ascribed to the strange appetite, as I may call it, of the fancy; which,
like that of a longing woman, often runs
out into the most extravagant desires; and is
better satisfied sometimes with loam, or
with the rinds of trees, than with the whole-
some nourishments of life.

Pref. Evening's Love, '71. K I 136
POETIC JUSTICE, c. Cf. CRITIC[s], b. SA-
TIRE, oo. CHARACTER[s], c.

d. [In a context concerning farce]
Laughter is indeed the propriety of a man,
but just enough to distinguish him from
his elder brother with four legs. . . . After
all, 'tis a good thing to laugh at any rate;
and if a straw can tickle a man, it is an
instrument of happiness.

Parallel, '95. K II 133
SATIRE, p. PRESENT AGE, p.

Lazar and Venus

ART AND LIFE, b. EPIC, a. BURLESQUE, a.

. . . there is as much of art, and as near
an imitation of nature, in a lazar, as in a
Venus.

Pref. Tyrannic Love, '70. S-S III 377
DRYDEN, LITERARY LIFE, k. CONTRAST.
COMEDY, h.

Lee, Nathaniel

CRITICASTER, e. Cf. DECORUM, h. DRY-
DEN, LITERARY LIFE, n.

a. Let the whole scene [*ii* of Act IV,
Duke of Guise (which is one of the best

in the tragedy, though murdered in the
acting) be read together . . .

Vindication, '83. S-S VII 209
b. I remember Poor Nat. Lee, who was
then upon the Verge of Madness, yet made
a Sober, and a Witty Answer to a Bad Poet,
who told him, *It was an easie thing to write
like a Madman: No,* said he, *'tis very difficult to write like a Madman, but 'tis a very
easie matter to write like a fool.* Otway and
He are safe by death from all Attacks . . .
[See PROSODY, y]

Letter to Dennis, 1693/94. Ward No. 31,
p. 72.

CHARACTER[s], d.

Leicester, Third Earl of [See PHILIP SID-
NEY]

Lemoyne, Father Pierre

FRENCH AUTHORS, b. EPIC POET, c.

Liaison des Scènes

a. (Crites) . . . that you may know it
[the place] to be the same, the stage is so
supplied with persons, that it is never
empty all the time . . .[1] This Corneille
calls *la liaison des scenes,* the continuity or
joining of the scenes; and 'tis a good mark
of a well-contrived play, when all the persons are known to each other, and every
one of them has some affairs with all the
rest.

Dram. Poesy, 65. K I 40
ANCIENTS, o. SCENE, a, b.

b. (Lisideius) . . . neither will I insist
on the care they take, that no person after
his first entrance shall ever appear, but the
business which brings him upon the stage
shall be evident; which, if observed, must
needs render all the events in the play more
natural; for there you see the probability
of every accident, in the cause that produced it; and that which appears chance in

the play, will seem so reasonable to you, that you will there find it almost necessary: so that in the exits of the actors you have a clear account of their purpose/and design in the next entrance . . . for there is nothing so absurd, says Corneille, as for an actor to leave the stage, only because he has no more to say.

Dram. Poesy, '65. K I 66–67

English vs. French, y. Unities (Dramatic), Place, d. Unities (Dramatic), General, b-2. Cf. Dryden, Works, m. Dryden, Works, z. Unities (Dramatic), General, c.

Livy (Titus Livius)

History, e. Polybius, b.

[Of Aeneid II] The destruction of Veii is here shadow'd under that of Troy. Livy in his description of it seems to have emulated in his prose, and almost equal'd, the beauty of Virgil's verse.

Notes and Observations on Virgil's Works, '97. N 711

Longinus, Dionysius Cassius*

a. And Longinus, who was undoubtedly, after Aristotle, the greatest critic amongst the Greeks . ./. has judiciously preferred the sublime genius that sometimes errs, to the middling or indifferent one, which makes few faults, but seldom or never rises to any excellence.

Author's Apology, '77. K I 179–180

Epic, f. Æschylus. Imitation of Models, b. Dryden, Literary Life, j. Passions, d, e, i.

b. [¶] Some think the famous critic, Longinus, was of Plutarch's family . . . but the proofs are so weak, that I will not

---

* See A. Rosenberg, *Longinus in England bis zum Ende des 18 Jahrhunderts,* Berlin, 1917.

insert them: they may both of them rely on their proper merits, and stand not in want of a relation to each other.

"Life of Plutarch," '83. S-S XVII 42

Persius, g. Homer and Virgil, d.

Lope de Vega

Rules, j.

Louis XIV

Boileau, b.

To what height the magnificence and encouragement of the present King of France may carry Painting and Sculpture, is uncertain; but by what he has done before the war in which he is engaged, we may/expect what he will do after . . .

Parallel, '95. K II 135–36

Patronage, d.

Love

Ancients, p, f, q. Beaumont and Fletcher. Cf. Comedy, e. Fletcher, d. Jonson, d. English Drama, a.

[¶] Prove also that love, being an heroic passion, is fit for tragedy, which cannot be denied, because of the example alleged of Phaedra; and how far Shakespeare has outdone them [the Ancients] in friendship, etc.

Heads of an Answer, '77. S-S XV 383

Tragedy, e, g. Shakespeare and Fletcher, b. Ovid, d. Opera, d. Donne, c. Spenser, c. Virgil, e.

Love and Honor

. . . an heroic play ought to be an imitation, in little, of an heroic poem; and, consequently . . . Love and Valour ought to be the subject of it. [See Heroic Play, d]

Essay of Heroic Plays, '72. K I 150

Epic Hero, d. Dryden, Literary Life, v.

Love Poetry

Donne, c.

Lucan (Marcus Annæus Lucanus)

a. For this reason (I mean not of length, but broken action, tied too severely to the laws of history), I am apt to agree with those who rank Lucan rather among historians in verse, than epic poets . . .

Pref. *Annus Mirabilis,* '66. K I 11

TECHNICAL TERMS, a.

b. [¶] In which sentence [*Non enim res gestae . . .*], and his own essay of a poem . . . it is thought he [Petronius] taxes Lucan, who followed too much the truth of history, crowded sentences together, was too full of points, and too often offered at somewhat which had more of the sting of an epigram, than of the dignity and state of an heroic poem. Lucan used not much the help of his heathen deities: there was neither the ministry of the gods, nor the precipitation of the soul, nor the fury of a prophet . . . in his *Pharsalia;* he treats you more like a philosopher than a poet, and instructs you, in verse, with what he had been taught by his uncle Seneca in prose. In one word, he walks soberly afoot, when he might fly.

Essay of Heroic Plays, '72. K I 152

c. [¶] As for hyperboles, I will neither quote Lucan, nor Statius, men of an unbounded imagination, but who often wanted the poise of judgment. The divine Virgil was not liable to that exception . . .

Author's Apology, '77. K I 184

SENECA, d. VIRGIL, oo.

d. [Virgil] is stately without ambition, which is the vice of Lucan.

Pref. *Sylvæ,* '85. K I 256

e. . . . Lucan is wanting [as an epic writer] both in design and subject, and is besides too full of heat and affectation . . .

Discourse of Satire, '93. K II 27

PERSIUS, l.

f. Our Author [Persius], living in the time of *Nero,* was Contemporary and Friend to the Noble Poet *Lucan* . . .

Argument of the Fourth Satire [Persius], '93. JK II 765

CRITIC[s], d. FIGURES, c. CRITIC[s], a. VIRGIL, bb. CHAUCER AND OVID.

Lucian*

SATIRE, pp.

a. . . . I think him either one of the Eclectic school, or else a Sceptic: I mean, that he either formed a body of philosophy . . . out of the opinions and dogmas of several heathen philosophers . . . or that he doubted of everything; weighed all opinions, and adhered to none of them; only used them as they served his occasion for the present dialogue, and perhaps rejected them in the next.

"Life of Lucian," '96. S-S XVIII 69

SCEPTICISM.

b. [¶] To conclude this article [Lucian's religion]: He was too fantastical, too giddy, too irresolute, either to be anything at all, or anything long; and in this view I cannot think he was either a steady atheist, or a deist, but a doubter, a sceptic . . .[1]

"Life of Lucian," '96. S-S XVIII 70

c. [¶] Lucian is accused likewise for his writing too lusciously in his "Dialogue of the Harlots." It has been the common fault of all satirists, to make vice too amiable, while they expose it; but of all men living, I am the most unfit to accuse Lucian, who am so little able to defend myself from the/same objection.

"Life of Lucian," '96. S-S XVIII 71–72

d. [¶] As for those who condemn our author [Lucian] for the too much gall

---

* See Hardin Craig, "Dryden's Lucian," *Classical Philology,* XVI (1921), 141–63.

and virulency of his satires, it is to be
suspected, says Dr. [Jasper] Mayne, that
they themselves are guilty of those hypocri-
sies, crimes, and follies, which he so sharply
exposes, and at the same time endeavours
to reform. I may add, that, for the most
part, he rather laughs like Horace, than
bites/like Juvenal. Indeed his genius was of
kin to both, but more nearly related to the
former. Some diseases are curable by leni-
tives; to others corrosives are necessary.
Can a man inveigh too sharply against the
cruelty of tyrants, the pride and vanity of
the great, the covetousness of the rich, the
baseness of the Sophists, and particularly
of the Cynics (who while they preach poverty to others, are heaping up riches, and
living in gluttony), besides the wrangling
of the sects among themselves about supreme happiness, which he describes at a
drunken feast, and calls it the battle of the
Lapithæ.

"Life of Lucian," '96. S-S XVIII 72–73

e. [¶] Some of his [Lucian's] cen-
surers accuse him of flatness and want of
wit in many places. These I suppose have
read him in some Latin translations, which,
I confess, are generally dull; and this is
the only excuse I can make for them. Otherwise they accuse themselves too manifestly
for want of taste or understanding. Of this
number is the wretched author of the *Lu-
cien en Belle Humeur,* who being himself
as insipid as a Dutch poet, yet arraigns
Lucian for his own fault . . .[1]/

. . . I wish I had the liberty to lash this
frog-land wit as he deserves; but when a
speech is not seconded in parliament, it
falls of course; and this author has the
whole senate of the learned to pull him
down: *incipient omnes pro Cicerone loqui.*

"Life of Lucian," '96. S-S XVIII 73–74

f. [Taking a cue from Dr. Mayne,
Dryden says of Lucian's wit, or satire]
Lucian's manner of convincing, was certainly more pleasant than that of the Christian writers, and we know the effect was
full as powerful; so easily can the Eternal
Wisdom draw good out of evil, and make
his enemy subservient to the establishment
of his faith.

"Life of Lucian," '96. S-S XVIII 75

g. If we compare his [Lucian's] style
with the Greek historians, his contemporaries, or near his time, we shall find it
much more pure than that of Plutarch,
Dion, or Appian, though not so grave; because his subjects and theirs required to be
treated after a different manner.

"Life of Lucian," '96. S-S XVIII 75
WIT, o.

h. [¶] I know not whom Lucian imitated, unless it might be Aristophanes . . .
but he, who has best imitated him in Latin,
is Erasmus; and in French, Fontenelle, in
his "Dialogues of the Dead," which I never
read but with a new pleasure.

"Life of Lucian," '96. S-S XVIII 76.
SATIRE, p.   DIALOGUE (GENRE), d, e.
SPENCE. TRANSLATION, g. FONTENELLE, b.

Lucilius, Caius
LAST AGE, k.

[¶] Lucilius . . . made satires after the
manner of Ennius, but he gave them a more
graceful turn . . . [See SATIRE, gg]
Discourse of Satire, '93. K II 61
HORACE, l, f. CHAUCER, c.

Lucretius (Titus Lucretius Carus)
IMITATION, j.

a. [Lucretius] refined [Roman po-
etry] to that degree of perfection . . .
that he left an easy task to Virgil; who . . .
copied his excellencies; for the method of
the *Georgics* is plainly derived from him.

Lucretius had chosen a subject naturally crabbed; he therefore adorned it with poetical descriptions, and precepts of morality . . . which you see Virgil has imitated . . .

Pref. *Sylvæ, '*85. K I 259

b. If I am not mistaken, the distinguishing character of Lucretius (I mean of his soul and genius) is a certain kind of noble pride, and positive assertion of his opinions. . . . [See Hobbes, b]/All this, too, with so much scorn and indignation, as if he were assured of the triumph, before he entered into the lists. From this sublime and daring genius of his, it must of necessity come to pass, that his thoughts must be masculine, full of argumentation, and that sufficiently warm. From the same fiery temper proceeds the loftiness of his expressions, and the perpetual torrent of his verse, where the barrenness of his subject does not too much constrain the quickness of his fancy. For there is no doubt to be made, but that he could have been everywhere as poetical, as he is in his descriptions, and in the moral part of his philosophy, if he had

not aimed more to instruct . . . than to delight. . . . in short, he was so much an atheist, that he forgot sometimes to be a poet.

Pref. *Sylvæ, '*85. K I 259–60

Dryden, Works, qq.

c. [¶] But there are other arguments in this poem [*De rerum natura*] . . . not belonging to the mortality of the soul, which are strong enough to a reasonable man, to make him less in love with life, and consequently in less apprehensions of death. . . .[1] These . . . so pathetically urged, so beautifully expressed, so adorned with examples, and so admirably raised by the *prosopopœia* of Nature, who is brought in speaking to her children with so much authority and vigour, deserve the pains I have taken with them . . .

Pref. *Sylvæ, '*85. K I 261

Dryden, Works, ss. Obscenity, **b.** Creech, b. Ovid, a. Coinage, c.

Lydgate, John

Chaucer, c.

❧ **M** ❧

Madrigal

English vs. French, n.

Mæcenas, Caius Cilnius

Maecenas took another course [than Lucan], and we know he was more than a great man, for he was witty too: but finding himself far gone in Poetry, which Seneca assures us was not his talent, he thought it his best way to be well with Virgil and with Horace; that at least he might be a poet at the second hand; and we see how

happily it has succeeded with him; for his own bad poetry is forgotten, and their panegyrics of him still remain.

Pref. *All for Love, '*78. K I 198

Patronage, a.

Malherbe, François de

As for the pauses, Malherbe first brought them into France within this last century . . . [See Prosody, c]

Ded. *Æneis, '*97. K II 217

Manners

TRAGEDY, m.

a. The manners, or decency of the characters, in speaking or acting what is proper for them, and proper to be shown by the poet. [See TRAGEDY, r]

Heads of an Answer, '77. S-S XV 389

b. [¶] The manners flow from the characters, and consequently must partake of their advantages and disadvantages.

Heads of an Answer, '77. S-S XV 388

c. [¶] After the plot, which is the foundation of the play, the next thing to which we ought to apply our judgment, is the manners; for now the poet comes to work above ground. The groundwork, indeed, is that which is most necessary, as that upon which depends the firmness of the whole fabric; yet it strikes not the eye so much, as the beauties or imperfections of the manners, the thoughts, and the expressions.

Pref. *Troilus,* '79. K I 213

d. [¶] The manners, in a poem, are understood to be those inclinations, whether natural or acquired, which move and carry us to actions, good, bad, or indifferent, in a play; or which incline the persons to such or such actions.

Pref. *Troilus,* '79. K I 213

e. I have anticipated part of this discourse already, in declaring that a poet ought not to make the manners/perfectly good in his best persons; but neither are they to be more wicked in any of his characters than necessity requires. To produce a villain, without other reason than a natural inclination to villainy, is, in Poetry, to produce an effect without a cause; and to make him more a villain than he has just reason to be, is to make an effect which is stronger than the cause.

Pref. *Troilus,* '79. K I 213–14

f. [¶] The manners arise from many causes; and are either distinguished by complexion, as choleric and phlegmatic, or by the differences of age or sex, of climates, or quality of the persons, or their present condition. They are likewise to be gathered from the several virtues, vices, or passions, and many other commonplaces, which a poet must be supposed to have learned from natural Philosophy, Ethics, and History . . .

Pref. *Troilus,* '79. K I 214

g. [¶] But as the manners are useful in this art, they may be all comprised under these general heads: first, they must be apparent; that is . . . some inclinations of the person must appear . . . Secondly . . . suitable, or agreeing to the persons . . . The third property of manners is resemblance; and this is founded upon the particular characters of men, as we have them . . . by relation or history; that is, when a poet has the known character of this or that man before him, he is bound to represent him such, at least not contrary to that which fame has reported him to have been. . . ./[1] Yet this is a rock on which ignorant writers daily split . . .

The last property of manners is, that they be constant and equal . . .[1] All these properties Horace has hinted . . . 1. *Notandi sunt tibi mores;* 2. *Aut famam sequere;* 3. *Aut sibi convenientia finge;* 4. *Servetur ad imum, qualis ab incepto processerit, et sibi constet.*

Pref. *Troilus,* '79. K I 214–15

h. Most comedies made up of accidents/ or adventures are liable to fall into this error [obscure manners]; and tragedies with many turns are subject to it; for the manners can never be evident, where the surprises of fortune take up all the business of the stage; and where the poet is more in

155

pain to tell you what happened to such a man, than what he was.[1]

Pref. *Troilus,* '79. K I 216–17

SHAKESPEARE AND FLETCHER AND JONSON. FLETCHER, f.

i. [In the 'fittingness' of their manners] Sophocles and Euripides have more excelled among the Greeks than Æschylus; and Terence more than Plautus, among the Romans.[1]

Pref. *Troilus,* '79. K I 217

j. The present French poets are generally accused, that where/soever they lay the scene, or in whatsoever age, the manners of their heroes are wholly French. Racine's Bajazet is bred at Constantinople; but his civilities are conveyed to him, by some secret passage, from Versailles into the Seraglio.

Pref. *Troilus,* '79. K I 217–18

PASSIONS, c. EPIC HERO, h. FARCE, e.

k. [¶] *Let every member be made for its own head,* says our author [Du Fresnoy]; not a withered hand to a young face. So, in the persons of a play, whatsoever is said or done by any of them must be consistent with the manners which the poet has given them distinctly; and even the habits must be proper to the degrees and humours of the persons, as well as in a picture.[1]

Parallel, '95. K II 142

PRESENT AGE, p. EPIC HERO, j. EPIC vs. TRAGEDY, f. EPIC, d.

l. Both of them [Chaucer and Ovid] understood the manners; under which name I comprehend the passions, and, in a larger sense, the descriptions of persons, and their very habits.[1]

Pref. *Fables,* 1700. K II 255

Manum de Tabula [Cf. JUDGMENT]

Cf. FLETCHER, c. OVID, h.

a. [¶] We have the proverb, *manum de tabula,* from the painters; which signifies, to know when to give over, and to lay by the pencil. Both Homer and Virgil practised this precept wonderfully well, but Virgil the better of the two . . .[1]

Parallel, '95. K II 151

DRYDEN, WORKS, gg. EXPRESSION, c.

b. Apelles said of Protogenes,—that he knew not when to give over. A work may be over-wrought, as well as under-wrought; too much labour often takes away the spirit by adding to the polishing, so that there remains nothing but a dull correctness, a piece without any considerable faults, but with few beauties; for when the spirits are drawn off, there is nothing but a *caput mortuum.*[1]

Parallel, '95. K II 152

Cf. CHAUCER, c, g.

Marino, Giovanni Battista

IMAGINATION, e.

Martial (Marcus Valerius Martialis)

WALSH, c. EPIC, j.

. . . if Virgil and Martial stood for Parliament-men, we know already who would carry it . . . [See CRITIC(s), a]

Ded. *Æneis,* '97. K II 223

CHAUCER AND OVID. Cf. POET, e.

Marvell, Andrew

SATIRE, ll.

Mascardi, Agostino

SATIRE, c. TRAGICOMEDY, f.

Masque

CORNEILLE (PIERRE), a-2.

Materia Poetica

POET, h.

The *materia/poetica* is as common to all writers as the *materia medica* to all physicians. [See FABLE, f]

Pref. *Don Sebastian,* '90. S-S VII 312–13

INVENTION, d.

Meanness [See also EXPRESSION; STYLE]
LAST AGE, c. TRAGEDY, s. JONSON, v.
SATIRE, f. VIRGIL, n. TRANSLATION, gg.

Medea (the Tragedy)
OVID, c.

Memory
Cf. FANCY, a. PLAY WRITING. WIT, d.
PLUTARCH, b. EPIC POET, a.

Menander
(Crites) . . . questionless we are de-
prived of a great stock of wit in the loss of
Menander . . . we may guess at Menan-
der's excellency by the plays of Terence,
who translated some of his; and yet wanted
so much of him, that he was called by
C. Cæsar the half-Menander . . .
Dram. Poesy, '65. K I 42
ANCIENTS, a. PROGRESS, f.

Milbourne, Luke
DRYDEN, LITERARY LIFE, o-2.

M—, who is/in orders, pretends,
amongst the rest, this quarrel to me, that I
have fallen foul on priesthood: if I have, I
am only to ask pardon of good priests, and
am afraid his part of the reparation will
come to little. Let him be satisfied, that he
shall not be able to force himself upon me
for an adversary. I contemn him too much
to enter into competition with him. His
own translations of Virgil have answered
his criticisms on mine. If (as they say, he
has declared in print) he prefers the version of Ogilby to mine, the world has made
him the same compliment; for 'tis agreed
on all hands, that he writes even below
Ogilby. That, you will say, is not easily to
be done; but what cannot M— bring about?
I am satisfied, however, that, while he and
I live together, I shall not be thought the
worst poet of the age.
Pref. *Fables,* 1700. K II 270–71
CRITICASTERS, k.

Milton, John
a. What I have borrowed [from *Paradise Lost* in *The State of Innocence*] will
be so easily discerned from my mean productions, that I shall/not need to point the
reader to the places: and truly I should be
sorry, for my own sake, that any one should
take the pains to compare them together;
the original being undoubtedly one of the
greatest, most noble, and most sublime
poems which either this age or nation has
produced.
Author's Apology, '77. K I 178–79
POETIC LICENSE, f.

b. Milton's *Paradise Lost* is admirable;
but am I therefore bound to maintain, that
there are no flats amongst his elevations,
when 'tis evident he creeps along sometimes for above an hundred lines together?
Cannot I admire the height of his invention, and the strength of his expression,
without defending his antiquated words,
and the perpetual harshness of their sound?
It is as much commendation as a man can
bear, to own him excellent; all beyond it is
idolatry.
Pref. *Sylvæ,* '85. K I 268
DRYDEN, WORKS, bbb. SPENSER, b.

c. [¶] As for Mr. Milton, whom we
all admire with so much justice, his subject
is not that of an Heroic Poem, properly so
called. His design is the losing of our happiness; his event is not prosperous, like that
of all other epic works; his heavenly machines are many, and his human persons
are but two. But I will not take Mr. Rymer's work out of his hands. He has prom-
ised the world a critique on that author;
wherein, though he will not allow his poem
for heroic, I hope he will grant us, that his
thoughts are elevated, his words sounding,
and that no man has so happily copied the

manner of Homer, or so copiously translated his Grecisms, and the Latin elegancies of Virgil. 'Tis true, he runs into a flat of thought, sometimes for a hundred lines together, but it is when he is got into a track of Scripture. His antiquated words were his choice, not his necessity; for therein he imitated Spenser, as Spenser did Chaucer. . . . Neither will I justify Milton for his blank verse, though I may excuse him, by the example of Hannibal Caro, and other Italians, who have used it; for whatever causes/he alleges for the abolishing of rhyme . . . his own particular reason is plainly this, that rhyme was not his talent . . . which is manifest in his *Juvenilia* . . . at an age when the soul is most pliant, and the passion of love makes almost every man a rhymer, though not a poet.

Discourse of Satire, '93. K II 29–30

ARCHAISMS, b. DRYDEN, LITERARY LIFE, b. EPIC POET, c. EPIC MACHINES, c. VIRGIL, ll.

d. Milton was the poetical son of Spenser, and Mr. Waller of Fairfax; for we have our lineal descents and clans as well as other families. Spenser more than once insinuates, that the soul of Chaucer was transfused into his body; and that he was begotten by him two hundred years after his decease. Milton has acknowledged to me, that Spenser was his original; and many besides myself have heard our famous Waller own, that he derived the harmony of his numbers from *Godfrey of Bulloign,* which was turned into English by Mr. Fairfax.

Pref. *Fables,* 1700. K II 247

Modernizing

CHAUCER, g.

[¶] But there are other judges, who

think I ought not to have translated Chaucer into English, out of a quite contrary notion: they suppose there is a certain veneration due to his old language; and that it is little less than profanation and sacrilege to alter it. They are farther of opinion, that somewhat of his good sense will suffer in this transfusion, and much of the beauty of his thoughts will infallibly be lost, which appear with more grace in their old habit. . . .[1] If the first end of a writer be to be understood, then, as his language grows obsolete, his thoughts must grow obscure—

Multa renascentur, quæ nunc cecidere . . .

When an ancient word for its sound and significancy deserves to be revived, I have that reasonable venera/tion for antiquity to restore it. All beyond this is superstition. Words are not like landmarks, so sacred as never to be removed; customs are changed, and even statutes are silently repealed, when the reason ceases for which they were enacted. As for the other part of the argument, that his thoughts will lose of their original beauty by the innovation of words; in the first place, not only their beauty, but their being is lost, where they are no longer understood, which is the present case. I grant that something must be lost in all transfusion, that is, in all translations; but the sense will remain, which would otherwise be lost, or at least be maimed, when it is scarce intelligible, and that to but a few. How few are there who can read Chaucer, so as to understand him perfectly? And if imperfectly, then with less profit, and no pleasure. 'Tis not for the use of some old Saxon friends, that I have taken these pains with him: let them neglect my version, because they have no need of it. I made it for their sakes who understand sense and poetry as well as they, when that poetry and sense is put into words which they understand. I will go farther, and dare to add, that what beauties I lose in some places, I give to others which had them not originally . . . Yet I think I have just occasion to complain of them, who because they understand Chaucer, would deprive the greater part of their countrymen of the same advantage, and hoard him up . . . In sum, I seriously protest, that no man ever had, or can have, a greater veneration for Chaucer than myself. I have translated some parts of his works, only that I might perpetuate his memory, or at least refresh it, amongst my countrymen./If I have altered him anywhere for the better, I must at the same time acknowledge, that I could have done nothing without him. *Facile est inventis addere* is no great commendation; and I am not so vain as to think I have deserved a greater.

Pref. *Fables*, 1700. K II 266–68

Moderns [See also ANCIENTS]

PRESENT AGE, a.

a. (Eugenius) . . . I cannot think so contemptibly of the age I live in, or so dishonourably of my own country, as not to judge we equal the Ancients in most kinds of poesy, and in some surpass them . . .

Dram. Poesy, '65. K I 33

ANCIENTS, k.

b. (Crites) [¶] If by these rules . . . we should judge our modern plays, 'tis probable that few of them would endure the trial: that which should be the business of a day, takes up in some of them an age; instead of one action, they are the epitomes of a man's life; and for one spot of ground (which the stage should represent) we are

sometimes in more countries than the map can show us.

Dram. Poesy, '65. K I 41

c. (Eugenius) . . . we own all the helps we have from them, and want neither veneration nor gratitude . . . but to these assistances we have joined our own industry; for, had we sat down with a dull imitation of them, we might then have lost somewhat of the old perfection, but never acquired any that was new. We draw not therefore/after their lines, but those of Nature; and having the life before us, besides the experience of all they knew, it is no wonder if we hit some airs and features which they have missed.

Dram. Poesy, '65. K I 43–44

d. (Crites) . . . [Eugenius] maintains the Moderns have acquired a new perfection in writing; I can only grant they have altered the mode of it.

Dram. Poesy, '65. K I 55

ANCIENTS, q.

e. (Narrator: Dryden) This moderation of Crites, as it was pleasing to all the company, so it put an end to that dispute; which Eugenius, who seemed to have the better of the argument, would urge no farther . . .

Dram. Poesy, '65. K I 55

ANCIENTS, d, a.

f. [¶] But suppose that Homer and Virgil were the only of their species, and that Nature was so much worn out in producing them, that she is never able to bear the like again, yet the example only holds in Heroic Poetry: in Tragedy and Satire, I offer myself to maintain against some of our modern critics, that this age and the last, particularly in England, have excelled the ancients in both those kinds; and I would instance in Shakespeare of the for-

159

mer, in your Lordship [Dorset] of the latter sort.

Discourse of Satire, '93. K II 26

BOILEAU, b. EPIC, CHRISTIAN, a. HORACE AND JUVENAL AND PERSIUS, k. ENGLISH DRAMA, i. DENNIS. RULES, g. FONTENELLE, b.

Molière (Jean Baptiste Poquelin)

a. (Neander) [¶] But of late years Molière, the younger Corneille, Quinault, and some others, have been imitating afar/off the quick turns and graces of the English stage.

Dram. Poesy, '65. K I 68–69

b. (Neander) . . . Molière has lately given them [the French] plays out of verse, which have not displeased them . . .

Dram. Poesy, '65. K I 88

c. . . . Plautus and Molière . . . the two greatest names of ancient and modern comedy . . .

Ded. *Amphitryon,* '90. S-S VIII 9

Monosyllables [See also PROSODY]

ACADEMY, b. LATIN, b. ENGLISH LANGUAGE, a.

Montague, Charles (afterwards Earl of Halifax)

DRYDEN, WORKS, yyy.

Montaigne, Michel Eyquem de

a. I have always been pleased to see him [Plutarch], and his imitator, Montaigne, when they strike a little out of the common road; for we are sure to be the better for their wandering.

"Life of Plutarch," '83. S-S XVII 64

b. And herein, even Montaigne himself is scarcely to be defended; for no man more esteemed Plutarch, no man was better acquainted with his excellencies; yet, this notwithstanding, he has done too great an honour to Seneca, by ranking him with our philosopher and historian; him, I say, who

was so much less a philosopher, and no historian.

"Life of Plutarch," '83. S-S XVII 72

ROME. PREFACES, d.

Moral (of a Literary Work)

POET, i.

[¶] The first rule which Bossu prescribes to the writer of an Heroic Poem, and which holds too by the same reason in all Dramatic Poetry, is to make the moral of the work . . . 'Tis the moral that directs the whole action of the play to one centre; and that action or fable is the example built upon the moral, which confirms the truth of it to our experience: when the fable is designed, then, and not before, the persons are to be introduced, with their manners, characters, and passions.

Pref. *Troilus,* '79. K I 213

SATIRE, c, d.

Moral Philosophy

PASSIONS, d. PLUTARCH, c. HISTORY, f.

Moral philosophy is divided into two parts, ethics and politics; the first instructs us in our private offices of virtue, the second in those which relate to the management of the commonwealth. Both of these teach by argumentation and reasoning, which rush as it were into the mind, and possess it with violence; but history rather allures than forces us to virtue.

"Life of Plutarch," '83. S-S XVII 61

SHAKESPEARE, h. EPIC POET, a. PERSIUS, i. HORRACE AND JUVENAL AND PERSIUS, c.

Moral Truth (in Poetry)

. . . moral truth is the mistress of the poet as much as of the philosopher . . . [See ETHICAL FUNCTION, a]

Defence of An Essay, '68. K I 121

Mulgrave (John Sheffield, Third Earl of)

a. . . . the *Essay on Poetry,* which I publicly valued before I knew the author of it . . . [See Obscenity, b]

Pref. *Sylvæ*, '85. K I 263

Chapman, b. Epic Hero, h.

b. I submit my opinion [of the superiority of the epic] to your [Mulgrave's] judgment, who are better qualified than any man I know, to decide this controversy. . . . Your *Essay of Poetry,* which was published without a name . . . I read over and over with much delight, and as much instruction . . . I gave the unknown author his due commendation, I must confess; but/who can answer for me and for the rest of the poets who heard me read the poem, whether we should not have been better pleased to have seen our own names at the bottom of the title-page? . . . But great excellencies will work their way through all sorts of opposition. I applauded rather out of decency than affection; and was ambitious, as some yet can witness, to be acquainted with a man with whom I had the honour to converse, and that almost daily, for so many years together. . . . You extorted a praise, which I should willingly have given, had I known you. Nothing had

been more easy than to commend a patron of long standing. The world would join with me, if the encomiums were just; and, if unjust, would excuse a grateful flatterer.

Ded. *Æneis,* '97. K II 162–63

c. . . . your Lordship, whose thoughts are always just; your numbers harmonious, your words chosen, your expressions strong and manly, your verse flowing, and your turns as happy as they are easy. . . . In the mean time, that little you have written is owned, and that particularly by the poets (who are a nation not over lavish of praise to their contemporaries), as a principal ornament of our language . . .

Ded. *Æneis,* '97. K II 178

Prosody, d. Translation, gg.

Music [See also Opera; Purcell]

Fancy, e. Italian Language and Literature, b.

Theatrical

Tragicomedy, b.

Church

Cf. Speeches (Dramatic), a. Ends of Poetry, k. ["our solemn music, which is inarticulate poesy . . ."]

❦ N ❦

Narrations (Dramatic)

a. (Eugenus) [Dorias's narration at the beginning of the fourth act of Terence's *Eunuch*] was very inartificial, because she was presumed to speak directly to the audience, and to acquaint them with what was necessary to be known, but yet should have been so contrived by the poet as to have been told by persons of the drama to

one another, and so by them to have come to the knowledge of the people . . .

Dram. Poesy, '65. K I 49

English vs. French, o, p.

b. (Lisideius) They therefore who imagine these relations [of action off stage] would make no concernment in the audience, are deceived, by confounding them with the other, which are of things antecedent to the play: those are made often in cold blood, as I may say . . . but these are warmed with our concernments, which were before awakened in the play. What the philosophers say of motion, that, when it is once begun, it continues of itself, and will do so to eternity, without some stop put to it, is clearly true on this occasion: the soul, being already moved with the characters and fortunes of those/imaginary persons, continues going of its own accord; and we are no more weary to hear what becomes of them when they are not on the stage, than we are to listen to the news of an absent mistress.

Dram. Poesy, '65. K I 63–64

c. (Lisideius) . . . some parts of the action are more fit to be represented, some to be related. Corneille says judiciously, that the poet is not obliged to expose to view all particular actions which conduce to the principal: he ought to select such of them to be seen, which will appear with the greatest beauty . . . and let the rest arrive . . . by narration.

Dram. Poesy, '65. K I 64

Decorum, c, d.

d. (Neander) To conclude on this subject of relations; if we are to be blamed for showing too much of the action, the French are as faulty for discovering too little of it: a mean betwixt both should be observed by every judicious writer, so as the audience may neither be left unsatisfied by not seeing what is beautiful, or shocked by beholding what is either incredible or undecent.

Dram. Poesy, '65. K I 75

Nature

Constancy

Age, Genius of, c. Poetry, c.

a. For Nature is still the same in all ages, and can never be contrary to herself.

Parallel, '95. K II 134

b. . . . for mankind is ever the same, and nothing lost out of Nature, though everything is altered.

Pref. *Fables,* 1700. K II 263

Depressed

Burlesque, a.

Distinguished from Learning

Shakespeare, b. Spenser, c.

Exhaustion [Cf. Decay]

Cf. Golden Ages, a. Moderns, f.

Faults

Imitation, h.

Idealized

Burlesque, a. Character[s], c. Imitation, h.

Imitation of

Ancients, k. Moderns, c. Tragedy, n.

c. Thus I grant you, that the knowledge of Nature was the original rule; and that all poets ought to study her, as well as Aristotle and Horace, her interpreters. But then this also undeniably/follows, that those things, which delight all ages, must have been an imitation of Nature . . . Therefore is Rhetoric made an art . . .

Author's Apology, '77. K I 183–84

Seneca, b. Rules, g. Imitation, i, h. See below, f. Chaucer, c.

Improvement

Good Sense.

as *Norm*

Passions, a. Burlesque, a. Rhyme (Debate), g. Imitation, j. Hero (Dramatic), d. Heightening, d. Ariosto, a. Epic, d. Chaucer, c.

Scientific Revelation of

Progress, a.

Source of Art

d. . . . Nature; a thing so almost infinite and boundless, as can never fully be comprehended, but where the images of all things are always present.

Ded. *Rival Ladies,* '64. K I 3

e. (Crites) . . . you have debauched the true old poetry so far, that Nature, which is the soul of it, is not in any of your writings.

Dram. Poesy, '65. K I 33

SHAKESPEARE, b.

FLETCHER, e. Cf. POET, o. Cf. OPERA, e. HORACE AND JUVENAL AND PERSIUS, c. Cf. RULES, j. OTWAY. OVID AND VIRGIL, b. Cf. INVENTION, c.

Source of Pleasure

FARCE, f. IMITATION, h. INVENTION, d.

f. Nothing but Nature can give a sincere pleasure; where that is not imitated, 'tis grotesque painting; the fine woman ends in a fish's tail.

Ded. *Æneis,* '97. K II 161

Unaided

RHYME (DEBATE), o.

Unequal to Art

WIT, e.

Necessity

He may be allowed sometimes to err, who undertakes to move so many characters and humours, as are requisite in a play, in those narrow channels which are proper to each of them; to conduct his imaginary persons through so many various intrigues and chances, as the labouring audience shall think them lost under every billow; and then at length to work them so naturally out of their distresses, that when the whole plot is laid open, the spectators may rest satisfied that every cause was powerful enough to produce the effect it had; and that the whole chain of them was with such due order linked together, that the first accident would naturally beget the second, till they all rendered the conclusion necessary.

Ded. *Rival Ladies,* '64. K I 2

LIAISON, b. FABLE, d. Cf. UNITIES (DRAMATIC), ACTION, d.

Nero (the Emperor)

ST. ÉVREMOND, b. HORACE AND JUVENAL AND PERSIUS, a, g.

Berecynthian Atys; or *Attin,* &c. Foolish verses of *Nero,* which the Poet [Persius, *First Satire,* line 185 in the translation] repeats; and which cannot be Translated properly into *English . . . Their crooked Horns,* &c. Other verses of *Nero* [line 198 of the translation], that were meer bombast.

Notes to the First Satire [Persius], '93. JK II 751

Nonsense

DRYDEN, LITERARY LIFE, e-2. Cf. SETTLE, b. POETIC LICENSE, b. ACADEMY, b. PATRONAGE, b. CHAPMAN, a.

North's *Plutarch*

. . . as that translation was only from the French, so it suffered this double disadvantage; first, that it was but a copy of a copy, and that too but lamely taken from the Greek original; secondly, that the/ English language was then unpolished, and far from the perfection which it has since attained; so that the first version is not only ungrammatical and ungraceful, but in many places almost unintelligible. . . . oppressed under the rubbish of antiquated words . . .

Ded. *Plutarch's Lives,* '83. S-S XVII 6–7

Numbers [See PROSODY]

❧ O ❧

Obscenity

a. . . . broad obscenities in words ought in good manners to be avoided . . . [See DECORUM, g]

Pref. *All for Love,* '78. K I 193
DRYDEN, WORKS, y. OVID, f. PLUTARCH, g. DRYDEN, WORKS, ss.

b. [In a passage considering Lucretius on the nature of love] 'Tis most certain, that barefaced bawdry is the poorest pretence to wit imaginable. If I should say otherwise, I should have two great authorities against me: the one is the *Essay on Poetry,* which I publicly valued before I knew the author of it [Mulgrave] . . . the other is no less than our admired Cowley . . . in his *Ode concerning Wit* . . .º But . . . I am only the translator, not the inventor; so that the heaviest part of the censure falls upon Lucretius, before it reaches me: in the next place, neither he nor I have used the grossest words, but the cleanliest metaphors we could find, to palliate the broadness of the meaning . . .

Pref. *Sylvæ,* '85. K I 263
DORSET, d. PERSIUS, d, e.

c. . . . as all stories are not proper subjects for an epic poem or a tragedy, so neither are they for a noble picture. The subjects both of the one and of the other ought to have nothing of immoral, low, or filthy in them . . . Only I must add, that though Catullus, Ovid, and others, were of another opinion,—that the subject of poets, and even their thoughts and expressions, might

be loose, provided their lives were chaste and holy, yet there are no such licences permitted in that art, any more than, in painting, to design and colour obscene nudities. *Vita proba est,* is no excuse; for it will scarcely be admitted, that either a poet or a painter can be chaste, who give us the contrary examples in their writings and their pictures. We see nothing of this kind in Virgil; that which comes the nearest to it is the adventure of the cave, where Dido and Æneas were driven by the storm; yet even there the poet pretends a marriage before the consummation . . . Neither is there any expression in that story, which a Roman matron might not read without a blush. Besides, the poet passes it over as hastily as he can . . . The altar-pieces and holy decorations of Painting shew *that* art may be applied to better uses, as well as Poetry . . .

Parallel, '95. K II 129
Cf. LUCIAN, c. Cf. THOMAS, b. DRYDEN, PERSONAL CHARACTER, e.

d. The King's Proclamation against vice and profaneness is issued out of print: but a deep disease is not to be cur'd with a slight Medicine. The parsons who must read it, will find as little effect from it, as from their dull Sermons: tis a Scare-Crow, wᶜʰ will not fright many birds from preying on the fields & orchards.

Letter to Mrs. Steward, 14 December 1699. Ward, No. 71, p. 131

e. In general I will only say, that I have

written nothing which savours of immorality or profaneness; at least, I am not conscious to myself of any such intention. If there happen to be found an irreverent expression, or a thought too wanton, they are crept into my verses through my inadvertency: if the searchers find any in the cargo, let them be staved or forfeited, like counterbanded goods; at least, let their authors be answerable for them, as being but imported merchandise, and not of my own manufacture. On the other side, I have endeavoured to choose such fables, both ancient and modern, as contain in each of them some instructive moral . . . I wish I could affirm with a safe conscience, that I had taken the same care in all my former writ/ings; for it must be owned, that supposing verses are never so beautiful or pleasing, yet, if they contain anything which shocks religion or good manners, they are at best what Horace says of good numbers without good sense, *Versus inopes rerum nugæque canoræ.* Thus far, I hope, I am right in court, without renouncing to my other right of self-defence, where I have been wrongfully accused, and my sense wire-drawn into blasphemy or bawdry, as it has often been by a religious lawyer, in a late pleading against the stage; in which he mixes truth with falsehood, and has not forgotten the old rule of calumniating strongly, that something may remain.

Pref. *Fables,* 1700. K II 250–51

f. I translated Chaucer . . . and, amongst the rest, pitched on the Wife of Bath's Tale; not daring, as I have said, to adventure on her *Prologue,* because 'tis too licentious.

Pref. *Fables,* 1700. K II 269

COLLIER.

Observation

. . . the characters and representations of folly are only the effects of observation; and observation is an effect of judgment. [See JUDGMENT, c]

Pref. *Evening's Love,* '71. K I 138

FABLE, c. FANCY, d, i.

Ogilby, John

What English readers, unacquainted with Greek or Latin, will believe me, or any other man, when we commend those authors, and confess we derive all that is pardonable in us from their fountains, if they take those [Homer and Virgil] to be the same poets whom our Oglebys have translated?

Pref. *Sylvæ,* '85. K I 253

DRYDEN, WORKS, oo. MILBOURNE.

Opera

HEROIC PLAY, b. WIT, m.

a. An opera is a poetical tale, or fiction, represented by vocal and instrumental music, adorned with scenes, machines, and dancing. The supposed persons of this musical drama are generally supernatural, as gods, and goddesses, and heroes . . . The subject, therefore, being extended beyond the limits of human nature, admits of that sort of marvellous and surprising conduct, which is rejected in other plays. Human impossibilities are to be received as they are in faith; because, where gods are introduced, a supreme power is to be understood, and second causes are out of doors.

Pref. *Albion and Albanius,* '85. K I 270

b. . . . the nature of an opera denies the frequent use of . . . poetical ornaments; for vocal music, though it often admits a loftiness of sound, yet always exacts an harmonious sweetness; or, to distinguish yet more justly, the recitative part of the opera requires a more masculine beauty of expression and sound; the other, which, for want of a proper English word, I must call the *songish part,* must abound in the softness and variety of numbers; its principal intention being to please hearing rather than to gratify the understanding.

Pref. *Albion and Albanius,* '85. K I 271
AUTHORITY, e.

c. . . . whosoever undertakes the writing of an opera (which is a modern invention, though built indeed on the foundation of ethnic worship), is obliged to imitate the design of the Italians, who have not yet invented, but brought to perfection, this sort of dramatic musical entertainment. I have not been able, by any search, to get any light, either of the time when it began, or of the first author. But I have probable reasons, which induce me to believe, that some Italians, having curiously observed the gallantries of the Spanish Moors, at their *zambras,* or royal feasts . . . may possibly have refined upon those Moresque divertisements, and produced this delightful entertainment . . . But however it began . . . we know that, for some centuries, the knowledge of Music has flourished principally in Italy, the mother of learning and of arts . . .

Pref. *Albion and Albanius,* '85. K I 272

d. I said in the beginning of this preface, that the persons represented in operas are generally gods, goddesses, and heroes descended from them, who are supposed to be their peculiar care; which hinders not, but that meaner persons may sometimes gracefully be introduced, especially if they have relation to those first times, which poets call the Golden Age; wherein, by reason of their innocence, those happy mortals were supposed to have had a more familiar

intercourse with superior beings; and therefore shepherds might reasonably be admitted, as of all callings the most innocent, the most happy, and who, by reason of the spare time they had, in their almost idle employment, had most leisure to make verses, and to be in love; without somewhat of which passion, no opera can possibly subsist.

Pref. *Albion and Albanius,* '85. K I 273

e. [Let the would-be critics of opera] first be assured that their ears are nice; for there is neither writing nor judgment on this subject without that good quality. 'Tis no easy matter, in our language, to make words so smooth, and numbers so harmonious, that they shall almost set themselves. And yet there are rules for this in Nature, and as great a certainty of quantity in our syllables, as either in the Greek or Latin: but let poets and judges understand those first, and then let them begin to study English. When they have chawed a while upon these preliminaries, it may be they will scarce adventure to tax me with want of thought and elevation of fancy in this work; for they will soon be satisfied, that those are not of the nature of this sort of writing. The necessity of double rhymes, and ordering of the words and numbers for the sweetness of the voice, are the main hinges on which an opera must move . . .

Pref. *Albion and Albanius,* '85. K I 277

f. [¶] The same reasons which depress thought in an opera have a stronger effect upon the words, especially in our language; for there is no maintaining the purity of English in short measures, where the rhyme returns so quick, and is so often female, or double rhyme, which is not natural to our tongue, because it consists too much of monosyllables, and those, too, most commonly clogged with consonants; for which reason I am often forced to coin new words, revive some that are antiquated, and botch others . . .

Pref. *Albion and Albanius,* '85. K I 278 Dryden, Works, ww.

g. The English, I confess, are not altogether so musical as the French; and yet they have been pleased already with *the Tempest,* and some pieces that followed, which were neither much better written nor so well composed as this.

Pref. *Albion and Albanius,* '85. K I 279

h. I see no opinion that I would retract or alter [in the Preface to *Albion and Albanius*], unless it be, that possibly the Italians went not so far as Spain for the invention of their operas. They might have it in their own country; and that by gathering up the shipwrecks of the Athenian and Roman theatres, which we know were adorned with scenes, music, dances, and machines, especially the Grecian. But of this the learned Monsieur Vossius . . . is the best, and perhaps the only judge now living.

Postscript *Albion and Albanius,* '85. K I 280

i. But the numbers of poetry and vocal music are sometimes so contrary, that, in many places, I have been obliged to cramp my verses, and make them rugged to the reader, that they may be harmonious to the hearer; of which I have no reason to repent me, because these sorts of entertainments [opera] are principally designed for/the ear and eye; and therefore, in reason, my art, on this occasion, ought to be subservient to his. And, besides, I flatter myself with an imagination, that a judicious audience will easily distinguish betwixt the songs wherein I have complied with him, and those in which I have fol-

lowed the rules of poetry, in the sound and cadence of the words.

Ded. *King Arthur,* '91. S-S VIII, 135–36

Opinion

Cf. Authority, c.

For stiffness of opinion is the effect of pride, and not of philosophy; it is a miserable presumption of that knowledge which human nature is too narrow to/contain; and the ruggedness of a stoic is only a silly affectation of being a god . . . True philosophy is certainly of a more pliant nature, and more accommodated to human use; *Homo sum, humani à me nihil alienum puto.*

Ded. *Don Sebastian,* '90. S-S VII 302–03 Cf. Lucian, a.

Ordonnance [Cf. Design]

[¶] To avoid absurdities and incongruities, is the same law established for both arts. The painter is not to paint a cloud at the bottom of a picture, but in the uppermost parts; nor the poet to place what is proper to the end or middle, in the beginning of a poem. . . . but there are few poets or painters who can be supposed to sin so grossly against the laws of nature and of art. I remember only one play . . . *The Slighted Maid,* where there is nothing in the first act but what might have been said or done in the fifth; nor anything in the midst, which might not have been placed as well in the beginning, or the end.

Parallel, '95. K II 145

Orinda, The Matchless (Katherine Philips)

Thomas, a.

Ornament[s]

Comedy, e. Plagiarism, b. Cf. Translation, u, q. Plutarch, g. Opera, b. Epic vs. Tragedy, d. Decorum, i. Tragicomedy, g. Translation, dd. Cf. Statius, c. English vs. French, n.

TURNS, a. Cf. PROSODY, s. BORROWING, c. DRYDEN, WORKS, 000. EPIC MACHINES, e.

Orrery (Roger Boyle, First Earl of)

. . . the kindness your Lordship has continually shown to all my writings. You have been pleased, my Lord, they should sometimes cross the Irish seas, to kiss your hands . . . Your favour has shone upon me at a remote distance, without the least knowledge of my person . . . [D]id I not consider you as my patron, I have little reason to desire you for my judge . . ./For who could so severely judge of faults as he, who has given testimony he commits none? Your excellent poems having afforded that knowledge of it to the world, that your enemies are ready to upbraid you with it, as a crime for a man of business to write so well.

Ded. *Rival Ladies,* '64. K I 2–3

COURT, a.

b. Thus in *Mustapha,* the play should naturally have ended with the death of Zanger, and not have given us the grace-cup after dinner, of Solyman's divorce from Roxolana.

Pref. *Troilus,* '79. K I 209

Otway, Thomas

PROSODY, y.

Mr. Otway possessed this part [ability to paint the passions] as thoroughly as any of the Ancients or Moderns. I will not defend everything in his *Venice Preserved;* but I must bear this testimony to his memory, that the passions are truly touched in it, though perhaps there is somewhat to be desired, both in the grounds of them, and in the height and elegance of expression; but nature is there, which is the greatest beauty.

Parallel, '95. K II 145

Ovid (Publius Ovidius Naso) [See also CHAUCER AND OVID; OVID AND VIRGIL]

a. [Ovid] is certainly more palatable to the reader, than any of the Roman wits; though some of them are more lofty, some more instructive, and others more correct. He had learning enough to make him equal to the best; but, as his verse came easily, he wanted the toil of application to amend it. He is often luxuriant both in his fancy and expressions, and, as it has lately been observed, not always natural. If wit be pleasantry, he has it to excess; but if it be propriety, Lucretius, Horace, and, above all, Virgil, are his superiors.

Examen Poeticum, '93. K II 9

a-2. . . . besides many of the learned, Ovid has almost all the *Beaux,* and the whole Fair Sex, his declared patrons.

Pref. *Fables,* 1700. K II 248

Art of Love

See below, d.

Dramatic Genius

b. (Eugenius) . . . yet he of them [the Ancients] who had a genius most proper for the stage, was Ovid; he had a way of writing so fit to stir up a pleasing admiration and concernment, which are the objects of tragedy, and to show the various movements of a soul combating betwixt two different passions . . .

Dram. Poesy, '65. K I 53

c. (*Eugenius*) . . . I am confident the *Medea* is none of his: for, though I esteem it for the gravity and sententiousness of it, which he himself concludes to be suitable to a tragedy . . . yet it moves not my soul enough to judge that he, who in the epic way wrote things so near the drama . . . should stir up no more concernment where he most endeavoured it.

Dram. Poesy, '65. K I 53

Dryden's Taste for
DRYDEN, WORKS, ccc.
Elegies

d. 'Tis true, they are not to be excused in the severity of manners, as being able to corrupt a larger Empire, if there were any, than that of Rome; yet this may be said in behalf of Ovid, that no man has ever treated the passion of love with so much delicacy of/thought, and of expression, or searched into the nature of it more philosophically than he.
Pref. *Ovid's Epistles,* '80. K I 230–31

e. In the most material part, which is the conduct, 'tis certain, that he [Ovid] seldom has miscarried; for if/his *Elegies* be compared with those of Tibullus and Propertius . . . it will be found that those poets seldom designed before they writ; and though the language of Tibullus be more polished, and the learning of Propertius, especially in his Fourth Book, more set out to ostentation; yet their common practice was to look no further before them than the next line . . . But our Poet has always the goal in his eye . . .
Pref. *Ovid's Epistles,* '80. K I 234–35
Epistles
PROPERTIUS.

f. . . . they [Ovid's *Epistles*] are generally granted to be the most perfect pieces of Ovid, and . . . the style of them . . . tenderly passionate and courtly . . . Yet where the characters were lower, as in Œnone and Hero, he has kept close to Nature, in drawing his images after a country life, though perhaps he has Romanized his Grecian dames too much . . . There seems to be no great variety in the particular subjects which he has chosen; most of the *Epistles* being written from ladies, who were forsaken by their lovers . . . but of

the general character of women, which is modesty, he has taken a most becoming care; for his amorous expressions go no further than virtue may allow, and therefore may be read, as he intended them, by matrons without a blush.
Pref. *Ovid's Epistles,* '80. K I 236
Excess

g. (Crites) . . . you find Ovid saying too much on every subject. *Nescivit* (says Seneca) *quod bene cessit relinquere* . . .
Dram. Poesy, '65. K I 93
WIT, h.

h. Yet, not to speak too partially in his [Ovid's] behalf, I will confess, that the copiousness of his wit was such, that he often writ/too pointedly for his subject, and made his persons speak more eloquently than the violence of their passion would admit: so that he is frequently witty out of season; leaving the imitation of Nature, and the cooler dictates of his judgment, for the false applause of Fancy. . . . Seneca's censure will stand good against him; *Nescivit quod bene cessit relinquere:* he never knew how to give over, when he had done well . . . This, then, is the allay of Ovid's writings, which is sufficiently recompensed by his other excellences: nay, this very fault is not without its beauties; for the most severe censor cannot but be pleased with the prodigality of his wit, though at the same time he could have wished that the master of it had been a better manager. Every thing which he does becomes him, and if sometimes he appears too gay, yet there is a secret gracefulness of youth which accompanies his writings . . .
Pref. *Ovid's Epistles,* '80. K I 233–34
TRANSLATION, r. DRYDEN, WORKS, pp. See above, a.

on *Morality in Poetry*
Obscenity, c.
Passions

i. [¶] If the imitation of Nature be the business of a poet, I know no author, who can justly be compared with ours [Ovid], especially in the description of the passions. . . . His thoughts, which are the pictures and results of those passions, are generally such as naturally arise from those disorderly motions of our spirits.

Pref. *Ovid's Epistles,* '80. K I 233
Pindar Contrasted
Translation, i.
Satire
Satire, kk.
Style

j. That he frequented the court of Augustus, and was well received in it, is most undoubted: all his poems bear the character of a court, and appear to be written, as the French call it, *cavalièrement* . . .

Pref. *Ovid's Epistles,* '80. K I 233
See below, k.
Theocritus Compared
Theocritus, a.
Tibullus Compared
Sedley, a.
Turns
Dryden, Literary Life, b. Turns, a, b.
Versification

k. On the contrary [to Virgil], Ovid and Claudian, though they write in styles differing . . . yet have each of them but one sort of music in their verses. . . . Ovid, with all his sweetness, has as little variety of numbers and sound as he [Claudian]: he is always, as it were, upon the hand-gallop, and his verse runs upon carpet-ground. He avoids, like the other, all synaloephas, or cutting off one vowel when it comes before another in the following

word; so that, minding only smoothness, he wants both variety and majesty.

Pref. *Sylvæ,* '85. K I 255
See above, a. Dryden, Works, eee. Prosody, b.
Miscellaneous
Wit, n.

Ovid and Virgil

a. For the two first of these [invention and fancy], Ovid is famous amongst the poets; for the latter [elocution], Virgil. Ovid images more often the movements and affections of the mind . . . His words therefore are the least part of his care; for he pictures nature in disorder, with which the study and choice of words is inconsistent. This is the proper wit of dialogue or discourse, and consequently of the Drama . . . On the other side, Virgil speaks not so often to us in the person of another, like Ovid, but in his own . . . and thereby gains more liberty than the other, to express his thoughts with all the graces of elocution,/to write more figuratively, and to confess as well the labour as the force of his imagination. Though he describes his *Dido* well and naturally, in the violence of her passions, yet he must yield in that to the *Myrrha,* the *Byblis,* the *Althœa,* of Ovid . . . But when action or persons are to be described . . . how bold, how masterly, are the strokes of Virgil!

Pref. *Annus Mirabilis,* '66. K I 15–16
Ethical Function, a. Cf. Diction, b.

b. Ovid takes it [the Aeneas-Dido story] up after him, even in the same age, and makes an ancient heroine of Virgil's new-created Dido; dictates a letter for her, just before her death, to the ungrateful fugitive; and, very unluckily for himself, is for measuring a sword with a man so much superior in force to him, on the same sub-

170

ject. I think I may be judge of this, because/I have translated both. The famous author of the *Art of Love* has nothing of his own; he borrows all from a greater master in his own profession; and, which is worse, improves nothing which he finds. Nature fails him; and, being forced to his old shift, he has recourse to witticism. This passes indeed with his soft admirers, and

gives him the preference to Virgil in their esteem. But let them like for themselves, and not prescribe to others: for our author needs not their admiration.

Ded. *Æneis,* '97. K II 193–94

TURNS, a.

Owen, John

EPIC, j.   CRITIC[s], a.

P

Painting [See also POETRY AND PAINTING]

And the great genius of Raphael, and others, having succeeded to the times of barbarism and ignorance, the knowledge of Painting is now arrived to a supreme perfection, though the performance of it is much declined in the present age.

Parallel, '95. K II 135

Panegyric*

a. . . . though the same images serve equally for the epic poesy, and for the historic and panegyric, which are branches of it, yet a several sort of sculpture is to be used in them . . .[1] [See IMAGES, c]

Pref. *Annus Mirabilis,* '66. K I 18

b. [¶] And now, My Lord, I must confess, that what I have written looks more like a Preface, than a Dedication; and truly it was thus far my design, that I might entertain you with somewhat in my own art which might be more worthy of a noble mind, than the stale exploded trick of fulsome panegyrics. 'Tis difficult to write

justly on anything, but almost impossible in praise.

Ded. *Spanish Friar,* '81. K I 249

SATIRE, h.   PROSODY, x.

c. [Speaking of having to draw the portrait in *Eleonora* from report rather than from direct knowledge] Every artist is apt enough to flatter himself, and I amongst the rest, that their own ocular observations would have discovered more perfections, at least others, than have been delivered to them . . .

Ded. *Eleonora,* '92. S-S XI 123

DONNE, b.   DORSET, b.   SATIRE, s.   IMITATION, d.

Paronomasia [Cf. CLENCHES]

Cf. WIT, a.

a. . . . the jingle of a . . . poor paronomasia . . . [See WIT, e]

Pref. *Annus Mirabilis,* '66. K I 15

Cf. WIT, k.

b. [Referring to Horace's play upon the name of Rupilius in the *Seventh Satire* of the *First Book*] A miserable clench, in my opinion, for Horace to record: I have heard honest Mr. Swan make many a better, and

---

* See James Kinsley, "Dryden and the Art of Praise," *English Studies,* XXXIV (1953), 57–64.

yet have had the grace to hold my countenance. But it may be puns were then in fashion, as they were wit in the sermons of the last age, and in the court of King Charles the Second. I am sorry to say it, for the sake of Horace; but certain it is, he has no fine palate who can feed so heartily on garbage.

Discourse of Satire, '93. K II 95

Pastoral

THEOCRITUS, a. OPERA, d.

. . . that humble style in which Pastoral delights, and which . . . is proper to the education and converse of shepherds . . . [See VIRGIL, t]

Ded. *Pastorals,* '97. S-S XIII 321

SPENSER, c. THEOCRITUS, c.

Passions (Representation)

a. (Eugenius) Any sudden gust of passion (as an extasy of love in an unexpected meeting) cannot better be expressed than in a word and a sigh, breaking one another. Nature is dumb on such occasions; and to make her speak, would be to represent her unlike herself.

Dram. Poesy, '65. K I 54

ENGLISH VS. FRENCH, bb. DECORUM, b.
SPEECHES (DRAMATIC), b. TRAGEDY, n.
FIGURES, a.

b. [Figures are to be chiefly used in passion] for then, *si vis me flere, dolendum est primum ipsi tibi;* the poet must put on the passion he endeavours/to represent: a man in such an occasion is not cool enough, either to reason rightly, or to talk calmly. Aggravations are then in their proper places; interrogations, exclamations, hyperbata, or a disordered connexion of discourse, are graceful there, because they are natural.

Author's Apology, '77. K I 185–86

TRAGEDY, c, e, f. FLETCHER, e.

c. [¶] Under this general head of manners, the passions are naturally included as belonging to the characters. I speak not of pity and terror, which are to be moved in the audience by the plot; but of anger, hatred, love, ambition, jealousy, revenge, etc., as they are shown in this or that person of the play.

Pref. *Troilus,* '79. K I 220

d. To describe these [the passions] naturally, and to move them artfully, is one of the greatest commendations which can be given to a poet: to write pathetically, says Longinus, cannot proceed but from a lofty genius. A poet must be born with this quality: yet, unless he help himself by an acquired knowledge of the passions, what they are in their own nature, and by what springs they are to be moved, he will be subject either to raise them where they ought not to be raised, or not to raise them by the just degrees of nature, or to amplify them beyond the natural bounds, or not to observe the crisis and turns of them, in their cooling and decay; all which errors proceed from want of judgment in the poet, and from being unskilled in the principles of Moral Philosophy.

Pref. *Troilus,* '79. K I 220

e. The roar of passion, indeed, may please an audience, three parts of which are ignorant enough to think all is moving which is noise, and it may stretch the lungs of an ambitious actor, who will die upon the spot for a thundering clap; but it will move no other passion than indignation and contempt from judicious men. Longinus, whom I have hitherto followed, continues thus: *If the passions be artfully employed, the discourse becomes vehement and lofty: if otherwise, there is nothing more ridiculous than a great passion out* *of season* . . .[1] He who would raise the passion of a judicious audience, says a learned critic [Le Bossu], must be sure to take his hearers along with him; if they be in a calm, 'tis in vain for him to be in a huff; he must move them by degrees, and kindle with 'em; otherwise he will be in danger of setting his own heap of stubble on fire, and of burning out by himself . . .

Pref. *Troilus, '79.* K I 221

f. Thus then the passions, as they are considered simply and in themselves, suffer violence when they are perpetually maintained at the same height . . . But this is not the worst: for the characters likewise bear a part in the general calamity . . . for it follows of necessity, that no man can be distinguished from another by his discourse, when every man is ranting, swaggering, and exclaiming with the same excess: as if it were the only business of all the characters to contend with each other for the prize at Billingsgate; or that the scene of the tragedy lay in Bet'lem . . .

Pref. *Troilus, '79.* K I 222

g. [¶] It is necessary therefore for a poet, who would concern an audience by describing of a passion, first to prepare it, and not to rush upon it all at once.[1]

Pref. *Troilus, '79.* K I 222

h. The next necessary rule is, to put nothing into the discourse which may hinder your moving of the passions. Too many accidents, as I have said, encumber the poet . . . for the variety of passions which they produce are ever crossing and jostling each other out of the way. He who treats of joy and grief together is in a fair way of causing neither of those effects. There is yet another obstacle . . . which is pointed wit, and sentences affected out of season; these are nothing of kin to the violence of pas-

sion: no man is at leisure to make sentences and similes, when his soul is in an agony.

Pref. *Troilus, '79.* K I 223

Shakespeare, r.

i. It is not that I would explode the use of metaphors from passion, for Longinus thinks 'em necessary to raise it: but to use 'em at every word, to say nothing without a metaphor, a simile, an image, or description, is, I doubt, to smell a little too strongly of the buskin.[1]

Pref. *Troilus, '79.* K I 224

Bombast, a. Shakespeare and Fletcher, b. Ovid, i. Theocritus, a. Cf. Imitation, h. Decorum, i.

j. To express the passions which are seated in the heart, by outward signs, is one great precept of the painters, and very difficult to perform. In poetry, the same passions and motions of the mind are to be expressed; and in this consists the principal difficulty, as well as the excellency of that art. This, says my author, is the gift of Jupiter; and, to speak in the same heathen language, we call it the gift of our Apollo —not to be obtained by pains or study, if we are not born to it; for the motions which are studied are never so natural as those which break out in the height of a real passion. [See Otway]

Parallel, '95. K II 145

k. [¶] *In the passions,* says our author, *we must have a very great regard to the quality of the persons who are actually possessed with them.* . . .[1] this is so much the same in both the arts, that it is no longer a comparison.

Parallel, '95. K II 146

Epic vs. Tragedy, f, j. Chaucer and Ovid, a. Turns, b.

Passions (Responsive)

Speeches, b.

a. 'Tis true, that to imitate well is a poet's work; but to affect the soul, and excite the passions . . . a bare imitation will not serve.

Defence of An Essay, '68. K I 113

SILENCE.

b. . . . it requires Philosophy, as well as Poetry, to sound the depth of all the passions; what they are in themselves, and how they are to be provoked: and in this science the best poets have excelled.

Author's Apology, '77. K I 183

FLETCHER, e. Cf. PASSIONS (REPRESENTATION), d, e, g, h. Cf. BOMBAST, a. STYLE, c. Cf. THEOCRITUS, a. Cf. HOMER, c. IMITATION, h. DECORUM, i. Cf. OTWAY. EPIC VS. TRAGEDY, f.

Patronage

DRYDEN, LITERARY LIFE, k. Cf. POET, a.

a. But they who should be our patrons are for no such expensive ways to fame; they have much of the poetry of Mæcenas, but little of his liberality. They are for persecuting Horace and Virgil, in the persons of their successors; for such is every man who has any part of their soul and fire, though in a less degree. Some of their little zanies yet go further; for they are persecutors even of Horace himself, as far as they are able, by their ignorant and vile imitations of him . . .

Pref. *All for Love,* '78. K I 198

b. [¶] Some few of our nobility are learned, and therefore I will not conclude an absolute contradiction in the terms of nobleman and scholar;/but as the world goes now, 'tis very hard to predicate one upon the other; and 'tis yet more difficult to prove, that a nobleman can be a friend to poetry. Were it not for two or three instances in Whitehall, and in the town, the poets of this age would find so little encour-

agement for their labours, and so few understanders, that they might have leisure to turn pamphleteers, and augment the number of those abominable scribblers, who, in this time of licence, abuse the press, almost every day, with nonsense, and railing against the government.

Ded. *Limberham,* '80. S-S VI 8–9

c. Tis enough for one Age to have neglected Mr Cowley, and sterv'd Mr Buttler; but neither of them had the happiness to live till your Lordship's Ministry.

Letter to Lawrence Hyde, 1683. Ward No. 10, p. 21

Cf. MULGRAVE, b.

c-2. . . . 'tis dangerous to offend an arbitrary master; and every patron who has the power of Augustus has not his clemency.

Ded. *Æneis,* '97. K II 179

d. If rewards could make good poets, their great master [the French poets' Louis] has not been wanting on his part in his bountiful encouragements: for he is wise enough to imitate Augustus, if he had a Maro.

Ded. *Æneis,* '97. K II 219

Pedantry

ENGLISH LANGUAGE, h. WIT, c. DIALOGUE (GENRE), a.

. . . Truewit was a scholar-like kind of man, a gentleman with an allay of pedantry, a man who seems mortified to the world, by much reading. [See PRESENT AGE, k]

Defence of the Epilogue, '72. K I 174

ANCIENTS, d. Cf. TRANSLATION, d. STYLE, d. DRYDEN, WORKS, mm. Cf. WALSH, b. WALSH, d. HOLYDAY, c. TRANSLATION, c. VIRGIL, n. CRITIC[s], a. BORROWING, c.

Pepys, Samuel

I remember last year, when I had the honour of dining with you, you were pleas'd to recommend to me, the Character of Chaucer's Good Parson. Any desire of yours is a Command to me; and accordingly I have put it into my English, with such additions and alterations as I thought fit.

Letter to Pepys, 14 July 1699. Ward No. 61, p. 115

Perfection (of Art)

Cf. MODERNS, c, d. Cf. PROSODY, w.

Perfection in any art is not suddenly obtained . . .

Pref. *Husband His Own Cuckold,* '96. S-S XV 410

CORRECTNESS, b. CHAUCER, c.

Perrault, Charles

ENGLISH DRAMA, i. DENNIS.

Persius (Aulus Persius Flaccus) [See also HORACE AND JUVENAL AND PERSIUS]

a. I will begin with him, who, in my opinion, defends the weakest cause, which is that of Persius; and labouring, as Tacitus professes of his own writing, to divest myself of partiality, or prejudice, con/sider Persius, not as a poet whom I have wholly translated, and who has cost me more labour and time than Juvenal, but according to what I judge to be his own merit; which I think not equal, in the main, to that of Juvenal or Horace, and yet in some things to be preferred to both of them.

Discourse of Satire, '93. K II 69–70

b. [¶] First, then, for the verse; neither Casaubon himself, nor any for him, can defend either his numbers, or the purity of his Latin . . . he is evidently beneath Horace and Juvenal in both.

Then, as his verse is scabrous, and hobbling, and his words not everywhere well chosen, the purity of Latin being more corrupted than in the time of Juvenal, and consequently of Horace, who writ when

the language was in the height of its perfection, so his diction is hard, his figures are generally too bold and daring, and his tropes, particularly his metaphors, insufferably strained.

In the third place, notwithstanding . . . Casaubon, Stelluti, and a Scotch gentleman [David Wedderburn: Ker] . . . yet he is still obscure: whether he affected not to be understood, but with difficulty; or whether the fear of his safety under Nero compelled him to this darkness in some places; or that it was occasioned by his close way of thinking, and the brevity of his style, and crowding of his figures; or . . . whether . . . many of his words have been corrupted, and many customs, and stories relating to them, lost to us . . .

Discourse of Satire, '93. K II 70

c. [¶] To come to a conclusion: he is manifestly below Horace, because he borrows most of his greatest beauties from him . . .[1]

. . . Scaliger . . . calls him . . . a silly writer and a trifler, full of ostentation of his learning, and, after all, un/worthy to come into competition with Juvenal and Horace.

After such terrible accusations, 'tis time to hear what his patron Casaubon can allege in his defence.

Discourse of Satire, '93. K II 71–72

Diction

See above, b.

Dryden's Study of

BUSBY, b.

Fulsomeness

d. [¶] To consider Persius yet more closely: he rather insulted over vice and folly, than exposed them, like Juvenal and Horace; and as chaste and modest as he is esteemed, it cannot be denied, but that in some places he is broad and fulsome, as the latter verses of the Fourth Satire, and of the Sixth, sufficiently witness.

Discourse of Satire, '93. K II 71

e. As for the chastity of his thoughts, Casaubon denies not but that one particular passage, in the Fourth Satire, *At si unctus cesses,* etc., is not only the most obscure, but the most obscene of all his works. I understood it; but for that reason turned it over.

Discourse of Satire, '93. K II 73

Judgment

f. [¶] After all, he was a young man, like his friend and contemporary Lucan; both of them men of extraordinary parts, and great acquired knowledge, considering their youth: but neither of them had arrived to that maturity of judgment which is necessary to the accomplishing of a formed poet. And this consideration, as, on the one hand, it lays some imperfections to their charge, so, on the other side, 'tis a candid excuse for those failings which are incident to youth and inexperience; and we have more reason to wonder how they, who died before the thirtieth year of their age, could write so well, and think so strongly, than to accuse them of those faults from which human nature, and more especially in youth, can never possibly be exempted.

Discourse of Satire, '93. K II 71

Majesty

PROGRESS, e.

Metaphoric Boldness

g. In/defence of his boisterous metaphors, he [Casaubon] quotes Longinus . . . To which it may be replied, that where the trope is far-fetched and hard it is fit for nothing but to puzzle the understanding; and may be reckoned amongst

those things of Demosthenes which Æschines called θαύματα, not ῥήματα, that is, prodigies, not words.

Discourse of Satire, '93. K II 73–74

Obscurity

See above, b.

h. The truth is, Persius is not sometimes, but generally, obscure; and therefore Casaubon, at last, is forced to excuse him, by alleging it was *se defendendo,* for fear of Nero; and that he was commanded to write so cloudily by Cornutus . . . I cannot help my own opinion; I think Cornutus needed not to have read many lectures to him on that subject. Persius was an apt scholar; and when he was bidden to be obscure in some places . . . took the same counsel for all his books; and never afterwards wrote ten lines together clearly.

Discourse of Satire, '93. K II 73

SATIRE, k.

Ostentation

SCALIGER, b.

Philosophic Consistency and Seriousness

i. In the meantime, I think myself obliged to give Persius his undoubted due, and to acquaint the world, with Casau/bon, in what he has equalled, and in what excelled, his two competitors.

. . . Casaubon, who saw that Persius could not laugh with a becoming grace, that he was not made for jesting, and that a merry conceit was not his talent, turned his feather, like an Indian, to another light . . . Moral doctrine, says he, and urbanity, or well-mannered wit, are the two things which constitute the Roman satire; but of the two, that which is most essential to this poem, and is, as it were, the very soul which animates it, is the scourging of vice, and exhortation to virtue. Thus wit . . . is already almost out of doors; and allowed only for . . . a weapon, as he calls it, of which the satirist makes use in the compassing of his design. . . . Satire [still according to Casaubon] is of the nature of moral philosophy, as being instructive: he, therefore, who instructs most usefully, will carry the palm . . . The philosophy in which Persius was educated, and which he professes . . . is the Stoic; the most noble, most generous, most beneficial . . . amongst all the sects, who have given us the rules of ethics, thereby to form a severe virtue in the soul; to raise in us an undaunted courage against the assaults of fortune; to esteem as nothing the things that are without us, because they are not in our power; not to value riches, beauty, honours, fame, or health, any further than as conveniences, and/so many [other] helps . . . In short, to be always happy, while we possess our minds with a good conscience, are free from the slavery of vices, and conform our actions and conversations to the rules of right reason. See here, my Lord, an epitome of Epictetus; the doctrine of Zeno, and the education of our Persius. . . . I will not lessen this commendation . . . by giving you an account of some absurdities in their doctrine, and some perhaps impieties, if we consider them by the standard of Christian faith. Persius has fallen into none of them . . . What he teaches might be taught from pulpits, with more profit . . . than all the nice speculations of divinity, and controversies concerning faith . . . Passions, interest, ambition, and all their bloody consequences of discord and of war, are banished from this doctrine. Here is nothing proposed but the quiet and tranquility of the mind . . . And therefore I

wonder not that the present Bishop of Salisbury has recommended this our author, and the Tenth Satire of Juvenal, in his Pastoral Letter . . . as the best commonplaces for . . . sermons . . . Herein then it is, that Persius has excelled both Juvenal and Horace. He sticks to his/own philosophy; he shifts not sides, like Horace, who is sometimes an Epicurean, sometimes a Stoic, sometimes an Eclectic . . . nor declaims like Juvenal against vices, more like an orator than a philosopher. Persius is everywhere the same . . . What he has learnt, he teaches vehemently; and what he teaches, that he practises himself. There is a spirit of sincerity in all he says; you may easily discern that he is in earnest, and is persuaded of that truth which he inculcates. In this I am of opinion that he excels Horace, who is commonly in jest . . . and is equal to Juvenal, who was as honest and serious as Persius, and more he could not be.

Hitherto I have followed Casaubon, and enlarged upon him, because I am satisfied that he says no more than truth; the rest is almost all frivolous.
Discourse of Satire, '93. K II 74–77
Tone
See above, d, g, i.
Satires: First

j. The Satyr [Persius's First] is in Dialogue, betwixt the Authour and his Friend or Monitor; who dissuades him from this dangerous attempt of exposing Great Men. But *Persius,* who is of a free Spirit, and has not forgotten that *Rome* was once a Commonwealth, breaks through . . . and boldly Arraigns the false Judgment of the Age in which he Lives. The Reader may observe that our Poet was a Stoick Philosopher; and that all his Moral Sentences, both here, and in all the rest of his Satyrs, are drawn from the Dogma's of that Sect.

Argument of the First Satire [Persius], '93. JK II 742

Satires: Second

k. The Satyr [Persius's Second] is divided into three parts. The first is the Exordium . . . which the Poet confines within the compass of four Verses. The second relates to the matter of the Prayers and Vows . . . wherein Men commonly Sinn'd against right Reason, and Offended in their Requests. The Third part consists, in shewing the repugnancies of those Prayers and Wishes, to those of other Men, and inconsistencies with themselves. . . . And Lastly, not only corrects the false Opinion of Mankind concerning them; but gives the True Doctrine of all Addresses made to Heaven . . . in excellent Precepts; and more worthy of a Christian than a Heathen.

Argument of the Second Satire [Persius], '93. JK II 752

See below, l.

Satires: Fourth

See above, d, e.

Satires: Fifth

Busby, b. Stoicism, b.

Satires: Sixth

l. [Of line 61 ff. in the translation of Persius's Sixth Satire] . . . this is the most Poetical Description of any in our Author: And since he and *Lucan* were so great Friends, I know not but *Lucan* might help him, in two/or three of these Verses, which seem to be written in his stile; certain it is, that besides this Description of a Shipwreck, and two Lines more, which are at the end of the Second Satyr, our Poet has written nothing Elegantly. I will therefore

Transcribe both the passages, to justifie my Opinion.

Notes to the Sixth Satire [Persius], '93. JK II 787–88

Satires, Unity of Theme

Satire, c.

Style

See above, b, c, d, g, h, i, l.

Verse

See above, b.

Petrarch (Francesco Petrarcha)

Boccaccio.

Petronius Arbiter

. . . Petronius Arbiter, the most elegant, and one of the most judicious authors of the Latin tongue . . .

Essay of Heroic Plays, '72. K I 152

Lucan, b. Horace, j, k. Satire, pp. Critic[s], d. Curiosa Felicitas.

Philips, Katherine [See Orinda]

Pindar

Pindar is generally known to be a dark writer, to want connection, (I mean as to our understanding,) to soar out of sight, and leave his reader at a gaze. [See Cowley, e]

Pref. *Ovid's Epistles,* '80. K I 240

Translation, i. Horace, c. Prosody, v. Authority, e. Prosody, x. Horace and Juvenal and Persius, b. Prosody, y.

Pindaric [See Prosody]

Plagiarism

a. (Crites) [Jonson] was not only a professed imitator of Horace, but a learned plagiary of all the others; you track him every where in their snow . . . .[See Jonson, e]

Dram. Poesy, '65. K I 43

Jonson, a. Dryden, Literary Life, m.

b. Those who have called Virgil, Terence, and Tasso, plagiaries (though they much injured them), had yet a better colour for their accusation; for Virgil has evidently translated Theocritus, Hesiod, and Homer, in many places . . . Terence was not only known to translate Menander . . . but was said also to be helped in those translations by Scipio . . . and Lælius. And Tasso, the most excellent of modern poets, and whom I reverence next to Virgil, has taken both from Homer . . . and from Virgil . . . Yet the bodies of Virgil's and Tasso's poems were their own; and so are all the ornaments of language and elocution . . ./Most of Shakespeare's plays, I mean the stories of them, are to be found in the *Hecatommuthi* . . . of Cinthio. . . . Beaumont and Fletcher had most of theirs from Spanish novels . . . Ben Johnson, indeed, has designed his plots himself; but no man has borrowed so much from the Ancients as he has done: and he did well in it, for he has thereby beautified our language.

Pref. *Evening's Love,* '71. K I 145–46
Cf. Poet, h. Fable, f. Boileau, b. Imitation of Models, d. Homer and Virgil, b. Dryden, Literary Life, o.

c. [Note to line 132 of the translation of *Æneid* III] Eustathius takes notice that the old poets were wont to take whole paragraphs from one another, which justifies our poet [Virgil] for what he borrows from Homer.

Notes and Observations on Virgil's Works, '97. N 711

Plato

a. . . . I must crave leave to say, that my whole discourse [in *Dramatic Poesy*] was sceptical, according to that way of reasoning which was used by Socrates, Plato, and all the Academics of old . . . [See Dryden, Works, d]

Defence of An Essay, '68. K I 124

Shakespeare, l. Ancients, a. Bellori. Epic Hero, g. Cf. Theocritus, a.

b. Plato, who borrowed so much from Homer, and yet concluded for the banishment of all poets, would at least have rewarded Virgil before he sent him into exile.

Ded. *Æneis,* '97. K II 189

c. [Of lines 980 f. of the translation of *Æneid VI*] The Platonists call God the *archetypal* sun . . . Now it was the receiv'd hypothesis amongst the Pythagoreans, that the sun was situate in the center of the world. Plato had it from them, and was himself of the same opinion, as appears by a passage in the *Timæus;* from which noble dialogue is this part of Virgil's poem taken.

Notes and Observations on Virgil's Works, '97. N 713

Platonism

Epic, Christian, b. Epic Poet, a. Epic, Christian, c. Plato, c.

Plautus, Titus Maccius

a. (Eugenius) . . . Plautus . . . is infinitely too bold in his metaphors and coining words, out of which many times his wit is nothing . . .

Dram. Poesy, '65. K I 51
Manners, i.

a-2. (Eugenius) [¶] Among their comedies [those of the Ancients], we find a scene or two of tenderness, and that where you would least expect it, in Plautus . . .

Dram. Poesy, '65. K I 54

b. . . . Plautus and Molière . . . the two greatest names of ancient and modern comedy . . .

Ded. *Amphitryon,* '90. S-S VIII 9

Play (Definition) [See also Comedy; Tragedy]

a. (Lisideius) . . . he conceived a play ought to be, *A just and lively image of hu-*

man nature, representing its passions and humours, and the changes of fortune to which it is subject, for the delight and instruction of mankind.

    Dram. Poesy, '65. K I 36

b. (Neander) . . . the soul of Poesy, which is imitation of humour and passions . . .

    Dram. Poesy, '65. K I 68

CORNEILLE (PIERRE), a-2.

c. [¶] As for what he urges, that *a play will still be supposed to be a composition of several persons speaking ex tempore* . . . I must crave leave to dissent from his opinion . . . for, if I am not deceived, a play is supposed to be the work of a poet, imitating or representing the conversation of several persons . . .

    Defence of An Essay, '68. K I 114

IMITATION, e. TRAGEDY, a.

d. . . . for writing a play, as I conceive, is not entering into the/Observator's province [*i.e.,* journalism]. . .

    Vindication, '83. S-S VII 197–98

Cf. DRYDEN, WORKS, ww.

Play (Parts)

(Eugenius) Aristotle . . . divides the/ integral parts of a play into four. First, the *Protasis,* or entrance . . . Secondly, the *Epitasis,* or working up of the plot; where the play grows warmer, the design or action of it is drawing on . . . Thirdly, the *Catastasis,* or counterturn, which destroys the expectation, imbroils the action in new difficulties, and leaves you far distant from that hope in which it found you . . . Lastly, the *Catastrophe,* which the Grecians called λύσις, the French *le denouement,* and we the discovery or unravelling of the plot: there you see all things settling again upon their first foundations; and, the obstacles which hindered the design or action

. . . once removed, it ends with that resemblance of truth and nature, that the audience are satisfied . . . Thus this great man delivered to us the image of a play; and I must confess it is so lively, that from thence much light has been derived to the forming it more perfectly into acts and scenes: but what poet first limited to five the number of the acts, I know not; only we see it so firmly established in the time of Horace, that he gives it for a rule in comedy; *Neu brevior quinto, neu sit productior actu.* So that you see the Grecians cannot be said to have consummated this art; writing rather by entrances, than by acts, and having rather a general/indigested notion of a play, than knowing how and where to bestow the particular graces of it.

    Dram. Poesy, '65. K I 44–46

Play Writing

Plotting and writing in this kind [drama] are certainly more troublesome employments than many which signify more, and are of greater moment in the world: the fancy, memory, and judgment, are then extended (like so many limbs) upon the rack; all of them reaching with their utmost stress at Nature; a thing so almost infinite and boundless, as can never fully be comprehended, but where the images of all things are always present.

    Ded. *Rival Ladies,* '64. K I 3

FLETCHER, b. FANCY, h. TRAGEDY, q.

Pliny the Younger (Gaius Plinius Cæcilius Secundus)

I know you [Howard] are not of the number of those, of whom the younger Pliny speaks; *Nec sunt parum multi, qui carpere amicos suos judicium vocant* . . .

    Pref. *Annus Mirabilis,* '66. K I 19

PROSODY, x.

Plot [See FABLE]

Plutarch

GOLDEN AGES, a.

a. For, like a true philosopher, who minded things, not words, he [Plutarch] strove not even to cultivate his mother tongue with any great exactness . . .

"Life of Plutarch," '83. S-S XVII 26

LATIN, a.

b. And as he [Plutarch] was continually in company with men of learning . . . so his memory was always on the stretch to receive and lodge their discourses; and his judgment perpetually employed in separating his notions, and distinguishing which were fit to be preserved, and which to be rejected.

"Life of Plutarch," '83. S-S XVII 30

c. Yet . . . in the midst of this moderation, he [Plutarch] opposed the two extremes of the Epicurean and Stoic sects, both of which he has judiciously combated . . . and both upon the same account,—because they pretend too much to certainty in their dogmas, and to impose them with too great arrogance; which he, who following the Academists, doubted more and pretended less, was no way able to support. The Pyrrhonians, or grosser sort of Sceptics, who bring all certainty in question, and startle even at the notions of common sense, appeared as absurd to him on the other side . . ./The moral philosophy, therefore, was his chiefest aim, because the principles of it admitted of less doubt; and because they were most conducing to the benefit of human life.

"Life of Plutarch," '83. S-S XVII 31–32

d. [¶] The religion he professed, to speak the worst of it, was heathen. I say, the religion he *professed;* for it is no way probable that so great a philosopher,/and so wise a man, should believe the superstitions and fopperies of Paganism . . .

"Life of Plutarch," '83. S-S XVII 32–33

e. . . . these [doctrines, *i.e.,* of Christianity] . . . might easily choke the faith of a philosopher [Plutarch], who believed no more than what he could deduce from the principles of nature . . . [H]e could not know without revelation, and the revelation was not to him.

"Life of Plutarch," '83. S-S XVII 35

LONGINUS, b. BIOGRAPHY, c.

f. Our author [Plutarch] therefore needs no excuse, but rather deserves a commendation, when he relates, as pleasant, some sayings of his heroes, which appear (I must confess it) very cold and insipid mirth to us. For it is not his meaning to commend the jest, but to paint the man; besides, we may have lost somewhat of the idiotism of that language in which it was spoken; and where the conceit is couched in a single word, if all the significations of it are not critically understood, the grace and the pleasantry are lost.

"Life of Plutarch," '83. S-S XVII 63

g. [¶] But in all parts of biography, whether familiar or stately . . . sublime or low . . . serious or merry, Plutarch equally excelled. . . . Dion Cassius is not so sincere; Herodian, a lover of truth, is oftentimes deceived . . ./Suetonius and Tacitus may be called alike either authors of histories, or writers of lives; but the first . . . runs too willingly into obscene descriptions . . . the other . . . often falls into obscurity; and both . . . have made so unlucky a choice of times, that they are forced to describe rather monsters than men . . . Our author, on the contrary . . . has generally chosen such great men as were famous for their several virtues . . .

Yet, as he was impartial, he disguised not the faults of any man . . .[1] Then he was more happy in his digressions . . ./Nor are the ornaments of poetry, and the illustrations of similitudes, forgotten by him; in both which he instructs, as well as pleases; or rather pleases, that he may instruct.

"Life of Plutarch," '83. S-S XVII 63–65
DIGRESSIONS.

h. [¶] This last reflection leads me naturally to say somewhat in general of his style . . . his elocution. . . . [I]n Plutarch, whose business was not to please the ear, but to charm and to instruct the mind, we may easily forgive the cadences of words, and the roughness of expression. Yet, for manliness of eloquence, if it abounded not in our author, it was not wanting in him. He neither/studied the sublime style, nor affected the flowery.

"Life of Plutarch," '83. S-S XVII 65–66
ST. ÉVREMOND, a. MONTAIGNE, b. VARRO. PREFACES, b. BIOGRAPHY, d. LUCIAN, g.

Plutarch and Seneca

If we consider them in their inclinations or humours, Plutarch was sociable and pleasant, Seneca morose and melancholy: Plutarch a lover of conversation, and sober feasts; Seneca reserved, uneasy to himself when alone, to others when in company. Compare them in their manners;/Plutarch everywhere appears candid, Seneca often is censorious. Plutarch, out of his natural humanity, is frequent in commending what he can; Seneca, out of the sourness of his temper, is prone to satire, and still searching for some occasion to vent his gall. Plutarch is pleased with an opportunity of praising virtue; and Seneca, to speak the best of him, is glad of a pretence to reprehend vice. Plutarch endeavours to teach others, but refuses not to be taught himself; for he is always doubtful and inquisitive: Seneca is altogether for teaching others, but so teaches them, that he imposes his opinions, for he was of a sect too imperious and dogmatical, either to be taught or contradicted; and yet Plutarch writes like a man of a confirmed probity, Seneca like one of a weak and staggering virtue. Plutarch seems to have vanquished vice . . . Seneca seems only to be combating and resisting, and that too but in his own defence: therefore Plutarch is easy in his discourse . . . Seneca is painful . . . Plutarch's virtue is humble and civilized; Seneca's haughty and ill-bred: Plutarch allures you, Seneca commands you. One would make virtue your companion, the other your tyrant. The style of Plutarch is easy and flowing, that of Seneca precipitous and harsh . . . The arguments of the Grecian, drawn from reason . . . make a deep and lasting impression . . . those of the Roman, drawn from wit, flash immediately on your imagination, but leave no durable effect . . .

"Life of Plutarch," '83. S-S XVII 72–73

Poet [See also EPIC POET; ENDS OF POETRY; ETHICAL FUNCTION; POETASTERS]
Boldness and Rashness
CRITIC[s], g. PROSODY, y.
Borrowing
INVENTION, d.
and *Critic*
CRITIC[s], d.
Desire of Fame
a. [¶] Ambition is so far from being a vice in poets, that it is almost impossible for them to succeed without it. Imagination must be raised, by a/desire of fame, to a desire of pleasing; and they whom, in all ages, poets have endeavoured most to please

have been the beautiful and the great. Beauty is their deity, to which they sacrifice, and greatness is their guardian angel, which protects them.

Ded. *State of Innocence,* '77. S-S V 100–01

Dignity

b. 'Tis no shame to be a poet, though 'tis to be a bad one. Augustus Cæsar of old, and Cardinal Richelieu of late, would willingly have been such; and David and Solomon were such.

Discourse of Satire, '93. K II 39

DRYDEN, LITERARY LIFE, t.

Distinguished from Historian

LUCAN, b. See below, f.

Distinguished from Rhymer

MILTON, c.

Envy Among

MULGRAVE, c.

Exaltation

POETIC LICENSE, a. SATIRE, f.

Inspired

INSPIRATION, b.

Instinct of a True

CURIOSA FELICITAS

Invention

See below, k. INVENTION, d.

as Judge

JONSON, a.

c. 'Tis a question variously disputed, whether an author may be allowed as a competent judge of his own works. As to the fabric and contrivance of them, certainly he may; for that is properly the employment of the judgment; which, as a master-builder, he may determine, and that without deception, whether the work be according to the exactness of the model; still granting him to have a perfect idea of that pattern by which he works, and that he keeps himself always constant to the discourse of his judgment, without admitting self-love, which is the false surveyor of his fancy, to intermeddle in it. These qualifications granted (being such as all sound poets are presupposed to have within them), I think all writers, of what kind soever, may infallibly judge of the frame and contexture of their works. But for the ornament of writing, which is greater, more various, and *bizarre* in poesy than in any other kind, as it is properly the child of fancy; so it can receive no measure, or at least but a very imperfect one, of its own excellencies or failures from the judgment. Self-love (which enters but rarely into the offices of the judgment) here predominates; and fancy (if I may so speak), judging of itself, can be no more certain, or demonstrative of its own effects, than two crooked lines can be the adequate measure of each other.

Pref. *Secret Love,* '67. S-S II 418

DRYDEN, WORKS, g. Cf. DRYDEN, LITERARY LIFE, g. CRITIC[s], e, f, g, h. DRYDEN, WORKS, dd.

d. If you like not my poem, the fault may possibly be in my writing; though it is hard for an author to judge against himself . . .

Pref. *Absalom and Achitophel,* '81. S-S IX 213

CRITICASTER, g. TRAGICOMEDY, d. CRITIC[s], f. Cf. DRYDEN, LITERARY LIFE, t. Cf. DRYDEN, WORKS, kkk. See below, l. DRYDEN, WORKS, vvv.

Language of

TECHNICAL TERMS, b.

Lawgiver

STYLE, c.

License of the Epic Poet [See POETIC LICENSE]

SUPERNATURAL, c.

Madness
POETRY, b.
Maturing of
FANCY, i, j.
Moral License
OBSCENITY, c.
Native Fund [Cf. SHAKESPEARE]
THEOCRITUS, a. SATIRE, b. Cf. PASSIONS, j.

d-2. But the author can give the stage no better than what was given him by Nature; and the actors must represent such things as they are capable to perform, and by which both they and the scribbler may get their living.

Parallel, '95. K II 133
SPENSER, c. HOPKINS.
Nimis Poeta

e. . . . there is a great difference of being *poeta* and *nimis poeta,* if we may believe Catullus [Martial: Ker II 258, n.], as much as betwixt a modest behaviour and affectation.

Pref. *Fables,* 1700. K II 258
Ostentation
HORACE AND JUVENAL AND PERSIUS, c.
Patriotic Role
DRYDEN, LITERARY LIFE, l.

f. [¶] To love our native country, and to study its benefit and its glory, to be interessed in its concerns, is natural to all men, and is indeed our common duty. A poet makes a further step; for endeavoring to do honour to it, 'tis allowable in him even to be partial in its cause; for he is not tied to truth, or fettered by the laws of history. Homer and Tasso are justly praised for choosing their heroes out of Greece and Italy; Virgil indeed made his a Trojan; but it was to derive the Romans and his own Augustus from him. But all the three poets are manifestly partial to their heroes, in favour of their country . . .¹ To apply this

to Virgil, he thought himself engaged in honour to espouse the cause and quarrel of his country against Carthage.

Ded. *Æneis,* '97. K II 191

g. And sure a poet is as much privileged to lie as an ambassador, for the honour and interest of his country; at least as Sir Henry Wotton has defined.

Ded. *Æneis,* '97. K II 192
Patron, Relation to
PATRONAGE, d.
Prerogative respecting History [Also above, *Distinguished from Historian*]
Cf. POETIC LICENSE, a. FABLE, e.
of *Present Age* [Cf. PRESENT AGE]
DONNE, d.
Profession of
THOMAS, b.
Proper Work
ACTION (DEFINED). IMAGING, a. ENGLISH vs. FRENCH, bb. HISTORICAL TRUTH, a. FABLE, c.

h. [¶] But in general, the employment of a poet is like that of a curious gunsmith, or watchmaker: the iron or silver is not his own; but they are the least part of that which gives the value: the price lies wholly in the workmanship.

Pref. *Evening's Love,* '71. K I 147

i. [¶] The great art of poets is either the adorning and beautifying of truth, or the inventing pleasing and probable fictions. If they invent impossible fables, like some of Æsop's, they ought to have such morals couched under them, as may tend to the instruction of mankind, or the regulation of manners, or they can be of no use; nor can they really delight any but such as would be pleased with Tom Thumb, without these circumstances.

Postscript *N and O,* '74. S-S XV 408
Cf. OVID, i. LUCRETIUS, b.

j. A poet, indeed, must live by the many; but a good poet will make it his business to please the few.

Pref. *Husband His Own Cuckold,* '96. S-S XV 411

k. They [critics] lay no less than want of invention to his charge [i.e., Virgil's]— a capital crime, I must acknowledge; for a poet is a maker, as the word signifies; and he who cannot make, that is, invent, has his name for nothing. [See INVENTION, d]

Ded. *Æneis,* '97. K II 197

Power over Great

SATIRE, d.

l. . . . this was the poetical revenge he [Virgil] took: for *genus irritabile vatum,* as Horace says. When a poet is thoroughly provoked, he will do himself justice, however dear it cost him; *animamque in vulnere ponit.* I think these are not bare imaginations of my own, though I find no trace of them in the commentators; but one poet may judge of another by himself. The vengeance we defer is not forgotten.

Ded. *Æneis,* '97. K II 173

Qualifications

See above, c.

m. . . . I am of opinion, that they cannot be good poets, who are not accustomed to argue well. False reasonings and colours of speech are the certain marks of one who does not understand the stage . . . [See ETHICAL FUNCTION, a]

Defence of An Essay, '68. K I 121

FABLE, c. UNIVERSITY, a. Cf. SETTLE, c.

n. [¶] A man should be learned in several sciences, and should have a reasonable, philosophical, and in some measure a mathematical head, to be a complete and excellent poet; and besides this, should have experience in all sorts of humours and manners of men; should be thoroughly skilled in conversation, and should have a great knowledge of mankind in general.

Postscript *N and O,* '74. S-S XV 406

FIGURES, b.

o. [The manners] are likewise to be gathered from the several virtues, vices, or passions, and many other commonplaces, which a poet must be supposed to have learned from natural Philosophy, Ethics, and History; of all which, whosoever is ignorant, does not deserve the name of poet.

Pref. *Troilus,* '79. K I 214

PASSIONS, d. TRAGICOMEDY, c. Cf. SHAKESPEARE, h. EPIC POET, a. EPIC VS. TRAGEDY, d. SHAKESPEARE, i. PERSIUS, f. See above, k. PROSODY, b. Cf. TECHNICAL TERMS, b.

Relation to Audience (Readers) [See also ENDS OF POETRY; ETHICAL FUNCTION]

p. . . . let it be yielded, that a writer is not to run down with the stream, or to please the people by their own usual methods, but rather to reform their judgments . . .

Heads of an Answer, '77. S-S XV 386

DRYDEN, LIFE, d.

Relation to Musician (Opera)

DRYDEN, WORKS, vv.

Satirical Poet, Function of [See ENDS OF POETRY]

SATIRE, s, n.

Sock and Buskin

ANCIENTS, i. Cf. PASSIONS, i.

Superiority to Philosopher and Priest

Cf. POETIC LICENSE, a. SUPERNATURAL, e.

Usefulness

q. [¶] There is somewhat of a tie in nature betwixt those who are born for worthy actions, and those who can transmit them to posterity; and though ours be much the inferior part, it comes at least within the verge of alliance; nor are we unprofitable members of the commonwealth, when we animate others to those virtues, which we copy and describe from you.

It is indeed their interest, who endeavour the subversion of governments, to discourage poets and historians; for the best which can happen to them, is, to be forgotten. But such who, under kings, are the fathers of their country, and by a just and prudent ordering of affairs preserve it, have the same reason to cherish the chroniclers of their actions, as they have to lay up in safety the deeds and evidences of their estates; for such records are their undoubted titles to the love and reverence of after ages.

Ded. *All for Love*, '78. S-S V 318

Poetasters [Cf. SATIRICASTER]

a. (Crites) [Crites could almost regret the naval victory at the price in 'ill verses' celebrating it] Adding, that no argument could scape some of those eternal rhymers, who watch a battle with more diligence than the ravens and birds of prey; and the worst of them surest to be first in upon the quarry: while the better able either out of modesty writ not at all, or set that due value upon their poems, as to let them be often called for and long expected!

Dram. Poesy, '65. K I 30

b. (Crites) . . . said, the public magistrate ought to send betimes to forbid them; and that it concerned the peace and quiet of all honest people, that ill poets should be as well silenced as seditious preachers.

Dram. Poesy, '65. K I 30

c. (Lisideius) . . . I ask you, if one of them does not perpetually pay us with clenches upon words, and a certain clownish kind of raillery? if now and then he does not offer at a catachresis or Clevelandism, wresting and torturing a word into

another meaning: in fine, if he be not one of those whom the French would call *un mauvais buffon* . . .

Dram. Poesy, '65. K I 31

d. (Crites) . . . his style [the poetaster's] and matter are everywhere alike: he is the most calm, peaceable writer you ever read: he never disquiets your passions with the least concernment, but still leaves you in as even a temper as he found you; he is a very Leveller in poetry: he creeps along with ten little words in every line, and helps out his numbers with *For to,* and *Unto,* and all the pretty expletives he/can find, till he drags them to the end of another line; while the sense is left tired half way behind it: he doubly starves all his verses, first for want of thought, and then of expression . . . [See WIT, a]

Dram. Poesy, '65. K I 31–32

WILD. SETTLE, a. POETIC LICENSE, b.

e. Men of pleasant conversation (at least esteemed so), and endued with a trifling kind of fancy, perhaps helped out with some smattering of Latin, are ambitious to distinguish themselves from the herd of gentlemen, by their Poetry . . .⁹

And is not this a wretched affectation, not to be contented with what fortune has done for them, and sit down quietly with their estates, but they must call their wits in question, and needlessly expose their nakedness to public view? Not considering that they are not to expect the same approbation from sober men, which they have found from their flatterers after the third bottle. If a little glittering in discourse has passed them on us for witty men, where was the necessity of undeceiving the world? . . . but what can be urged in their defence, who, not having the vocation of poverty to scribble, out of mere wantonness take pains to make themselves ridiculous?

Pref. *All for Love,* '78. K I 196

FLECKNOE. Cf. PATRONAGE, b. SATIRICASTER, b.

f. A dissenter in poetry from sense and English will make as good a Protestant rhymer as a Dissenter from the Church of England a Protestant parson.

"Epistle to the Whigs," Prefixed to *The Medal,* '82. S-S IX 431

CRITICASTER, h.

g. [Dorset is encouraged, among other reasons, to write so that] in relation to a multitude of scribblers, who daily pester the world with their insufferable stuff . . . they might be discouraged from writing any more.

Discourse of Satire, '93. K II 21

DRYDEN, LITERARY LIFE, e. DORSET, d.

h. And I care not much if I give this handle [the rule of pleasing at any price: see AUDIENCE, POPULAR, j] to our bad illiterate poetasters, for the defence of their *scriptions,* as they call them.

Examen Poeticum, '93. K II 7

PROSODY, y. Cf. FARCE, f. CURIOSA FELICITAS. PRESENT AGE, p. Cf. SATIRE, j. CRITIC[s], a.

Poetesses

THOMAS, a.

Poetic Justice

a. (Eugenius) . . . instead of punishing vice and rewarding virtue, they [the Ancients] have often shown a prosperous wickedness, and an unhappy piety: they have set before us a bloody image of revenge in Medea . . . [See ANCIENTS, r]

Dram. Poesy, '65. K I 50

FABLE, b. ENDS OF POETRY, k.

b. [In defence of Maximin, in *Tyrannic*

Love] Nay, as if I had foreseen this objection, I purposely removed the scene of the play, which ought to have been at Alexandria in Egypt, where S. Catherine suffered, and laid it under the walls of Aquileia in Italy, where Maximin was slain; that the punishment of his crime might immediately succeed its execution.

Pref. *Tyrannic Love,* '70. S-S III 378

COMEDY, f.

c. In Tragedy, where the actions and persons are great, and the crimes horrid, the laws of justice are more strictly observed; and examples of punishment to be made, to deter mankind from the pursuit of vice. . . . Thus Tragedy fulfils one great part of its institution; which is, by example, to instruct. But in Comedy it is not so; for the chief end of it is/divertisement and delight: and that so much, that it is disputed, I think, by Heinsius, before Horace his *Art of Poetry,* whether instruction be any part of its employment. At least I am sure it can be but its secondary end: for the business of the poet is to make you laugh . . . And if he works a cure on folly, and the small imperfections in mankind, by exposing them to public view, that cure is not performed by an immediate operation. For it works first on the ill-nature of the audience; they are moved to laugh by the representation of deformity; and the shame of that laughter teaches us to amend what is ridiculous in our manners. This being then established, that the first end of Comedy is delight, and instruction only the second; it may reasonably be inferred, that Comedy is not so much obliged to the punishment of faults which it represents, as Tragedy. For the persons in Comedy are of a lower quality, the action is little, and the faults and vices are but the sallies of youth, and the frailties of human nature, and not premeditated crimes . . . such as move pity and commiseration, not detestation and horror; such, in short, as may be forgiven, not such as must of necessity be punished. But, lest any man should think that I write this to make libertinism amiable, or that I cared not to debase the end and institution of Comedy, as I might thereby maintain my own errors, and those of better poets, I must further declare . . . that we make not vicious persons happy, but only as Heaven makes sinners so; that is, by reclaiming them first from vice. For so it is to be supposed they are,/when they resolve to marry; for then, enjoying what they desire in one, they cease to pursue the love of many.[1]

Pref. *Evening's Love*, '71. K I 142–44

d. . . . consider, if pity and terror be enough for tragedy to move; and I believe, upon a true definition of tragedy, it will be found, that its work extends farther, and that is to reform manners, by a delightful representation of human life in great persons, by way of dialogue. If this be true, then not only pity and terror are to be moved, as the only means to bring us to virtue, but generally love to virtue, and hatred to vice, by showing the rewards of one, and punishments of the other; at least by rendering virtue always amiable, though it be shown unfortunate, and vice detestable, though it be shown triumphant.

Heads of an Answer, '77. S-S XV 383
TRAGEDY, c. Cf. TRAGEDY, d.

e. [In defense of *Rollo*] . . . poetic justice is not neglected . . . for we stab him in our minds for every offence which he commits; and the point which the poet is to gain on the audience is not so much in the

death of an offender, as the raising an horror of his crimes.

Heads of an Answer, '77. S-S XV 387

f. [¶] After all, we need not yield, that the English way is less conducing to move pity and terror, because they often show virtue oppressed and vice punished; where they do not both, or either, they are not to be defended.

Heads of an Answer, '77. S-S XV 388
TRAGEDY, f, g. Cf. ANTONY AND CLEOPATRA. Cf. SHAKESPEARE, t. HERO (DRAMATIC), d.

g. . . . the learned Mr. Rymer has well observed, that in all punishments we are to regulate ourselves by poetical justice . . .

Pref. *Don Sebastian*, '90. S-S VII 312
CHARACTER[s], c. EPIC vs. TRAGEDY, e.

Poetic License

FABLE, b.

a. (Neander) But if no latitude is to be allowed a poet, you take from him not only his license of *quidlibet audendi,* but you tie him up in a straiter compass than you would a philosopher. This is indeed *Musas colere severiores.* You would have him follow Nature, but he must follow her on foot: you have dismounted him from his Pegasus.

Dram. Poesy, '65. K I 103
HISTORICAL TRUTH, a. Cf. HISTORICAL TRUTH, b.

b. . . . some little friends of his [Settle's], who are smatterers in poetry, will be ready for most of his gross errors to use that much mistaken plea of *poetica licentia,* which words fools are apt to use for the palliating the most absurd nonsense in any poem. I cannot find when any poets had liberty, from any authority, to write nonsense, more than any other men. Nor is that plea of *poetica licentia* used as a subterfuge by any but weak professors of that art, who are commonly given over to a mist of fancy, a buzzing of invention, and a sound of something like sense, and have no use of judgment. . . . The licentious wildness and extravagance of such men's conceits have made poetry contemned by some, though it be very unjust for any to condemn the science for the weakness of some of the professors.

Postscript *N and O*, '74. S-S XV 405
FANCY, e.

c. [¶] But some will say after this, what license is left for poets? Certainly the same that good poets ever took, without being faulty (for surely the best were so sometimes, because they were but men),/and that license is fiction; which kind of poetry is like that of landscape-painting; and poems of this nature, though they be not *vera,* ought to be *verisimilia.*

Postscript *N and O*, '74. S-S XV 407–8
IMITATION, j.

d. Poetic Licence I take to be the liberty which poets have assumed to themselves, in all ages, of speaking things in verse, which are beyond the severity of prose. 'Tis that particular character which distinguishes and sets the bounds betwixt *oratio soluta* and poetry. This, as to what regards the thought or imagination of a poet,/consists in fiction: but then those thoughts must be expressed; and here arise two other branches of it; for if this license be included in a single word, it admits of tropes; if in a sentence or proposition, of figures; both which are of a much larger extent, and more forcibly to be used in verse than prose. This is that birthright which is derived to us from our great forefathers, even from Homer down to Ben; and they who would deny it to us, have, in plain terms,

the fox's quarrel to the grapes—they cannot reach it. [See following entry]

Author's Apology, '77. K I 188–89

e. [¶] How far these liberties [of poetic license] are to be extended, I will not presume to determine here, since Horace does not. But it is certain that they are to be varied, according to the language and age in which an author writes. . . . And 'tis evident that the English does more nearly follow the strictness of the latter [Roman] than the freedoms of the former [Greek].

Author's Apology, '77. K I 189

f. [¶] Horace a little explains himself on this subject of *Licentia Poetica,* in these verses—

. . . Pictoribus atque Poetis
Quidlibet audendi semper fuit æqua potestas:
Sed non, ut placidis coeant immitia, non ut
Serpentes avibus geminentur, tigribus hædi.

He would have a poem of a piece; not to begin with one thing, and end with another: he restrains it so far, that thoughts of an unlike nature ought not to be joined together. That were indeed to make a chaos. He taxed not Homer, nor the divine Virgil, for interesting/their gods in the wars of Troy and Italy; neither, had he now lived, would he have taxed Milton, as our false critics have presumed to do, for his choice of a supernatural argument; but he would have blamed my author, who was a Christian, had he introduced into his poem heathen deities, as Tasso is condemned by Rapin . . . and as Camoens . . . ought to be censured by all his readers, when he brings in Bacchus and Christ into the same adventure of his fable.

Author's Apology, '77. K I 189–90
DRYDEN, WORKS, u. UNITIES (DRAMATIC), GENERAL, c, d. DRYDEN, WORKS, lll. OBSCENITY, c. UNITIES (DRAMATIC), TIME, e.

Poetry [See also MATERIA POETICA]*

See TRAGEDY, h.

Abuse

POETIC LICENSE, b.

April Poetry

a. [In panegyric of Dorset's poetry] We are not kept in expectation of two good lines, which are to come after a long parenthesis of twenty bad; which is the April poetry of other writers, a mixture of rain and sunshine by fits . . .

Discourse of Satire, '93. K II 41

Distinguishing Trait

POETIC LICENSE, d.

Expression

POET, c. BORROWING (VERBAL), c. EPIC, d.

Foundation

ENGLISH VS. FRENCH, e. RULES, d.

Furor Poeticus

b. They who would justify the madness of Poetry from the authority of Aristotle, have mistaken the text, and consequently the interpretation: I imagine it to be false read, where he says of Poetry, that it is Εὐφυοῦς ἤ/μανικοῦ, that it had always somewhat in it either of a genius, or of a madman. 'Tis more probable that the original ran thus, that Poetry was Εὐφυοῦς οὐ μανικοῦ, that it belongs to a witty man, but not to a madman.

Pref. *Troilus,* '79. K I 221–22

Livelihood

b-2. We who write, if we want the talent, yet have the excuse that we do it for a poor subsistence . . . [See POETASTERS, e]

Pref. *All for Love,* '78. K I 196

Lower Orders

COMEDY, h.

---

* See R. P. Cowl, *The Theory of Poetry in England: Its Development in Doctrines and Ideas from the Sixteenth to the Nineteenth Century,* London, 1914.

190

Moral Basis [See MORAL (OF A LITERARY WORK)]

POET, i.

Moral License

OBSCENITY, c.

Origin [See also SATIRE, *Original and Progress*]

c. Mankind, even the most barbarous, have the seeds of poetry implanted in them. The first specimen of it was certainly shown in the praises of the Deity, and prayers to him; and as they are of natural obligation, so they are likewise of divine institution . . .[1] The first/poetry was thus begun, in the wild notes of natural poetry, before the invention of feet, and measures. The Grecians and Romans had no other original of their poetry. Festivals and holidays soon succeeded to private worship . . . But . . . both the Grecians and Romans agreed, after their sacrifices were performed, to spend the remainder of the day in sports and merriments; amongst which, songs and dances, and that which they called wit, (for want of knowing better,) were the chiefest entertainments. The Grecians . . . habited themselves like . . . rural deities, and imitated them in their rustic dances, to which they joined songs, with some sort of rude harmony, but without certain numbers; and to these they added a kind of chorus.

The Romans, also, (as Nature is the same in all places,) . . ./had certain young men, who, at their festivals, danced and sung . . . to a certain kind of verse, which they called Saturnian. . . . Those ancient Romans, at these holidays . . . had a custom of reproaching each other with their faults, in a sort of *ex tempore* poetry, or rather of tunable hobbling verse . . .

Discourse of Satire, '93. K II 45–47

Progress of Poesy and Painting

d. . . . I profess to have no other ambition in this *Essay,* than that poetry may not go backward, when all other arts and sciences are advancing.

Defence of the Epilogue, '72. K I 163

e. The greatest age for Poetry amongst the Romans was certainly that of Augustus Cæsar: and yet we are told that painting was then at its lowest ebb . . . In the reign of Domitian, and some who succeeded him, Poetry was but meanly cultivated, but Painting eminently flourished. . . . [Both arts] were . . . in a manner extinguished by the irruption of the barbarous nations, and both restored about the times of Leo the Tenth, Charles the Fifth, and Francis the First; though I might observe, that neither Ariosto, nor any of his contemporary poets, ever arrived at the excellency of Raphael, Titian, and the rest, in painting. But in revenge, at this time, or lately, in many countries, Poetry is better practiced than her sister-art.

Parallel, '95. K II 135

CHAUCER, c.

Proper Critics of [See also POET, as *Judge*]
CRITIC[s], h.

Prophetic Function

f. [In a panegyric vein to Robert, Earl of Sunderland] . . . I am almost ready to reassume the ancient rights of poetry; to point out, and prophesy the man, who was born for no less an undertaking . . .

Ded. *Troilus,* '79. S-S VI 250

Subtlety

DENHAM, b.

Subject of

f-2. All other greatness in subjects is only counterfeit; it will not endure the test of danger; the greatness of arms is only real.

Pref. *Annus Mirabilis,* '66. K I 14

EPIC, M. OBSCENITY, c.

f-3. The subject of a poet, either in Tragedy or in an Epic Poem, is a great action of some illustrious hero. It is the same in painting; not every action, nor every person, is considerable enough to enter into the cloth. . . .[1] but the parallel is more complete in tragedy, than in an epic poem. For as a tragedy may be made out of many particular episodes of Homer or of Virgil, so may a noble picture . . . History is also fruitful of designs both for the painter and the Tragic poet . . .[1]

Parallel, '95. K II 130

Unprofitableness

THOMAS, b.

Miscellaneous

g. [In panegyric of Dorset's poetry] 'Tis that which the Romans call *cæna dubia;* where there is such plenty, yet withal so much diversity, and so good order, that the choice is difficult betwixt one excellency and another; and yet the conclusion, by a due climax, is evermore the best; that is, as a conclusion ought to be, ever the most proper for its place.

Discourse of Satire, '93. K II 41

Poetry and Painting [See *A Parallel of Poetry and Painting*]

RHYME (DEBATE), g.

a. For so says Horace,

Ut pictura poesis . . .

[See IMITATION, g]

Defence of An Essay, '68. K I 114

b. But some will, I doubt not, object, that poetry should not be reduced to the strictness of mathematics; to which I answer, it ought to be so far mathematical as to have likeness and proportion, since they will all confess that it is a kind of painting. But they will perhaps say, that a poem is a picture to be seen at a distance, and there-

fore ought to be bigger than the life. I confess there must be a due distance allowed
for the seeing of any thing in the world;
for an object can no more be seen at all too
near, than too far off the eye: but granting
that a poem is a picture to be viewed at a
great distance, the distance and the bigness
ought to be so suited, as though the picture
be much bigger than the life, yet it must
not seem so . . . and by the way, let us consider that dramatic poetry, especially the
English, brings the picture nearer the eye,
than any other sort of poetry.

Postscript *N and O,* '74. S-S XV 407

POETIC LICENSE, c, f. UNITIES (DRA-
MATIC), ACTION, c. FANCY, h. Cf. CRITI-
CASTERS, h. PROSODY, v. CHARACTER[s], c.
EPIC HERO, e. ENDS OF POETRY, j. FIC-
TION. OBSCENITY, c. POETRY, f-3. UNITIES
(DRAMATIC), GENERAL, e.

c. . . . I must say this to the advantage
of Painting, even above Tragedy, that what
this last represents in the space of many
hours, the former shews us in one moment.
The action, the passion, and the manners
of so many persons as are contained in a
picture are to be discerned at once, in the
twinkling of an eye; at least they would
be so, if the sight could travel over so
many different objects all at once, or the
mind could digest them all at the same in-
stant, or point of time. Thus, in the famous picture of Poussin, which repre/sents
the *Institution of the Blessed Sacrament,*
you see our Saviour and his twelve disciples,
all concurring in the same action, after different manners, and in different postures;
only the manners of Judas are distinguished
from the rest. Here is but one indivisible
point of time observed; but one action performed by so many persons, in one room,

and at the same table; yet the eye cannot
comprehend at once the whole object, nor
the mind follow it so fast; 'tis considered
at leisure, and seen by intervals.

Parallel, '95. K II 131–32

COMEDY, h. FARCE, e, f. RULES, f, g.
IMITATION, i, h. INVENTION, b. AUTHOR-
ITY, f. SUBJECT, INTEGRITY OF. DECORUM,
i. POSTURE. CHARACTER[s], d. MANNERS,
k. HERO (DRAMATIC), f. EPIC, b.
CHORUS, c. SCENARIO. ORDONNANCE. PAS-
SIONS, j, k. TRAGICOMEDY, g. CHARAC-
TER[s], e. EXPRESSION, b. FIGURES, c.
CHIAROSCURO. MANUM DE TABULA, a.
EXPRESSION, c. EPIC HERO, j.

Points

. . . Lucan . . . was too full of points,
and too often offered at somewhat which
had more of the sting of an epigram,
than of the dignity and state of an heroic
poem. [See LUCAN, b]

Essay of Heroic Plays, '72. K I 152

SETTLE, c. SENECA, b. PASSIONS, h. OVID,
h. BOILEAU, b. TASSO, b.

Polybius*

ENGLISH LANGUAGE, c. HISTORY, e.

a. I had read him [Polybius], in English,
with the pleasure of a boy, before I was ten
years of age; and yet, even then, had some
dark notions of the prudence with which he
conducted his design . . . But when being of a riper age, I took him again into my
hands, I must needs say, that I have profited
more by reading him than by Thucydides, Appian, Dion Cassius, and all the rest
of the Greek historians/together; and
amongst all the Romans, none have reached

---

* See L. R. N. Strachan, "Dryden's 'Character of
Polybius,' " *Notes and Queries,* 11th ser., IX (1914),
103–05.

him, in this particular, but Tacitus, who is equal with him.

"Character of Polybius," '93. S-S XVIII 32–33

COMINES. HISTORIAN, b.

b. [¶] Another part of this veracity [of Polybius] . . . an effect of a sound judgment, [is] that he perpetually explodes the legends of prodigies and miracles, and instead of them, most accurately searches into the natural causes . . . You hear not in Polybius that it rained blood or stones . . . or a thousand such impossibilities, with which Livy perpetually crowds the calends of almost every consulship.

"Character of Polybius," '93. S-S XVIII 43

c. [Polybius's] digressions are . . . so instructive, that we may truly say, they transcend the profit which we receive from the matter of fact. Upon the whole, we may conclude him to be a great talker; but we must grant him to be a prudent man.

"Character of Polybius," '93. S-S XVIII 49

ROME.

Polybius and Tacitus

[¶] I will not undertake to compare Polybius and Tacitus; though, if I should attempt it upon the whole merits of the cause, I must allow to Polybius the greater comprehension, and the larger soul; to Tacitus, the greater eloquence, and the more close connection of his thoughts. The manner of Tacitus in writing is more like the/force and gravity of Demosthenes; that of Polybius more like the copiousness and diffusive character of Cicero. . . . They are both of them, without dispute, the best historians in their several kinds. . . . But it is not my business to defend Tacitus;

neither dare I decide the preference betwixt him and our Polybius. They are equally profitable and instructive . . . but Tacitus more useful to those who are born under a monarchy, Polybius to those who live in a republic.

"Character of Polybius," '93. S-S XVIII 51–52

Portrait Painting (Portraiture)

IMITATION, g.

What calumny your Grace [Ormond] may expect from such writers, is already evident: but it will fare with them as it does with ill painters; a picture so unlike in all its features and proportions, reflects not on the original, but on the artist; for malice will make a piece more unresembling than ignorance; and he who studies the life, yet bungles, may draw some faint imitation of it, but he who purposely avoids nature, must fall into grotesque,/and make no likeness.

Ded. *Plutarch's Lives,* '83. S-S XVII 16–17

TRANSLATION, x.

Possibility

[¶] After all this, the very absurdity, to which he [Howard] would reduce me, is none at all: for he only drives at this, that, if his argument be true, I must then acknowledge that there are degrees in impossibilities, which I easily grant him without dispute; and, if I mistake not, Aristotle and the School are of my opinion. For there are some things which are absolutely impossible, and others which are only so *ex parte* . . .

Defence of An Essay, '68. K I 132

SUPERNATURAL, a. LAUGHTER, c. LAST AGE, c. SUPERNATURAL, d, e, f. POET, i. PROBABILITY, b. Cf. SHAKESPEARE, l.

193

Opera, a. Cf. Polybius, b. Cf. Ariosto, a.

Posture

Cf. Translation, x.

[¶] Du Fresnoy . . . makes *design,* or *drawing,* the second part of painting; but the rules which he gives concerning the posture of the figures are almost wholly proper to that art, and admit not any comparison, that I know, with poetry. The posture of a poetic figure is, as I conceive, the description of his heroes in the performance of such or such an action; as of Achilles, just in the act of killing Hector . . .[1] Both the poet and the painter vary the posture, according to the action or passion which they represent, of the same person; but all must be great and graceful in them.[1]

Parallel, '95. K II 140

Prefaces

a. [¶] The writing of prefaces to plays was probably invented by some very ambitious poet, who never thought he had done enough: Perhaps by some ape of the French eloquence, which uses to make a business of a letter of gallantry, an examen of a farce; and, in short, a great pomp and ostentation of words on every trifle.

Pref. *Tempest,* '69. S-S III 105

Panegyric, b.

b. [¶] And now with the usual vanity of Dutch prefacers, I could load our author [Plutarch] with the praises and commemorations of writers . . . but to cumber pages with this kind of stuff, were to raise a distrust in common readers that Plutarch wants them.

"Life of Plutarch," '83. S-S XVII 76

Dryden, Works, uu.

c. In the meantime I beg the reader's pardon, for entertaining him so long with myself: 'tis an usual part of ill manners in all authors, and almost in all mankind, to

trouble others with their business . . .

Parallel, '95. K II 117

Dryden, Works, ttt. Correctness, b.

d. . . . I am of the temper of most kings, who love to be in debt, are all for present money, no matter how they pay it afterwards: besides, the nature of a preface is rambling, never wholly out of the way, nor in it. This I have learned from the practice of honest Montaigne . . .

Pref. *Fables,* 1700. K II 255

Present Age

a. (Crites) There are so few who write well in this age . . . that methinks any praises should be welcome; they neither rise to the dignity of the last age, nor to any of the Ancients . . .

Dram. Poesy, '65. K I 33

Nature, e. Moderns, a.

b. (Eugenius) . . . neither know I any reason why I may not be as zealous for the reputation of our age, as we find the Ancients themselves in reference to those who lived before them. For you hear your Horace saying,

Indignor quidquam reprehendi . . ./

And after

Si meliora dies . . .

Dram. Poesy, '65. K I 33–34

c. (Eugenius) . . . those [English plays] we now see acted come short of many which were written in the last age . . .

Dram. Poesy, '65. K I 34

d. (Eugenius) . . . in the epic or lyric way, it will be hard for them [the last age] to show us one such amongst them, as we have many now living, or who lately were so: they can produce nothing so courtly/ writ, or which expresses so much the conversation of a gentleman, as Sir John Suckling; nothing so even, sweet, and flowing, as Mr. Waller; nothing so majestic, so correct, as Sir John Denham; nothing so elevated, so copious, and full of spirit, as Mr. Cowley . . . [See next entry]

Dram. Poesy, '65. K I 34–35

e. (Eugenius) . . . as for the Italian, French, and Spanish plays, I can make it evident, that those [in English] who now write surpass them; and that the Drama is wholly ours.

Dram. Poesy, '65. K I 35

f. (Narrator: Dryden) . . . every one was willing to acknowledge how much our poesy is improved by the happiness of some writers yet living; who first taught us to mould our thoughts into easy and significant words; to retrench the superfluities of expression, and to make our rime so properly a part of the verse, that it should never mislead the sense, but itself be led and governed by it.

Dram. Poesy, '65. K I 35
CRITICASTERS, a. ENGLISH VS. FRENCH, a.

g. (Neander) . . . our present poets . . . have far surpassed all the Ancients, and the modern writers of other countries.

Dram. Poesy, '65. K I 89
LAST AGE, b. RHYME (DEBATE), 1. DRYDEN, PERSONAL CHARACTER, f.

h. Yet I would so maintain my opinion of the present age, as not to be wanting in my veneration for the past . . .

Defence of the Epilogue, '72. K I 162

i. For we live in an age so sceptical, that as it determines little, so it takes nothing from antiquity on trust . . .

Defence of the Epilogue, '72. K I 163

j. Neither would I be understood, when I/speak of impropriety of language, either wholly to accuse the last age, or to excuse the present, and least of all myself; for all writers have their imperfections and failings: but I may safely conclude in the general, that our improprieties are less frequent, and less gross than theirs.[1]

Defence of the Epilogue, '72. K I 164–65
Cf. BORROWING (VERBAL), b.

k. [¶] That the wit of this age is much more courtly, may easily be proved, by viewing the characters of gentlemen which were written in the last. First, for Johnson: —Truewit, in the *Silent Woman,* was his masterpiece; and Truewit was a scholarlike kind of man, a gentleman with an allay of pedantry, a man who seems mortified to the world, by much reading. The best of his discourse is drawn, not from the knowledge of the town, but books; and, in short, he would be a fine gentleman in an university.

Defence of the Epilogue, '72. K I 174

l. I cannot, therefore, conceive it any insolence to affirm, that, by the knowledge and pattern of their wit who writ before us, and by the advantage of our own conversation, the discourse and raillery of our comedies excel what has been written by them.

Defence of the Epilogue, '72. K I 175
LAST AGE, j.

m. Wit seems to have lodged itself more nobly in this age, than in any of the former; and people of my mean condition are only writers, because some of the nobility, and your Lordship in the first place, are above the narrow praises which poesy could give you.

Ded. *Marriage à la Mode, '73.* S-S IV 257
CRITICASTERS, e. SHAKESPEARE, n. Cf. SHAKESPEARE, g. ACADEMY, b. NORTH'S *Plutarch*

n. [¶] It is an age, indeed, which is only fit for satire, and the sharpest I have shall never be wanting to lance its villainies, and its ingratitude to the government.

Ded. *Plutarch's Lives,* '83. S-S XVII 8

CRITICASTERS, h. SATIRE, h. CRITIC[s], c. Cf. SATIRE, i. FARCE, c, d. DONNE, d. PROSODY, z. CRITIC[s], d. LAST AGE, l.

o. What then would he [Homer] appear in the harmonious version of one of the best writers [Congreve], living in a much better age than was the last? I mean for versification, and the art of numbers; for in the drama we have not arrived to the pitch of Shakespeare and Ben Johnson.

Examen Poeticum, '93. K II 14

DENNIS, a. PAINTING. SCEPTICISM, b.

p. This I dare venture to maintain, that the taste of the age is wretchedly depraved in all sorts of poetry; nothing almost but what is abominably bad can please. The young hounds, who ought to come behind, now lead the pack; but they miserably mistake the scent. Their poets, worthy of such an audience, know not how to distinguish their characters; the manners are all alike inconsistent, and interfering with each other. There is scarce a man or woman of God's making in all their farces, yet they raise an unnatural sort of laughter, the common effect of buffoonery; and the rabble, which takes this for wit, will endure no better, because it is above their understanding. This account I take from the best judges; for I thank God, I have had the grace hitherto to avoid the seeing or reading of their gallimaufries. But it is the latter end of a century, and I hope the next will begin better.

Pref. *Husband His Own Cuckold,* '96. S-S XV 410

IMAGINATION, e. COLLIER.

Probability [Cf. VERISIMILITY]

Cf. NECESSITY. UNITIES (DRAMATIC), PLACE, b. FABLE, b. Cf. TUMULT, a.

LIAISON, b. DECORUM, d. CORNEILLE (PIERRE), a-2. RHYME (DEBATE), g.

a. . . . it [is] not the business of a poet to represent historical truth, but probability.

Ded. *Indian Emperor,* '67. S-S II 288

IMAGINATION (*Responsive*), b. VERISIMILITY, b. SUPERNATURAL, c, d. Cf. LAST AGE, c. TRAGEDY, a.

b. The last quality of the action is, that it ought to be probable, as well as admirable and great. 'Tis not necessary that there should be historical truth in it; but always necessary that there should be a likeness of truth, something that is more than barely possible; *probable* being that which succeeds, or happens, oftener than it misses. To invent therefore a probability, and to make it wonderful, is the most difficult undertaking in the art of Poetry; for that which is not wonderful is not great; and that which is not probable will not delight a reasonable audience.

Pref. *Troilus,* '79. K I 209

Cf. SHAKESPEARE, l. RULES, d. TRAGEDY, q. FABLE, e. EPIC MACHINES, *a.*

Profaneness [See OBSCENITY]

Progress

a. (Crites) [¶] Is it not evident, in these last hundred years (when the study of philosophy has been the business of all the Virtuosi in Christendom), that almost a new Nature has/been revealed to us?— that more errors of the school have been detected, more useful experiments in philosophy have been made, more noble secrets in optics, medicine, anatomy, astronomy, discovered, than in all those credulous and doting ages from Aristotle to us?—so true is it, that nothing spreads more fast than science, when rightly and generally cultivated.

Dram. Poesy, '65. K I 36–37

b. (Eugenius) . . . if natural causes be

more known now than in the time of Aristotle, because more studied, it follows that poesy and other arts may, with the same pains, arrive still nearer to perfection . . .

Dram. Poesy, '65. K I 44

POETRY, d.

c. And, both in the whole course of that satire [I.10], and in his most admirable *Epistle to Augustus,* he [Horace] makes it his business to prove, that antiquity alone is no plea for the excellency of a poem; but that, one age learning from another, the last (if we can suppose an equality of wit in the writers) has the advantage of knowing more and better than the former. And this, I think, is the state of the question in dispute [in the Epilogue to The Second Part of 'The Conquest of Granada' and in the *Defence of the Epilogue*].

Defence of the Epilogue, '72. K I 163

LAST AGE, c, k. Cf. ANCIENTS, a. GOOD SENSE. Cf. GOLDEN AGES, b.

d. [In connection with a proposal to render Christian machinery in the epic effective] Yet we see the art of war is improved in sieges, and new instruments of death are/invented daily; something new in philosophy and the mechanics is discovered almost every year; and the science of former ages is improved by the succeeding.

Discourse of Satire, '93. K II 33–34

HORACE AND JUVENAL AND PERSIUS, j.

e. The majestic way of Persius and Juvenal was new when they began it, but 'tis old to us; and what poems have not, with time, received an alteration in their fashion? 'Which alteration,' says Holyday, 'is to aftertimes as good a warrant as the first.' Has not Virgil changed the manners of Homer's heroes in his *Æneis?* Certainly he has, and for the better: for Virgil's age

was more civilised, and better bred;/and he writ according to the politeness of Rome, under the reign of Augustus Cæsar, not to the rudeness of Agamemnon's age, or the times of Homer. Why should we offer to confine free spirits to one form, when we cannot so much as confine our bodies to one fashion of apparel?

Discourse of Satire, '93. K II 101–2

f. I was afraid that I had been the inventor of a new sort of designing, when, in my third act, I make a discovery of my Alphonso's true parentage. If it were so, what wonder had it been that dramatic poetry, though a/limited art, yet might be capable of receiving some innovations for the better? But afterwards I casually found that Menander and Terence, in the "Heautontimoroumenos," had been before me, and made the same kind of discovery in the same act.

Ded. *Love Triumphant,* '94. S-S VIII 374–75

PRESENT AGE, p. MODERNIZING.

Pronunciation (English)

PROSODY, ll. ACADEMY, b. ENGLISH LANGUAGE, a.

Propertius, Sextus

OVID, e.

Except Sabinus, who writ some answers to Ovid's *Letters* . . .º I remember not any of the Romans who have treated this subject, save only Propertius, and that but once, in his Epistle of *Arethusa to Lycotas,* which is written so near the style of Ovid, that it seems to be but an imitation; and therefore ought not to defraud our poet of the glory of his invention.

Pref. *Ovid's Epistles,* '80. K I 236

Propriety [Cf. DECORUM]

PRESENT AGE, j. JONSON, u. FLETCHER, d. Cf. FLETCHER, f. ACADEMY, b. SUBLIME. SUPERNATURAL, g. Cf. EPIC, j.

. . . in all things we are to imitate the customs and the times of those persons and things which we represent . . .

Parallel, '95. K II 139

Cf. IMITATION, b. PASSIONS, k. TECHNICAL TERMS, b.

Propriety of Thoughts and Words

Cf. FABLE, c.

[Wit] is a propriety of thoughts and words; or, in other terms, thoughts and words elegantly adapted to the subject. [See WIT, 1]

Author's Apology, '77. K I 190

Cf. TRAGEDY, m. Cf. SYLVESTER'S *Du Bartas.* ACTING AND ACTORS, b. VIRGIL, oo. WIT, m. Cf. DRAMA READ AND ACTED, b. Cf. JUVENAL, a. Cf. OVID, a. WIT, o. Cf. VIRGIL, mm. Cf. HOMER AND VIRGIL, d. Cf. CHAUCER AND OVID.

Prose

PROSODY, f. RHYME (DEBATE), c. PROSODY, g, h. RHYME (DEBATE), u.

a. . . . one great reason why prose is not to be used in serious plays, is, because it is too near the nature of converse: there may be too great a likeness . . .

Defence of An Essay, '68. K I 114

JONSON, l. RHYME (DEBATE), x, r. POETIC LICENSE, d. TRANSLATION, j. ETHEREGE. Cf. SATIRE, aa. TRANSLATION, c. Cf. VIRGIL, mm. Cf. PROSODY, s. DRYDEN, LIFE, e. CHAUCER AND BOCCACCIO.

b. . . . prose allows more liberty of thought, and the expression is more easy when unconfined by numbers.

Pref. *Fables,* 1700. K II 269

Prosody*

Cf. PRESENT AGE, f, o. DONNE, c. POETRY, c. SATIRE, aa.

a. But versification and numbers are

---

* See R. D. Jameson, "Notes on Dryden's Lost Prosodia," *MP,* XX (1923), 241–53.

the greatest pleasures of poetry . . . when there is anything deficient in numbers and sound, the reader is uneasy and unsatisfied; he wants something of his complement, desires somewhat which he finds not . . .

Discourse of Satire, '93. K II 86

DONNE, d. PRESENT AGE, o. EXPRESSION, b. DRYDEN, WORKS, iii.

b. But Virgil, who never attempted the lyric verse, is everywhere elegant, sweet, and flowing in his hexameters. His words are not only chosen, but the places in which he ranks them for the sound. . . . I cannot boast that I have been thus exact in my verses; but I have endeavoured to follow the example of my master, and am the first Englishman, perhaps, who made it his design to copy him in his numbers, his choice of words, and his placing them for the sweetness of the sound. On this last consideration I have shunned the *cæsura* [*i.e.,* synaloepha] as much as possibly I could: for, wherever that is used, it gives a roughness to the verse; of which we can have little need in a language which is overstocked with consonants. Such is not the Latin, where the vowels and consonants are mixed in proportion to each other: yet Virgil judged the vowels to have somewhat of an over-balance, and therefore tempers their sweetness with *cæsuras.* Such difference there is in tongues, that the same figure, which roughens one, gives majesty to another: and that was it which Virgil studied in his verses. Ovid uses it but rarely; and hence it is that his versification cannot so properly be called sweet, as luscious. The Italians are forced upon it once or twice in every line, because they have a redundancy of vowels . . . On the other side . . . 'tis all we can do to give sufficient sweetness to our language: we must not only/choose our words for elegance, but for sound; to perform which, a mastery in the language is required; the poet must have a magazine of words, and have the art to manage his few vowels to the best advantage, that they may go the further. He must also know the nature of the vowels, which are more sonorous, and which more soft and sweet, and so dispose them as his present occasions require: all which, and a thousand secrets of versification beside, he may learn from Virgil . . . If he be above Virgil, and is resolved to follow his own *verve,* (as the French call it), the proverb will fall heavily upon him: *Who teaches himself, has a fool for his master.*

Ded. *Æneis,* '97. K II 215–16

c. [¶] You may please also to observe [of the translation of the *Æneid*], that there is not, to the best of my remembrance, one vowel gaping on another for want of a *cæsura,* in this whole poem: but,/where a vowel ends a word, the next begins either with a consonant, or what is its equivalent; for our *W* and *H* aspirate, and our diphthongs, are plainly such. The greatest latitude I take is in the letter *Y,* when it concludes a word, and the first syllable of the next begins with a vowel. Neither need I have called this a latitude, which is only an explanation of this general rule, that no vowel can be cut off before another when we cannot sink the pronunciation of it; as *he, she, me, I,* etc. Virgil thinks it sometimes a beauty to imitate the license of the Greeks, and leave two vowels opening on each other . . .⁹

But *nobis non licet esse tam disertis,* at least if we study to refine our numbers. I have long had by me the materials of an English *Prosodia,* containing all the mechanical rules of versification, wherein I have treated, with some exactness, of the feet, the quantities, and the pauses. The French and Italians know nothing of the two first; at least their best poets have not practised them. As for the pauses, Malherbe first brought them into France within this last century; and we see how they adorn their Alexandrines.

Ded. *Æneis,* '97. K II 216–17

d. I am sure there are few who make verses, have observed the sweetness of these two lines in *Cooper's Hill—*

Though deep, yet clear; though gentle, yet not dull;
Strong without rage; without o'erflowing, full.

And there are fewer who can find the reason of that/sweetness. I have given it to some of my friends in conversation; and they have allowed the criticism to be just. But, since the evil of false quantities is difficult to be cured in any modern language; since the French and the Italians, as well as we, are yet ignorant what feet are to be used in Heroic Poetry; since I have not strictly observed those rules myself, which I can teach others; since I pretend to no dictatorship among my fellow-poets; since, if I should instruct some of them to make well-running verses, they want genius to give them strength as well as sweetness; and, above all, since your Lordship has advised me not to publish that little which I know, I look on your counsel as your command, which I shall observe inviolably, till you shall please to revoke it, and leave me at liberty to make my thoughts public.

Ded. *Æneis,* '97. K II 217–18

ENGLISH VS. FRENCH, n.

Accent
See below, p.

Alexandrine
RHYME (PROSODIC), gg. RHYME (DEBATE), f, k. See below, v.

e. . . . I must acknowledge that Virgil in Latin, and Spenser in English, have been my masters. Spenser has also given me the boldness to make use sometimes of his Alexandrine line, which we call, though improperly, the Pindaric, because Mr. Cowley has often employed it in his *Odes*. It adds a certain majesty to the verse, when it is used with judgment, and stops the sense from overflowing into another line.

Ded. *Æneis*, '97. K II 218

See below, jj. Cf. above, c.

Blank Verse [See also RHYME (DEBATE)]

f. [Shakespeare invented] that kind of writing which we call blank verse, but the French, more properly, *prose mesurée;* into which the English tongue so naturally slides, that, in writing prose, it is hardly to be avoided. [See SHAKESPEARE, a]

Ded. *Rival Ladies,* '64. K I 6

See below, n. RHYME (DEBATE), d, f, g, h, i.

g. (Neander) As for that place of Aristotle, where he says, plays should be writ in that kind of verse which is nearest prose, it makes little for you [Crites]; blank verse being properly but measured prose. Now measure alone, in any modern language, does not constitute verse . . .

Dram. Poesy, '65. K I 96

h. (Neander) Neither do the Spanish, French, Italian, or Germans, acknowledge at all, or very rarely, any such kind of poesy as blank verse amongst them. Therefore, at most 'tis but a poetic prose, a *sermo pedestris;* and as such, most fit for comedies, where I acknowledge rhyme to be improper.

Dram. Poesy, '65. K I 97

RHYME (DEBATE), k, m, p, x. Cf. DRYDEN, WORKS, v. CARO. MILTON, c. TRANSLATION, gg. See below, hh.

Burlesque

BUTLER, b. See below, m. BOILEAU, c.

Cadence

DONNE, a. See below, ee. RHYME (DEBATE), q. Cf. PLUTARCH, h. See below, v. DRYDEN, WORKS, bbb. OPERA, i. DRYDEN, WORKS, eee. EXPRESSION, b.

Caesura [See below, *Synaloepha*]

Closed Couplet [See below, *Enjambement*]

WALLER, a. RHYME (DEBATE), d. See below, ee, bb.

Consonants [See CONSONANTS]

Distich

WALLER, a. See below, ee. RHYME (DEBATE), k. See below, bb, m, k.

Ear

Cf. PLUTARCH, h. See below, v, w. OPERA, e. DRYDEN, WORKS, ooo, sss. HOMER AND VIRGIL, d. Cf. CHAUCER, c.

Enjambement

Cf. WALLER, a. See below, ee. RHYME (DEBATE), k. See above, e.

Expletives

POETASTERS, d.

Feet [Cf. below, *Measure*]

See below, p.

i. (Neander) No man is tied in modern poesy to observe any farther rule in the feet of his verse, but that they be dissyllables; whether spondee, trochee, or iambic, it matters not; only he is obliged to rhyme.

Dram. Poesy, '65. K I 97

See below, ff. SATIRE, aa. See above, c, d.

Fourteener

CHAPMAN, b.

"Golden" Verse

j. . . . that verse . . . which they call golden, or two substantives and two adjectives, with a verb betwixt them to keep the peace. [See CLAUDIAN]

Pref. *Sylvæ,* '85. K I 255

Hemistich
See below, dd, ee. RHYME (DEBATE), k, p.
VIRGIL, oo.

k. [¶] There is another thing in which
I have presumed to deviate from him
[Cowley] and Spenser. They both make
hemistichs (or half verses), breaking off in
the middle of a line. I confess there are not
many such in the *Fairy Queen;* and even
those few might be occasioned by his unhappy choice of so long a stanza. Mr.
Cowley had found out that no kind of
staff is proper for a heroic poem, as being
all too lyrical: yet, though he wrote in
couplets, where rhyme is freer from constraint, he frequently affects half verses; of
which we find not one in Homer, and I
think not in any of the Greek poets, or the
Latin, excepting only Virgil; and there is
no question but he thought he had Virgil's
authority for that licence. But, I am confident, our poet never meant to leave him,
or any other, such a precedent: and I
ground my opinion on these two reasons:
first, we find no example of a hemistich in
any of his *Pastorals* or *Georgics;* for he had
given the last finishing strokes to both these
poems: but his *Æneis* he left so incorrect,
at least so short of that perfection at which
he aimed, that we know how hard a sentence he passed upon it: and . . . I reasonably presume, that he intended to have
filled up all those hemistichs . . .[1]/On
these considerations I have shunned hemistichs; not being willing to imitate Virgil
to a fault . . .[1] I am confident your Lordship is by this time of my opinion, and that
you will look on those half lines hereafter
as the imperfect products of a hasty Muse;
like the frogs and serpents in the Nile; part
of them kindled into life, and part a lump

of unformed unanimated mud.
   Ded. *Æneis,* '97. K II 230–31
l. That Virgil never intended to have
left any hemistich, I have prov'd already
in the preface.
   Notes and Observations on Virgil's
Works, '97. N 711
Heroic Line
VIRGIL, pp. See below, v, x.

m. [Speaking of the versification of
Satire] . . . I would prefer the verse of
ten syllables, which we call the English
heroic, to that of eight. . . . For this sort
of number is more roomy; the thought can
turn itself with greater ease in a larger
compass. When the rhyme comes too thick
upon us, it straitens the expression; we are
thinking of the close, when we should be
employed in adorning the thought. It
makes a poet giddy with turning in a space
too narrow for his imagination; he loses
many beauties, without gaining one advantage. For a burlesque rhyme I have already concluded to be none; or, if it were,
'tis more easily purchased in ten syllables
than in eight. In both occasions 'tis as in a
tennis-court, when the strokes of greater
force are given, when we strike out and
play at length.
   Discourse of Satire, '93. K II 106
BOILEAU, c. HOLYDAY, c. Cf. CHAPMAN, b.
See above, d. ENGLISH VS. FRENCH, n. See
below, r. TRANSLATION, n. CHAU-
CER, c, f.
Hiatus
See above, c.
Hudibrastics [See below, *Octosyllabics*]
Inversion

n. . . . I admire some men should perpetually stumble in a way so easy [blank
verse], and inverting the order of their

words, constantly close their lines with verbs, which though commended sometimes in writing Latin, yet we were whipt at Westminster if we used it twice together. I know some, who, if they were to write in blank verse, *Sir, I ask your pardon,* would think it sounded more heroically to write, *Sir, I your pardon ask.* [See next entry]

Ded. *Rival Ladies,* '64. K I 6

o. I should judge him to have little command of English, whom the necessity of rhyme should force/often upon this rock [inversion]; though sometimes it cannot easily be avoided; and indeed this is the only inconvenience with which rhyme can be charged.

Ded. *Rival Ladies,* '64. K I 6–7
RHYME (DEBATE), c.
Measure [Cf. above, *Feet*]
RHYME (DEBATE), g, i, j.

p. (Neander) Now measure alone, in any modern language, does not constitute verse; those of the Ancients in Greek and Latin consisted in quantity of words, and a determinate number of feet. But . . . by the inundation of the Goths and Vandals into Italy, new languages were brought in, and . . . /a new way of poesy . . . This new way consisted in measure of number of feet, and rhyme; the sweetness of rhyme, and observation of accent, supplying the place of quantity. [See above, i]

Dram. Poesy, '65. K I 96–97
JUDGMENT, b.

q. [¶] I have not everywhere [in *Tyrannic Love*] observed the equality of numbers, in my verse; partly by reason of my haste; but more especially, because I would not have my sense a slave to syllables.

Pref. *Tyrannic Love,* '70. S-S III 379

OPERA, f. SATIRE, aa. See below, y.
Monosyllables
POETASTERS, d. Cf. LATIN, b. OPERA, f. WALSH, c. HOLYDAY, c.

r. . . . I am excluded from it [literal translation of Virgil] by the narrow compass of our heroic verse, unless I would make use of monosyllables only, and those clogged with consonants, which are the dead weight of our mother-tongue. [See next entry]

Ded. *Æneis,* '97. K II 226

s. 'Tis possible, I confess, though it rarely happens, that a verse of monosyllables may sound harmoniously; and some examples of it I have seen. My first line of the *Æneis* is not harsh—

> Arms, and the Man I sing, who forc'd
> by Fate, &c.

But a much better instance may be given from the last line of Manilius, made English by our learned and judicious Mr. Creech—

> Nor could the World have borne so
> fierce a Flame—

where the many liquid consonants are placed so artfully, that they give a pleasing sound to the words, though they are all of one syllable.

'Tis true, I have been sometimes forced upon it in other places of this work: but I never did it out of/choice; I was either in haste, or Virgil gave me no occasion for the ornament of words; for it seldom happens but a monosyllable line turns verse to prose; and even that prose is rugged and unharmonious.[1]

Ded. *Æneis,* '97. K II 226–27
BORROWING (VERBAL), c.   DRYDEN, WORKS, sss.
Numbers: Harshness
SETTLE, c. PERSIUS, b. CHAPMAN, b.

Numbers: Roughness
DRYDEN, WORKS, bbb, sss.
Numbers: Smoothness
WALSH, c. THOMAS, c.
Numbers: Variety
See below, ee, t-2. VIRGIL, oo. OVID, k.
OPERA, b. EPIC POET, a. SPENSER, b.
Numerousness
HORACE, j. See above, d. SPENSER, b.
Octosyllabics
BUTLER, b. See above, m.
Onomatopoeia

t. . . . the very sound of his [Virgil's]
words have often somewhat that is con-
natural to the subject . . . [See VIRGIL, 1]
Pref. *Annus Mirabilis,* '66. K I 17
VIRGIL, oo. DRYDEN, WORKS, sss.
Pause
See above, c.
Pindaric

t-2. (Neander) . . . we may use the
benefit of the Pindaric way practised in
The Siege of Rhodes; where the numbers
vary, and the rhyme is disposed carelessly,
and far from often chiming. [See RHYME
(DEBATE), k]
Dram. Poesy, '65. K I 97
TRANSLATION, h. COWLEY, e. DRYDEN,
WORKS, tt.

u. [Pindaric verse] allows more latitude
than any other. Every one knows it was
introduced into our language, in this age,
by the happy genius of Mr. Cowley. The
seeming easiness of it has made it spread;
but it has not been considered enough, to
be so well cultivated. It languishes in almost every hand but his . . . He, indeed,
has brought it as near perfection as was
possible in so short a time. But if I may be
allowed to speak my mind modestly, and
without injury to his sacred ashes, somewhat of the purity of English, somewhat of

more equal thoughts, somewhat of sweetness in the numbers, in one word, somewhat of a finer turn and more lyrical
verse, is yet wanting. As for the soul of it,
which consists in the warmth and vigour
of fancy, the masterly figures, and the
copiousness of imagination, he has excelled
all others in this kind.
Pref. *Sylvæ,* '85. K I 267

v. Since Pindar was the prince of lyric
poets, let me have leave to say, that, in imitating him, our numbers should, for the
most part, be lyrical: for variety, or rather
where the majesty of thought requires it,
they may be stretched to the English heroic
of five feet, and to the French Alexandrine
of six. But the ear must preside, and direct
the judgment to the choice of numbers:
without the nicety of this, the harmony of
Pindaric verse can never be complete; the
cadency of one line must be a rule to that
of the next; and the sound of the former
must slide gently into that which follows,
without leaping from one extreme into
another. It must be done like the shadowings of a picture, which fall by degrees into
a darker colour. I shall be glad, if I have
so explained myself as to be understood; but
if I have not, *quod nequeo dicere, et sentio
tantum,* must be my excuse.
Pref. *Sylvæ,* '85. K I 268

w. [The Pindaric ode is] a noble sort
of poetry . . . happily restored by one man
[Cowley], and . . . grossly copied by almost all the rest. A musical ear,/and a great
genius, if another Mr. Cowley could arise
in another age, may bring it to perfection.
Pref. *Sylvæ,* '85. K I 268–69

x. But I defend them not [the extravagant similitudes of *Eleonora*]; let them pass
for beautiful faults amongst the better sort
of critics; for the whole poem, though writ-

ten in that which they call heroic verse, is of the pindaric nature, as well in the thought as the expression; and, as such, requires the same grains of allowance for it. It was intended . . . not for an elegy, but a panegyric: a kind of apo/theosis, indeed, if a heathen word may be applied to a Christian use. And on all occasions of praise, if we take the ancients for our patterns, we are bound by prescription to employ the magnificence of words, and the force of figures, to adorn the sublimity of thoughts. Isocrates . . . and Cicero, and the younger Pliny . . . have left us their precedents for our security; for I think I need not mention the inimitable Pindar, who stretches on these pinions out of sight, and is carried upward, as it were, into another world.

Ded. *Eleonora,* '92. S-S XI 122–23

y. There is another part of Poetry in which the English stand almost upon an equal foot with the Ancients; and 'tis that which we call Pindarique; introduced but not perfected by our famous Mr. Cowley: and of this, Sir, you are certainly one of the greatest Masters. You have the Sublimity of Sense as well as Sound, and know how far the Boldness of a Poet may lawfully extend. I could wish you would cultivate this kind of Ode; and reduce it either to the same Measures which Pindar us'd, or give new Measures of your own. For, as it is, it looks like a vast Tract of Land newly discover'd. The Soil is wonderfully Fruitful, but unmanur'd, overstock'd with Inhabitants; but almost all Salvages, without Laws, Arts, Arms, or Policy. I remember Poor Nat. Lee, who was then upon the Verge of Madness, yet made a Sober, and a Witty Answer to a Bad Poet, who told him, *It was an easie thing to write like*

a Madman: No, said he, *'tis very difficult to write like a Madman, but 'tis a very easie matter to write like a fool.* Otway and He are safe by death from all Attacks, but we poor Poets Militant (to use Mr. Cowley's Expression) are at the Mercy of Wretched Scribblers: And when they cannot fasten upon our Verses, they fall upon our Morals, our Principles of State and Religion.

Letter to Dennis, March 1694. Ward No. 31, p. 72

See above, e. See below, jj.

Prosodia

HOMER, e.

z. I might descend also to the mechanic beauties of heroic verse; but we have yet no English *prosodia,* not so much as a tolerable dictionary, or a grammar; so that our language is in a manner barbarous; and what government will encourage any one, or more, who are capable of refining it, I know not: but nothing under a public expense can go through with it. And I rather fear a declination of the language, than hope an advancement of it in the present age.

Discourse of Satire, '93. K II 110

See above, c, d.

Quantity

See above, p. See below, ff. OPERA, e. See above, c, d.

Quatrain

aa. I have chosen to write my poem in quatrains, or stanzas of four in alternate rhyme, because I have ever judged them more noble, and of greater dignity, both for the sound and number, than any other verse in use amongst us . . .

Pref. *Annus Mirabilis,* '66. K I 11

bb. But in this necessity of our rhymes, I have always found the couplet verse most easy (though not so proper for this occasion [i.e., the *Annus Mirabilis*]), for there the work is sooner at an end, every two lines concluding the labour of the poet; but in quatrains he is to carry it farther on, and not only so, but to bear along in his head the troublesome sense of four lines together. For those who write correctly in this kind must needs acknowledge, that the last line of the stanza is to be considered in the composition of the first.

Pref. *Annus Mirabilis*, '66. K I 12

Rhyme (*Prosodic*) [Cf. RHYME (DE-BATE)]

PRESENT AGE, f.

cc. (Neander) . . . what other conditions are required to make rhyme natural in itself, besides an election of apt words, and a right disposing of them? For the due choice of your words expresses your sense naturally, and the due placing them adapts the rhyme to it. . . . so that the necessity of rhyme never forces any but bad or lazy writers to say what they would not otherwise. [See next entry]

Dram. Poesy, '65. K I 95

dd. (Neander) 'Tis true, there is both care and art required to write in verse. A good poet never concludes upon the first line, till he has sought out such a rhyme as may fit the sense, already prepared to heighten the second: many times the close of the sense falls into the middle of the next verse, or farther off, and he may often prevail himself of the same advantages in English which Virgil had in Latin; he may break off in the hemistich, and begin another line. [See next entry]

Dram. Poesy, '65. K I 95

ee. (Neander) Indeed, the not/observing these two last things [the concluding of the sense in the middle of a second verse 'or farther off'] makes plays which are writ in verse so tedious: for though, most commonly, the sense is to be confined to the couplet, yet nothing that does *perpetuo tenore fluere,* run in the same channel, can please always. 'Tis like the murmuring of a stream, which not varying in the fall, causes at first attention, at last drowsiness. Variety of cadences is the best rule; the greatest help to actors, and refreshment to the audience.

Dram. Poesy, '65. K I 95–96

ff. The learned languages have certainly a great advantage of us, in not being tied to the slavery of any rhyme; and where less constrained in the quantity of every syllable, which they might vary with spondees or dactyls, besides so many other helps of grammatical figures, for the lengthening or abbreviation of them, than the modern are in the close of that one syllable, which often confines, and more often corrupts, the sense of all the rest.

Pref. *Annus Mirabilis,* '66. K I 12

gg. Neither can we give ourselves the liberty of making any part of a verse for the sake of rhyme, or concluding with a word which is not current English, or using the variety of female rhymes, all which our fathers practised; and for the female rhymes, they are still in use amongst other nations; with the Italian in every line, with the Spaniard promiscuously, with the French alternately, as those who have read the *Alaric,* the *Pucelle,* or any of their later poems, will agree . . . And besides this, they write in Alexandrines, or verses of six feet; such as, amongst us, is the old translation of Homer by Chapman: all which, by lengthening of their chain, makes the sphere of their activity the larger.

Pref. *Annus Mirabilis,* '66. K I 12.

RHYME (DEBATE), x. Cf. SETTLE, c.
WALSH, c. BUTLER, b. See above, m.
TRANSLATION, gg.

hh. [Caro, in his translation of the
Æneis] has taken the advantage of writing
in blank verse, and freed himself from the
shackles of modern rhyme, if it be modern;
for Le Clerc has told us lately, and I believe has made it out, that David's Psalms
were written in as arrant rhyme as they are
translated. Now, if a Muse cannot run
when she is unfettered, it is a sign she has
but little speed. I will not make a digression here, though I am strangely tempted
to it; but will only say, that he who can
write well in rhyme may write better in
blank verse. Rhyme is certainly a constraint
even to the best poets, and those who make
it with most ease; though perhaps I have
as little reason to complain of that hardship
as/any man, excepting Quarles and Withers. What it adds to sweetness, it takes
away from sense; and he who loses the least
by it may be called a gainer. It often makes
us swerve from an author's meaning . . .

    Ded. *Æneis*, '97. K II 220–21

DRYDEN, WORKS, nnn.

Rhyme (Prosodic), Feminine

See above, gg. ENGLISH LANGUAGE, a.
OPERA, e, f. BUTLER, b. See above, m.

Rhyme (Prosodic), Half

WALSH, c.

Rhyme (Prosodic), Triplet [See below,
Triplet Rhyme]

Rhyme (Prosodic), Rhythms of

See above, i, ff.

Stanza (General) [See also *Quatrain*]

See above, k.

Stanza of Eight

TASSONI.

Stanza: Spenserian

SPENSER, b. See above, k.

Sweetness

DENHAM, a. RHYME (DEBATE), d. PRES-
ENT AGE, d. LAST AGE, a. RHYME (DE-
BATE), i, q. ETHICAL FUNCTION, a. See be-
low, ll. SUCCESS. TRANSLATION, z.
OVID, k. See above, u. OPERA, b. ITAL-
IAN LANGUAGE AND LITERATURE, b.
OPERA, e. FRENCH LANGUAGE, a. DRYDEN,
WORKS, eee. See above, b, d, hh. VIRGIL, i.
Cf. TRANSLATION, ff. DRYDEN, WORKS, ooo.
Cf. CHAUCER, c.

Syllabism

See above, q.

Synaloepha

VIRGIL, oo. OVID, k. DRYDEN, WORKS, eee.

ii. Since I have named the/synalœpha,
which is the cutting off one vowel immediately before another, I will give an example
of it from Chapman's *Homer* . . .

    Apollo's priest to th'Argive fleet doth bring, &c.

There we see he makes it not *the Argive,*
but *th'Argive,* to shun the shock of the
two vowels, immediately following each
other. But in his second argument, in the
same page, he gives a bad example of the
quite contrary kind—

    Alpha the pray'r of Chryses sings:
    The army's plague, the strife of kings.

In these words, *the army's, the* ending with
a vowel, and *army's* beginning with another vowel, without cutting off the first
. . . there remains a most horrible ill-
sounding gap betwixt those words. I cannot say that I have everywhere observed the
rule of synalœpha in my translation; but
wheresoever I have not, 'tis a fault in sound.
The French and the Italians have made it
an inviolable precept in their versification;
therein following the severe example of the
Latin poets. Our countrymen have not yet
reformed their poetry so far, but content
themselves with following the licentious

practice of the Greeks . . .¹ But it becomes us, for the sake of euphony, rather *Musas colere severiores,* with the Romans, than to give into the looseness of the Grecians.

Examen Poeticum, '93. K II 10–11
See above, b, c. [in these places, called *cæsura*]

Trimeter
ENGLISH VS. FRENCH, n.

Triplet Rhyme

jj. [¶] When I mentioned the Pindaric line, I should have added, that I take another licence in my verses: for I frequently make use of triplet rhymes, and for the same reason, because they bound the sense. And therefore I generally join these two licences together,/and make the last verse of the triplet a Pindaric: for, besides the majesty which it gives, it confines the sense within the barriers of three lines, which would languish if it were lengthened into four. Spenser is my example for both these privileges of English verses; and Chapman has followed him in his translation of Homer. Mr. Cowley has given into [*sic*] them after both; and all succeeding writers after him. I regard them now as the *Magna Charta* of heroic poetry, and am too much an Englishman to lose what my ancestors have gained for me.

Ded. Æneis, '97. K II 228–29

Word Order
See above, cc. RHYME (DEBATE), i.

kk. (Neander) . . . no poet need constrain himself at all times to it [naturalness in expression and rhyme]. It is enough he makes it his general rule; for I deny not but sometimes there may be a greatness in placing the words otherwise; and sometimes they may sound better, sometimes also the variety itself is excuse enough.

Dram. Poesy, '65. K I 98

ll. [¶] Well-placing of words, for the sweetness of pronunciation, was not known till Mr. Waller introduced it . . .

Defence of the Epilogue, '72. K I 169
See above, b. THOMAS, c.

Protatic Persons
ENGLISH VS. FRENCH, o.

Pulci, Luigi
ASTROLOGY. EPIC POET, c.

Pun, Punning [See PARONOMASIA]

Purcell, Henry

a. But what has been wanting on my part, has been abundantly supplied by the excellent composition of Mr. Purcell; in whose person we have at length found an Englishman equal with the best abroad. At least, my opinion of him has been such, since his happy and judicious performances in the late opera ["The Prophetess" of Beaumont and Fletcher: Scott] and the experience I have/had of him, in the setting of my three songs for this "Amphitryon" . . .

Ded. Amphitryon, '90. S-S VIII 9–10

b. There is nothing better than what I intended, but the music; which has since [c. 1683 or 1684, when the play was first written] arrived to a greater perfection in England than ever formerly; especially passing through the artful hands of Mr. Purcell, who has composed it with so great a genius, that he has nothing to fear but an ignorant, ill-judging audience.

Ded. King Arthur, '91. S-S VIII 135
OPERA, i.

Purgation [See ENDS OF POETRY; ETHICAL FUNCTION]

Pyrrhonism [See the Index to Bredvold's *Intellectual Milieu of John Dryden*]
PLUTARCH, c. HOBBES, a. See also SCEPTICISM.

Q

Quarles, Francis
PROSODY, hh.
Quatrain [See PROSODY]
Quinault, Philippe
MOLIÈRE, a.
Quintilian (Marcus Fabius Quintilianus)
COMEDY, e. ENGLISH LANGUAGE, f-2. AES-CHYLUS, a. SATIRE, z, bb, nn.

Quotation
I am no admirer of quotations; but you shall hear, if you please, one of the Ancients delivering his judgment on this question . . .
Essay of Heroic Plays, '72. K I 152.
EPIC, f.

R

Rabble [See AUDIENCE, POPULAR; HOI POL-LOI; VOX POPULI]
Racine, Jean-Baptiste
   a. In the meantime we may take notice, that where the poet ought to have preserved the character [of Hippolytus, in Racine's *Phèdre*] as it was delivered to us by antiquity, when he should have given us the picture of a rough young man, of the Amazonian strain, a jolly huntsman, and both by his profession and his early rising a mortal enemy to love, he [Racine] has chosen to give him the turn of gallantry, sent him /to travel from Athens to Paris, taught him to make love, and transformed the Hippolytus of Euripides into Monsieur Hippolyte.
   Pref. *All for Love,* '78. K I 194–95
MANNERS, j. Cf. ST. ÉVREMOND, d.
   b. [¶] Monsieur Racine has, indeed, used it [the chorus] in his *Esther;* but not that he found any necessity of it . . . The cho-rus at St. Cyr was only to give the young ladies an occasion of entertaining the king with vocal music, and of commending their own voices. The play itself was never intended for the public stage, nor, without disparagement to the learned author, could possibly have succeeded there; and much less the translation of it here.
   Parallel, '95. K II 144

Raillery
POETASTERS, c.
   . . . the discourse and raillery of our comedies excel what has been written by them [the poets of the last age]. [See PRESENT AGE, 1]
   Defence of the Epilogue, '72. K I 175
HORACE, g. HORACE AND JUVENAL AND PERSIUS, g. SATIRE, b. HORACE, e. HOR-ACE AND JUVENAL AND PERSIUS, h. SATIRE, c. DIALOGUE (GENRE), d. TRANSLATION, g.

Rant [See BOMBAST]

Rapin, René

. . . amongst the French, the greatest of this age, Boileau and Rapin; the latter of which is alone sufficient, were all other critics lost, to teach anew the rules of writing.
Author's Apology, '77. K I 181
Cf. Poetic License, f. Tragedy, e, h. Diction, a. Tragedy, k. Rules, c, d. Cf. French Authors, c. [Noyes suggests Rapin: see Noyes, p. 513 and note].

Readers (Types)
Critic[s], a.

Reading
Cf. Settle, c, d. Cf. History, a. Satire, b. Translation, cc.

Reason

. . . Reason . . . will refuse to take the leap, when the distance . . . appears too large. [See Imagination (Responsive), b]
Defence of An Essay, '68. K I 128.
Verisimility, b. Unities (Dramatic), Place, g. Authority, d. Age, Genius of, c. Rules, d. Dryden, Works, cc. Cf. Style, c. Religion. Plutarch and Seneca. Authority, e. Criticism, e. Persius, i. Unities (Dramatic), Action, g.

Reformation of Stage [Cf. Collier; Milbourne]

Neither can we accept of those Lay-Bishops, as some call them, who, under pretence of reforming the stage, would intrude themselves upon us, as our superiors; being indeed incompetent judges of what/is manners, what religion, and, least of all, what is poetry and good sense. I can tell them, in behalf of all my fellows, that when they come to exercise a jurisdiction over us, they shall have the stage to themselves, as they have the laurel.
Examen Poeticum, '93. K II 6–7

Regularity [Cf. also Rules]
a. (Neander) Now what, I beseech you, is more easy than to write a regular French play, or more difficult than write an irregular English one . . . ?
Dram. Poesy, '65. K I 77
French vs. English, r, u.

b. [¶] For what else concerns this play, I would tell the reader, that it is regular, according to the strictest of dramatic laws; but that it is a commendation which many of our poets now despise, and a beauty which our common audiences do not easily discern. Neither indeed do I value myself upon it; because, with all that symmetry of parts, it may want an air and spirit (which consists in the writing) to set it off.
Pref. Secret Love, '67. S-S II 418
Rules, d. Unities (Dramatic), General, c.

Rehearsal, The [See also Buckingham]
Dryden, Literary Life, e.

Religion

[¶] I have ever thought, that the wise men in all ages have not much differed in their opinions of religion; I mean, as it is grounded on human reason: for reason, as far as it is right, must be the same in all men; and truth being but one, they must consequently think in the same train.
"Life of Plutarch," '83. S-S XVII 33
Plutarch, e. Audience, Popular, j. Obscenity, e.

Religious Function (in Literature)
. . . religion was first taught in verse . . . [See Ends of Poetry, k]
Pref. Tyrannic Love, '70. S-S III 376
Persius, i. Obscenity, c.

Repartee
Rhyme (Debate), d.
a. (Neander) As for Comedy, repartee is one of its chiefest graces . . . [See Speeches (Dramatic), b]
Dram. Poesy, '65. K I 72

BEAUMONT AND FLETCHER. RHYME (DE-BATE), p, q. DIALOGUE (DRAMATIC).

b. As for repartie, in particular; as it is the very soul of conversation, so it is the greatest grace of Comedy, where it is proper to the characters. There may be much of acuteness in a thing well said; but there is more in a quick reply: *sunt enim longe venustiora omnia in respondendo quam in provocando.*

Pref. *Evening's Love,* '71. K I 139

Representation [See IMITATION; IMAGING; etc.]

. . . the stage being the representation of the world . . . [See THEATER]

Ded. *Rival Ladies,* '64. K I 2

RHYME (DEBATE), i. TRAGEDY, a. EPIC vs. TRAGEDY, f, h.

Restoration, The

(Neander) And though the fury of a civil war, and power for twenty years together abandoned to a barbarous race of men, enemies of all good learning, had buried the Muses under the ruins of monarchy; yet, with the restoration of our/happiness, we see revived Poesy lifting up its head, and already shaking off the rubbish which lay so heavy on it.

Dram. Poesy, '65. K I 88–89

Cf. CONVERSATION, b.

Revival

[Of the report of a French translation of Chaucer at the same time as his] But the matter of fact being true, it makes me think that there is something in it like fatality; that, after certain periods of time, the fame and memory of great Wits should be renewed, as Chaucer is both in France and England.

Pref. *Fables,* 1700. K II 268

Rhetoric * [Cf. CICERO, QUINTILIAN, FIGURES, *etc.*]

. . . those things, which delight all ages, must have been an imitation of Nature . . . Therefore is Rhetoric made an art; therefore the names of so many tropes and figures were invented . . .

Author's Apology, '77. K I 184

Rhyme (Debate)

a. . . . to speak properly, 'tis not so much a new way amongst us [i.e., 'writing scenes in verse'], as an old way new revived; for many years before Shakespeare's plays, was the tragedy of Queen *Gorboduc,* in English/verse . . .

Ded. *Rival Ladies,* '64. K I 5–6

b. But supposing our countrymen had not received this writing [rhymed drama] till of late; shall we oppose ourselves to the most polished and civilized nations of Europe? . . . All the Spanish and Italian tragedies I have yet seen, are writ in rhyme. For the French, I do not name them . . .

Ded. *Rival Ladies,* '64. K I 6

PROSODY, o.

c. This [inversion of word order] is that which makes them say, rhyme is not natural, it being only so, when the poet either makes a vicious choice of words, or places them, for rhyme sake, so unnaturally as no man would in ordinary speaking; but when 'tis so judiciously ordered, that the first word in the verse seems to beget the second, and that the next, till that becomes the last word in the line, which, in the negligence of prose, would be so; it must then be granted, rhyme has all the advantages of prose, besides its own.

Ded. *Rival Ladies,* '64. K I 7

WALLER, a. DENHAM, a. DAVENANT, a.

d. [¶] The advantages which rhyme has

---

* See Lillian Feder, "John Dryden's Use of Classical Rhetoric," *PMLA,* LXIX (1954), 1258–78.

over blank verse are so many, that it were lost time to name them. Sir Philip Sidney, in his *Defence of Poesy,* gives us one, which in my opinion, is not the least considerable; I mean the help it brings to memory . . . Then, in the quickness of reparties . ./. it has so particular a grace, and is so aptly suited to them, that the sudden smartness of the answer, and the sweetness of the rhyme, set off the beauty of each other. But that benefit which I consider most in it . . . is, that it bounds and circumscribes the fancy. For imagination in a poet is a faculty so wild and lawless, that like an high-ranging spaniel, it must have clogs tied to it, lest it outrun the judgment. The great easiness of blank verse renders the poet too luxuriant . . . but when the difficulty of artful rhyming is interposed, where the poet commonly confines his sense to his couplet . . . the fancy then gives leisure to the judgment to come in . . .

Ded. *Rival Ladies,* '64. K I 7–8

e. But as the best medicines may lose their virtue by being ill applied, so is it with verse, if a fit subject be not chosen for it. Neither must the/argument alone, but the characters and persons be great and noble; otherwise (as Scaliger says of Claudian) the poet will be *ignobiliore materiâ depressus.* The scenes which in my opinion most commend it, are those of argumentation and discourse, on the result of which the doing or not doing some considerable action should depend.

Ded. *Rival Ladies,* '64. K I 8–9

PRESENT AGE, f. ENGLISH VS. FRENCH, s.

f. (Neander) Not to name our old comedies before Shakespeare, which were all writ in verse of six feet, or Alexandrines, such as the French now use, I can show in Shakespeare, many scenes of rhyme to-

gether, and the like in Ben Johnson's tragedies . . .¹ which . . . showed Ben no enemy to this way of writing, especially if you look upon his *Sad Shepherd,* which goes sometimes on rhyme, sometimes on blank verse, like an horse who eases himself on trot and amble.

Dram. Poesy, '65. K I 78

g. (Crites) I have . . . only to affirm, that it [rhyme] is not allowable in serious plays; for comedies, I find you already concluding with me. To prove this, I might satisfy myself to tell you, how much in vain it is for you to strive against the stream of the people's inclination; the greatest part of which are prepossessed so much with those excellent plays of Shakespeare, Fletcher, and Ben Johnson, which have been written out of rhyme, that except you could bring them such as were written better in it . . . it will be impossible for you to gain your cause with them, who will still be judges. . . ./ First then, I am of opinion, that rhyme is unnatural in a play, because dialogue there is presented as the effect of sudden thought: for a play is the imitation of Nature; and since no man without premeditation speaks in rhyme, neither out he to do it on the stage. . . . For this reason, says Aristotle, 'tis best to write tragedy in that kind of verse which is the least such, or which is nearest prose: and this amongst the Ancients was the iambic, and with us is blank verse, or the measure of verse kept exactly without rhyme. These numbers therefore are fittest for a play; the others for a paper of verses, or a poem; blank verse being as much below them, as rhyme is improper for the Drama. . . . But there are two particular exceptions, which many besides myself have had to verse . . ./The hand of art will be too visible in it, against that maxim of all professions, *Ars est celare artem* . . . For . . . we know we are to be deceived, and we desire to be so; but no man ever was deceived but with a probability of truth . . . Nay, rather ought they [the very scenes themselves] not to be laboured with so much the more diligence and exactness, to help the imagination? since the mind of man does naturally tend to, and seek after truth; and therefore the nearer/any thing comes to the imitation of it, the more it pleases.

. . . But verse, you say, circumscribes a quick and luxuriant fancy . . . Yet this argument . . . would only prove that we may write better in verse, but not more naturally. . . . for he who wants judgment to confine his fancy in blank verse, may want it as much in rhyme: and he who has it will avoid errors in both kinds.

Dram. Poesy, '65. K I 90–93

h. (Neander) . . . I exclude all Comedy from my defence [of rhyme]; and . . . I deny not but blank verse may also be used; [I] content myself only to assert, that in serious plays where the subject and characters are great, and the plot unmixed with mirth . . . rhyme is . . . as natural and more effectual than blank verse.

Dram. Poesy, '65. K I 94

PROSODY, cc, dd, ee.

i. (Neander) You [Crites] say the stage is the representation of Nature, and no man in ordinary conversation speaks in rhyme. But you foresaw when you said this, that it might be answered—neither does any man speak in blank verse, or in measure without rhyme. Therefore you concluded, that which is nearest Nature is still to be preferred. But you took no notice that rhyme might be made as natural as blank verse, by

the well placing of the words, &c. All the difference between them, when they are both correct, is, the sound in one, which the other wants; and if so, the sweetness of it, and all the advantage resulting from it, which are handled in the Preface to *The Rival Ladies,* will yet stand good.

Dram. Poesy, '65. K I 96

j. (Neander) But when, by the inundation of the Goths and Vandals into Italy, new languages were brought in . ./. a new way of poesy was practised; new . . . in those countries, for in all probability it was that of the conquerors in their own nations. This new way consisted in measure or number of feet, and rhyme . . .

Dram. Poesy, '65. K I 96–97

PROSODY, h.

k. (Neander) . . . our couplet verses may be rendered as near prose as blank verse itself, by using those advantages I lately named, as breaks in a hemistich, or running the sense into another line, thereby making art and order appear as loose and free as nature: or not tying ourselves to couplets strictly, we may use the benefit of the Pindaric way practised in *The Siege of Rhodes;* where the numbers vary, and the rhyme is disposed carelessly, and far from often chiming. Neither is that other advantage of the Ancients to be despised, of changing the kind of verse when they please . . .

Dram. Poesy, '65. K I 97

LAST AGE, b.

l. (Neander) [¶] This way of writing in verse they have only left free to us; our age is arrived to a perfection in it, which they never knew; and which (if we may guess by what of theirs we have seen in verse, as *The Faithful Shepherdess,* and *Sad Shep-*

herd) 'tis probable they never could have reached. For the genius of every age is different; and though ours excel in this, I deny not but that to imitate Nature in that perfection which they did in prose, is a greater commendation than to write in verse exactly.

Dram. Poesy, '65. K I 99

m. (Neander) Tragedy, we know, is wont to image to us the minds and fortunes of noble persons, and to portray these exactly; heroic rhyme is nearest Nature, as being the noblest kind of modern verse. . . .ᵠ Blank verse is acknowledged to be too low for a poem, nay more, for a paper of verses; but if too low for an ordinary sonnet, how much more for Tragedy, which is by Aristotle, in the dispute betwixt the epic poesy and the dramatic, for many reasons he there alleges, ranked above it?

Dram. Poesy, '65. K I 101

n. (Neander) . . . the epic way is every where interlaced with dialogue, or discursive scenes; and therefore you [Crites] must either grant rhyme to be improper there, which is contrary to your assertion, or admit it into plays by the same title which you have given it to poems.

Dram. Poesy, '65. K I 101

o. (Neander) Verse, 'tis true, is not the effect of sudden thought; but this hinders not that sudden thought may be represented in verse, since those thoughts are such as must be higher than Nature can raise them without premeditation, especially to a continuance of them, even out of verse; and consequently you cannot imagine them to have been sudden either in the poet or in the actors.

Dram. Poesy, '65. K I 102

p. (Neander) [¶] This, I confess, is an objection [i.e., that it is unnatural that in repartee one speaker would give the rhyme to another] which is in every one's mouth, who loves not rhyme: but suppose . . . the repartee were made only in blank verse, might not part of the same argument be turned against you? for the measure is as often supplied there, as it is in rhyme; the latter half of the hemistich as commonly made up, or a second line subjoined as a reply to the former . . .¹

Dram. Poesy, '65. K I 102

q. (Neander) I acknowledge the hand of art appears in repartee, as of necessity it must in all kinds of verse. But there is also the quick and poynant brevity of it (which is an high imitation of Nature in those sudden gusts of passion) to mingle with it; and this, joined with the cadency and sweetness of the rhyme, leaves nothing in the soul of the hearer to desire. 'Tis an art which appears; but it appears only like the shadowings of painture, which being to cause the rounding of it, cannot be absent; but while that is considered, they are lost: so while we attend to the other beauties of the matter, the care and labour of the rhyme is carried from us, or at least/drowned in its own sweetness, as bees are sometimes buried in their honey. When a poet has found the repartee, the last perfection he can add to it, is to put it into verse. However good the thought may be, however apt the words in which 'tis couched, yet he finds himself at a little unrest, while rhyme is wanting: he cannot leave it till that comes naturally, and then is at ease, and sits down contented.

Dram. Poesy, '65. K I 103–4.

Judgment, b.

r. (Neander) Thus then the second thoughts being usually the best, as receiving the maturest digestion from judgment, and the last and most mature product of those thoughts being artful and laboured verse, it may well be inferred, that verse is a great help to a luxuriant fancy . . .

Dram. Poesy, '65. K I 107
PROSODY, ff, gg.

s. For the way of writing plays in verse, which I have seemed to favour, I have, since that time, laid the practice of it aside, till I have more leisure, because I find it troublesome and slow. But I am no way altered from my opinion of it, at least/with any reasons which have opposed it.

Epistle Ded. *Dram. Poesy,* '67. K I 23–24
COURT, b.

t. For my own part, if, in treating of this subject [rhymed drama], I sometimes dissent from the opinion of better wits, I declare it is not so much to combat their opinions, as to defend my own, which were first made public.

Epistle Ded. *Dram. Poesy,* '67. K I 26
HEROIC PLAY, a.

u. As for the question as he [Howard] states it, whether rhyme be nearest the nature of what it represents, I wonder he should think me so ridiculous as to dispute whether prose or verse be nearest to ordinary conversation.

Defence of An Essay, '68. K I 113

v. [¶] But to return to verse; whether it be natural or not in plays, is a problem which is not demonstrable of either side . . . I am satisfied if it cause delight . . .

Defence of An Essay, '68. K I 113

w. You see in *Catiline* and *Sejanus,* where the argument is great, he [Jonson] sometimes ascends to verse, which shows he thought it not unnatural in serious plays; and had his genius been as proper for rhyme as it was for humour, or had the age in

which he lived attained to as much knowledge in verse as ours, it is probable he would have adorned those subjects with that kind of writing.

Defense of An Essay, '68. K I 115

x. [¶] Thus Prose, though the rightful prince, yet is by common consent deposed, as too weak for the government of serious plays: and he failing, there now start up two competitors; one, the nearer in blood, which is Blank Verse; the other, more fit for the ends of government, which is Rhyme. Blank Verse is, indeed, the nearer Prose, but he is blemished with the weakness of his predecessor. Rhyme (for I will deal clearly) has somewhat of the usurper in him; but he is brave, and generous, and his dominion pleasing. For this reason of delight, the Ancients (whom I will still believe as wise as those who so confidently correct them) wrote all their tragedies in verse, though they knew it most remote from conversation.

Defence of An Essay, '68. K I 115

y. [¶] But I have said too much in the defence of verse; for, after all, it is a very indifferent thing to me whether it obtain or not. I am content hereafter to be ordered by his rule, that is, to write it sometimes because it pleases me, and so much the rather, because he has declared that it pleases him [Howard].

Defence of An Essay, '68. K I 118

z. [¶] Whether Heroic Verse ought to be admitted into serious plays, is not now to be disputed: 'tis already in possession of the stage; and I dare confidently affirm, that very few tragedies, in this age, shall be received without it. [See next entry]

Essay of Heroic Plays, '72. K I 148

aa. All the arguments which are formed against it [rhyme] can amount to no more than this, that it is not so near conversation as prose, and therefore not so natural. But it is very clear to all who understand poetry, that serious plays ought not to imitate conversation too nearly. If nothing were to be raised above that level, the foundation of Poetry would be destroyed. And if you once admit of a latitude, that thoughts may be exalted, and that images and actions may be raised above the life, and described in measure without rhyme, that leads you insensibly from your own principles to mine: you are already so far onward of your way, that you have forsaken the imitation of ordinary converse. . . . and to continue where you are, is to lodge in the open fields, betwixt two inns. You have lost that which you call natural, and have not acquired the last perfection of Art.

Essay of Heroic Plays, '72. K I 148

bb. 'Tis indeed so difficult to write verse, that the adversaries of it have a good plea against many who undertake that task, without being formed by Art or Nature for it. Yet, even they who have written worst in it, would have written worse without it: they have cozened many with their sound, who never took the pains to examine their sense.

Essay of Heroic Plays, '72. K I 149

DRYDEN, WORKS, v. TRAGICOMEDY, c. AUTHORITY, e. Cf. MILTON, c. PROSODY, hh.

Rhyme (Prosodic) [See PROSODY]

Richelieu (Armand Jean du Plessis, Cardinal and Duc de)

. . . the great Cardinal of Richelieu . . . [See ENGLISH VS. FRENCH, b]

Dram. Poesy, '65. K I 56

SPEECHES (DRAMATIC), a. ACADEMY, b. POET, b.

Rochester (John Wilmot, Second Earl of)

DRYDEN, WORKS, o, p. PRESENT AGE, m.

a. I find it is not for me to contend any way with your Lordship, who can write better on the meanest Subject than I can on the best.

Letter to Wilmot, 1673. Ward No. 4, p. 8

b. You are that Rerum Natura of your own Lucretius, Ipsa suis pollens opibus, nihil indiga nostri.

Letter to Rochester, 1673. Ward No. 4, p. 9

PATRONAGE, a.

c. [Dryden pretends to be unaware of Rochester's authorship of the *Allusion to the Tenth Satire* of the First Book of Horace: see Ker's note to I, 199] [¶] For my part, I would wish no other revenge, either for myself, or the rest of the poets, from this rhyming judge of the twelvepenny gallery, this legitimate son of Sternhold, than that he would subscribe his name to his censure, or (not to tax him beyond his learning) set his mark: for, should he own himself publicly . . . they whom he condemns would be thankful to him, they whom he praises would choose to be condemned; and the magistrates, whom he has elected, would modestly withdraw . . . to avoid the scandal of his nomination. The sharpness of his satire, next to himself, falls most heavily on his friends, and they ought never to forgive him for commending them perpetually the wrong way, and sometimes by contraries.

Pref. *All for Love*, '78. K I 199

DORSET, b. CRITIC[s], a. COWLEY, i.

Rome

This [the contemplation of the great Romans of the republic] sets me so on fire, when I am reading either here [in Polybius], or in any ancient author, their lives and actions, that I cannot hold from breaking out with Monta[i]gne into this expression: "It is just . . . for every honest man

215

to be content with the government and laws of his native country, without endeavouring to alter or subvert them; but if I were to choose, where I would have been born, it should have been in a commonwealth." He indeed names Venice, which, for many reasons, should not be my wish; but rather Rome in such an age, if it were possible, as that wherein Polybius lived; or that of Sparta, whose constitution for a republic is by our author compared with Rome, to which he justly gives the preference.

"Character of Polybius," '93. S-S XVIII 51

HORACE AND JUVENAL AND PERSIUS, f.

Roscommon (Wentworth Dillon, Fourth Earl of)

Cf. TRANSLATION, d.

a. For my Lord Roscommons Essay [*of Translated Verse*], I am of your opinion, that you shou'd reprint it, & that you may safely venture on a thousand/more. in my verses before it, pray let the printer mend his errour . . .¹

Letter to Tonson, 1684. Ward No. 11, pp. 22–23

b. [Besides 'my natural' impulses to translate, for the *Sylvæ*] there was an accidental motive which was full as forcible, and God forgive him who was the occasion of it. It was my Lord Roscommon's *Essay on Translated Verse,* which made me uneasy till I tried whether or no I was capable of following his rules, and/of reducing the speculation into practice . . . I think I have generally observed his instructions; I am sure my reason is sufficiently convinced both of their truth and usefulness . . .

Pref. *Sylvæ,* '85. K I 251–52

TRANSLATION, gg. LANSDOWNE.

c. [¶] My Lord Roscommon's notes on

this pastoral [Virgil's Sixth] are equal to his excellent translation of it; and thither I refer the reader.

Notes and Observations on Virgil's Works, '97. N 709

Royal Society

DRYDEN, WORKS, d.

Rules *

a. (Crites) . . . all the rules by which we practise the Drama at this day . . . were delivered to us from the observations which Aristotle made . . .

Dram. Poesy, '65. K I 38

ENGLISH VS. FRENCH, c. AUTHORITY, a.

b. . . . if Nature be to be imitated, then there is a rule for imitating Nature rightly; otherwise there may be an end, and no means conducing to it.

Defence of An Essay, '68. K I 123

ARISTOTLE, d. NATURE, c.

c. [¶] After all, if any one will ask me, whether a tragedy cannot be made upon any other grounds than those of exciting pity and terror in us;—Bossu, the best of modern critics, answers thus in general: That all excellent arts, and particularly that of poetry, have been invented and brought to perfection by men of a transcendent genius; and that, therefore, they, who practise afterwards the same arts, are obliged to tread in their footsteps, and to search in their writings the foundation of them; for it is not just that new rules should destroy the authority of the old. But Rapin writes more particularly thus, that no passions in a story are so proper to move our concernment as fear and pity . . .

Pref. *Troilus, '79.* K I 211

d. . . . because many men are shocked

---

* See Hoyt Trowbridge, "The Place of Rules in Dryden's Criticism," *MP,* XLIV (1946), 84–96.

at the name of rules, as if they were a kind of magisterial prescription upon poets, I will conclude with the words of Rapin, in his *Reflections* on Aristotle's work *of Poetry:* 'If the rules be well considered, we shall find them to be made only to reduce Nature into method . . . : 'tis only by these, that probability in fiction is maintained, which is the soul of poetry. They are founded upon good sense, and sound reason, rather than on authority . ./. but 'tis evident, by the ridiculous mistakes and gross absurdities which have been made by those poets who have taken their fancy only for their guide, that if this fancy be not regulated, it is a mere caprice, and utterly incapable to produce a reasonable and judicious poem.'

Pref. *Troilus,* '79. K I 228–29

DRYDEN, WORKS, cc. TRAGICOMEDY, c. Cf. DECORUM, h. Cf. SATIRE, jj.

e. [In a context of theory of translation] For many a fair precept in poetry is, like a seeming demonstration in the mathematics, very specious in the diagram, but failing in the mechanic operation.

Pref. *Sylvæ,* '85. K I 252

AUTHORITY, e. Cf. UNITIES (DRAMATIC), GENERAL, d. Cf. DRYDEN, LITERARY LIFE, a. SATIRE, b, c.

f. . . . as they [poetry and painting] are arts, they must have rules, which may direct them to their common end.

Parallel, '95. K II 133

g. . . . the way to please being to imitate Nature, both the poets and the painters in ancient times, and in the best ages, have studied her; and from the practice of both these arts the rules have been drawn by which we are instructed how to please, and to compass that end which they obtained, by following their example. For Nature is still the same in all ages, and can never be con-

trary to herself. Thus, from the practice of Æschylus, Sophocles, and Euripides, Aristotle drew his rules for tragedy . . . Thus, amongst the moderns, the Italian and French critics, by studying the precepts of Aristotle and Horace, and having the example of the Grecian poets before their eyes, have given us the rules of modern tragedy; and thus the critics . . . in the art of painting . . .

Parallel, '95. K II 134

IMITATION, i.

h. To inform our judgments, and to reform our tastes, rules were invented, that by them we might discern when Nature was imitated, and how nearly.

Parallel, '95. K II 137.

i. [¶] Having thus shewn that imitation pleases, and why . . . it follows, that some rules of imitation are necessary to obtain the end; for without rules there can be no art, any more than there can be a house without a door to conduct you into it.

Parallel, '95. K II 138

j. [We are] not to make new rules of the drama, as Lopez de Vega has attempted unsuccessfully to do, but to be content to follow our masters, who understood Nature better than we.

Parallel, '95. K II 139

UNITIES (DRAMATIC), TIME, e. VIRGIL, gg.

k. [¶] The motives that induced Virgil to coin this fable [Dido and Æneas], I have shewed already; and have also begun to show that he might make this anachronism, by superseding the mechanic rules of poetry, for the same reason that a monarch may dispense with or suspend his own laws, when he finds it necessary so to do, especially if those laws are not altogether fundamental. Nothing is to be called a fault in poetry, says Aristotle, but what is against the art; therefore a man may be an admirable poet without being an exact chronologer.

Ded. *Æneis,* '97. K II 194

Rymer, Thomas [See Heads of an Answer to Rymer, S-S XV]*

PQ,

a. . . . Mr. Rymer sent me his booke [*Tragedies of the Last Age*], which has been my best entertainment hetherto: tis certainly very learned, & the best piece of Criticism in the English/tongue; perhaps in any other of the modern. If I am not altogether of his opinion, I am so, in most of what he sayes: and thinke my selfe happy that he has not fallen upon me, as severely and as wittily as he has upon Shakespeare, and Fletcher. for he is the only man I know capable of finding out a poets blind sides: and if he can hold heere without exposeing his Edgar to be censurd by his Enemyes; I think there is no man will dare to answer him, or can.

Letter to Dorset, mid-1677. Ward No. 6, pp. 13–14

b. . . . this excellent critique of Mr. Rymer [*Tragedies of the Last Age*] . . .

Heads of an Answer, '77. S-S XV 381

ANCIENTS, u. AGE, GENIUS OF, c.

c. [¶] My judgment on this piece is this: that it is/extremely learned, but that the author of it is better read in the Greek than in the English poets; that all writers ought to study this critique, as the best account I have ever seen of the ancients; that the model of tragedy he has here given is excellent, and extreme correct; but that it is not the only model of all tragedy, because it is

* See Fred G. Walcott, "John Dryden's Answer to Thomas Rymer's *The Tragedies of the Last Age,"* XV (1936), 194–214.

218

too much circumscribed in plot [characters], etc.; and lastly, that we may be taught here justly to admire and imitate the ancients, without giving them the preference, with this author, in prejudice to our [own] country.

Heads of an Answer, '77. S-S XV 390–91

d. [¶] Want of method in this excellent treatise, makes the thoughts of the author sometimes obscure.

Heads of an Answer, '77. S-S XV 391

ANCIENTS, m. SHAKESPEARE, s. DECORUM, h. POETIC JUSTICE, g. MILTON, c.

e. I spoke to Mr Tonson to send you down the Bookes . . . you desir'd; in order to the writeing of a preface before my next Play [See Ward, n. 9, p. 164] . . . For I shall be very proud, of your entring into the lists, though not against Rymer; yet as a champion for our cause, who defy the Chorus of the Ancients.

Letter to Walsh, May 1693. Ward No. 24, p. 54

f. About a fortnight ago I had an intimation/from a friend by letter, That one of the Secretaryes, I suppose Trenchard had informd the Queen, that I had abusd her Government . . . in my Epistle to my Lord Radclyffe [Ded. *Examen Poeticum*]; & that thereupon, she had commanded her Historiographer Rymer, to fall upon my Playes; wᶜʰ he assures me is now doeing. I doubt not his malice, from a former hint you gave me: & if he be employd, I am confident tis of his own seeking; who you know has spoken slightly of me in his last Critique [*A Short View of Tragedy*]: & that gave me occasion to snarl againe.

Letter to Tonson, 30 August 1693. Ward No. 26, pp. 58–59

SHAKESPEARE, i.

g. Chaucer (as you have formerly been

told by our learned Mr. Rymer) first adorned and amplified our barren tongue from the Provençal, which was then the most polished of all the modern languages;

but this subject has been copiously treated by that great critic, who deserves no little commendation from us his countrymen.

Pref. *Fables*, 1700. K II 249

S

St. Évremond (Charles de Marguetel de Saint-Denis, Seigneur de)*

a. . . . casually casting my eye on the works of a French gentleman, deservedly famous for wit and criticism, I wondered, amongst many commendations of Plutarch, to find this one reflection . . .º

. . . .

This judgment could not have proceeded but from a man who has a nice taste in authors; and if it be not altogether just, it is at least delicate . . ./

. . . But this is sufficient to vindicate our author's [Plutarch's] judgment from being superficial; and I desire not to press the argument more strongly against this gentleman, who has honoured our country by his long residence amongst us.

"Life of Plutarch," '83. S-S XVII 70–71

b. An ingenious Frenchman esteems, as he tells us, his [Seneca's] person rather than his works; and values him more as the preceptor of Nero, a man ambitious of the empire, and the gallant of Agrippina, than as a teacher of morality. For my part, I dare not push the commendation so far.

"Life of Plutarch," '83. S-S XVII 74

SENECA, c.

* See John M. Aden, "Dryden and St. Évremond," *Comparative Literature*, VI (1954), 232–39.

c. There is not only a justness in his conceptions, which is the foundation of good writing, but also a purity of language, and a beautiful turn of words, so little understood by modern writers . . .

"Character of St. Evremont," '92. S-S XVIII 13

VIRGIL, a.

d. Be this [defense of Virgil] said with all manner of respect and deference to the opinion of Monsieur St. Evremont; amongst whose admirable talents, that of penetration is not the least. He generally dives into the very bottom of his authors; searches into the inmost recesses of their souls, and brings up with him those hidden treasures which had escaped the diligence of others. His examination of the *"Grand Alexandre,"* in my opinion, is an admirable piece of criticism; and I doubt not, but that his observations on the English theatre had been as absolute in their kind, had he seen with his own eyes, and not with those of other men. But conversing in a manner wholly with the court, which is not always the truest judge, he has been unavoidably led into mistakes, and given to some of our coarsest poets a reputation abroad, which they never had at home.

"Character of St. Evremont," '92. S-S XVIII 16

e. [¶] I will trouble your Lordship but with one objection more, which I know not whether I found in Le Fèvre, or Valois; but I am sure I have read it in another/French critic [St. Évremond: Ker], whom I will not name, because I think it is not much for his reputation.

Ded. *Æneis,* '97. K II 201–2

FRENCH AUTHORS, c.

Sallust (Caius Sallustius Crispus)

DRYDEN, WORKS, bbb.

Salt

. . . I would have more of the *urbana, venusta, salsa, faceta,* and the rest which Quintilian reckons up as the ornaments of wit . . . [See COMEDY, e]

Pref. *Evening's Love,* '71. K I 139

DORSET, b.   HORACE AND JUVENAL AND PERSIUS, d.   TRANSLATION, g.

Sandys, George

VOX POPULI.   TRANSLATION, c.

. . . the ingenious and learned Sandys, the best versifier of the former age . . . [See TRANSLATION, o]

Pref. *Fables,* 1700. K II 247

Sannazaro, Jacopo

LATIN, c.

Satire

Art of [Cf. SUCCESS]

a. And I confess I have laid in for those [the moderate sort], by rebating the satire, where justice would allow it, from carrying too sharp an edge. They who can criticise so weakly, as to imagine I have done my worst, may be convinced, at their own cost, that I can write severely, with more ease than I can gently. I have but laughed at some men's follies, when I could have declaimed against their vices; and other men's virtues I have commended, as freely as I have taxed their crimes.

Pref. *Absalom and Achitophel,* '81. S-S IX 212

HORACE, g.   HORACE AND JUVENAL AND PERSIUS, c.

b. . . . Holyday says, 'a perpetual grin, like that of Horace, rather angers than amends a man.' I cannot give him up the manner of Horace in low satire so easily. Let the chastisement of Juvenal be never so necessary for this new kind of satire; let him declaim as wittily and sharply as he pleases; yet still the nicest and most delicate touches of satire consist in fine raillery. This, my Lord [Dorset], is your particular talent, to which even Juvenal could not arrive. 'Tis not reading, 'tis not imitation of an author, which can produce this fineness; it must be inborn; it must proceed from a genius, and particular way of thinking, which is not to be taught; and therefore not to be imitated by him who has it not from nature. How easy it is to call rogue and villain,/and that wittily! But how hard to make a man appear a fool, a blockhead, or a knave, without using any of those opprobrious terms! To spare the grossness of the names, and to do the thing yet more severely, is to draw a full face, and to make the nose and cheeks stand out, and yet not to employ any depth of shadowing. This is the mystery of that noble trade, which yet no master can teach to his apprentice; he may give the rules, but the scholar is never the nearer in his practice. Neither is it true, that this fineness of raillery is offensive. A witty man is tickled when he is hurt in this manner, and a fool feels it not. The occasion of an offence may possibly be given, but he cannot take it. If it be granted, that in effect this way does more mischief . . . yet there is still a vast difference betwixt the slovenly butchering of a man, and the fineness of a stroke that separates the head from the body, and leaves it standing in its place. A man may be capable, as Jack

Ketch's wife said of his servant, of a plain piece of work, a bare hanging; but to make a malefactor die sweetly was only belonging to her husband. I wish I could apply it to myself, if the reader would be kind enough to think it belongs to me. The character of Zimri in my *Absalom* is, in my opinion, worth the whole poem: it is not bloody, but it is ridiculous enough; and he, for whom it was intended, was too witty to resent it as an injury. If I had railed, I might have suffered for it justly; but I managed my own work more happily, perhaps more dexterously. I avoided the mention of great crimes, and applied myself to the representing of blindsides, and little extravagancies; to which, the wittier a man is, he is generally the more obnoxious. It succeeded as I wished; the jest went/round, and he was laught at in his turn who began the frolic.

Discourse of Satire, '93. K II 92–94
HORACE, e.

c. Will your Lordship be pleased to prolong my audience . . . till I tell you my own trivial thoughts, how a modern satire should be made? I will not deviate in the least from the precepts and examples of the Ancients, who were always our best masters. I will only illustrate them, and discover some of the hidden beauties in their designs, that we thereby may form our own in imitation of them. Will you please but to observe, that Persius, the least in dignity . . . has notwithstanding been the first who has discovered to us this important secret, in the designing of a perfect satire; that it ought only to treat of one subject; to be confined to one particular theme; or at least, to one principally. If other vices occur in the management of the chief, they should only be transiently lashed, and not be insisted on, so as to make the

design double. As in a play of the English fashion, which we call a tragi-comedy, there is to be but one main design; and though there be an underplot, or second walk of comical characters and adventures, yet they are subservient to the chief fable, carried along under it, and helping to it; so that the drama may not/seem a monster with two heads. . . . Mascardi, in his discourse of the *Doppia Favola* . . . gives an instance of it in the famous pastoral of Guarini, called *Il Pastor Fido* . . .[1] 'Tis certain, that the divine wit of Horace was not ignorant of this rule . . . for he gives this very precept, *sit quodvis simplex duntaxat et unum;* yet he seems not much to mind it in his *Satires* . . . I know it may be urged in defence of Horace, that this unity is not necessary; because the very word *satura* signifies a dish plentifully stored with all variety of fruit and grains. Yet Juvenal, who calls his poems a *farrago,* which is a word of the same signification with *satura,* has chosen to follow the same method of Persius, and not of Horace; and Boileau, whose example alone is a sufficient authority, has wholly confined himself, in all his *Satires,* to this unity of design. That variety, which is not to be found in any one satire, is, at least, in many, written on several occasions. And if variety be of absolute necessity in every one of them, according to the etymology of the word, yet it may arise naturally from one subject, as it is diversely treated, in the several/subordinate branches of it, all relating to the chief. It may be illustrated accordingly with variety of examples in the subdivisions of it, and with as many precepts as there are members of it; which, altogether, may complete that *olla,* or hotchpotch, which is properly a satire.

Under this unity of theme, or subject, is comprehended another rule . . . The poet is bound, and that *ex officio,* to give his reader some one precept of moral virtue, and to caution him against some one particular vice or folly. Other virtues, subordinate to the first, may be recommended under that chief head; and other vices or follies may be scourged . . .¹

¹. . . In general, all virtues are everywhere to be praised and recommended to practice; and/all vices to be reprehended, and made either odious or ridiculous; or else there is a fundamental error in the whole design.

I have already declared who are the only persons that are the adequate object of private satire, and who they are that may properly be exposed by name for public examples . . . Of the best and finest manner of Satire, I have said enough in the comparison betwixt Juvenal and Horace: 'tis that sharp, well-mannered way of laughing a folly out of countenance . . . I will proceed to the versification . . . [See BUTLER]

Discourse of Satire, '93. K II 102–5

d. Herein he [Juvenal, in the First Satire] confines himself to no one Subject, but strikes indifferently at all Men in his way: In every following Satyr he has chosen some particular Moral which he wou'd inculcate; and lashes some particular/Vice or Folly, (An Art with which our Lampooners are not much acquainted.) But our Poet being desirous to reform his own Age, and not daring to attempt it by an Overt act of naming living Persons, inveighs only against those who were infamous in the times immediately preceding his, whereby he not only gives a fair warning to Great Men, that their Memory lies at the mercy of future Poets and Historians, but also with a finer stroke of his Pen, brands ev'n the living,

and personates them under dead mens Names.

Argument of the First Satire [Juvenal], '93. JK II 670–71

e. The great Art of this Satyr [Juvenal's Third] is particularly/shown, in Common Places; and drawing in as many Vices, as cou'd naturally fall into the compass of it.

Argument of the Third Satire [Juvenal], '93. JK II 679–80

PERSIUS, j, k. LUCIAN, d.

Burlesque

BURLESQUE, b. Cf. BUTLER, b.

Definition [See below, o, t]

f. [¶] 'Tis but necessary, that after so much has been said of Satire some definition of it should be given. Heinsius, in his dissertations on Horace, makes it for me . . . : 'Satire is a kind of poetry, without a series of action, invented for the purging of our minds; in which human vices, ignorance, and errors, and all things besides, which are produced from them . . . are severely reprehended; partly dramatically, partly simply, and sometimes in both kinds . . . but, for the most part, figuratively, and occultly; consisting in a low familiar way, chiefly in a sharp and pungent manner of speech; but partly, also, in a facetious and civil way of jesting; by which either hatred, or laughter, or indignation, is moved.'—Where I cannot but observe, that this obscure and perplexed definition, or rather description, of satire, is wholly accommodated to the Horatian way; and ex/cluding the works of Juvenal and Persius, as foreign from that kind of poem. The clause in the beginning of it *without a series of action* distinguishes satire properly from stage-plays . . . The end or scope of satire is to purge the passions . . . The rest which follows is . . . generally belonging to all three [satirists]; till he comes upon us, with the excluding clause *consisting in a low familiar way of speech,* which is the proper character of Horace; and from which the other two, for their honour be it spoken, are far distant. But how come lowness of style, and the familiarity of words, to be so much the propriety of satire . . . ? Is the fault of Horace to be made the virtue and standing rule of this poem? Is the *grande sophos* of Persius, and the sublimity of Juvenal, to be circumscribed with the meanness of words and vulgarity of expression? If Horace refused the pains of numbers, and the loftiness of figures, are they bound to follow so ill a precedent? Let him walk afoot, with his pad in his hand, for his own pleasure; but let not them be accounted no poets, who choose to mount, and show their horsemanship.

Discourse of Satire, '93. K II 100–101
See above, c.
Derivation
See below, v.

g. Casaubon judged better [than Scaliger], and his opinion is grounded on sure authority, that Satire was derived from *satura,* a Roman word, which signifies full and abundant, and full also of variety, in which nothing is wanting to its due perfection.

Discourse of Satire, '93. K II 54
Difficile est satiram non scribere
PRESENT AGE, n.

h. There are few in any age who can bear the load of a dedication; for where praise is undeserved, it is satire; though satire on folly is now no longer a scandal to any one person, where a whole age is dipt together.

Ded. *Don Sebastian,* '90. S-S VII 305
i. They say, my talent is satire; if it be so, it is a fruitful age, and there is an ex-

traordinary crop to gather. But a single hand is insufficient for such a harvest: they have sown the dragon's teeth themselves, and it is but just they should reap each other in lampoons.

Ded. *Eleonora,* '92. S-S XI 126
j. Here [among the present poetasters] is a field of satire opened to me: but, since the Revolution, I have wholly renounced that talent. For who would give physic to the great, when he is uncalled?—to do his patient no good, and endanger himself for his prescription.

Postscript *Æneis,* '97. K II 241
Dorset's Satire
DORSET, b. MODERNS, f.
Ends [See ENDS OF POETRY]
PERSIUS, i. See above, f. See also below, *Function.*
Form [See above, c, f.]

k. [Speaking of Persius's satire] It must be granted to Casaubon . . . that Satire is a poem of a difficult nature in itself, and is not written to vulgar readers: and through the relation which it has to comedy, the frequent change of persons makes the sense perplexed, when we can but divine who it is that speaks; whether Persius himself, or his friend and monitor; or, in some places, a third person.

Discourse of Satire, '93. K II 74
DONNE, d. BUTLER. PROSODY, m. BOILEAU, c.
Function [See also above, *Ends*]

l. . . . satire lashes vice into reformation . . .

Author's Apology, '77. K I 182
DRYDEN, WORKS, y.

m. [¶] The true end of satire is the amendment of vices by correction. And he who writes honestly is no more an enemy to the offender, than the physician to the patient, when he prescribes harsh remedies to an inveterate disease; for those are only in order to prevent the chirurgeon's work of an *Ense rescindendum,* which I wish not to my very enemies. To conclude all; if the body politic have any analogy to the natural, in my weak judgment, an act of oblivion were as necessary in a hot distempered state, as an opiate would be in a raging fever.

Pref. *Absalom and Achitophel,* '81. S-S IX 214

See below, t. PERSIUS, i. HORACE, h. See below, s. CHARACTER[s], c.

n. A satirical poet is the check of the laymen on bad priests. We are only to take care, that we involve not the innocent with the guilty in the same condemnation. The good cannot be too much honoured, nor the bad too coarsely used . . .

Pref. *Fables,* 1700. K II 260

Genre

o. Had I time, I could enlarge on the beautiful turns of words and thoughts, which are as requisite in this, as in heroic poetry itself, of which the satire is undoubtedly a species.

Discourse of Satire, '93. K II 108

Irony

p. If the pleasure/arising from comedy and satire be either laughter, or some nobler sort of delight, which is above it, no man is so great a master of irony as our author [Lucian]. That figure is not only a keen, but a shining weapon in his hand; it glitters in the eyes of those it kills; his own gods, his greatest enemies, are not butchered by him, but fairly slain: they must acknowledge the hero in the stroke, and take the comfort which Virgil gives to a dying captain:

Æneæ magni dextrâ cadis

"Life of Lucian," '96. S-S XVIII 75–76

224

Lampoon

q. These observations [on Buckingham's folly] would easily run into a lampoon, if I had not forsworn that dangerous part of/ wit, not so much out of good nature, But at least from the inborn vanity of poets. I should show it to others, and betray my self to a worse mischief than what I do give my Enemy. This has been lately the case of Etherege, who translateing a Satyre of Boileau's, and changing the French names for English, read it so often that it came to their eares who were concernd; and forc'd him to leave off the design e're it was half finish'd.

Letter to Rochester, c. 1 May 1673. Ward No. 4, pp. 9–10

See below, ll. See above, i.

r. But these dull makers of lampoons, as harmless as they have been to me, are yet of dangerous example to the public. Some witty men may perhaps succeed to their designs, and, mixing sense with malice, blast the reputation of the most innocent amongst men, and the most virtuous amongst women.

Heaven be praised, our common libellers are as free from the imputation of wit as of morality; and therefore whatever mischief they have designed, they have performed but little of it. Yet these ill-writers, in all justice, ought themselves to be exposed; as Persius has [done] . . . in his First Satire . . . and none is so fit to correct their faults, as he [Dorset] who is not only clear from any in his own writings, but is also so just, that he will never defame the good; and is armed with the power of verse, to punish and make examples of the bad.

Discourse of Satire, '93. K II 22

DORSET, d. See below, t, kk.

s. In a word, that former sort of satire

[personal], which is known in England by the name of lampoon, is a dangerous sort of weapon, and for the most part unlawful. We have no moral right on the reputation of other men. 'Tis taking from them what we cannot restore to them. There are only two reasons for which we may be permitted to write lampoons; and I will not promise that they can always justify us. The first is revenge, when we have been affronted in the same nature, or have been any ways notoriously abused, and can make ourselves no other reparation. And yet we know, that, in Christian charity, all offences are to be forgiven, as we expect the like pardon from those which we daily commit against Almighty God. And this consideration has often made me tremble when I was saying our Saviour's prayer;/ . . . for which reason I have many times avoided the commission of that fault, even when I have been notoriously provoked . . . [See DRYDEN, PERSONAL CHARACTER, d]

. . . I will . . . proceed to give the second reason which may justify a poet when he writes against a particular person; and that is, when he is become a public nuisance. . . . 'Tis an action of virtue to make examples of vicious men. They may and ought to be upbraided . . . both for their own amendment, if they are not yet incorrigible, and for the terror of others . . . The/first reason was only an excuse for revenge; but this second is absolutely of a poet's office to perform: but how few lampooners are there now living, who are capable of this duty! . . . [H]ow remote they are, in common justice, from the choice of such persons as are the proper subject of satire! And how little wit . . . ! The weaker sex is their most ordinary theme; and the best and fairest are sure to be the most severely handled. Amongst men, those who are prosperously unjust are entitled to a panegyric; but afflicted virtue is insolently stabbed . . . No decency is considered, no fulsomeness omitted; no venom is wanting, as far as dulness can supply it. For there is a perpetual dearth of wit; a barrenness of good sense and entertainment. The neglect of the readers will soon put an end to this sort of scribbling. There can be no pleasantry where there is no wit; no impression can be made where there is no truth for the foundation.

Discourse of Satire, '93. K II 79–81

DRYDEN, PERSONAL CHARACTER, d. See above, d.

Lucianic

LUCIAN, d.

Meaning of the Word [See also above, *Definition*]

See below, u.

t. . . . as Dacier has observed before me, we may take notice, that the word *satire* is of a more general signification in Latin, than in French, or English. For amongst the Romans it was not only used for those discourses which decried vice, or exposed folly, but for others also, where virtue was recommended. But in our modern languages we apply it only to invective poems, where the very name of Satire is formidable to those persons who would appear to the world what they are not in themselves; for in English, to say satire, is to mean reflection, as we use that word in the worst sense; or as the French call it, more properly, *médisance.*

Discourse of Satire, '93. K II 67

Modern

See above, r. MODERNS, f. See above, s.

Original and Progress

u. If we take Satire in the general signification of the word . . . for an invective, it is certain that it is almost as old as verse; and though hymns, which are praises of God, may be allowed to have been before it, yet the defamation of others was not long after it.[1]

Discourse of Satire, '93. K II 44

v. But, considering Satire as a species of poetry, here the war begins amongst the critics. Scaliger, the father, will have it descend from Greece to Rome; and derives the word Satire from *Satyrus,* that mixed kind of animal . . .[1] But Casaubon, and his followers, with reason, condemn this derivation; and prove, that from *Satyrus,* the word *satira,* as it signifies a poem, cannot possibly descend.[1] . . . 'tis allowed that the Grecians had such poems; but [maintained] that they were wholly different *in specie* from that to which the Romans gave the name of Satire.

Discourse of Satire, '93. K II 45

Poetry, c. Cf. Farce, d.

w. . . . satyric tragedy, and the Roman Satire, have little resemblance in any of their features. The very kinds are different; for what has a pastoral tragedy to do with a paper of verses satirically written? . . . And the first farces of the Romans, which were the rudiments of their poetry, were written before they had any communication with the Greeks . . .

Discourse of Satire, '93. K II 51

x. [¶] The Grecians, besides these satyric tragedies, had another kind of poem, which they called *silli,* which were more of kin to the Roman satire. Those *silli* were indeed invective poems, but of a different species from the Roman poems of Ennius, Pacuvius, Lucilius, Horace, and the rest of their successors.

Discourse of Satire, '93. K II 51
See below, kk.

y. [¶] Thus . . . I . . . have proved, I hope, from the best critics, that the Roman Satire was not borrowed from thence [Greece], but of their own manufacture.

Discourse of Satire, '93. K II 53

z. [¶] Quintilian says, in plain words, *Satira quidem tota nostra est;* and Horace had said the same thing before him, speaking of his predecessor in that sort of poetry, *et Græcis intacti carminis auctor.* Nothing can be clearer than the opinion of the poet, and the orator, both the best critics of the two best ages of the Roman Empire, that Satire was wholly of Latin growth . . .

Discourse of Satire, '93. K II 53

aa. [Citing Dacier on *Saturnian* and *Fescennine* verse] They were made *ex tempore,* and were, as the French call them, *impromptus;* for which the Tarsians of old were much renowned; and we see the daily examples of them in the Italian farces of Harlequin and Scaramucha. Such was the poetry of that savage people, before it was turned into numbers, and the harmony of verse. Little of the Saturnian verses is now remaining; we only know from authors that they were nearer prose than poetry, without feet, or measure. They were ἔνρυθμοι, but not ἔμμετροι; perhaps they might be used in the/solemn part of their ceremonies; and the Fescenine, which were invented after them, in the afternoon's debauchery, because they were scoffing and obscene.

Discourse of Satire, '93. K II 55–56

bb. Dacier . . . only says, that one Livius Andronicus was the first stage-poet at Rome; but I will adventure on this hint, to advance another proposition, which I hope the learned will approve. And though we have not anything of Andronicus remaining to justify my conjecture, yet it is ex-

ceeding probable, that, having read the
works of those Grecian wits, his countrymen, he imitated not only the groundwork,
but also the manner of their writing; and
how grave soever his tragedies might be,
yet, in his comedies, he expressed the way of
Aristophanes, Eupolis, and the rest, which
was to call some persons by their own
names, and to expose their defects to the
laughter of the people . . .[1] Now, if this be
granted, we may easily suppose that the
first hint of satirical plays on the Roman
stage was given by the Greeks: not from
their *Satyrica* . . . but from their Old
Comedy, which was imitated first by Livius
Andronicus. And then Quintilian and
Horace must be cautiously interpreted,
where they affirm that Satire is wholly
Roman, and a sort of verse, which was not
touched on by the Grecians. . . . they
spoke of Satire, not as in its first elements,
but as it was formed into a separate work;
begun by Ennius, pursued by Lucilius, and
completed afterwards by Horace.

Discourse of Satire, '93. K II 58

cc. So that the ancient Satire of the Romans was in extemporary reproaches; the
next was farce, which was brought from
Tuscany; to that succeeded the plays of
Andronicus, from the Old Comedy of the
Grecians; and out of all these sprung two
several branches of new Roman Satire, like
different scions from the same root, which
I shall prove . . .

Discourse of Satire, '93. K II 59

dd. [Ennius, according to Dacier, hit
upon the idea of writing satires, not for the
stage, but to be read] He made discourses
in several sorts of verse, varied often in the
same paper; retaining still in the title their
original name of Satire. Both in relation to
the subjects, and the variety of matters con-

tained in them, the satires of Horace are
entirely like them; only Ennius . . . confines not himself to one sort of verse, as
Horace does; but taking example from the
Greeks, and even from Homer himself in
his *Margites,* which is a kind of Satire, as
Scaliger observes, gives himself the licence, when one sort of numbers comes
not easily, to run into another, as his fancy
dictates.[1] . . . Horace has thought him
worthy to be copied . . .[1]

Discourse of Satire, '93. K II 60

ee. [¶] Here we have Dacier making out
that Ennius was the first satirist in that
way of writing, which was of his invention;
that is, Satire abstracted from the stage, and
new-modelled into papers of verses on several subjects. But he will have Ennius take
the groundwork of Satire/from the first
farces of the Romans, rather than from the
formed plays of Livius Andronicus, which
were copied from the Grecian comedies. It
may possibly be so; but Dacier knows no
more of it than I do. And it seems to me the
more probable opinion, that he rather imitated the fine railleries of the Greeks, which
he saw in the pieces of Andronicus . . .

Discourse of Satire, '93. K II 60–61

ff. Most evident it is, that whether he
[Ennius] imitated the Roman farce, or
the Greek comedies, he is to be acknowledged for the first author of Roman Satire,
as it is properly so called, and distinguished
from any sort of stage-play.

Discourse of Satire, '93. K II 61

gg. [¶] Lucilius . . . made satires after
the manner of Ennius, but he gave them a
more graceful turn, and endeavoured to
imitate more closely the *vetus comœdia* of
the Greeks . . . And though Horace/
seems to have made Lucilius the first author of satire in verse amongst the Romans

. . .ᵍ he is only thus to be understood; that Lucilius had given a more graceful turn to the satire of Ennius and Pacuvius, not that he invented a new satire of his own . . .

Discourse of Satire, '93. K II 61–62

hh. . . . Dacier justly taxes Casaubon, saying, that the Satires of Lucilius were wholly different in *specie* from those of Ennius and Pacuvius. . . ./But this, as we say in English, is only a distinction without a difference; for the reason of it is ridiculous, and absolutely false. This was that which cozened honest Casaubon, who, relying on Diomedes, had not sufficiently examined the origin and nature of those two satires; which were entirely the same . . .

Discourse of Satire, '93. K II 62–63

CASAUBON, b. HORACE AND JUVENAL AND PERSIUS, j.

Personal

ii. Neither was it more allowable in him [Jonson], than it is in our present poets, to represent the follies of particular persons; of which many have accused him. *Parcere personis, dicere de vitiis,* is the rule of plays. And Horace tells you, that the Old Comedy amongst the Grecians was silenced for the too great liberties of the poets . . .ᵍ

Pref. *Evening's Love,* '71. K I 137

jj. [Of the *Duke of Guise*] It is known that noble person [Henry, Earl of Arlington, Lord Chamberlain] to whom it was referred is a severe critic on good sense, decency, and morality; and I can assure the world, that the rules of Horace are more familiar to him than they are to me. He remembers too well that the *vetus comœdia* was banished from the Athenian theatre for its too much license in representing persons . . .

Vindication, '83. S-S VII 160

kk. To these *silli,* consisting of parodies, we may properly add the satires which were

written against particular persons; such as were the iambics of Archilochus against Lycambes, which Horace undoubtedly imitated in some of his Odes and Epodes . . . I might also name the invective of Ovid against Ibis . . . but these are the underwood of Satire, rather than the timber-trees: they are not of general extension, as reaching only to some individual person. And Horace seems to have purged himself from those/splenetic reflections in his Odes and Epodes, before he undertook the noble work of Satires, which were properly so called.

Discourse of Satire, '93. K II 52–53

HORACE, h.

Roman [See above, *Original and Progress*]

PERSIUS, i.

Scurrility

ll. Those not succeeding [i.e., anti-prelatical petitions to Parliament], satire and railing was the next; and Martin Marprelate, (the Marvel of those times), was the first Presbyterian scribbler, who sanctified libels and scurrility to the use of the good old cause: which was done (says my author), upon this account, that their serious treatises having been fully answered and refuted, they might compass by railing what they had lost by reasoning; and, when their cause was sunk in court and Parliament, they might at least hedge in a stake amongst the rabble, for to their ignorance all things are wit which are abusive; but if Church and State were made the theme, then the doctoral degree of wit was to be taken at Billingsgate . . .

Pref. *Religio Laici,* '82. S-S X 27

Seneca's Disposition to

PLUTARCH AND SENECA.

Spelling

mm. In the criticism of spelling, it [satire] ought to be with *i,* and not with *y,* to distinguish its true derivation from *sa-tura,* not from *satyrus.* And if this be so, then it is false spelled throughout this book; for here it is written *Satyr:* which having not considered at the first, I thought it not worth correcting afterwards.

Discourse of Satire, '93. K II 67.

Varronian

nn. In the meanwhile, following the order of time, it will be necessary to say somewhat of another kind of Satire . . . that which we call the Varronian Satire, (but which Varro himself calls the Menippean,) because Varro, the most learned of the Romans, was the first author of it, who imitated . . . the manner of Menippus the Gardarenian, who professed the philosophy of the Cynics.

This sort of Satire was not only composed of several sorts of verse, like those of Ennius, but was also mixed with prose; and Greek was sprinkled amongst the Latin. Quintilian . . . tells us, that this satire of Varro was of a former kind. [But] how can we possibly imagine this to be, since Varro, who was contemporary to Cicero, must consequently be after/Lucilius? But Quintilian meant not . . . in order of time . . . ; he would only give us to understand, that the Varronian Satire, with mixture of several sorts of verses, was more after the manner of Ennius and Pacuvius, than that of Lucilius, who was more severe, and more correct, and gave himself less liberty in the mixture of his verses . . .

Discourse of Satire, '93. K II 64–65

oo. [Having cited Cicero on Varro] Thus it/appears, that Varro was one of those writers whom they called σπουδογέλοιοι, studious of laughter; and that, as learned as he was, his business was more to divert his reader, than to teach him. And he entitled his own satires *Menippean;* not that

Menippus had written any satires (for his were either dialogues or epistles), but that Varro imitated his style, his manner, and facetiousness. . . . But Varro, in imitating him, avoids his impudence and filthiness, and only expresses his witty pleasantry.

Discourse of Satire, '93. K II 65–66

pp. . . . those authors who are acknowledged to have written Varronian satires, in imitation of his [Varro's]; of whom the chief is Petronius Arbiter . . . Many of Lucian's dialogues may also properly/be called Varronian satires, particularly his *True History;* and consequently the *Golden Ass* of Apuleius, which is taken from him. Of the same stamp is the mock deification of Claudius, by Seneca: and the *Symposium* or *Cæsars* of Julian, the Emperor. Amongst the moderns, we may reckon the *Encomium Moriæ* of Erasmus, Barclay's *Euphormio,* and a volume of German authors [*Epistolæ Obscurorum Virorum?* Ker], which my ingenious friend, Mr. Charles Killigrew, once lent me. In the English, I remember none which are mixed with prose, as Varro's were; but of the same kind is *Mother Hubbard's Tale,* in Spenser; and (if it be not too vain to mention anything of my own), the poems of *Absalom* and *MacFleckno.*

Discourse of Satire, '93. K II 66–67

Butler, b. Tassoni.

Virgilian

Virgil, ii, nn.

Satiricaster

a. (Lisideius) . . . one that is so much a well-willer to the satire, that he spares no man; and though he cannot strike a blow to hurt any, yet ought to be punished for the malice of the action . . .

Dram. Poesy, '65. K I 31

b. [¶] I have only one favour to desire

of you at parting; that, when you think of answering this Poem, you would employ the same pens against it who have combated with so much success against "Absalom and Achitophel;" for then you may assure yourselves of a clear victory, without the least reply. Rail at me abundantly; and, not to break a custom, do it without wit . . ./If God has not blessed you with the talent of rhyming, make use of my poor stock, and welcome; let your verses run upon my feet; and for the utmost refuge of notorious blockheads, reduced to the last extremity of sense, turn my own lines upon me, and in utter despair of your own satire, make me satirise myself.

"Epistle to the Whigs," prefixed to *The Medal*, '82. S-S IX 428–29

Satirists [See specific authors]
Lucian, c.

Scaliger, Julius Caesar
Rhyme (Debate), e. Satire, v.

a. [In connection with Scaliger's contention that satire was of Greek origin] . . . Scaliger, the father, according to his custom, that is, insolently enough, contradicts them both [Quintilian and Horace] . . .
Discourse of Satire, '93. K II 53
Satire, g, dd. Persius, c.

b. Persius [alleges Casaubon, attempting to put the best construction on Scaliger's criticism] showed his learning, but was no boaster of it; he did *ostendere*, but not *ostentare*; and so, he says, did Scaliger: where, methinks, Casaubon turns it handsomely upon that supercilious critic, and silently insinuates that he himself was sufficiently vainglorious, and a boaster of his own knowledge.
Discourse of Satire, '93. K II 72
Critic[s], d. Dryden, Works, ttt.

Scarron, Paul
Boileau, c.
Scenario
Cf. Dryden, Literary Life, n.

[¶] To make a sketch, or a more perfect model of a picture, is, in the language of poets, to draw up the/scenary of a play; and the reason is the same for both; to guide the undertaking, and to preserve the remembrance of such things, whose natures are difficult to retain.
Parallel, '95. K II 144–45

Scene
Cf. Play (Parts), a.

a. (Eugenius) [¶] 'Tis true, they [the Ancients] have kept the continuity, or, as you called it, *liaison des scenes,* somewhat better: two do not perpetually come in together, talk, and go out together; and other two succeed them, and do the same throughout the act, which the English call by the name of single scenes . . .
Dram. Poesy, '65. K I 49

b. (Eugenius) . . . for it is to be accounted a new scene, not every time the stage is empty; but every person who enters, though to others, makes it so; because he introduces a new business.
Dram. Poesy, '65. K I 49

Scepticism*
Dryden, Works, d.

a. For we live in an age so sceptical, that as it determines little, so it takes nothing from antiquity on trust.
Defence of the Epilogue, '72. K I 163
Dryden, Personal Character, i. Dryden, Works, qq. Lucian, a.

b. And this derision [of his 'gentle gods'

---

* See Louis I. Bredvold, *The Intellectual Milieu of John Dryden* (University of Michigan Publications in Language and Literature, XII), Ann Arbor, 1934.

by Lucian], as it shews the man himself, so it gives us an idea of the age in which he lived; for if that had been devout or ignorant, his scoffing humour would either have been restrained, or had not passed unpunished; all knowing ages being naturally sceptic, and not at all bigotted; which, if I am not much deceived, is the proper character of our own.

"Life of Lucian," '96. S-S XVIII 70
Lucian, b.

Schools of Poetry
Milton, d.

Scudéry, Georges de
Prosody, gg. Epic Hero, d. French Authors, b. Epic Poet, c.

Sedley, Sir Charles

a. I can make my boast to have found a better Mæcenas in the person of my Lord Treasurer Clifford, and a more elegant Tibullus in that of Sir Charles Sedley. I have chosen that poet to whom I would resemble you, not only because I think him at least equal, if not superior, to Ovid, in his elegies; nor because of his quality, for he was, you know, a Roman knight . . . but for his candour, his wealth, his way of living, and particularly because of this testimony which is given him by Horace, which I have a thousand times in my mind applied to you:

Non tu corpus eras sine pectore . . .

Ded. *Assignation,* '73. S-S IV 372
Criticasters, d. Juvenal, c.

b. [Of line 234 in the translation of Persius's Fifth Satire] This alludes to the Play of *Terence,* call'd the *Eunuch;* which was excellently imitated of late in English, by Sir *Charles Sedley* . . .

Notes to the Fifth Satire [Persius], '93.
JK II 781

Segrais, Jean Regnauld de

a. . . . I now casually remember out of . . . Segrais . . . or . . . Bossu, no matter which . . . [See Epic vs. Tragedy, j]
Ded. *Æneis,* '97. K II 165

b. . . . his [Segrais's] admirable preface to his translation of the *Æneis,* as the author of the Dauphin's *Virgil* justly calls it . . .
Ded. *Æneis,* '97. K II 178

c. . . . his [Segrais's] preface [to the translation of the *Æneis*] is a perfect piece of criticism, full and clear, and digested/ into an exact method; mine is loose, and, as I intended it, epistolary. . . . His notes and observations on every book are of the same excellency . . .
Ded. *Æneis,* '97. K II 178–79
Translation, gg. Critic[s], a. English Language, f.

Self-Love

. . . self-love, which is the false surveyor of . . . fancy . . . [See Poet, c]
Pref. *Secret Love,* '67. S-S II 418
Dryden, Works, cc.

Seneca, Lucius Annaeus [See also Plutarch and Seneca]

a. (Eugenius) The master-piece of Seneca I hold to be that scene in the *Troades,* where Ulysses is seeking for Astyanax to kill him; there you see the tenderness of a mother so represented in Adromache, that it raises compassion to a high degree . . . and bears the nearest resemblance of any thing in their tragedies to the/excellent scenes of passion in Shakespeare, or in Fletcher . . .
Dram. Poesy, '65. K I 53–54

b. Seneca . . . as if there were no such thing as nature to be minded in a play, is always running after pompous expression, pointed sentences, and philosophical notions, more proper for the study than the stage: the Frenchman [Corneille] followed a wrong scent; and the Roman was absolutely at cold hunting.

Pref. *Œdipus,* '79. S-S VI 132
OVID, h. MONTAIGNE, b. PLUTARCH AND SENECA. ST. ÉVREMOND, b.

c. For his . . . style . . . we may call it a shattered eloquence, not vigorous, not united, not embodied, but broken into fragments; every part by itself pompous, but the whole confused and unharmonious. His Latin, as Monsieur St. Evremont has well observed, has nothing in it of the purity and elegance of Augustus his times . . .

"Life of Plutarch," '83. S-S XVII 75

d. After all that has been said, he is certainly to be allowed a great wit, but not a good philosopher; not fit to be compared with Cicero, of whose reputation he was emulous, any more than Lucan is with Virgil.

"Life of Plutarch," '83. S-S XVII 76
SATIRE, pp.

Sententiae

OVID, c.

. . . neither is it [wit] so much the morality of a grave sentence . . . [See WIT, e]

Pref. *Annus Mirabilis,* '66. K I 15
LUCAN, b. SENECA, b. PASSIONS, h. DRYDEN, WORKS, h. DESIGNING. HORACE AND JUVENAL AND PERSIUS, c. Cf. PERSIUS, j.

Settle, Elkanah*

a. This upstart illiterate scribbler, who lies more open to censure than any writer of the age . . .

Pref. *N and O,* '74. S-S XV 398

b. Never did I see such a confused heap

---

* See Roswell G. Ham, "Dryden versus Settle," *MP,* XXV (1928), 409–16.

of false grammar, improper English, strained hyperboles, and downright bulls. His plot is incoherent, and full of absurdities, and the characters of his persons so ill chosen, that they are all either knaves or fools . . ./They all speak alike, and without distinction of character; that is, every one rants, and swaggers, and talks nonsense abundantly.

Pref. *N and O,* '74. S-S XV 398–99

c. In short, he is an animal of a most deplored understanding, without reading and conversation: his being is in a twilight of sense, and some glimmering of thought, which he can never fashion either into wit or English. His style is boisterous and roughhewn; his rhyme incorrigibly lewd, and his numbers perpetually harsh and ill-sounding. That little talent which he has, is fancy. He sometimes labours with a thought, but with the pudder he makes . . . it is commonly still-born; so that, for want of learning and elocution, he will never be able to express any thing either naturally or justly. This subjects him . . . to false allusions, and mistaken points of wit. As for judgment, he has not the least grain of it . . .

Pref. *N and O,* '74. S-S XV 399
AUDIENCE, POPULAR, e. POETIC LICENSE, b.

d. Mr. Settle . . . /himself declares, he neither reads, nor cares for conversation; so that he would persuade us he is a kind of fanatic in poetry, and has a light within him, and writes by inspiration; which (like that of the heathen prophets) a man must have no sense of his own when he receives; and no doubt he would be thought inspired, and would be reverenced extremely in the country where Santons are worshipped.

Postscript *N and O,* '74. S-S XV 406–7
SHADWELL, e.

Sextus Empiricus

HOBBES, a.

Shadwell, Thomas

a. . . . "The Lancashire Witches" were without doubt the most insipid jades that ever flew upon a stage . . .

Vindication, '83. S-S VII 151

HISTORICAL TRUTH, c. Cf. AUDIENCE, POPULAR, h. [Scott's conjecture]

b. [¶] Yet even this their celebrated writer [Thomas Hunt, author of "A Defence . . . of the City of London," a Whig tract] knows no more of style and English than the Northern dedicator [Shadwell]; as if dulness and clumsiness were fatal to the name of *Tom.* It is true, he is a fool in three languages more than the poet; for, they say, "he understands Latin, Greek, and Hebrew," from all which, to my certain knowledge, I acquit the other. Og may write against the king, if he pleases, so long as he drinks for him, and his writings will never do the government so much harm as his drinking does it good; for true subjects will not be much perverted by his libels; but the wine-duties rise considerably by his claret. He has often called me an atheist in print; I would believe more charitably of him, and that he only goes the broad way, because the other is too narrow for him. He may see, by this, I do not delight to meddle with his course of life, and his immoralities, though I have a long bead-roll of them. I have hitherto contented myself with the ridiculous part of him, which is enough, in all conscience, to employ one man; even without/the story of his late fall at the Old Devil, where he broke no ribs, because the hardness of the stairs could reach no bones; and, for my part, I do not wonder how he came to fall, for I have always known him heavy: the miracle is, how

he got up again. . . . But to leave him, who is not worth any further consideration, now I have done laughing at him,—would every man knew his own talent, and that they, who are only born for drinking, would let both poetry and prose alone!

Vindication, '83. S-S VII 180–81

c. [Retorting to the charge that in *The Duke of Guise* a mountain was delivered of a mouse] I have been gossip to many such labours of a dull fat scribbler, where the mountain has been bigger, and the mouse less.

Vindication, '83. S-S VII 198

d. And may the same dulness preserve him ever from public justice; it is a sufficient thick mud-wall betwixt him and law; it is his guardian angel that protects him from punishment, because, in spite of him, he cannot deserve it. . . . He can never offend enough, to need the mercy of government, for it is beholding to him, that he writes against it; and he never offers at a satire, but he converts his readers to the contrary opinion.

Vindication, '83. S-S VII 204

e. Bear your good fortune moderately, Mr. Poet [Shadwell]; for, as loose and infamous as I am, if I had written for your party, your pension would have been cut off as useless. But they must take up with Settle, and such as they can/get: Bartholomew-Fair writers, and Bartholomew-Close printers; there is a famine of wit amongst them; they are forced to give unconscionable rates, and, after all, to have only carrion for their money.

Vindication, '83. S-S VII 205–6

f. But if Jack Ketch must needs have the handling of us poets, let him begin first where he may take the deepest say; let me be hanged, but in my turn; for I am sure I am neither the fattest scribbler, nor the worst . . .

Vindication, '83. S-S VII 210

Sᴛ. Éᴠʀᴇᴍᴏɴᴅ, d.

Shakespeare, William [See also combinations with Shakespeare, following]*

a. Shakespeare (who, with some errors not to be avoided in that age, had undoubtedly a larger soul of poesy than ever any of our nation) was the first who . . . invented . . . blank verse.

Ded. *Rival Ladies,* '64. K I 6

Jᴏɴsᴏɴ, h.

b. (Neander) [¶] To begin, then, with Shakespeare. He was the man who of all modern, and perhaps ancient poets, had the largest and most comprehensive soul. All the images of Nature were still present to him, and he drew/them, not laboriously, but luckily; when he describes any thing, you more than see it, you feel it too. Those who accuse him to have wanted learning, give him the greater commendation: he was naturally learn'd; he needed not the spectacles of books to read Nature; he looked inwards, and found her there. I cannot say he is everywhere alike; were he so, I should do him injury to compare him with the greatest of mankind. He is many times flat, insipid; his comic wit degenerating into clenches, his serious swelling into bombast. But he is always great, when some great occasion is presented to him; no man can say he ever had a fit subject for his wit, and did not then raise himself as high above the rest of poets,

Quantum lenta solent inter viburna cupressi.

---

* See John O. Eidson, "Dryden's Criticism of Shakespeare," *SP,* XXXIII (1936), 273–80. See also Augustus Ralli, *A History of Shakespeare Criticism* (London: Oxford University Press, 1932).

The consideration of this made Mr. Hales of Eaton say, that there was no subject of which any poet ever writ, but he would produce it much better treated of in Shakespeare . . .

Dram. Poesy, '65. K I 79–80

Bᴇᴀᴜᴍᴏɴᴛ ᴀɴᴅ Fʟᴇᴛᴄʜᴇʀ. Dʀʏᴅᴇɴ, Wᴏʀᴋs, v.

c. . . . it is almost a miracle that much of his [Shakespeare's] language remains so pure; and that he who began Dramatic Poetry amongst us, untaught by any, and as Ben Johnson tells us, without learning, should by the force of his own genius perform so much, that in a manner he has left no praise for any who come after him.

Pref. *All for Love,* '78. K I 201

Aᴇsᴄʜʏʟᴜs.

d. They who think to do me an injury by saying that it [his scene between Troilus and Hector, concluding the third act of *Troilus and Cressida*] is an/imitation of the scene betwixt Brutus and Cassius, do me an honour by supposing I could imitate the incomparable Shakespeare . . .

Pref. *Troilus,* '79. K I 204–5

e. [Of the Brutus-Cassius scene compared with Amintor-Melantius scene in *The Maid's Tragedy* and with Agamemnon-Menelaus in *Iphigenia*] But the particular groundwork which Shakespeare has taken is incomparably the best . . .

Pref. *Troilus,* '79. K I 205

f. [¶] Here, therefore, the general answer may be given to the first question, how far we ought to imitate Shakespeare and Fletcher in their plots; namely, that we ought to follow them so far only as they have copied the excellencies of those who invented and brought to perfection Dramatic Poetry; those things only excepted, which religion, custom of countries, idioms of langues, etc., have altered in the super-structures, but not in the foundation of the design.

Pref. *Troilus*, '79. K I 211

g. If Shakespeare were stripped of all the bombasts in his passions, and dressed in the most vulgar words, we should find the beauties of his thoughts remaining; if his embroideries were burnt down, there would still be silver at the bottom of the melting-pot: but I fear (at least let me fear it for myself) that we, who ape his sound-ing words, have nothing of his thought, but are all outside; there is not so much as a dwarf within our giant's clothes. There-fore, let not Shakespeare suffer for our sakes; 'tis our fault, who succeed him in an age which is more refined, if we imitate him so ill, that we copy his failings only, and make a virtue of that in our writings which in his was an imperfection.

Pref. *Troilus,* '79. K I 227
HISTORICAL TRUTH, c.

h. [Dorset's talents as literary critic] are as inborn to you [Dorset], as they were to Shakespeare; and, for aught I know, to Homer; in either of whom we find all arts and sciences, all moral and natural philosophy, without knowing that they ever studied them.

Discourse of Satire, '93. K II 18
MODERNS, f. LAST AGE, l. PRESENT AGE, o.

i. After I have confess'd thus much of our Modern Heroick Poetry, I cannot but conclude with Mr. Rym[er], that our Eng-lish Comedy is far beyond anything of the Ancients. And notwithstanding our ir-regularities, so is our Tragedy. Shakespear had a Genius for it; and we know, in spite of Mr. R—— that Genius alone is a greater Virtue (if I may so call it) than all other Qualifications put together. You see/what

success this Learned Critick has found in the World, after his Blaspheming Shake-spear. Almost all the Faults which he has discover'd are truly there; yet who will read Mr. Rym—— or not read Shakespear? For my own part I reverence Mr. Rym——s Learning, but I detest his Ill Nature and his Arrogance. I indeed, and such as I, have reason to be afraid of him, but Shakespear has not.

Letter to Dennis, March, 1694. Ward No. 31, pp. 71–72

Characters [See also below, *Falstaff, Mercutio*]
ENGLISH VS. FRENCH, s. COMEDY, e. AN-CIENTS, e. See below, t, o, p, l. FLETCHER, g. See below, r.
Design
DAVENANT, b.
Diction
TRAGEDY, e. DICTION, b, a.
English Language, Contribution to
GRAFFING, b.
Falstaff
HUMORS, a.

j. . . . so in a comical character, or hu-mour (which is an inclination to this or that particular folly), Falstaff is a liar, and a coward, a glutton, and a buffoon, because all these qualities may agree in the same man . . .

Pref. *Troilus,* '79. K I 215
Cf. CRITICASTERS, g.
Friendship Motif
LOVE. SHAKESPEARE AND FLETCHER, b.
History Plays

k. (Lisideius) . . . if you consider the historical plays of Shakespeare, they are rather so many chronicles of kings, or the business many times of thirty or forty years, cramped into a representation of two hours and an half; which is not to imitate or paint nature, but rather to draw her in miniature, to take her in little; to look upon her through the wrong end of a perspective, and receive her images not only much less, but infinitely more imperfect than the life . . .

Dram. Poesy, '65. K I 59

Tragedy, t.

Invention

l. I will instance but in one [character], to show the copiousness of his [Shakespeare's] invention [corrected from Ker's *intention*]; it is that of Caliban, or the monster, in the *Tempest.* He seems there to have created a person which was not in Nature, a boldness which, at first sight, would appear intolerable; for he makes him a species of himself, begotten by an incubus on a witch; but this, as I have elsewhere proved, is not wholly beyond the bounds of credibility, at least the vulgar still believe it. We have the separated notions of a spirit, and of a witch (and spirits, according to Plato, are vested with a subtle body; according to some of his followers, have different sexes); therefore, as from the distinct apprehensions of a horse, and of a man, imagination has formed a centaur; so, from those of an incubus and a sorceress, Shakespeare has produced his monster. Whether or no his generation can be defended, I leave to philosophy; but of this I am certain, that the poet has most judiciously furnished him with a person, a language, and a character, which will suit him, both by father's and mother's side: he has all the discontents and malice of a witch, and of a devil, besides a convenient proportion of the deadly sins; gluttony, sloth, and lust, are/manifest; the dejectedness of a slave is likewise given him, and the ignorance of one bred up in a desert island. His person is

monstrous, and he is the product of unnatural lust; and his language is as hobgoblin as his person; in all things he is distinguished from other mortals.

Pref. *Troilus,* '79. K I 219–20

Irregularity, Vigorous

English vs. French, u.

Language Improprieties

m. But, malice and partiality set apart, let any man, who understands English, read diligently the works of Shakespeare and Fletcher, and I dare undertake, that he will find in every page either some solecism of speech, or some notorious flaw in sense . . .

Defence of the Epilogue, '72. K I 165

n. Yet it must be allowed to the present age, that the tongue in general is so much refined since Shakespeare's time, that many of his words, and more of his phrases, are scarce intelligible. And of those which we understand, some are ungrammatical, others coarse; and his whole style is so pestered with figurative expressions, that it is as affected as it is obscure. 'Tis true, that in his latter plays he had worn off somewhat of the rust; but the tragedy which I have undertaken to correct was in all probability one of his first endeavours on the stage.

Pref. *Troilus,* '79. K I 203

Dryden, Works, aa.

Magic Effects, Use of

Imitation, j.

Manners

Shakespeare and Fletcher and Jonson.

o. But our Shakespeare [by contrast to the French], having ascribed to Henry the Fourth the character of a king and of a father, gives him the perfect manners of each relation . . .

Pref. *Troilus,* '79. K I 218

p. To return once more to Shakespeare; no man ever drew so many characters, or generally distinguished 'em better from one another, excepting only Johnson.

Pref. *Troilus*, '79. K I 219
See above, l.
Mercutio

q. [¶] Shakespeare showed the best of his skill [at portraying a gentleman] in his Mercutio; and he said himself, that he was forced to kill him in the third act, to prevent being killed by him. But, for my part, I cannot find he was so dangerous a person: I see nothing in him but what was so exceeding harmless, that he might have lived to the end of the play, and died in his bed, without offence to any man.

Defence of the Epilogue, '72. K I 174
Native Genius
See above, b, c. Dryden, Literary Life, a.
See above, h, i.
Passions
Seneca, a.

r. [¶] If Shakespeare be allowed, as I think he must, to have made his characters distinct, it will easily be inferred that he understood the nature of the passions . . . yet I cannot deny that he has his failings; but they are not so much in the passions themselves, as in his manner of expression: he often obscures his meaning by his words . . . I will not say of so great a poet, that he distinguished not the blown puffy style from true sublimity; but I may venture to maintain, that the fury of his fancy often transported him beyond the bounds of judgment, either in coining of new words and phrases, or racking words which were in use, into the violence of a catachresis.

Pref. *Troilus*, '79. K I 224
Bombast, a. See above, g. Shakespeare
and Fletcher, b.

Plotting
Last Age, c. Shakespeare and Fletcher, a.

s. [¶] How defective Shakespeare and Fletcher have been in all their plots, Mr. Rymer has discovered in his criticisms . . . cisms . . .

Pref. *Troilus*, '79. K I 211
Plots, Source
Plagiarism, b.
Poetic Justice
See below, t.
Reflection of Age
Age, Genius of, c.
Troilus and Cressida
See above, n.

t. . . . so lamely is it [Shakespeare's *Troilus and Cressida*] left to us, that it is not divided into acts; which fault I ascribe to the actors who printed it after Shakespeare's death; and that too so carelessly, that a more uncorrect copy I never saw. For the play itself, the author seems to have begun it with some fire; the characters of Pandarus and Thersites are promising enough; but as if he grew weary of his task, after an entrance or two, he lets them fall: and the latter part of the tragedy is nothing but a confusion of drums and trumpets, excursions and alarms. The chief persons . . . are left alive; Cressida is false, and is not punished. Yet, after all, because the play was Shakespeare's, and that there appeared in some places of it/the admirable genius of the author, I undertook to remove that heap of rubbish under which many excellent thoughts lay wholly buried.

Pref. *Troilus*, '79. K I 203–4
Tumult
Tumult, b. See above, t.
Wit (Excess)
Wit, h.

u. Shakespeare, who many times has written better than any poet, in any language, is yet so far from writing wit always, or expressing that wit according to the dignity of the subject, that he writes, in many places, below the dullest writer of ours, or any precedent age. Never did any author precipitate himself from such height of thought to so low expressions, as he often does. He is the very Janus of poets . . .

Defence of the Epilogue, '72. K I 172
FLETCHER, c.

v. [¶] Let us therefore admire the beauties and the heights of Shakespeare, without falling after him into a carelessness, and, as I may call it, a lethargy of thought, for whole scenes together.

Defence of the Epilogue, '72. K I 176

Shakespeare and Fletcher

a. [¶] The difference between Shakespeare and Fletcher in their plotting seems to be this; that Shakespeare generally moves more terror, and Fletcher more compassion: for the first had a more masculine, a bolder and more fiery genius; the second, a more soft and womanish. In the mechanic beauties of the plot . . . the three Unities . . . they are both deficient; but Shakespeare most. Ben Johnson reformed those errors in his comedies, yet one of Shakespeare's was regular before him; which is, *The Merry Wives of Windsor.*

Pref. *Troilus,* '79. K I 212

b. [¶] For what remains, the excellency of that poet [Shakespeare] was, as I have said, in the more manly passions; Fletcher's in the softer: Shakespeare writ better betwixt man and/man; Fletcher, betwixt man and woman: consequently, the one described friendship better; the other love: yet Shakespeare taught Fletcher to write love: and Juliet and Desdemona are origi-

nals. 'Tis true, the scholar had the softer soul; but the master had the kinder. . . . Shakespeare had an universal mind, which comprehended all characters and passions; Fletcher a more confined and limited: for though he treated love in perfection, yet honour, ambition, revenge, and generally all the stronger passions, he either touched not, or not masterly. To conclude all, he was a limb of Shakespeare.

Pref. *Troilus,* '79. K I 227–28

Shakespeare and Fletcher and Jonson

'Tis one of the excellencies of Shakespeare, that the manners of his persons are generally apparent, and you see their bent and inclinations. Fletcher comes far short of him in this, as indeed he does almost in everything: there are but glimmerings of manners in most of his comedies, which run upon adventures; and in his tragedies . . . are but pictures shown you in the twilight . . . But of all poets, this commendation is to be given to Ben Johnson, that the manners, even of the most inconsiderable persons in his plays, are everywhere apparent.

Pref. *Troilus,* '79. K I 217

Shakespeare and Jonson

(Neander) If I would compare him [Jonson] with Shakespeare, I must acknowledge him the more correct poet, but Shakespeare the greater wit. Shakespeare was the Homer, or father of our dramatic poets; Johnson was the Virgil, the pattern of elaborate writing; I admire/him, but I love Shakespeare.

Dram. Poesy, '65. K I 82–83
SHAKESPEARE AND FLETCHER, a.

Sidney, Sir Philip

RHYME (DEBATE), d. WIT, k.

a. Connexion of epithets, or the conjunction of two words in one, are frequent and elegant in the Greek, which yet Sir Philip

Sidney, and the translator of Du Bartas, have unluckily attempted in the English . . .

Author's Apology, '77. K I 189

b. . . . like the painter in the *Arcadia* . . .

Ded. *Æneis,* '97. K II 229

Silence

. . . the greatest note of admiration is silence. It is that noble passion, to which poets raise their audience in highest subjects, and they have then gained over them the greatest victory, when they are ravished into a pleasure which is not to be expressed by words.

Ded. *Amboyna,* '73. S-S V 5

Cf. VIRGIL, dd.

Sobriety (Political)

DRYDEN, MISCELLANEOUS.

Sonnet

RHYME (DEBATE), m. DRYDEN, LITERARY LIFE, b. ENGLISH VS. FRENCH, n.

Sophists

LUCIAN, d.

Sophocles

ANCIENTS, e.

a. . . . "Œdipus" was the most celebrated piece of all antiquity; . . . Sophocles, not only the greatest wit, but one of the greatest men in Athens, made it for the stage at the public cost; and . . . it had the reputation of being his masterpiece . . .

Pref. *Œdipus,* '79. S-S VI 131

MANNERS, i.

b. Sophocles has been more judicious [than Fletcher] in his *Antigona;* for, though he represents in Creon a bloody prince, yet he makes him not a lawful king, but an usurper, and Antigona herself is the heroine of the tragedy.

Pref. *Troilus,* '79. K I 218

ANCIENTS, a. CHARACTER[s], c. AUTHORITY, f. IMITATION, d.

Spanish Critics

[¶] Dryden has assured me that he got more from the Spanish critics alone, than from the Italian and French, and all other critics put together. [Bolingbroke]

Joseph Spence, *Anecdotes* (1820), 14

Spanish Literature [See also LOPE DE VEGA]

PROSODY, gg.

Spanish Plays

RHYME (DEBATE), b. PRESENT AGE, e. PROSODY, h.

a. (Eugenius) . . . the Spaniards at this day allow but three acts, which they call *Jornadas,* to a play . . .

Dram. Poesy, '65. K I 46

b. (Lisideius) [¶] Another thing in which the French differ from us/and from the Spaniards, is, that they do not embarrass, or cumber themselves with too much plot . . .

Dram. Poesy, '65. K I 59–60

c. (Neander) [¶] I grant the French have performed what was possible on the ground-work of the Spanish plays; what was pleasant before, they have made regular: but there is not above one good play to be writ on all those plots; they are too much alike to please often . . .

Dram. Poesy, '65. K I 69

UNITIES (DRAMATIC), ACTION, d. DRYDEN, WORKS, xx.

Sparta.

ROME.

Speeches (Dramatic)

a. (Neander) . . . I confess their [the French] verses are to me the coldest I have ever read. . . . being so many declamations, which tire us with the length . . . When the French stage came to be reformed by Cardinal Richelieu, those long harangues were introduced, to comply with the gravity of a churchman. Look upon the *Cinna* and the *Pompey;* they are not so properly to be called plays, as long discourses of reasons of state; and *Polieucte* in matters of religion is as solemn as the long stops upon our organs. Since that time it is grown into a custom, and their actors /speak by the hour-glass, as our parsons do . . .

Dram. Poesy, '65. K I 71–72

ENGLISH VS. FRENCH, x.

b. (Neander) But to speak generally: it cannot be denied that short speeches and replies are more apt to move the passions and beget concernment in us, than the other [long speeches]; for it is unnatural for any one in a gust of passion to speak long together, or for another in the same condition to suffer him, without interruption. Grief and passion are like floods raised in little brooks by a sudden rain; they are quickly up; and if the concernment be poured unexpectedly in upon us, it overflows us: but a long sober shower gives them leisure to run out as they came in, without troubling the ordinary current. As for Comedy, repartee is one of its chiefest graces; the greatest pleasure of the audience is a chace of wit, kept up on both sides, and swiftly managed.

Dram. Poesy, '65. K I 72

POET, m. SHAKESPEARE, m.

Speght, Thomas

CHAUCER, c.

Spenser, Edmund

SUPERNATURAL, b.

a. I remember, when I was a boy, I thought inimitable Spenser a mean poet, in comparison of Sylvester's *Dubartas* . . .

Ded. *Spanish Friar, '81.* K I 247

SYLVESTER's *Du Bartas,* a. THEOCRITUS, a. EPIC, j.

b. The English have [in epic] only to boast of Spenser and Milton, who neither of them wanted either genius or learning to have been perfect poets, and yet both of them are liable to many censures. For there is no uniformity in the design of Spenser: he aims at the accomplishment of no one action; he raises up a hero for every one of his adventures; and endows each of them with some particular moral virtue, which renders them all equal, without subordination, or preference. Every one is most valiant in his own legend: only we must do him that justice to observe, that magnanimity, which is the character of Prince Arthur, shines throughout the whole poem; and succors the rest, when they are in distress. The original of every knight was then living in the court of Queen Elizabeth . . . an ingenious piece of flattery, though it turned not much to his account. Had he lived to finish his poem, in the six remaining legends, it had certainly been more of a piece; but could not have been perfect, because the model was not true. . . . for the rest, his obsolete language, and the ill choice of his stanza, are faults but of the second magnitude; for, notwithstanding the first, he is still intelligible, at least after a little practice; and for the last, he is the more to be admired, that, labouring under such a difficulty, his verses are so numerous,/so various, and so harmonious, that only Virgil, whom he profestly imitated, has surpassed him among the Romans; and only Mr. Waller among the English.

Discourse of Satire, '93. K II 28–29

MILTON, c. ARCHAISMS, b. SATIRE, pp. DRYDEN, LITERARY LIFE, b.

c. [¶] Our own nation has produced a third poet in this kind [pastoral], not inferior to the two former [Virgil, Theocritus]: for the *Shepherd's Kalendar* of Spenser is not to be matched in any modern language, not even by Tasso's *Aminta,* which infinitely transcends Guarini's *Pastor Fido,* as having more of nature in it, and being almost wholly clear from the wretched affectation of learning. . . ./

But Spenser, being master of our northern dialect, and skilled in Chaucer's English, has so exactly imitated the Doric of Theocritus, that his love is a perfect image of that passion . . . before it was corrupted with the knowledge of arts, and the ceremonies of what we call good manners.

Ded. *Pastorals,* '97. S-S XIII 324–25

EPIC POET, c. PROSODY, e. ENGLISH vs. FRENCH, m. VIRGIL, ll. PROSODY, jj, k. COINAGE, c.

d. For Spenser and Fairfax both flourished in the reign of Queen Elizabeth; great masters in our language, and who saw much farther into the beauties of our numbers than those who immediately followed them.

Pref. *Fables,* 1700. K II 247

MILTON, d. CHAUCER, c.

Stage Production

In a play-house, everything contributes to impose upon the judgment; the lights, the scenes, the habits, and, above all, the grace of action . . . [See JUDGMENT (RESPONSIVE)]

Ded. *Spanish Friar,* '81. K I 245

ACTING AND ACTORS, b. DESIGNING. DRAMA READ AND ACTED, b.

Statius, Publius Papinius

SUPERNATURAL, b.

a. . . . I will neither quote Lucan, nor Statius, men of unbounded imagination, but who often wanted the poise of judgment. [See LUCAN, c]

Author's Apology, '77. K I 184

CHAPMAN, a. DRYDEN, WORKS, n. SUBLIME, b.

b. . . . Statius, the best versifactor next to/Virgil, knew not how to design after him . . .

Discourse of Satire, '93. K II 26–27

FIGURES, c. VIRGIL, ee.

c. Statius, as Bossu has well observed, was ambitious of trying his strength with his master Virgil, as Virgil had before tried his with Homer. The Grecian gave the two Romans an example, in the games . . . at the funerals of Patroclus. Virgil imitated the invention of Homer, but changed the sports. But both the Greek and Latin poet took their occasions from the subject; though, to confess the truth, they were both ornamental, or, at best, convenient parts of it . . . Statius, who, through his whole poem, is noted for want of conduct and judgment, instead of staying . . . for the death of Capaneus, Hippomedon, Tydeus, or some other of his seven champions . . ./. went out of his way . . . to commit a fault. For he took his opportunity to kill a royal infant . . . to make way for those funeral honours which he intended for him.

Ded. *Æneis,* '97. K II 155–56

CRITIC[s], a. VIRGIL, bb, j.

Sternhold, Thomas

VOX POPULI.

. . . this rhyming judge of the twelve-penny gallery, this legitimate son of Sternhold . . . [See ROCHESTER, c]

Pref. *All for Love,* '78. K I 199

DRYDEN, LITERARY LIFE, d.

Stoicism

PLUTARCH, C.

a. . . . the ruggedness of a stoic is only a silly affectation of being a god . . . [See OPINION]

Ded. *Don Sebastian,* '90. S-S VII 303

PERSIUS, i. HORACE AND JUVENAL AND PERSIUS, c. PERSIUS, j. Cf. HOWARD, b.

b. Here [Persius's Fifth Satire] our Author excellently Treats that Paradox of the Stoicks, which affirms, that the Wise or Virtuous Man is only Free; and that all Vicious Men, are Naturally Slaves. And, in the Illustration of this Dogma, he takes up the remaining part of this inimitable Satyr.

Argument of the Fifth Satire [Persius], '93. JK II 772

Style [See BOMBAST; FIGURES; MEANNESS; PROSODY (*Sweetness*); TECHNICAL TERMS]

Ciceronian

a-0. . . . his [Louis Maimbourg, author of the *History of the League*] style . . . is rather Ciceronian, copious, florid, and figurative, than succinct . . .

Postscript, *History of the League,* '84. S-S XVII 185

Curiosa Felicitas

HORACE, j.

English Style, Taste in

a. There are many who understand Greek and Latin, and yet are ignorant of their mother-tongue. The proprieties and delicacies of the English are known to few; 'tis impossible even for a good wit to understand and practise them, without the help of a liberal education, long reading, and digesting of those few good authors we have amongst us, the knowledge of men and manners, the freedom of habitudes and conversation with the best company of both sexes; and, in short, without wearing off the rust which he contracted while he was lay-

ing in a stock of learning. Thus difficult it is to understand the purity of English, and critically to discern not only good writers from bad, and a proper style from a corrupt, but also to distinguish that which is pure in a good author, from that which is vicious and corrupt in him.

Pref. *Sylvæ,* '85. K I 253

Hudibrastic

BUTLER, b.

High (Grand) Style

TRAGEDY, s. EPIC, i. See below, c. VIRGIL, oo. LUCRETIUS, b. DRYDEN, WORKS, yy. PROSODY, x. ARIOSTO, a. TASSO, b. EPIC, j. Cf. JUVENAL, a. Cf. BELLORI, v. TRANSLATION, n.

Middle Style

b. Some, who have seen a paper of verses, which I wrote last year to her Highness the Duchess, have accused them of that only thing I could defend in them. They said, I did *humi serpere,*—that I wanted not only height of fancy, but dignity of words, to set it off. I might well answer with that of/ Horace, *Nunc non erat his locus;* I knew I addressed them to a lady, and accordingly affected the softness of expression, and the smoothness of measure, rather than the height of thought . . .

Pref. *Annus Mirabilis,* '66. K I 18–19

c. [¶] If any one be so lamentable a critic as to require the smoothness, the numbers, and the turn of heroic poetry in this poem [*Religio*], I must tell him, that if he has not read Horace, I have studied him, and hope the style of his Epistles is not ill imitated here. The expressions of a poem, designed purely for instruction, ought to be plain and natural, and yet majestic; for here the poet/is presumed to be a kind of lawgiver, and those three qualities, which I have named, are proper to the legislative style. The florid, elevated, and figurative way, is for the passions; for love and hatred, fear and anger, are begotten in the soul by showing their objects out of true proportion, either greater than the life, or less; but instruction is to be given by showing them what they naturally are. A man is to be cheated into passion, but to be reasoned into truth.

Pref. *Religio Laici,* '82. S-S X 32–33

History, d, e. Plutarch, h. Lucretius, b. Dryden, Works, yy. Walsh, b. Horace and Juvenal and Persius, a. Virgil, mm.

Low (Familiar) Style [See also Meanness]

Dryden, Works, yy. Horace and Juvenal and Persius, a. Horace, l. Butler, b. Chaucer and Boccaccio.

Satiric, defined

Satire, f.

Senecan

Seneca, c.

Shakespearean

Dryden, Works, v. Shakespeare, n.

Varied

Biography, b.

Miscellaneous

Settle, c.

d. The difference is as plainly seen betwixt sophistry and truth, as it is betwixt the style of a gentleman and the clumsy stiffness of a pedant.

Ded. *Plutarch's Lives,* '83. S-S XVII 16

Subject, Integrity of

Satire, c.

[¶] As in the composition of a picture the painter is to take care that nothing enter into it which is not proper or convenient to the subject, so likewise is the poet to reject all incidents which are foreign to his poem, and naturally no parts of it . . . No

person, no incident, in the piece, or in the play, but must be of use to carry on the main design.

Parallel, '95. K II 139

Sublime*

Style, b. Dryden, Literary Life, e-2. Cf. Silence. Cf. Milton, a.

a. . . . the sublime genius that sometimes errs . . . [See Longinus, a]

Author's Apology, '77. K I 180

Cf. Heightening, c. Epic, i. Shakespeare, r. Cf. Bombast, b. Cf. Plutarch, g, h. Cf. Lucretius, b.

b. Neither do I discommend the lofty style in Tragedy, which is naturally pompous and magnificent; but nothing is truly sublime that is not just and proper. . . ./ Virgil had all the majesty of a lawful prince, and Statius only the blustering of a tyrant. But when men affect a virtue which they cannot easily reach, they fall into a vice which bears the nearest resemblance to it. Thus an injudicious poet who aims at loftiness runs easily into the swelling puffy style, because it looks like greatness.

Ded. *Spanish Friar,* '81. K I 246–47

Prosody, x. Juvenal, a. Satire, f. Boileau, c. Dryden, Literary Life. b. Prosody, y. Cf. English vs. French, k. Cf. Virgil, u. Epic, g. Critic[s], a. Virgil, s.

Sublime, False [See Bombast, *passim*]

. . . I will not say of [Shakespeare] . . . that he distinguished not the blown puffy style from true sublimity . . . [See Shakespeare, r]

Pref. *Troilus,* '79. K I 224

Bombast, b. Chapman, a. Dryden,

---

* See S. H. Monk, *The Sublime: A Study of Critical Theories in XVIII-Century England* (New York: Modern Language Association of America, 1935).

WORKS, n. SUBLIME, b. SYLVESTER's *Du Bartas.* HEIGHTENING, d. CRITIC[s], a.

Success (Poetic)

Yet, if a poem have a genius, it will force its own reception in the world; for there is a sweetness in/good verse which tickles even while it hurts; and no man can be heartily angry with him who pleases him against his will.

Pref. *Absalom and Achitophel,* '81. S-S IX 211–12

Suckling, Sir John

(Eugenius) . . . nothing so courtly/writ . . . as Sir John Suckling . . . [See PRESENT AGE, d]

Dram. Poesy, '65. K I 34–35

DAVENANT, b. GRAFFING, b.

Suetonius (Caius Suetonius Tranquillus)

PLUTARCH, g.

Supernatural [See also EPIC MACHINES, DEUS EX MACHINA]

a. [¶] As for what I have said [in *Tyrannic Love*] of astral or aërial spirits, it is no invention of mine, but taken from those who have written on that subject. Whether there are such beings or not, it concerns not me; it is sufficient for my purpose, that many have believed the affirmative; and that these heroic representations, which are of the same nature with the epic, are not limited, but with the extremest bounds of what is credible.

Pref. *Tyrannic Love,* '70. S-S III 381

Cf. LUCAN, b.

b. For my part, I am of opinion, that neither Homer, Virgil, Statius, Ariosto, Tasso, nor our English Spencer, could have formed their poems half so beautiful, without those gods and spirits, and those enthusiastic parts of/poetry, which compose the most noble parts of all their writings.

Essay of Heroic Plays, '72. K I 152–53

c. And if any man object the improbabilities of a spirit appearing, or of a palace raised by magic; I boldly answer him, that an heroic poet is not tied to a bare representation of what is true, or exceeding probable; but that he may let himself loose to visionary objects, and to the representation of such things as depending not on sense, and therefore not to be comprehended by knowledge, may give him a freer scope for imagination.

Essay of Heroic Plays, '72. K I 153

d. 'Tis enough that, in all ages and religions, the greatest part of mankind have believed the power of magic, and that there are spirits or spectres which have appeared. This, I say, is foundation enough for poetry . . .

Essay of Heroic Plays, '72. K I 153

e. . . . and I dare further affirm, that the whole doctrine of separated beings, whether those spirits are incorporeal substances (which Mr. Hobbs, with some reason, thinks to imply a contradiction), or that they are a thinner or more aërial sort of bodies (as some of the Fathers have conjectured), may better be explicated by poets than by philosophers or divines. For their speculations on this subject are wholly poetical; they have only their fancy for their guide; and that, being sharper in an excellent poet, than it is likely it should be in a phlegmatic, heavy gownman, will see further in its own empire, and produce more satisfactory notions on those dark and doubtful problems.

Essay of Heroic Plays, '72. K I 153

f. [¶] Some men think they have raised a great argument against the use of spectres and magic in heroic poetry,/by saying they are unnatural; but whether they or I believe there are such things, is not material; 'tis enough that, for aught we know, they may be in Nature; and whatever is, or may be, is not properly unnatural.

Essay of Heroic Plays, '72. K I 153–54

Cowley, b. Imitation, j. Poetic License, f. Opera, a.

g. [Speaking of the supernatural in opera] Yet propriety is to be observed even here./The gods are all to manage their peculiar provinces; and what was attributed by the heathens to one power ought not to be performed by any other. . . .[1] To conclude, they must all act according to their distinct and peculiar characters.

Pref. *Albion and Albanius,* '85. K I 270–71

Dryden, Works, ww. Imagination, d. Epic, Christian, b. Cf. Epic Poet, c.

Sweetness [See Prosody]

Sylvester's *Du Bartas*

Sidney, a.

I remember, when I was a boy, I thought inimitable Spenser a mean poet, in comparison of Sylvester's *Dubartas,* and was rapt into an ecstasy when I read these lines:—

Now, when the Winter's keener breath began
To chrystallize the Baltic Ocean;
To glaze the Lakes, to bridle up the Floods,
And periwig with Snow the bald-pate Woods.

I am much deceived if this be not abominable fustian, that is, thoughts and words ill-sorted, and without the least relation to each other; yet I dare not answer for an audience, that they would not clap it on the stage . . . [See Audience, Popular, f]

Ded. *Spanish Friar,* '81. K I 247

Synaloepha [See Prosody]

T

Tacitus, Cornelius [See also Polybius and Tacitus]

History, d, e. Plutarch, g. Polybius, a. Persius, a. Chaucer, c.

Tasso, Torquato

Plagiarism, b.

a. And Tasso, the most excellent of modern poets . . . whom I reverence next to Virgil . . .

Pref. *Evening's Love,* '71. K I 145

Epic Hero, b. Supernatural, b. Cf. Cowley, b. Epic Hero, d. Poetic License, f. Theocritus, a.

b. Tasso, whose design was regular, and who observed the rules of unity in time and place more closely than Virgil, yet was not so happy in his action; he confesses himself to have been too lyrical, that is, to have written beneath the dignity of heroic verse, in his episodes of Sophronia, Erminia, and Armida; his story is not so pleasing as Ariosto's; he is too flatulent sometimes, and sometimes too dry; many times unequal, and almost always forced; and, besides, is full of conceits, points of epigram, and witticisms; all which are not only below the dignity of heroic verse, but contrary to its nature: Virgil and Homer have not one of them. . . . But to return to Tasso: he borrows from the invention of Boiardo, and in his alteration of his poem, which is infinitely for the worse, imitates Homer . . . very servilely . . .[1]

Discourse of Satire, '93. K II 27

FRENCH AUTHORS, b. DRYDEN, LITERARY LIFE, b. EPIC, CHRISTIAN, c. SPENSER, c. EPIC POET, c. ENGLISH vs. FRENCH, l. EPIC HERO, k. POET, f.

Tassoni, Alessandro

The *Secchia Rapita*/is an Italian poem, a satire of the Varronian kind. 'Tis written in the stanza of eight, which is their measure for heroic verse. The words are stately, the numbers smooth, the turn both of thoughts and words is happy. The first six lines of the stanza seem majestical and severe; but the two last turn them all into a pleasant ridicule.

Discourse of Satire, '93. K II 106–7

BOILEAU, c.

Taste

Were there neither judge, taste, nor opinion in the world, yet they [tragedy and comedy] would differ in their natures . . . [See GENRE, b]

Defence of An Essay, '68. K I 120

AUDIENCE, POPULAR, a. EPIC vs. TRAGEDY, c. Cf. POET, p. Cf. CRITIC[s], h. Cf. ST. ÉVREMOND, a. DRYDEN, LITERARY LIFE, a. Cf. PARONOMASIA, b. ENGLISH vs. FRENCH, k. IMITATION, i. RULES, h. LUCIAN, e. PRESENT AGE, p. Cf. VIRGIL, bb.

Tautology

WALSH, c. VIRGIL, o.

Technical Terms

a. . . . I have never yet seen the description of any naval fight in the proper terms which are used at sea; and if there be any such, in another language, as that of Lucan in the third of his *Pharsalia,* yet I could not prevail myself of it in the English; the

terms of art in every tongue bearing more of the idiom of it than any other words. We hear indeed among our poets, of the thundering of guns, the smoke, the disorder, and the slaughter, but all these are common notions. And . . . as those who, in a logical dispute, keep in general terms, would hide a fallacy; so those, who do it in any poetical description, would veil their ignorance . . .[q]

For my own part, if I had little knowledge of the sea, yet I have thought it no shame to learn . . .

Pref. *Annus Mirabilis,* '66. K I 13

TRANSLATION, g.

b. . . . I will not give the reasons why I writ not always in the proper terms of navigation, land-service, or in the cant of any profession. I will only say, that Virgil has avoided those proprieties, because he writ not to mariners, soldiers, astronomers, gardeners, peasants, etc., but to all in general, and in particular to men and ladies of the first quality, who have been better bred than to be too nicely knowing in the terms. In such cases, it is enough for a poet to write so plainly, that he may be understood by his readers; to avoid impropriety, and not affect to be thought learned in all things.

Ded. *Æneis,* '97. K II 236

Terence (Publius Terentius Afer)

a. (Crites) . . . not but that there may be many actions in a play . . . but they must be all subservient to the great one . . . such as in Terence's *Eunuch* is the difference and reconcilement of Thais and Phædria . . .

Dram. Poesy, '65. K I 41

MENANDER.

a-2. (Crites) To read Macrobius, explaining . . . Virgil . . . is enough to assure me that I ought to think the same of Terence; and that in the purity of his style (which Tully so much valued that he ever carried his works about him) there is yet left in him great room for admiration, if I knew but where to place it.

Dram. Poesy, '65. K I 42

b. (Eugenius) The Unity of Time, even Terence himself (who was the best and most regular of them) has neglected: his *Heautontimorumenos* . . . takes up visibly two days . . .

Dram. Poesy, '65. K I 48

NARRATIONS (DRAMATIC), a.

c. (Eugenius) . . . to which unnatural way of narration Terence is subject in all his plays. In his *Adelphi* . . . Syrus and Demea enter after the scene was broken . . . and indeed you can scarce look into any of his comedies, where you will not presently discover the same interruption.

Dram. Poesy, '65. K I 50

d. (Eugenius) . . . yet a thing well said will be wit in all languages . . . When Phædria, in the *Eunuch,* had a command from his mistress to be absent two days . . . said, *Tandem ego non illa caream, si sit opus, vel totum triduum?*—Parmeno, to mock the softness of his master . . . cries out . . . *Hui! universum triduum!* the elegancy of which *universum,* though it cannot be rendered in our language, yet leaves an impression on our souls: but this happens seldom in him . . .

Dram. Poesy, '65. K I 51

PLAGIARISM, b.

e. But Terence made an innovation in the Roman [stage]: all his plays have double actions; for it was his custom to translate two Greek comedies, and to weave them into one of his, yet so, that both their actions were comical, and one was principal,

the other but secondary or subservient. And this has obtained on the English stage, to give us the pleasure of variety.

Pref. *Troilus,* '79. K I 208

MANNERS, i. PROGRESS, f. COINAGE, c.

Theater

For the stage being the representation of the world, and the actions in it, how can it be imagined, that the picture of human life can be more exact than life itself is?

Ded. *Rival Ladies,* '64. K I 2

Theocritus

a. [¶] That which distinguishes Theocritus from all other poets, both Greek and Latin, and which raises him even above Virgil in his *Eclogues,* is the inimitable tenderness of his passions, and the natural expression of them in words so becoming of a pastoral. A simplicity shines through all he writes: he shows his art and learning, by disguising both. His shepherds never rise above their country education in their complaints of love: there is the same difference betwixt him and Virgil, as there is betwixt Tasso's *Aminta* and the *Pastor Fido* of Guarini. Virgil's shepherds are too well read in the philosophy of Epicurus and of Plato, and Guarini's seem to have been bred in courts; but Theocritus and Tasso have taken theirs from cottages and plains. It was said of Tasso, in relation to his similitudes, *mai esce del bosco:* that he never departed from the woods; that is, all his comparisons were taken from the country. The same may be said of our Theocritus: he is softer than Ovid; he touches the passions more delicately, and performs all this out of his own fond, without diving into the arts and sciences for a supply. Even his Doric dialect has an incomparable sweetness in its clownishness . . . This was impossible for Virgil to imitate; because the/severity of the Roman language denied him that advantage. Spenser has endeavoured it in his *Shepherd's Calendar;* but neither will it succeed in English; for which reason I forbore to attempt it. For Theocritus writ to Sicilians, who spoke that dialect; and I direct this part of my translations to our ladies, who neither understand, nor will take pleasure in such homely expressions.

Pref. *Sylvæ,* '85. K I 265–66

VIRGIL, V.

b. [¶] After all, I must confess that the boorish dialect of Theocritus has a secret charm in it/which the Roman language cannot imitate, though Virgil has drawn it down as low as possibly he could . . .¹ But Theocritus may justly be preferred as the original, without injury to Virgil . . .

Ded. *Pastorals,* '97. S-S XIII 323–24

SPENSER, C.

c. [¶] In the mean Time, I would advise you not to trust too much to Virgil's Pastorals; for as excellent as they are, yet, Theocritus is far before him, both in Softness of Thought, and Simplicity of Expression. Mr. Creech has translated that Greek Poet, which I have not read in English.

Letter to Elizabeth Thomas, November 1699. Ward No. 69, p. 127

Thinking

You may thinke of what you please, and that as little as you please; (for in my opinion), thinking it selfe, is a kind of paine to a witty man; he finds so much more in it to disquiet, than to please him.

Letter to Rochester, 1673. Ward No. 4, p. 9

Thomas, Elizabeth (Corinna)

a. . . . your Verses were, I thought, too good to be a Woman's; some of my Friends to whom I read them were of the same Opinion. 'Tis not over gallant, I must con-

fess, to say this of the fair Sex; but most certain it is, that they generally write with more Softness than Strength. On the contrary, you want neither Vigour in your Thoughts, nor force in your Expressions, nor Harmony in your Numbers, and methinks I find much of Orinda [Katherine Phillips] in your Manner (to whom I had the Honour to be related, and also to be Known.)

Letter to Elizabeth Thomas, 12 November 1699. Ward No. 68, p. 125

b. [¶] The great Desire which I observe in you to write well, and those good Parts which God Almighty and Nature have bestowed on you, make me not to doubt that by Application to Study, and the Reading of the best Authors, you may be absolute Mistress of Poetry. 'Tis an unprofitable Art, to those who profess it; but you, who write only for your Diversion, may pass your Hours with Pleasure in it, and without Prejudice, always avoiding (as I know you will) the Licenses which Mrs. Behn allowed herself, of writing loosely, and giving . . . some Scandal to the Modesty of her Sex. I confess, I am last Man who ought, in Justice to arraign her, who have been myself too much a Libertine in most of my Poems, which I should be well contented I had Time either to purge or to see them fairly burned.

Letter to Elizabeth Thomas, November 1699. Ward No. 69, p. 127

c. If you have any considerable/Faults, they consist chiefly in the Choice of Words and the placing them so as to make the Verse run smoothly . . .

Letter to Elizabeth Thomas, November 1699. Ward No. 69, pp. 127–28

Thoughts

. . . when it [*The Rival Ladies*] was only a confused mass of thoughts, tumbling over one another in the dark . . . [See FANCY, a]

Ded. *Rival Ladies,* '64. K I 1

RHYME (DEBATE), r. WIT, d. IMAGINATION, c. Cf. SHAKESPEARE, v. POETIC LICENSE, d. WIT, l. ENGLISH DRAMA, h. TRAGEDY, e, r. MANNERS, c. OVID, i. Cf. TRANSLATION, q. Cf. PROSODY, u. WIT, m. Cf. EXPRESSION, c. Cf. EPIC, d. CHAUCER AND OVID.

Thucydides

ANCIENTS, a. HISTORY, d. POLYBIUS, a.

Tibullus, Albius

SEDLEY, a. OVID, e.

Time

ACTING AND ACTORS, b. DRYDEN, WORKS, ff.

Timeservers

DRYDEN, LITERARY LIFE, t.

Tragedy [See also EPIC VS. TRAGEDY] *

Ancient: Faults of

ANCIENTS, v.

Ancients: Authority

AUTHORITY, f.

Aristotle's Definition

ARISTOTLE, e.

a. [¶] Tragedy is thus defined by Aristotle (omitting what I thought unnecessary in his definition). It is an imitation of one entire, great, and probable action; not told, but represented; which, by moving in us fear and pity, is conducive to the purging of those two passions in our minds.

Pref. *Troilus,* '79. K I 207

Design

ANCIENTS, u.

---

* See C. C. Green, *The Neo-Classic Theory of Tragedy in England During the Eighteenth Century* (Cambridge, Mass.: Harvard University Press, 1934). See also Margaret Sherwood, *Dryden's Dramatic Theory and Practice* (Boston: Lamson, Wolff & Co., 1898).

Ends

OVID, b, c. TRAGICOMEDY, a. POETIC JUSTICE, c. ANCIENTS, u.

b. [¶] Secondly, [the answerer to Rymer ought to prove] that other ends [than those of terror and pity], as suitable to the nature of tragedy, may be found in the English, which were not in the Greek.

Heads of an Answer, '77. S-S XV 381

POETIC JUSTICE, d.

c. [¶] If, then, the encouragement of virtue, and discouragement of vice, be the proper ends of poetry in tragedy, pity and terror, though good means, are not the only. For all the passions, in their turns, are to be set in a ferment; as joy, anger, love, fear, are to be used as the poet's commonplaces, and a general concernment for the principal actors is to be raised, by making them appear such in their characters, their words, and actions, as will interest the audience in their fortunes.

Heads of an Answer, '77. S-S XV 383

d. [¶] And if, after all, in a larger sense, pity comprehends this concernment for the good, and terror/includes detestation for the bad, then let us consider whether the English have not answered this end of tragedy, as well as the ancients, or perhaps better.

Heads of an Answer, '77. S-S XV 383–84

e. [¶] That we may the less wonder why pity and terror are not now the only springs on which our tragedies move, and that Shakespeare may be more excused, Rapin confesses that the French tragedies now all run on the *tendre;* and gives the reason, because love is the passion which most predominates in our souls; and that therefore the passions represented become insipid, unless they are conformable to the/thoughts of the audience. But it is to be concluded, that this passion works not now amongst the French so strongly as the other two did amongst the ancients. Amongst us, who have a stronger genius for writing, the operations from the writing are much stronger; for the raising of Shakespeare's passions is more from the excellency of the words and thoughts, than the justness of the occasion; . . . by the genius of poetry in writing, he has succeeded.

Heads of an Answer, '77. S-S XV 388–89

f. If terror and pity are only to be raised, certainly this author follows Aristotle's rules, and Sophocles' and Euripides's example; but joy may be raised too, and that doubly, either by seeing a wicked man punished, or a good man at last fortunate; or perhaps indignation, to see wickedness prosperous,/and goodness depressed: both these may be profitable to the end of tragedy, reformation of manners; but the last improperly, only as it begets pity in the audience; though Aristotle, I confess, places tragedies of this kind in the second form.

Heads of an Answer, '77. S-S XV 389–90

g. [¶] And if we should grant that the Greeks performed this better, perhaps it may admit of dispute, whether pity and terror are either the prime, or at least the only ends of tragedy.

It is not enough that Aristotle has said so, for Aristotle drew his models of tragedy from Sophocles and Euripides; and if he had seen ours, might have changed his mind. And chiefly we have to say . . . that the punishment of vice and reward of virtue are the most adequate ends of tragedy, because most conducing to good example of life. Now pity is not so easily raised for a criminal (and the ancient tragedy always represented its chief person such), as it is for an innocent man; and the suffering of innocence and punishment of the offender

is of the nature of English tragedy: contrarily, in the Greek, innocence is unhappy often, and the offender escapes. Then we are not touched with the sufferings of any sort of men so much as of lovers, and this was almost unknown to the ancients: so that they neither administered poetical justice . . . so well as we; neither knew they the best common-place of pity, which is love.

Heads of an Answer, '77. S-S XV 390

h. [¶] His [Rymer's] meaning, that pity and terror are to be moved, is, that they are to be moved as the means conducing to the ends of tragedy, which are pleasure and instruction.

And these two ends may be thus distinguished. The chief end of the poet is to please; for his immediate reputation depends on it.

The great end of the poem is to instruct, which is performed by making pleasure the vehicle of that instruction; for poesy is an art, and all arts are made to profit. [Rapin.]

The pity . . . is for the criminal, not for those or him whom he has murdered, or who have been the occasion of the tragedy. The terror is likewise in the punishment of the same criminal, who, if he be represented too great an offender, will not be pitied; if altogether innocent, his punishment will be unjust.

Heads of an Answer, '77. S-S XV 391
See above, a.

i. . . . I hasten to the end or scope of Tragedy, which is, to rectify or purge our passions, fear and pity.

Pref. *Troilus,* '79. K I 209

j. To purge the passions by example, is therefore the particular instruction which belongs to/Tragedy.

Pref. *Troilus,* '79. K I 209–10

k. Rapin, a judicious critic, has observed from Aristotle, that pride and want of commiseration are the most predominant vices in mankind; therefore, to cure us of these two, the inventors of Tragedy have chosen to work upon two other passions, which are fear and pity.

Pref. *Troilus*, '79. K I 210

Rules, c.

Fable

l. [¶] But the answerer [of Rymer] ought to prove two things: First, that the fable is not the greatest masterpiece of a tragedy, though it be the foundation of it.

Heads of an Answer, '77. S-S XV 381

m. [¶] Aristotle places the fable first; not *quoad dignitatem, sed quoad fundamentum:* for a fable,/never so movingly contrived to those ends of his, pity and terror, will operate nothing on our affections, except the characters, manners, thoughts, and words are suitable.

Heads of an Answer, '77. S-S XV 381–82

Greatness of Subject

Rhyme (Debate), h.

n. (Neander) . . . a serious play . . . is indeed the representation of Nature, but 'tis Nature wrought up to an higher pitch. The plot, the characters, the wit, the passions, the descriptions, are all exalted above the level of common converse, as high/as the imagination of the poet can carry them, with proportion to verisimility.

Dram. Poesy, '65. K I 100–101

Rhyme (Debate), m. Genre, b. Unities (Dramatic), Time, c. Poetic Justice, c.

o. [The tragic action] ought to be great, and to consist of great persons, to distinguish it from Comedy, where the action is trivial, and the persons of inferior rank.

Pref. *Troilus*, '79. K I 209

Poetry, f-3.

p. . . . so in Poetry, Tragedy is more beautiful than Comedy; because . . . the persons are greater whom the poet instructs, and consequently the instructions of more benefit to mankind: the action is likewise greater and more noble, and thence is derived the greater and more noble pleasure.

Parallel, '95. K II 136

Decorum, i.

Greek Tragedy, Development of

Chorus, b.

Happy Ending

See above, f. Fletcher, e.

q. Neither is it so trivial an undertaking, to make a tragedy end happily; for 'tis more difficult to save than 'tis to kill. The dagger and the cup of poison are always in a readiness; but to bring the action to the last extremity, and then by probable means to recover all, will require the art and judgment of a writer, and cost him many a pang in the performance.

Ded. *Spanish Friar*, '81. K I 249

Love as Subject

Love, a. Dryden, Literary Life, v.

Manners

Manners, h.

Moral [See Moral (of a Literary Work)]

Parts

English Drama, h.

r. The parts of a poem, tragic or heroic, are—

1. The fable itself.

2. The order or manner of its contrivance, in relation of the parts to the whole.

3. The manners, or decency of the characters, in speaking or acting what is proper for them, and proper to be shown by the poet.

4. The thoughts, which express the manners.

5. The words, which express those thoughts.

Heads of an Answer, '77. S-S XV 389

EPIC, c.

Passions [See PASSIONS, *passim*]

FIGURES, e. EPIC vs. TRAGEDY, f.

Picture: Tragedy compared with
POETRY AND PAINTING, c.

Probability [See main heading]

Satiric Tragedy

SATIRE, W, X.

Scope of Representation

DRAMA: EPIC ORIGINS.

Style

s. [¶] But meanness of expression one would not think to be his [Jonson's] error in a tragedy, which ought to be more high and sounding than any other kind of poetry . . .

Defence of the Epilogue, '72. K I 169

DICTION, a. SUBLIME, b.

Subject [See above, *Greatness of Subject*]

OBSCENITY, c.

Unity of Action

See above, a.

t. [Tragedy, according to Aristotle, represents an action which] must be one or single; that is, it must not be a history of one man's/life . . . but one single action of [it]. This condemns all Shakespeare's historical plays, which are rather chronicles represented, than tragedies; and all double action of plays.

Pref. *Troilus*, '79. K I 207–8

UNITIES (DRAMATIC), ACTION, c.

Tragicomedy

ENGLISH vs. FRENCH, z.

a. (Lisideius) There is no theatre in the world has any thing so absurd as the English tragi-comedy; 'tis a drama of our own invention, and the fashion of it is enough to proclaim it so; here a course of mirth, there another of sadness and passion, a third of honour, and/fourth a duel: thus, in two hours and a half, we run through all the fits of Bedlam. The French affords you as much variety on the same day, but they do it not so unseasonably, or *mal à propos,* as we: our poets present you the play and the farce together; and our stages still retain somewhat of the original civility of the *Red Bull:*

Atque ursum et pugiles media inter carmina poscunt.

The end of tragedies or serious plays, says Aristotle, is to beget admiration, compassion, or concernment; but are not mirth and compassion things incompatible? and is it not evident that the poet must of necessity destroy the former by intermingling of the latter? . . . Would you not think that physician mad, who, having prescribed a purge, should immediately order you to take restringents upon it?

Dram. Poesy, '65. K I 57–58

JONSON, t.

b. (Neander) As for their [the French] new way of mingling mirth with serious plot, I do not, with Lisideius, condemn the thing, though I cannot approve their manner of doing it. He tells us, we cannot so speedily recollect ourselves after a scene of great passion and concernment, as to pass to another of mirth and humour, and to enjoy it with any relish: but why should he imagine the soul of man more heavy than his senses? Does not the eye pass from an unpleasant object to a pleasant in a much shorter time than is required to this? and does not the unpleasantness of the first commend the beauty of the latter? The old rule of logic might have convinced him, that/contraries, when placed near, set off each other. A continued gravity keeps the spirit too much bent; we must refresh it sometimes . . . A scene of mirth, mixed with tragedy, has the same effect upon us which our music has betwixt the acts . . . I must therefore have stronger arguments, ere I am convinced that compassion and mirth in the same subject destroy each other; and in the mean time cannot but conclude, to the honour of our nation, that we have invented, increased, and perfected a more pleasant way of writing for the stage, than was ever known to the ancients or moderns of any nation, which is tragi-comedy.

Dram. Poesy, '65. K I 69–70.

ENGLISH VS. FRENCH, q. DRYDEN, WORKS, i. Cf. ANCIENTS, w. UNITIES (DRAMATIC), ACTION, c. Cf. PASSIONS, h.

c. [Speaking of *The Spanish Friar*] There are evidently two actions in it; but it will be clear to any judicious man, that with half the pains I could have raised a play from either of them; for this time I satis-fied my own humour, which was to tack two plays together; and to break a rule for the pleasure of variety. The truth is, the audience are grown weary of continued melancholy scenes; and I dare venture to prophesy, that few tragedies except those in verse shall succeed in this age, if they are not lightened with a course of mirth. For the feast is too dull and solemn without the fiddles. But how difficult a task this is, will soon be tried; for a several genius is re-quired to either way; and, without both of 'em, a man, in my opinion, is but half a poet for the stage.

Ded. *Spanish Friar,* '81. K I 249

d. [¶] To avoid the imputation of too much vanity (for all writers, and especially poets, will have some,) I will give but one other instance, in relation to the uniform-ity of the design. I have observed, that the English will not bear a thorough tragedy; but are pleased that it should be lightened with underparts of mirth. It had been easy for me to have given my audience a better course of comedy, I mean a more diverting, than that of Antonio and Morayma; but I dare appeal, even to my enemies, if I, or any man, could have invented one, which had been more of a piece, and more depending on the serious part of the design.

Pref. *Don Sebastian,* '90. S-S VII 316

e. After all, it was a bold attempt of mine, to write upon a single plot, unmixed with comedy; which, though it be the natu-ral and true way, yet is not to the genius of the nation. Yet, to gratify the barbarous part of my audience, I gave them a short rabble scene . . . They may thank me, if they please, for this indulgence; for no French poet would have allowed them any more than a bare relation of that scene, which debases a tragedy to show upon the stage.

Pref. *Cleomenes,* '92. S-S VIII 220

SATIRE, c.

f. In the meane time, I am affrayd, for my sake, you dis/cover not your Opinion, concerning my Irregular way, of Tragicom-edies, in my doppia favola. . . . I will never defend that practice: for I know it distracts the Hearers. But I know, withall, that it has hitherto pleasd them, for the sake of va-riety; & for the particular tast, which they have to low Comedy. Mascardi, in some of his Miscellany Treatises, has a Chapter con-cerning this; & exemplifies, in the Satyr & Corsica, of the Pastor Fido . . .

Letter to Walsh, 12 December 1693. Ward No. 28, pp. 61–62

UNITIES (DRAMATIC), ACTION, g.

g. [¶] The Gothic manner, and the barbarous ornaments, which are to be avoided in a picture, are just the same with those in an ill-ordered play. For example, our English tragi-comedy must be confessed to be wholly Gothic, notwithstanding the success which it has found/upon our theatre, and in the *Pastor Fido* of Guarini . . . Neither can I defend my *Spanish Friar,* as fond as otherwise I am of it, from this imputation: for though the comical parts are diverting, and the serious moving, yet they are of an unnatural mingle: for mirth and gravity destroy each other, and are no more to be allowed for decent than a gay widow laughing in a mourning habit.

Parallel, '95. K II 146–47

Dryden, Works, gg.

Translation [See also Modernizing, Ogilby, Roscommon] *

Modes

a. [¶] All translation, I suppose, may be reduced to these three heads.

First, that of metaphrase, or turning an author word by word, and line by line, from one language into another. Thus, or near this manner, was Horace his *Art of Poetry* translated by Ben Johnson. The second way is that of paraphrase, or translation with latitude, where the author is kept in view by the translator, so as never to be lost, but his words are not so strictly followed as his sense; and that too is admitted to be amplified, but not altered. Such is Mr. Waller's translation of Virgil's Fourth *Æneid.* The third way is that of imitation, where the translator (if now he has not lost that name) assumes the liberty, not only to vary from the words and

---

* See William Frost, *Dryden and the Art of Translation* (Yale Studies in English, vol. 128), New Haven, 1955.

254

sense, but to forsake them both as he sees occasion; and taking only some general hints from the original, to run division on the groundwork, as he pleases. Such is Mr. Cowley's practice in turning two Odes of Pindar, and one of Horace, into English.

Pref. Ovid's Epistles, '80. K I 237

b. Imitation and verbal version are, in my opinion, the two extremes which ought to be avoided; and therefore, when I have proposed the mean betwixt them, it will be seen how far his [Denham's] argument will reach. [See Denham, b]

Pref. Ovid's Epistles, '80. K I 241

See below, x.

c. Mr. Chapman, in his *Translation of Homer,* professes to have done it somewhat paraphrastically . . . I remember not the reason . . . but I suppose it is for fear of omitting any of his excellencies. Sure I am, that if it be a fault, 'tis much more pardonable than that of those, who run into the other extreme of a literal and close translation, where the poet is confined so straitly to his author's words, that he wants elbow-room to express his elegancies. He leaves him obscure; he leaves him prose,/ where he found him verse; and no better than thus has Ovid been served by the so-much-admired Sandys. This is at least the idea which I have remaining of his translation; for I never read him since I was a boy. . . . But this proceeded from the wrong judgment of the age in which he lived. They neither knew good verse, nor loved it; they were scholars, 'tis true, but they were pedants; and for a just reward of their pedantic pains, all their translations want to be translated into English.

Ded. Examen Poeticum, '93. K II 9–10

Metaphrase

d. [¶] Concerning the first of these

methods [metaphrase], our master Horace has given us this caution:

Nec verbum verbo curabis reddere, fidus
Interpres . . .
Nor word for word too faithfully translate;

as the Earl of Roscommon has excellently rendered it. Too faithfully is, indeed, pedantically . . ./

'Tis almost impossible to translate verbally, and well, at the same time; for the Latin (a most severe and compendious language) often expresses that in one word, which either the barbarity or the narrowness of modern tongues cannot supply in more. 'Tis frequent, also, that the conceit is couched in some expression, which will be lost in English . . .[1]

In short, the verbal copier is encumbered with so many difficulties at once, that he can never disentangle himself from all.[1]

Pref. *Ovid's Epistles,* '80. K I 237–38
See below, k.

e. A noble author would not be pursued too close by a translator. We lose his spirit, when we think to take his body. . . . Thus Holyday . . . seized the meaning of Juvenal, but the poetry has always escaped him.

Discourse of Satire, '93. K II 112

f. These gentlemen [translators of Lucian] know very well, that they are not to creep after the words of their author, in so servile a manner as some have done; for that must infallibly throw them on a necessity of introducing a new mode of diction and phraseology with which we are not at all acquainted, and would/incur that censure which my Lord Dorset made formerly on those of Mr. Spence, viz. that he was so cunning a translator, that a man must consult the original, to understand the version. For every language has a propriety and

idiom peculiar to itself, which cannot be conveyed to another without perpetual absurdities.

"Life of Lucian," '96. S-S XVIII 82–83

g. [¶] A translator that would write with any force or spirit of an original, must never dwell on the words of his author. He ought to possess himself entirely, and perfectly comprehend the genius and sense of his author, the nature of the subject, and the terms of the art or subject treated of; and/then he will express himself as justly, and with as much life, as if he wrote an original; whereas, he who copies word for word, loses all the spirit in the tedious transfusion.

I would not be understood that he should be at liberty to give such a turn as Mr. Spence has in some of his; where for the fine raillery and attic salt of Lucian, we find the gross expressions of Billingsgate, or Moorfields and Bartholomew Fair. For I write not to such translators, but to men capacious of the soul and genius of their authors, without which all their labour will be of no use but to disgrace themselves, and injure the author that falls into their slaughter-house.

"Life of Lucian," '96. S-S XVIII 83–84

Imitation

h. [¶] The consideration of these difficulties, in a servile, literal translation, not long since made two of our famous wits, Sir John Denham and Mr. Cowley, to contrive another way of turning authors into our tongue, called, by the latter of them, imitation. . . . I take imitation . . . in their sense, to be an endeavour of a later poet to write like one who has written before him, on the same subject; that is, not to translate his words, or to be confined to his sense, but only to set him as a pattern, and to write, as he supposes that author would have done, had he lived in our age, and in our country. Yet I dare not say, that either of them have carried this libertine way . . . so far as my definition reaches; for in the *Pindaric Odes,* the customs and ceremonies/of ancient Greece are still preserved. But I know not what mischief may arise hereafter from the example of such an innovation, when writers of unequal parts to him shall imitate so bold an undertaking.

Pref. *Ovid's Epistles,* '80. K I 239–40

Cowley, e.

i. But if Virgil, or Ovid, or any regular intelligible authors [by contrast to Pindar], be thus used [translated by the method of Imitation, as Cowley uses with Pindar], 'tis no longer to be called their work, when neither the thoughts nor words are drawn from the original; but instead of them there is something new produced, which is almost the creation of another hand. By this way, 'tis true, somewhat that is excellent may be invented, perhaps more excellent than the first design; though Virgil must be still excepted, when that *perhaps* takes place. . . . To state it fairly; imitation of an author is the most advantageous way for a translater to show himself, but the greatest wrong which can be done to the memory and reputation of the dead.

Pref. *Ovid's Epistles,* '80. K I 240

Denham, b. See below, k. Cowley, h.

Dryden's Own Translations

Dryden, Works, kk. Roscommon, a, b.

j. [¶] For this last half year I have been troubled with the disease (as I may call it) of translation; the cold prose fits of it, which are always the most tedious with me, were spent in the *History of the League:* the hot, which succeeded them, in

this volume of Verse Miscellanies.

Pref. *Sylvæ,* '85. K I 251

Dryden, Works, mm, nn, oo, ss. Obscenity, b. Creech, b.

k. [Of the translation of Juvenal and Persius] The common way which we have taken is not a literal translation, but a kind of paraphrase; or somewhat, which is yet more loose, betwixt a paraphrase and imitation. It was not possible for us, or any men, to have made it pleasant any other way. If rendering the exact sense . . . almost line for line, had been our business, Barten Holyday had done it already to our hands: and by the help of his learned notes and illustrations not only of Juvenal and Persius, but what is yet more obscure, his own verses, might be understood.

But he wrote for fame, and wrote to scholars: we write only for the pleasure and entertainment of those . . . who, though they are not scholars, are not ignorant: persons of understanding and good sense, who, not having been conversant in the original, or at least not having made Latin verse so much their business as to be critics in it, would be glad to find if the wit of our two great authors be answerable to their fame and reputation in the world. We have, therefore, endeavoured to give the public all the satisfaction we are able in this kind.

Discourse of Satire, '93. K II 111

Dryden, Works, ggg.

l. [¶] I have avoided as much as I cou'd possibly the borrow'd Learning of Marginal Notes and Illustrations, and for that Reason have Translated this Satyr somewhat largely. And freely own (if it be a fault) that I have likewise omitted most of the Proper Names, because I thought they wou'd not much edifie the

Reader. To conclude, if in two or three places I have deserted all the Commentators, 'tis because I thought they first deserted my Author, or at least have left him in so much obscurity, that too much room is left for guessing.

Argument of the First Satire [Juvenal], '93. JK II 671

DRYDEN, WORKS, hhh, mmm.

m. [¶] I had long since considered that the way to please the best judges is not to translate a poet literally, and Virgil least of any other . . . / The way I have taken is not so strait as metaphrase, nor so loose as paraphrase: some things too I have omitted, and sometimes have added of my own. Yet the omissions, I hope, are but of circumstances, and such as would have no grace in English; and the additions, I also hope, are easily deduced from Virgil's sense.

Ded. *Æneis,* '97. K II 226–27

n. [Of the *Æneis*] . . . I thought fit to steer betwixt the two extremes of paraphrase and literal translation; to keep as near my author as I could, without losing all his graces, the most eminent of which are in the beauty of his words; and those words, I must add, are always figurative. Such of these as would retain their elegance in our tongue, I have endeavoured to graff on it; but most of them are of necessity to be lost, because they will not shine in any but their own. Virgil has sometimes two of them in a line; but the scantiness of our heroic verse is not capable of receiving more than one; and that too must expiate for many others which have none. Such is the difference of the languages, or such my want of skill in choosing words. Yet I may presume to say, and I hope with as much reason as the French translator, that, taking all the materials of this divine au-

thor, I have endeavoured to make Virgil speak such English as he would himself have spoken, if he had been born in England, and in this present age. I acknowledge, with Segrais, that I have not succeeded in this attempt according to my desire: yet I shall not be wholly without praise, if in some sort I may be allowed to have copied the clearness, the purity, the easiness, and the magnificence of his style.

Ded. *Æneis,* '97. K II 228

o. [Of his translations from the *Metamorphoses*] . . . which I hope I have translated closely enough, and given them the same turn of verse which they had in the original; and this, I may say, without vanity, is not the talent of every poet. He who has arrived the nearest to it, is the ingenious and learned Sandys, the best versifier of the former age; if I may properly call it by that name, which was the former part of this concluding century.

Pref. *Fables,* 1700. K II 247

p. . . . I have not [in the Chaucer] tied myself to a literal translation; but have often omitted what I judged unnecessary, or not of dignity enough to appear in the company of better thoughts. I have presumed farther in some places, and added somewhat of my own where I thought my author was deficient, and had not given his thoughts their true lustre, for want of words in the beginning of our language. And to this I was the more emboldened, because (if I may be permitted to say it of myself) I found I had a soul congenial to his, and that I had been conversant in the same studies. Another poet, in another age, may take the same liberty with my writings; if at least they live long enough to deserve correction. It was also necessary sometimes to restore the sense of

Chaucer, which was lost or mangled in the errors of the press.[1]

Pref. *Fables,* 1700. K II 265

MODERNIZING.

License

See below, u.

q. . . . for thought, if it be translated truly, cannot be lost in another language; but the words that convey it to our apprehension (which are the image and ornament of that thought,) may be so ill chosen, as to make it appear in an unhandsome dress, and rob it of its native lustre. There is, therefore, a liberty to be allowed for the expression; neither is it necessary that words and lines should be confined to the measure of their original. The sense of an author, generally speaking, is to be sacred and inviolable.

Pref. *Ovid's Epistles,* '80. K I 242

r. If the fancy of Ovid be luxuriant, 'tis his character to be so; and if I retrench it, he is no longer Ovid. It will be replied, that he receives advantage by this lopping of his superfluous branches; but I rejoin, that a translator has no such right. . . . In two cases only there may a seeming difficulty arise; that is, if the thought be notoriously trivial or dishonest; but the same answer will serve for both, that then they ought not to be translated . . .ᵠ

Pref. *Ovid's Epistles,* '80. K I 242

s. The word, perish, usd by Mr Creech [in translating *De rerum natura,* I, 225–28] is a verb neuter, where Lucretius puts (perimit) which is active: a license, which in translating a philosophicall Poet, ought not to be taken, for some reasons, which I have not room to give.

Letter to an Unidentified Person, 1682. Ward No. 7, p. 16

Practical Difficulties

t. [¶] This has brought me to say a word or two about translation in general; in which no nation might more excel than the English, though, as matters are now managed, we come so far short of the French. There may indeed be a reason assigned . . . and that is, that here the booksellers are the undertakers of works of this nature, and they are persons more devoted to their own gain than the public honour. . . . [See BOOKSELLERS] While translations are thus at the disposal of the booksellers, and have no better judges or rewarders of the performance, it is impossible that we should make any progress in an art so very useful to an enquiring people, and for the improvement and spreading of knowledge, which is none of the worst preservatives against slavery.

It must be confessed, that when the bookseller has interest with gentlemen of genius and quality . . . as in that of Plutarch's Lives, and this of Lucian, the reader may satisfy himself that he shall have the author's spirit and soul in the traduction.

"Life of Lucian," '96. S-S XVIII 82

Translator

u. [¶] No man is capable of translating poetry, who, besides a genius to that art, is not a master both of his author's language, and of his own; nor must we understand the language only of the poet, but his particular turn of thoughts and expression, which are the characters that distinguish, and as it were individuate him from all other writers. When we are come thus far, 'tis time to look into ourselves, to conform our genius to his, to give his thought either the same turn, if our tongue will bear it, or, if not, to vary but the dress, not to alter or destroy the substance. The like care must be taken of the more outward ornaments, the words. When they appear (which is but seldom) literally graceful, it were an injury to the author that they should be changed. But since every language is so full of its own proprieties, that what is beautiful in one, is often barbarous, nay sometimes nonsense, in another, it would be unreasonable to limit a translator to the narrow compass of his author's words: 'tis enough if he choose out some expression which does not vitiate the sense. I suppose he may stretch his chain to such a latitude; but by innovation of thoughts, methinks he breaks it.

Pref. *Ovid's Epistles*, '80. K I 241

v. In the meantime it seems to me that the true reason why we have so few versions which are tolerable, is not from the too close pursuing of the author's sense, but because there are so few who have all the talents which are requisite for translation, and that there is so little praise and so small encouragement for so considerable a part of learning.

Pref. *Ovid's Epistles*, '80. K I 243
DRYDEN, LITERARY LIFE, h.

w. [¶] Having received the honour of your Majesty's commands to translate the *History of the League*, I have applied myself . . . to obey them: First, by a thorough understanding of my author . . . then by giving his thoughts the same beauty in our language which they had in the original, and, which I most of all endeavoured, the same force and perspicuity . . .

Ded. *History of the League*, '84. S-S XVII 83

x. [¶] For, after all, a translator is to make his author appear as charming as possibly he can, provided he maintains his character, and makes him not unlike himself. Translation is a kind of drawing after the life; where every one will acknowledge there is a double sort of likeness, a good one and a bad. 'Tis one thing to draw the outlines true, the features like, the propor-

tions/exact, the colouring itself perhaps tolerable; and another thing to make all these graceful, by the posture, the shadowings, and, chiefly, by the spirit which animates the whole.

Pref. *Sylvæ*, '85. K I 252–53

y. Thus it appears necessary, that a man should be a nice critic in his mothertongue before he attempts to translate a foreign language. Neither is it sufficient, that he be able to judge of words and style; but he must be a master of them too; he must perfectly understand his author's tongue, and absolutely command his own. So that to be a thorough translator, he must be a thorough poet. Neither is it enough to give his author's sense in good English, in poetical expressions, and in musical numbers; for . . . there yet remains an harder task; and 'tis a secret which few translators have sufficiently thought. I have already hinted a word or two concerning it; that is, the maintaining the character of an author, which distinguishes him from all others, and makes him appear that individual poet whom you would interpret.

Pref. *Sylvæ*, '85. K I 254

z. Suppose two authors/are equally sweet, yet there is a great distinction to be made in sweetness, as in that of sugar and that of honey.[1]

Pref. *Sylvæ*, '85. K I 254–55

aa. [¶] Besides all this [the greater succinctness of Latin over modern tongues], an author has the choice of his own thoughts and words, which a translator has not; he is confined by the sense of the inventor to those expressions which are the nearest to it . . .[1]

Pref. *Sylvæ*, '85. K I 257

bb. For 'tis not enough to give us the meaning of a poet . . . but he [the translator] must also imitate his genius and his numbers, as far as the English will come up to the elegance of the original. In few words, 'tis only for a poet to translate a poem. Holyday and Stapylton had not enough considered this, when they attempted Juvenal . . .

Discourse of Satire, '93. K II 92

IMITATION OF MODELS, d.

cc. [¶] The qualification of a translator, worth reading, must be, a mastery of the language he translates out of, and that he translates into; but if a deficience be to be allowed in either, it is in the original; since if he be but master enough of the tongue of his author, as to be master of his sense, it is possible for him to express that sense with eloquence in his own, if he have a thorough command of that. But without the latter, he can never arrive at the useful and the delightful; without which reading is a penance and a fatigue.

"Life of Lucian," '96. S-S XVIII 83

dd. [¶] It is true that there will be a great many beauties, which in every tongue depend on the diction, that will be lost in the version of a man not skilled in the original language of the author; but then on the other side, first it is impossible to render all those little ornaments of speech in any two languages; and if he have a mastery in the sense and spirit of his author, and in his own language have a style and happiness of expression, he will easily supply all that is lost by that defect.

"Life of Lucian," '96. S-S XVIII 83

See above, g.

ee. But [to] a man who wants these natural qualifications which are necessary for such an undertaking [translation], all particular precepts are of no other use than to make him a more remarkable coxcomb.

"Life of Lucian," '96. **S-S XVIII 84**

260

ff. We [translators] are bound to our author's sense, though with the latitudes already mentioned; for I think it not so sacred, as that one iota must not be added or diminished, on pain of an *Anathema.* But slaves we are, and labour on another man's plantation . . . : if the soil be sometimes barren, then we are sure of being scourged: if it be fruitful, and our care succeeds, we are not thanked; for the proud read will only say, the poor drudge has done his duty. But this is nothing to what follows; for, being obliged to make his sense intelligible, we are forced to untune our own verses, that we may give his meaning to the reader. He, who invents, master of his thoughts and words: he can turn and vary them as he pleases, till he renders/them harmonious; but the wretched translator has no such privilege: for, being tied to the thoughts, he must make what music he can in the expression; and, for this reason, it cannot always be so sweet as that of the original.

Ded. *Æneis,* '97. K II 232–33

Translating Virgil

VIRGIL, pp, p, i. ENGLISH LANGUAGE, b, e. See above, n.

Translations of Virgil's Aeneid

gg. Segrais, whose preface is so wonderfully good, yet is wholly destitute of elevation, though his version is much better than that of the two brothers [Robert and Antoine le Chevalier d'Agneaux: Ker], or any of the rest who have attempted Virgil. Hannibal Caro is a great name amongst the Italians; yet his translation of the *Æneis* is most scandalously mean, though he has taken the advantage of writing in blank verse, and freed himself from the shackles of modern rhyme . . ./He is a foot poet, he lacqueys by the side of Virgil at the best, but never mounts behind him. . . ./

What I have said, though it has the face of arrogance, yet is intended for the honour of my country; and therefore I will boldly own, that this English translation has more of Virgil's spirit in it than either the French or the Italian. Some of our countrymen have translated episodes and other parts of Virgil, with great success; as particularly your Lordship [Mulgrave], whose version of *Orpheus and Eurydice* is eminently good. Amongst the dead authors, the *Silenus* of my Lord Roscommon cannot be too much commended. I say nothing of Sir John Denham, Mr. Waller, and Mr. Cowley; 'tis the utmost of my ambition to be thought their equal, or not to be much inferior to them, and some others of the living. But 'tis one thing to take pains on a fragment, and translate it perfectly; and another thing to have the weight of a whole author on my shoulders. They who believe the burthen light, let them attempt the Fourth, Sixth, or Eighth *Pastoral;* the First or Fourth *Georgic;* and, amongst the *Æneids,* the Fourth, the Fifth, the/Seventh, the Ninth, the Tenth, the Eleventh, or the Twelfth; for in these I think I have succeeded best.

Ded. *Æneis,* '97. K II 220–23

Travesty [See BURLESQUE, a, b]

Triplet [See PROSODY]

Tropes

PROSODY, ff. VIRGIL, l. DIALOGUE (DRAMATIC). ARISTOTLE, d. PASSIONS, b. POETIC LICENSE, d. PERSIUS, b, g. EXPRESSION, b.

Truth

(Lisideius) For the spirit of man cannot be satisfied but with truth . . . [See VERISIMILITY, a]

Dram. Poesy, '65. K I 59

RHYME (DEBATE), g. VERISIMILITY, b. UNITIES (DRAMATIC), PLACE, g. ACTING AND ACTORS, b. DRYDEN, WORKS, ff. STYLE, c. RELIGION. HISTORY, b, e. COMINES, b. HISTORIAN, b. SATIRE, s. IMITATION, h. Cf. POET, g.

Tuke, Sir Samuel

a. (Neander) Most of their [the French] new plays are, like some of ours, derived from the Spanish novels. There is scarce one of them without a veil, and a trusty Diego, who drolls much after the rate of the *Adventures.*

Dram. Poesy, '65. K I 69

b. (Neander) [The action of Jonson's *Silent Woman* extends in time no more than is required for presentation on the stage] A beauty perhaps not much observed; if it had, we should not have looked on the Spanish translation of *Five Hours* with so much wonder.

Dram. Poesy, '65. K I 83

c. At least, as Sir Samuel Tuke has said before me, a modest man may praise what is not his own.

Ded. *Examen Poeticum,* '93. K II 14

Tumidity [See BOMBAST]

Tumult [See also DECORUM]

ENGLISH VS. FRENCH, p.

a. (Lisideius) For what is more ridiculous than to represent an army with a drum and five men behind it; all which the hero of the other side is to drive in before him; or to see a duel fought, and one slain with two or three thrusts of the foils, which we know are so blunted, that we might give a man an hour to kill another in good earnest with them.

Dram. Poesy, '65. K I 62

DECORUM, c, d.

b. [¶] To those who object my frequent use of drums and trumpets, and my representation of battles, I answer, I introduced them not on the English stage: Shakespeare used them frequently; and though Johnson shows no battle in his *Cataline,* yet you hear from behind the scenes the sounding of trumpets, and the shouts of fighting armies. But I add farther, that these warlike instruments, and even their presentations of fighting on the stage, are no more than necessary to produce the effects of an heroic play; that is, to raise the imagination of the audience, and to per/suade them, for the time, that what they behold on the theatre is really performed.

Essay of Heroic Plays, '72. K I 154–55

SHAKESPEARE, t.

Turns

Cf. TRANSLATION, u. LATIN, a. Cf. PROSODY, u. WALSH, c. ST. ÉVREMOND, c. HORACE AND JUVENAL AND PERSIUS, b. Cf. PROSODY, m. TASSONI. SATIRE, o. DRYDEN, LITERARY LIFE, b. DRYDEN, WORKS, eee. EXPRESSION, b. Cf. MULGRAVE, c. ENGLISH VS. FRENCH, n.

a. The turn on thoughts and words is their [the French] chief talent; but the Epic Poem is too stately to receive those little ornaments. . . . Virgil is never fre-

quent in those turns, like Ovid, but much more sparing of them in his *Æneis* than in his *Pastorals* and *Georgics* . . .[1] I have used that licence in his *Æneis* sometimes; but I own it as my fault. 'Twas given to those who understand no better. 'Tis like Ovid's

Semivirumque bovem, semibovemque virum.

The poet found it before his critics, but it was a darling sin, which he could not be persuaded to reform.

Ded. *Æneis,* '97. K II 219

b. As for the turn of words, in which Ovid particularly excels all poets, they are sometimes a fault, and sometimes a beauty, as they are used properly or improperly; but in strong passions always to be shunned, because passions are serious, and will admit no playing. The French have a high value for them; and, I confess, they are often what they call delicate, when they are introduced with judgment; but Chaucer writ with more simplicity, and followed Nature more closely, than to use them.

Pref. *Fables,* 1700. K II 257

❧ U ❧

Underplot

(Crites) [¶] For two actions, equally laboured and driven on by the writer, would destroy the unity of the poem; it would no longer be one play, but two: not but that there may be many actions in a play, as Ben Johnson has observed in his *Discoveries;* but they must be all subservient to the great one, which our language happily expresses in the name of *underplots* . . .

Dram. Poesy, '65. K I 41

ENGLISH VS. FRENCH, z, aa. ENGLISH DRAMA, c. DRYDEN, WORKS, u. ANCIENTS, w. TRAGEDY, t. TERENCE, e. DRYDEN, WORKS, q. TRAGICOMEDY, c. Cf. UNITIES (DRAMATIC), GENERAL, c. TRAGICOMEDY, d, e. SATIRE, c. ENGLISH VS. FRENCH, k. TRAGICOMEDY, f. UNITIES (DRAMATIC), ACTION, g. IMITATION, i.

Unities (Dramatic), General*

a. (Crites) [¶] Out of these two [Aristotle and Horace] have been extracted the famous Rules, which the French call *Des Trois Unitez,* or, the Three Unities, which ought to be observed in every regular play . . .

Dram. Poesy, '65. K I 38

b. (Crites) [¶] If by these rules . . . we should judge our modern plays, 'tis probable that few of them would endure the trial . . . [See MODERNS, b]

Dram. Poesy, '65. K I 41

* See L. S. Friedland, "The Dramatic Unities in England," *JEGP,* X (1911), 56–89, 280–99, 453–67.

ENGLISH VS. FRENCH, y. JONSON, m.

b-2. (Neander) [*The Silent Woman*] is all included in the limits of three hours and a half . . . the latitude of place is almost as little as you can imagine . . . The continuity of scenes is observed more than in any of our plays, except his own *Fox* and *Alchymist.* . . . The action of the play is entirely one . . .

Dram. Poesy, '65. K I 83

DRYDEN, WORKS, m, u. SHAKESPEARE AND FLETCHER, a. HISTORICAL TRUTH, c.

c. . . . I have not exactly kept the three mechanic rules of unity. I knew them, and had them in my eye, but followed them only at a distance; for the genius of the English cannot bear too regular a play: we are given to variety, even to a debauchery of pleasure. My scenes are therefore sometimes broken, because my underplot required them so to be, though the general scene remains,—of the same castle; and I have taken the time of two days, because the variety of accidents which are here represented could not naturally be supposed to arrive in one: but to gain a greater beauty, it is lawful for a poet to supersede a less.

Pref. *Don Sebastian,* '90. S-S VII 313

d. [¶] For the rest, some of the mechanic rules of unity are observed, and others are neglected. The action is but one . . . and every scene in the play is tending to the accomplishment of the main design. The place is likewise one; for it is all in the compass of Alexandria, and the port of that city. The time might easily have been reduced into the space of twenty-four hours, if I would have omitted the scene of famine in the fifth act; but it pleased me . . ./and, in such a case, it is better to trespass on a rule, than leave out a beauty.

Pref. *Cleomenes,* '92. S-S VIII 220–21
Epic vs. Tragedy, d. English vs. French, v. Dryden, Works, lll.

e. Tragedy and Picture are more narrowly circumscribed by the mechanic rules of time and place, than the Epic Poem. The time of this is left/indefinite. 'Tis true, Homer took up only the space of eight-and-forty days for his *Iliads;* but whether Virgil's action was comprehended in a year, or somewhat more, is not determined by Bossu. Homer made the place of his action Troy, and the Grecian camp besieging it. Virgil introduces his Æneas sometimes in Sicily, sometimes in Carthage, and other times at Cumæ, before he brings him to Laurentum; and even after that, he wanders . . .[1] But Tragedy, according to the practice of the ancients, was always confined within the compass of twenty-four hours, and seldom takes up so much time. As for the place of it, it was always one, and that not in a larger sense (as for example, a whole city, or two or three several houses in it), but the market, or some other public place, common to the chorus and all the actors; which established law of theirs . . . seems too strict at the first appearance, because it excludes all secret intrigues, which are the beauties of the modern stage; for nothing can be carried on with privacy, when the chorus is supposed to be always present. But to proceed; I must say this to be the advantage of Painting, even above Tragedy, that what this last represents in the space of many hours, the

former shows us in one moment.[1]

Parallel, '95. K II 130–31
Poetry and Painting, c. Drama: Epic Origins.

Unities (Dramatic), Action

a. (Crites) . . . the poet is to aim at one great and complete action, to the carrying on of which all things in his play, even the very obstacles, are to be subservient . . .

For two actions, equally laboured and driven on by the writer, would destroy the unity of the poem . . . not but that there may be many actions in a play, as Ben Johnson has observed in his *Discoveries;* but they must be all subservient to the great one . . . There ought to be but one action, says Corneille . . . but this cannot be brought to pass but by many other imperfect actions, which conduce to it, and hold the audience in a delightful suspense of what will be.

Dram. Poesy, '65. K I 41
English vs. French, z, aa. Fletcher, a.

b. (Neander) [¶] Eugenius [It was actually Crites; see K I 41] has already shown us, from the confession of the French poets, that the Unity of Action is sufficiently preserved, if all the imperfect actions of the play are conducing to the main design; but when those petty intrigues . . . are so ill ordered, that they have no coherence with the other, I must grant that Lisideius has reason to tax that want of due connexion; for co-ordination in a play is as dangerous and unnatural as in a state. In the mean time he must acknowledge, our variety, if well ordered, will afford a greater pleasure to the audience.

Dram. Poesy, '65. K I 71
Design. English Drama, c. An-

CIENTS, w. TRAGEDY, t. DRYDEN, WORKS, q.

c. The natural reason of this rule [Unity of Action] is plain; for two different independent actions distract the attention and concernment of the audience, and consequently destroy the intention of the poet; if his business be to move terror and pity, and one of his actions be comical, the other tragical, the former will divert the people, and utterly make void his greater purpose. Therefore, as in perspective, so in Tragedy, there must be a point of sight in which all the lines terminate; otherwise the eye wanders, and the work is false.

Pref. *Troilus,* '79. K I 208

d. [¶] As the action ought to be one, it ought, as such, to have order in it; that is, to have a natural beginning, a middle, and an end. . . . This consideration will arraign all plays after the new model of Spanish plots, where accident is heaped upon/accident, and that which is first might as reasonably be last; an inconvenience not to be remedied, but by making one accident naturally produce another, otherwise it is a farce and not a play.

Pref. *Troilus,* '79. K I 208–9

e. [In a context relating to biography] For this reason [that "when the understanding is intent and fixed on a single thing, it carries closer to the mark; every part of the object sinks into it; and, the soul receives it unmixed and whole."] Aristotle commends the unity of action in a poem; because the mind is not capable of digesting many things at once, nor of conceiving fully any more than one idea at a time. Whatsoever distracts the pleasure, lessens it . . .

"Life of Plutarch," '83. S-S XVII 61

f. If any be so curious to inquire what became of Cassandra, whose fortune was left in suspense at the conclusion of the play, I must first inform them, that, after the death of Cleomenes (the hero of my poem), I was obliged by the laws of the drama to let fall the curtain immediately, because the action was then concluded.

Pref. *Cleomenes,* '92. S-S VIII 227

SATIRE, c.

g. For my action, it is evidently double; and in that I have the most of the ancients for my examples. Yet I dare not defend this way by reason, much less by their authority; for their actions, though double, were of the same species; that is to say, in their comedies, two amours; and their persons were better linked in interest than mine. Yet even/this is a fault which I should often practise, if I were to write again, because it is agreeable to the English genius. We love variety more than any other nation; and so long as the audience will not be pleased without it, the poet is obliged to humour them. On condition they were cured of this public vice, I could be content to change my method, and gladly give them a more reasonable pleasure.

Ded. *Love Triumphant,* '94. S-S VIII 375–76

SUBJECT, INTEGRITY OF. DRAMA: EPIC ORIGINS.

Unities (Dramatic), Place

a. (Crites) . . . the stage . . . being but one and the same place, it is unnatural to conceive it many; and those far distant from one another.

Dram. Poesy, '65. K I 40

b. (Crites) I will not deny but, by the variation of painted scenes, the fancy, which in these cases will contribute to its own deceit, may sometimes imagine it [the stage] several places, with some appearance of probability; yet it still carries the greater likelihood of truth, if those places be supposed so near each other, as in the same town or city . . .

Dram. Poesy, '65. K I 40

c. (Crites) . . . for the observation of this [Unity of Place], next to the Ancients, the French are to be most commended.

Dram. Poesy, '65. K I 40

ANCIENTS, x. ENGLISH VS. FRENCH, cc, y.

d. (Neander) [Following a summary of the action in Thomas Corneille's *L'Amour à la Mode,* 1651] In this ridiculous manner the play goes on, the stage being never empty all the while: so that the street, the window, the houses, and the closet, are made to walk about, and the persons to stand still.

Dram. Poesy, '65. K I 77

e. . . . I must crave leave to tell him [Howard], that though the stage cannot be two places, yet it may properly represent them successively, or at several times. His argument is indeed no more than a mere fallacy, which will evidently appear when we distinguish place, as it relates to plays, into real and imaginary.

Defence of An Essay, '68. K I 126

f. [As to] that other part of his [Howard's] argument . . . that 'tis as impossible for a stage to represent two rooms or houses, as two countries or kingdoms . . . because both were alike impossible. This is manifestly otherwise . . . for the imagination being judge of what is represented, will in reason be less shocked with the appearance of two rooms in the same house, or two houses in the same city, than with two distant cities in the same country, or two remote countries in the same universe.

Defence of An Essay, '68. K I 127

VERISIMILITY, b.

g. [¶] For what else concerns the Unity of Place, I have already given my opinion of it in my *Essay,* that there/is a latitude to be allowed to it, as several places in the same town or city, or places adjacent to each other in the same country; which may all be comprehended under the larger denomination of one place; yet with this restriction, that the nearer and fewer those imaginary places are, the greater resemblance they will have to truth; and reason, which cannot make them one, will be more easily led to suppose them so.

Defence of An Essay, '68. K I 128–29

DRYDEN, WORKS, lll.

Unities (Dramatic), Time

a. (Crites) . . . the time of the feigned action, or fable . . . should be proportioned as near as can be to the duration of that time in which it is represented: since therefore, all plays are acted on the theatre in a space of time much within the compass of twenty-four hours, that play is to be thought the nearest imitation of nature, whose plot or action is confined within that time; and, by the same rule . . . it follows, that all the parts of it are to be equally subdivided; as namely, that one act take not up . . . time . . . out of proportion to the rest . . .

Dram. Poesy, '65. K I 39

EURIPIDES. ENGLISH VS. FRENCH, dd. Cf. SHAKESPEARE, k. FLETCHER, a. Cf. DECORUM, c. ENGLISH VS. FRENCH, y. JONSON, m.

b. [¶] What has been said of the Unity of Place, may easily be applied to that of

Time: I grant it to be impossible, that the greater part of time should be comprehended in the less, that twenty-four hours should be crowded into three: but there is no necessity of that supposition; for as *place,* so *time* relating to a play, is either imaginary or real . . . [Therefore] where is the absurdity of affirming, that the feigned business of twenty-four imagined hours, may not more naturally be represented in the compass of three real hours, than the like feigned business of twenty-four years in the same proportion of real time?

Defence of An Essay, '68. K I 129

c. I say not this [animadverting on the extended time of the *Duke of Lerma*] with the least design of limiting the stage too servilely to twenty-four hours . . . In few words, my own opinion is this . . . that the imaginary time of every play ought to be contrived into as narrow a compass, as the nature of the plot, the quality of the persons, and variety of accidents will allow. In Comedy, I would not exceed twenty-four or thirty hours; for the plot, accidents, and persons, of Comedy are small, and may be naturally turned in a little compass: but in/ Tragedy, the design is weighty, and the persons great; therefore, there will naturally be required a greater space of time in which to move them.

Defence of An Essay, '68. K I 130–31

d. [¶] But as it is an error, on the one side, to make too great a disproportion betwixt the imaginary time of the play, and the real time of its representation; so, on the other side, 'tis an oversight to compress the accidents of a play into a narrower compass than that in which they could naturally be produced. Of this last error the

French are seldom guilty . . . but few Englishmen, except Ben Johnson, have ever made a plot, with variety of design in it, included in twenty-four hours, which was altogether natural. . . . Yet, of the two, I think that error the most pardonable which in too strait a compass crowds together many accidents, since it produces more variety, and, consequently, more pleasure to the audience; and because the nearness of proportion betwixt the imaginary and real time, does speciously cover the compression of the accidents.

Defence of An Essay, '68. K I 131
Last Age, c. Dryden, Works, lll. Drama: Epic Origins.

e. . . . I was almost running into a long digression, to prove that there is no such absolute necessity that the time of a stage action should so strictly be confined to twenty-four hours as never to exceed them, for which Aristotle contends, and the Grecian stage has practised. Some longer space, on some occasions, I think, may be allowed, especially for the English theatre, which requires more variety of incidents than the French. Corneille himself, after long practice, was inclined to think that the time allotted by the Ancients was too short to raise and finish a great/action: and better a mechanic rule were stretched or broken, than a great beauty were omitted. To raise, and afterwards to calm the passions—to purge the soul from pride, by the examples of human miseries, which befall the greatest—in few words, to expel arrogance, and introduce compassion, are the great effects of tragedy. Great, I must confess, if they were altogether as true as they are pompous. But are habits to be introduced at three hours' warning? are radical diseases

Universities

so suddenly removed. . . . An epic poem is not in so much haste: it works leisurely . . . but the cure is likely to be more perfect. The effects of tragedy, as I said, are too violent to be lasting.

Ded. *Æneis,* '97. K II 157–58

Universities

PRESENT AGE, k.

a. I am, ridiculously enough, accused to be a contemner of universities; that is, in other words, an enemy of learning; without the foundation of which, I am sure, no man can pretend to be a poet.

Ded. *Assignation,* '73. S-S IV 375

b. Because I deale not in Satyre, I have sent Your Lordship a prologue and epilogue which I made for our players when they went down to Oxford. I heare, since they have succeeded; And by the event your Lordship will judge how easy 'tis to passe any thing upon an University; and how grosse flattery the learned will endure.

Letter to Rochester, 1673. Ward No. 4, p. 10

ACADEMY, b.

c. . . . I particularly observed . . . when I read Plutarch in the library of Trinity College, in Cambridge, to which foundation I gratefully acknowledge a great part of my education.

"Life of Plutarch," '83. S-S XVII 55

CRITIC[s], a.

Urbanity

COMEDY, e. PERSIUS, i. HORACE AND JUVENAL AND PERSIUS, d.

Variety

(Neander) [¶] And this leads me to wonder why Lisideius . . . should cry up the barrenness of the French plots, above the variety and copiousness of the English. [See ENGLISH VS. FRENCH, q]

Dram. Poesy, '65. K I 70

UNITIES (DRAMATIC), ACTION, b. DESIGN. DRAMATIS PERSONAE, a. ENGLISH VS. FRENCH, s, u. PROSODY, kk. HERO (DRAMATIC), a. ETHICAL FUNCTION, a. UNITIES (DRAMATIC), TIME, d. FABLE, c. HEROIC PLAY, c. ANCIENTS, v. Cf. ENGLISH DRAMA, c. ANCIENTS, w. TERENCE, e. Cf. OVID, f. TRAGICOMEDY, c. Cf. BIOGRAPHY, a. Cf. OVID, k. PROSODY, v.

UNITIES (DRAMATIC), GENERAL, c. DONNE, c. POETRY, g. EPIC VS. TRAGEDY, d. SATIRE, c. ENGLISH VS. FRENCH, k. TRAGICOMEDY, f. UNITIES (DRAMATIC), ACTION, g. UNITIES (DRAMATIC), TIME, e.

Varro, Marcus Terentius [See also SATIRE, *Varronian*]

[¶] If I had been to find out a parallel for Plutarch, I should rather have pitched on Varro, the most learned of the Romans . . . or Pomponius Atticus, if he had written.

"Life of Plutarch," '83. S-S XVII 72

Vega Carpio, Lope Felix de [See LOPE DE VEGA]

Verisimility [See also PROBABILITY]*

UNITIES (DRAMATIC), PLACE, b. PLAY (PARTS). FABLE, b.

a. (Lisideius) For the spirit of man cannot be satisfied but with truth, or at least verisimility; and a poem is to contain, if not τὰ ἔτυμα, yet ἐτύμοισιν ὁμοῖα, as one of the Greek poets has expressed it.

Dram. Poesy, '65. K I 59

TRAGEDY, n. Cf. ETHICAL FUNCTION, a.

b. So, then, the less change of place there is, the less time is taken up in transporting the persons of the drama, with analogy to reason; and in that analogy, or resemblance of fiction to truth, consists the excellency of the play.

Defence of An Essay, '68. K I 128

UNITIES (DRAMATIC), PLACE, g. POETIC LICENSE, c. PROBABILITY, b.

Versification [See PROSODY]

Vida, Marco Girolamo

EPIC VS. TRAGEDY, d.

Villain

MANNERS, e.

Virgil (Publius Vergilius Maro)

Æneas

a. [¶] It is true, that as I am a religious admirer of Virgil, I could wish that he [St. Évremond] had not discovered [in *Observations on Segrais' Translation of Virgil*] our father's nakedness. But, after all, we must confess, that Æneas was none of the greatest heroes, and that Virgil was sensible of it himself.

"Character of St. Evremont," '92. S-S XVIII 14

EPIC HERO, e, f, g, h, k, l.

b. But he [Æneas] is arraigned with

* See R. M. Alden, "The Doctrine of Verismilitude in French and English Criticism of the Seventeenth Century," *Matzke Memorial Volume*, Stanford, 1911, pp. 38–48.

more show of reason by the ladies, who will make a numerous party against him, for being false to love, in forsaking Dido. And I cannot much blame them; for, to say the truth, it is an ill precedent for their gallants to follow. Yet, if I can bring him off with flying colours, they may learn experience at her cost, and, for her sake, avoid a cave, as the worst shelter they can choose from a shower of rain, especially when they have a lover in their company.

Ded. *Æneis, '97.* K II 186

c. [¶] Upon the whole matter [Æneas's desertion of Dido], and humanly speaking, I doubt there was a fault somewhere; and Jupiter is better able to bear the blame, than either Virgil or Æneas.

Ded. *Æneis, '97.* K II 189

See below, e.

Æneid

ANCIENTS, q.

d. But However I will not fail in my paines of translating the Sixth Eneid with the same exactness as I have performed the Fourth: because that Book is my greatest Favourite.

Letter to Tonson, April 1695. Ward No. 32, p. 75

e. [¶] But let us consider the secret reasons which Virgil had for thus framing this noble episode [of Æneas and Dido], wherein the whole passion of love is more exactly described than in any other poet.

Ded. *Æneis, '97.* K II 190

PROSODY, k. DRYDEN, WORKS, rrr.

Art

HORACE AND JUVENAL AND PERSIUS, c. INVENTION, c.

Beauties

f. Virgil has a thousand secret beauties . . .

Ded. *Æneis, '97.* K II 183

Canon

g. [¶] I have omitted the four preliminary lines of the First Æneid, because I think them inferior to any four others in the whole poem, and consequently believe they are not Virgil's.

Ded. *Æneis,* '97. K II 236

Chasteness

OBSCENITY, c.

Chaucer compared with

CHAUCER, h.

Coinage

COINAGE, c.

Conciseness

h. He [Virgil] studies brevity more than any other poet . . .

Ded. *Æneis,* '97. K II 227

ENGLISH LANGUAGE, b.

i. But having before observed that Virgil endeavours to be short, and at the same time elegant, I pursue the excellence [i.e., in the translation] and forsake the/brevity: for there he is like ambergris, a rich perfume, but of so close and glutinous a body, that it must be opened with inferior scents of musk or civet, or the sweetness will not be drawn out into another language.

Ded. *Æneis,* '97. K II 227–28

Correctness

CORRECTNESS, a.

Debts

PLAGIARISM, b. LUCRETIUS, a. AUTHORITY, e. PLAGIARISM, c.

j. [¶] [Of Æneid V] A great part of this book is borrow'd from Apollonius Rhodius; and the reader may observe the great judgment and distinction of our author, in what he borrows from the ancients, by comparing them. I conceive the reason why he omits the horse race in the funeral games, was, because he shews Ascanius afterwards on horseback, with his troops of boys, and would not wear that subject threadbare, which Statius, in the next age, describ'd so happily. Virgil seems to me to have excell'd Homer in all those sports . . .

Notes and Observations on Virgil's Works, '97. N 712

k. [¶] [Æneid VIII, line 34 of the translation] This similitude is literally taken from Apollonius Rhodius, and 'tis hard to say whether the original or the translation excels. But in the shield which he describes afterwards in this *Æneid,* he as much transcends his master Homer . . .

Notes and Observations on Virgil's Works, '97. N 714

Diction

l. [¶] See . . . in his *Georgics* . . . those . . . excellent images of Nature, most of which are neither great in themselves, nor have any natural ornament to bear them up; but the words wherewith he describes them are so excellent, that . . ./ *Materiam superabat opus:* the very sound of his words have often somewhat that is connatural to the subject . . . To perform this, he made frequent use of tropes . . .

Pref. *Annus Mirabilis,* '66. K I 16–17

DICTION, b.

m. There is an inimitable grace in Virgil's words, and in them principally consists that beauty, which gives so unexpressible a pleasure . . . This diction . . . is never to be copied; and . . . will appear but lame in the best translation.

Pref. *Sylvæ,* '85. K I 258

HORACE, j. HORACE AND JUVENAL AND PERSIUS, b. See below, ii.

n. Of the two ancient epic poets, who have so far excelled all the moderns, the invention and design were the particular talents of Homer. Virgil must yield to him in both; for the design of the Latin was borrowed from the Grecian: but the *dictio Virgiliana,* the expression of Virgil, his colouring, was incomparably the better; and in that I have always endeavoured to copy him. Most of the pedants, I know, maintain the contrary, and will have Homer excel even in this part. But of all people, as they are the most ill-mannered, so they are the worst judges. Even of words, which are their province, they seldom know more than the grammatical construction, unless they are born with a poetical genius, which is a rare portion amongst them. Yet some I know may stand excepted; and such I honour. Virgil is so exact in every word, that none can be changed but for a worse;/ nor any one removed from its place, but the harmony will be altered. He pretends sometimes to trip; but . . . like a skilful dancer on the ropes (if you will pardon the meanness of the similitude) . . . makes a seeming stumble, that you may think him in great hazard . . . while . . . he is only giving you a proof of his dexterity.

Parallel, '95. K II 148–49

CURIOSA FELICITAS. See below, mm. PROSODY, b. TRANSLATION, n. TECHNICAL TERMS, b.

o. Our author is too frugal of his words and sense to commit tautologies in either.

Notes and Observations on Virgil's Works, '97. N 713

Difficulty of Translating
See below, pp.

p. In short, they, who have called him the torture of grammarians, might also have called him the plague of translators; for he seems to have studied not to be translated.

Pref. *Sylvæ,* '85. K I 257

DRYDEN, WORKS, oo, pp. DENNIS.

q. . . . I repent nothing of it [the agreement with Tonson about the Virgil] that is passd, but that I do not find my self capable of translating so great an Authour, & therefore feare to loose my own Credit, & to hazard your profit, which it wou'd grieve me if you shou'd loose, by your too good opinion of my Abilities.

Letter to Tonson, 8 June 1695. Ward No. 33, p. 76

r. It wou'd require seaven yeares to translate Virgil exactly.

Letter to Tonson, December 1695 (?). Ward No. 36, p. 80

TRANSLATION, m. See above, i. TRANSLATION, n. ENGLISH LANGUAGE, e.

s. [¶] If I cannot copy his harmonious numbers, how shall I imitate his noble flights, where his thoughts and words are equally sublime? . . .ᵠ

What modern language, or what poet, can express the majestic beauty of this one verse, amongst a thousand others?

> *Aude, hospes, contemnere opes, et te quoque*
> *dignum*
> *Finge deo . . .*

For my part, I am lost in the admiration of it: I contemn the world when I think on it, and myself when I translate it.

Ded. *Æneis,* '97. K II 233

Eclogues
THEOCRITUS, a.

t. And, though this version is not void of errors, yet it comforts me that the faults of others are not worth finding. Mine are neither gross nor frequent in those Eclogues wherein my master has raised himself above that humble style in which Pastoral delights, and which, I must confess, is proper to the education and converse of shepherds: for he found the strength of his genius betimes, and was, even in his youth, preluding to his *Georgics* and his *Æneis*.

Ded. *Pastorals,* '97. S-S XIII 321

u. The Fourth, the Sixth, and the Eighth Pastorals are clear evidences of this truth [Virgil's versatility of style in the *Pastorals*]. In the three first, he contains himself within his bounds: but, addressing to Pollio, his great patron, and himself no vulgar poet, he no longer could restrain the freedom of his spirit, but began to assert his native character, which is sublimity . . .

Ded. *Pastorals,* '97. S-S XIII 322

v. In all the rest, he [Virgil] is equal to his Sicilian master [Theocritus], and observes, like him, a just decorum both of the subject and the persons . . .¹

Ded. *Pastorals,* '97. S-S XIII 323

THEOCRITUS, b. SPENSER, c. THEOCRITUS, c.

Figures

AUTHORITY, d. See below, oo.

Georgics

w. . . . his *Georgics,* which I esteem the divinest part of all his writings . . .

Pref. *Annus Mirabilis,* '66. K I 16

See above, l. LUCRETIUS, a.

x. [The *Georgics*] are more perfect in their kind than even his divine *Æneids.*

Pref. *Sylvæ,* '85. K I 259

x-2. . . . Virgil in his fourth Georgic . . . perpetually raises the lowness of his subject, by the loftiness of his words, and ennobles it by comparisons drawn from empires, and from monarchs . . .¹

Discourse of Satire, '93. K II 107

y. . . . if I durst presume so farr, I would humbly offer the Georgiques to your Lordships patronage. They are not I confess the most specious part of Virgil, but in revenge they are his Masterpiece in which

he has not onely out done all other Poets, but him self. Accordingly I have labour'd and I may say I have cultivated the Georgiques with more care than any other part of him, and as I think my self with more success.

Letter to Chesterfield, 17 February 1697. Ward No. 41, p. 86

z. . . . the best poem of the best poet.

Ded. *Georgics,* '97. S-S XIV 2

aa. Virgil wrote his *Georgics* in the full strength and vigour of his age, when his judgment was at the height, and before his fancy was declining. He had (according to our homely saying) his full swing at this poem . . .

Ded. *Georgics,* '97. S-S XIV 2

bb. [¶] The poetry of this book [*Georgic* I] is more sublime than any part of Virgil, if I have any taste. And if ever I have copied his majestic style, 'tis here. The compliment he makes Augustus, almost in the beginning, is ill imitated by his successors, Lucan and Statius. They dedicated to tyrants, and their flatteries are gross and fulsome. Virgil's address is both more lofty and more just.

Notes and Observations on Virgil's Works, '97. N 710

Hemistich

See below, oo. PROSODY, k, l.

Images

IMAGES, c.

Influence in English Poetry

PROGRESS, e.

Invention [See also INVENTION]

See below, dd.

cc. Is there no invention in some other parts of Virgil's *Æneis*? The disposition of so many various matters, is not that his own?¹

Ded. *Æneis,* '97. K II 198

HOMER AND VIRGIL, d.
Judgment
WIT, h. LUCAN, c.

dd. Virgil, I am confident, would have omitted such a work of superogation [as Andromache's digression to Hector on her pedigree, in Homer]. But Virgil had the gift of expressing much in little, and sometimes in silence; for, though he yielded much to Homer in invention, he more excelled him in his admirable judgment. He drew the passion of Dido for Æneas, in the most lively and most natural colours that are imaginable.

Ded. *Examen Poeticum,* '93. K II 13
FIGURES, c. MANUM DE TABULA, a.

ee. Statius never thought an expression could be bold enough; and if a bolder could be found, he rejected the first. Virgil had judgment enough to know daring was necessary; but he knew the difference betwixt a glowing colour and a glaring . . .[1]

Parallel, '95. K II 152
FANCY, i.

ff. . . . the critics make it one of Virgil's beauties, that, having said what he thought convenient, he always left somewhat for the imagination of his readers to supply; that they might gratify their fancies, by finding more in what he had written, than at first they could; and think they had added to his thought, when it was all there before-hand, and he only saved himself the expense of words.

Ded. *Georgics,* '97. S-S XIV 4
AUGUSTUS.

gg. [On the Dido-Æneas anachronism] To moralize this story, Virgil is the Apollo who has this dispensing power. His great judgment made the laws of poetry; but he never made himself a slave to them; chronology, at best, is but a cobweb-law,

and he broke through it with his weight. They who will imitate him wisely, must choose, as he did, an obscure and a remote era, where they may invent at pleasure, and not be easily contradicted.

Ded. *Æneis,* '97. K II 193
FIGURES, e. DRYDEN, LIFE, d. TURNS, a. CRITIC[s], a. IMAGINATION, e. CHAUCER AND OVID.

Lapses
CRITICISM, d.

License
CATACHRESIS. RULES, k. PROSODY, c.

Machinery [See also EPIC MACHINERY]
POETIC LICENSE, f.

as *Model*
Cf. SHAKESPEARE AND JONSON.

hh. Yet before I leave Virgil, I must own the vanity to tell you . . . that he has been my master in this poem.

Pref. *Annus Mirabilis,* '66. K I 17
OGILBY. EPIC VS. TRAGEDY, d. AUTHORITY, f. PROSODY, e.

Moral Truth
ETHICAL FUNCTION, a.

Numbers
See below, oo. HOMER, e. STATIUS, b. SPENSER, b.

ii. But versification and numbers are the greatest pleasures of poetry: Virgil knew it, and practised both so happily, that, for aught I know, his greatest excellency is in his diction. In all other parts of poetry, he is faultless; but in this he placed his chief perfection. And give me leave . . . to say that Virgil could have written sharper satires than either Horace or Juvenal, if he would have employed his talent that way.[1]

Discourse of Satire, '93. K II 86
See below, mm. PROSODY, b, c. LIVY. DRYDEN, WORKS, sss.

Patriotism
POET, f.
Platonism
EPIC POET, a.
Pre-eminence
Cf. SENECA, d.

jj. [¶] Virgil has confined his works within the compass of eighteen thousand lines, and has not treated many subjects; yet he ever had, and ever will have, the reputation of the best poet.

Discourse of Satire, '93, K II 24
HOMER, d.

kk. [¶] Thus at least I have shewn, that in the most perfect poem, which is that of Virgil, a perfect idea was required and followed; and consequently that all succeeding poets ought rather to imitate him, than even Homer.

Parallel, '95. K II 128
EPIC POET, c. Cf. PLATO, b.

ll. Spenser and Milton are the nearest, in English, to Virgil and Horace in the Latin; and I have endeavoured to form my style by imitating their masters. I will further own . . . that my chief ambition is to please those readers who have discernment enough to prefer Virgil before any other poet in the Latin tongue.

Ded. Æneis, '97. K II 223
CHAUCER, c.
Propriety
See below, oo. TASSO, b. OVID, a.

mm. And, indeed what I have already written, either in justification or praise of Virgil, is against myself, for presuming to copy, in my coarse English, the thoughts and beautiful expressions of this inimitable poet, who flourished in an age when his language was brought to its last perfection, for which it was particularly owing to him and Horace. I will give your Lordship my

opinion, that those two friends had consulted each other's judgment, wherein they should endeavour to excel; and they seem to have pitched on propriety of thought, elegance of words, and harmony of numbers. According to this model, Horace writ his *Odes* and *Epodes:* for his *Satires* and *Epistles,* being intended wholly for instruction, required another style:

Ornari res ipsa negat, contenta doceri:

and therefore, as he himself professes, are *sermoni propiora,* nearer prose than verse.

Ded. Æneis, '97. K II 214–15
Satire
See above, ii.

nn. . . . *varium et mutabile semper femina* is the sharpest satire, in the fewest words, that ever was made on womankind; for both the adjectives are neuter, and *animal* must be understood, to make them grammar. Virgil does well to put those words into the mouth of Mercury. *If a God had not spoken them, neither durst he have written them, nor I translated them.*

Ded. Æneis, '97. K II 192
Style
SUBLIME, b.

oo. I looked [at the time of translating for *Sylvæ*] on Virgil as a succinct and grave majestic writer; one who weighed not only every thought, but every word and syllable; who was still aiming to crowd his sense into as narrow a compass as possibly he could; for which reason he is so very figurative, that he requires (I may almost say) a grammar apart to construe him. His verse is everywhere sounding the very thing in your ears, whose sense it bears; yet the numbers are perpetually varied . . . so that the same sounds are never repeated twice together. . . . But to return . . .

though he is smooth where/smoothness is required, yet he is so far from affecting it, that he seems rather to disdain it; frequently makes use of synaloephas, and concludes his sense in the middle of his verse. He is everywhere above conceits of epigrammatic wit, and gross hyperboles; he maintains majesty in the midst of plainness; he shines, but glares not; and is stately without ambition, which is the vice of Lucan. I drew my definition of poetical wit from my particular consideration of him: for propriety of thoughts and words are only to be found in him . . . This exact propriety of Virgil I particularly regarded as a great part of his character . . .

Pref. *Sylvæ,* '85. K I 255–56

pp. Virgil therefore, being so very sparing of his words, and leaving so much to be imagined by the reader, can never be translated as he ought, in any modern tongue. To make him copious, is to alter

his character; and to translate him line for line, is impossible . . ./Virgil is much the closest of any Roman poet, and the Latin hexameter has more feet than the English heroic.

Pref. *Sylvæ,* '85. K I 256–57

HORACE AND JUVENAL AND PERSIUS, b. See above, bb. HOMER, a.

Supernatural [See also above, *Machinery*]

SUPERNATURAL, b.

Unities

UNITIES (DRAMATIC), GENERAL, e.

Vox Populi [Cf. AUDIENCE, POPULAR; HOI POLLOI]

RHYME (DEBATE), g.

(Neander) Do we not see them [the people] stick to/Hopkins' and Sternhold's psalms, and forsake those of David, I mean Sandys his translation of them?

Dram. Poesy, '65. K I 99–100

POET, p. CRITIC[s], h.

Waller, Edmund

a. But the excellence and dignity of it [rhyme] were never fully known till Mr. Waller taught it; he first made writing easily an art; first showed us to conclude the sense most commonly in distichs, which, in the verse of those before him, runs on for so many lines together, that the reader is out of breath to overtake it.

Ded. *Rival Ladies,* '64. K I 7

PRESENT AGE, d. PROSODY, ll. GRAFFING, b. TRANSLATION, a. WALSH, c.

b. . . . Mr. Waller,/the father of our

English numbers. . . . Here . . . I hope the reader need not be told, that Mr. Waller is only mentioned for honour's sake; that I am desirous of laying hold on his memory, on all occasions, and thereby acknowledging to the world, that unless he had written, none of us could write.

Pref. Walsh's *Dialogue,* '91. S-S XVIII 5–6

SPENSER, b. DRYDEN, LITERARY LIFE, b. CHAPMAN, b. TRANSLATION, gg. MILTON, d. CHAUCER, c.

Walsh, William

a. [¶] Nothing cou'd please me better, than to know you as well by the endowments of your Mind, as by those of your person. I knew before this discovery, that you were ingenious, but not that you were a Poet, & one of the best that these times produce, or the Succeeding times can expect.

Letter to Walsh, 1690 (?). Ward No. 15, p. 30

b. [¶] You command me Deare Sir, to make a kind of critique on your Essay [*Dialogue Concerning Women*] . . . There is not the least occasion of reflecting on your disposition of the piece, nor the thoughts. I see nothing to censure in either of them. Besides this the style is easy and naturall; as fit for Dialogue, as if you had set Tully before you; and as gallant as Fontenelle in his plurality of Worlds. In the correctness of the English there is not much for me to animadvert. Be pleasd therefore, to avoid the words, don't, can't, shan't, and the like abbreviations of syllables; which seem to me to savour of a little rus/ticity. As for Pedantry you are not to be taxd with it. I remember I hinted somewhat of concludding your Sentences with prepositions or conjunctions sometimes, which is not elegant . . .[1] I find likewise, that you make not a due distinction betwixt that, and who . . .[1] *That,* ought always to signify a thing; *who,* a person.[1]

Letter to Walsh, c. 1691. Ward No. 17, pp. 33–34

c. Philareque, or the Critique on Balzac, observes it as a fault in his style, that he has in many places written twenty words together (en suitte) which were all Monosyllables. I observe this in some lines of your Noble Epigramm ["Gripe and Shifter"]: and am often guilty of it myselfe through hastinesse. Mr. Waller counted this a vertue of the English tongue, that it cou'd bring so many words of the Teutonique together, and yet the smoothness of the Verse not vitiated. Now I am speaking of your Epigramm, I am sure you will not be offended with me for saying, there is some imperfection in the two last lines.

Blend 'em together, Fate, ease both theire paine; And of two wretches make one happy man. The word blend includes the sense of *together;* ease both their paine: paine is Singular, both is Plurall. . . . Then the Rhyme is not full of pain and Man. An half/rhyme is not always a fault; but in the close of any paper of verses, tis to be avoyded. And after all, tell me truly, if those words, ease both their paine; were not superfluous in the sence, and onily put, for the sake of the rhyme, and filling up the verse. It came into my head to alter them, and I am affrayd for the worse.

. . . [Dryden's alteration] Now I begin, to be in for Cakes and Ale; and why should I not put a quere on those other lines? [verses 3–4] Poor Shift, does all his whole contrivance set, To spend that wealth he wants the Sence to get. All his whole Contrivance, is but all his Contrivance, or his whole Contrivance; thus, one of those words, lookes a little like tautology . . . But this is trifling, in me. For your sence is very intelligible . . . And, by your favour, so is Martial's: Viribus hic non est, hic non est utilis annis: and yet in exactness of Criticism, your censure [See Ward, Letter 16, p. 32] stands good upon him . . ./

276

[P.S.] Your apostrophe's to your Mistresse [in the *Dialogue*] . . . are . . . as fine turnes of gallantry, as I have mett with anywhere.

Letter to Walsh, c. 1691. Ward No. 17, pp. 34–36

d. . . . it was not easy for me to imagine, that one [Walsh] so young could have treated so nice a subject [women] with so much judgment. It is true, I was not ignorant, that he was naturally ingenious, and that he had improved himself by travelling . . . but so much variety of reading, both in ancient and modern authors, such digestion of that reading, so much justness of thought, that it leaves no room for affectation, or pedantry, I may venture to say, are not over-common amongst practised writers, and very rarely to be found amongst beginners.

Pref. Walsh's *Dialogue*, '91. S-S XVIII 5
Dryden, Literary Life, b.   Rymer, e.
Wycherley, b.   Ancients, n.

e. . . . William Walsh, of Abberley, Esq. (who has long honoured me with his friendship, and who, without flattery, is the best critic of our nation) . . .

Postscript *Æneis*, '97. K II 244
Chudleigh.

Wild, Robert

(Eugenius) . . . he is the very Withers of the city: they have bought more editions of his works than would serve to lay under all their pies at the Lord Mayor's Christmas.

Dram. Poesy, '65. K I 32

Wilmot, John [See Rochester]

Wit

a. (Crites) . . . his [the Leveller in poetry] poetry neither has wit in it, nor seems to have it . . .[1]

He affects plainness, to cover his want of imagination: when he writes the serious way, the highest flight of his fancy is some miserable antithesis, or seeming contradiction; and in the comic he is still reaching at some thin conceit, the ghost of a jest, and that too flies before him, never to be caught; these swallows which we see before us on the Thames are the just resemblance of his wit . . .

Dram. Poesy, '65. K I 32
Emulation. Ancients, y.

b. (Eugenius) . . . yet a thing well said will be wit in all languages . . .

Dram. Poesy, '65. K I 51
Plautus, a.

c. (Eugenius) But to do this [catachresis] always, and never be able to write a line without it, though it may be admired by some few pedants, will not pass upon those who know that wit is best conveyed to us in the most easy language; and is most to be admired when a great thought comes dressed in words so commonly received, that it is understood by the meanest apprehensions . . .

Dram. Poesy, '65. K I 52
Donne, a.   Cleveland, b.   Cf. Shakespeare, b.   Cf. Humors, a.   Tragedy, n.

d. The composition of all poems is, or ought to be, of wit; and wit in the poet, or *Wit writing,* (if you will give me leave to use a school-distinction), is no other than the faculty of imagination in the writer, which, like a nimble spaniel, beats over and ranges through the field of memory, till it springs the quarry it hunted after; or, without metaphor, which searches over all the memory for the species or ideas of those things which it designs to represent. *Wit written* is that which is well defined, the happy result of thought, or product of imagination. [See next entry]

Pref. *Annus Mirabilis, '66.* K I 14

e. But to proceed from wit, in the general notion of it, to the proper wit of an Heroic or Historical Poem, I judge it chiefly to consist in the delightful imagining of persons, actions, passions, or things. 'Tis not the jerk or sting of an epigram, nor the seeming contradiction of/a poor antithesis (the delight of an ill-judging audience in a play of rhyme), nor the jingle of a more poor paronomasia; neither is it so much the morality of a grave sentence . . . but it is some lively and apt description, dressed in such colours of speech, that it sets before your eyes the absent object, as perfectly, and more delightfully than nature.

Pref. *Annus Mirabilis, '66.* K I 14–15

OVID AND VIRGIL, a.

f. *A great wit's great work is to refuse,* as my worthy friend Sir John Berkenhead has ingeniously expressed it . . .

Defence of An Essay, '68. K I 122

JUDGMENT, c.

g. Some ingenious men, for whom I have a particular esteem, have thought I have much injured Ben Johnson, when I have not allowed his wit to be extraordinary: but they confound the notion of what is witty, with what is pleasant. That Ben Johnson's plays were pleasant, he must want reason who denies: but that pleasantness was not properly wit, or the sharpness of conceit, but the natural/imitation of folly . . .

Pref. *Evening's Love, '71.* K I 138–39

COMEDY, e.

h. [Speaking of repartee] Yet, as Mr. Cowley (who had a greater portion of it

[wit] than any man I know) tells us in his *Character of Wit,* rather than all wit, let there be none. I think there is no folly so great in any poet of our age, as the superfluity and/waste of wit was in some of our predecessors: particularly we may say of Fletcher and of Shakespeare, what was said of Ovid, *in omni ejus ingenio, facilius quod rejici, quam quod adjici potest, invenies.* The contrary of which was true in Virgil, and our incomparable Johnson.

Pref. *Evening's Love, '71.* K I 139–40

i. But . . . there are as different characters in wit as in folly [i.e., humours characters]. Neither is all kind of wit proper in the mouth of every ingenious person. A witty coward, and a witty brave, must speak differently.

Pref. *Evening's Love, '71.* K I 140

j. [¶] However, if I should grant, that there were a greater latitude in characters of wit, than in those of humour; yet that latitude would be of small advantage to such poets, who have too narrow an imagination to write it. And to entertain an audience perpetually with humour, is to carry them from the conversation of gentlemen,/ and treat them with the follies and extravagancies of Bedlam.

Pref. *Evening's Love, '71.* K I 140–41

Cf. SHAKESPEARE, u. JONSON, u, v.

k. [¶] This was then the mode of wit, the vice of the age, and not Ben Johnson's; for you see, a little before him, that admirable wit, Sir Philip Sidney, perpetually playing with his words. In his time, I believe, it ascended first into the pulpit, where (if you will give me leave to clench too) it yet finds benefit of its clergy; for they are/commonly the first corrupters of eloquence, and the last reformed from vicious oratory . . .

Defence of the Epilogue, '72. K I 173–74
Cf. PRESENT AGE, k. FLETCHER, d.

l. [¶] From that which has been said,
it may be collected, that the definition of
Wit (which has been so often attempted,
and ever unsuccessfully by many poets) is
only this: that it is a propriety of thoughts
and words; or, in other terms, thoughts
and words elegantly adapted to the subject.

Author's Apology, '77. K I 190
PASSIONS, h. DRYDEN, WORKS, h. OVID, h.
Cf. CHAPMAN, a. Cf. SYLVESTER's *Du
Bartas.* SATIRE, ll. Cf. PLUTARCH AND
SENECA. VIRGIL, oo. OBSCENITY, b.

m. [¶] If Wit has truly been defined,
'a propriety of thoughts and words,' then
that definition will extend to all sorts of
Poetry: and, among the rest, to this present
entertainment of an opera. Propriety of
thought is that fancy which arises naturally
from the subject, or which the poet adapts
to it. Propriety of words is the clothing of
those thoughts with such expressions as are
naturally proper to them; and from both
these, if they are judiciously performed, the
delight of poetry results.

Pref. *Albion and Albanius, '85.* K I 270

n. Ovid, going to his banishment, and
writing from on shipboard to his friends,
excused the faults of his poetry by his misfortunes; and told them, that good verses
never flow, but from a serene and composed spirit. Wit, which is a kind of Mercury, with wings fastened to his head and
heels, can fly but slowly in a damp air.

Ded. *Eleonora, '92.* S-S XI 121
FIGURES, d. POETRY, c. PERSIUS, i. SAT-
IRE, s. HORACE AND JUVENAL AND PER-
SIUS, d. DONNE, d. DRYDEN, LITERARY
LIFE, b. OVID, a.

o. [¶] If wit consists in the propriety
of thoughts and words (which I imagined
I had first found out, but since am pleas-
ingly convinced that Aristotle has made the
same defintion in other terms), then Lucian's thoughts and words are always
proper to his characters and his subject.

"Life of Lucian," '96. S-S XVIII 75
PRESENT AGE, p. CRITIC[s], a. CHAU-
CER AND OVID. Cf. CHAUCER, g.

Withers, George
WILD. PROSODY, hh.

Words [Cf. DICTION]
ENGLISH DRAMA, h. TRANSLATION, q.
EXPRESSION, b. MODERNIZING.

Writing, Good
WALLER, a. TRAGEDY, e. ST. ÉVREMOND, c.

Wycherley, William

a. Many of our present writers are eminent in both these kinds [comedy and sat-
ire]; and, particularly, the author of the
Plain Dealer, whom I am proud to call my
friend, has obliged all honest and virtuous
men, by one of the most bold, most general,
and most useful satires, which has ever
been presented on the English theatre.

Author's Apology, '77. K I 182
HORACE, b. JUVENAL, a.

b. Mr Wycherleys Poems will not come
out, till Michaelmass term: if his versifica-
tions prove as [well?] as his wit, I shall
believe it will be extraordinary. However
Congreve & Southern & I, shall not faile to
appeare before it. & if you will come in, he
will have reason to acknowledge it for a
favour.

Letter to Walsh, May 1693. Ward No. 24,
p. 54

c. But as well as I love Mr. Wycherley, I
confess I love my self so well, that I will not
shew how much I am inferiour to him in

Wit and Judgment; by undertaking any thing after him. [This concerns Wycherley's judgment respecting the marriage of a friend.]

Letter to Dennis, March 1694. Ward No. 31, p. 73

d. Mr. Wycherley, when we read it [Racine's *Esther*] together, was of my opinion [that it could not succeed on the public stage] in this, or rather I of his; for it becomes me so to speak of so excellent a poet, and so great a judge.

Parallel, '95. K II 144

CHUDLEIGH.

Youth

OVID, h. MILTON, c. PERSIUS, f.

Selective Index

of Familiar Phrases, Quotations, Titles, Topics, and Allusions

ab abusu ad usum, non valet consequentia
[COLLIER]

abhor: what we abhor we never imitate
[EPIC HERO, i]

Achilles and Rinaldo [EPIC HERO, d]

Achilles . . . roaring along the salt sea-shore
[EPIC HERO, m]

acorns before . . . bread [LAST AGE, e]

acumen of wit [JUDGMENT, c]

acuteness in a thing well said [REPARTEE, b]

Aeschines [PERSIUS, g]

afoot: he walks soberly afoot, when he might
fly [LUCAN, b]

age, a green old [FANCY, i]

age: where a whole age is dipt together
[SATIRE, h]

ages: those credulous and doting [PROGRESS,
a]

Agesilaus riding on a hobby horse
[BIOGRAPHY, c]

Ajax, a man-killing idiot! [EPIC HERO, n]

Alit æmulatio ingenia [EMULATION, a]

anatomy [PROGRESS, a; Cf. DRYDEN, WORKS,
ss]

Andronicus (Livius) [SATIRE, bb, cc, ee]

animal, the poor reasonable [BIOGRAPHY, c]

animamque in vulnere ponit [POET, l]

Anthologia, the Greek [EPIC, j]

Antony and Cleopatra: I never writ anything
for myself but *Antony and Cleopatra*
[DRYDEN, WORKS, gg]

Apelles [INVENTION, e]

Apollo, gift of [PASSIONS (RESPONSIVE), j]

Apollo, priests of [INSPIRATION, b]

Apollonius Rhodius [VIRGIL, j, k]

Appian [ENGLISH LANGUAGE, c. POLYBIUS, a.
LUCIAN, g]

April poetry [POETRY, a]

Apuleius [SATIRE, pp]

Archilochus [SATIRE, kk]

argue well, when poets do not [ETHICAL
FUNCTION, a]

Aristotle and the School [POSSIBILITY. Cf.
PROGRESS, a]

Arlington (Henry, Earl of; Lord Chamberlain) [SATIRE, jj]

Ars est celare artem [RHYME (DEBATE), g.
THEOCRITUS, a]

aspirate (vb.) [PROSODY, c]

astronomy [PROGRESS, a]

atheist: so much an atheist, that he forgot
sometimes to be a poet [LUCRETIUS, b]

Atticus [DIALOGUE (GENRE), a. VARRO]

Augustus playing at bounding-stones
[BIOGRAPHY, c]

auribus istius temporis accommodata
[CHAUCER, c]

Bajazet, Racine's [MANNERS, j]

Balzac, J. L. G. de [WALSH, c]

Barine, Ode to [HORACE, k]

Barry, Mrs. Elizabeth [S-S, VIII, 220]

Bartholomew-Fair writers and Bartholomew-
Close printers [SHADWELL, e]

Bartholomew Fair, gross expressions of
[TRANSLATION, g]

bawdry, barefaced [OBSCENITY, b]

beautiful monster [EPIC, d]

Bedlam (Hospital) [PASSIONS (REPRESENTA-
TIVE), f. WIT, j]

beef: lovers of beef broiled upon the coals
[EPIC HERO, a]

bells: the prudence of a carter to put bells
upon his horses [FARCE, g]

281

Selective Index

Berkenhead, Sir John [WIT, f]

best good man, with the worst-natur'd Muse [DORSET, b]

Billingsgate [PASSIONS (REPRESENTATIVE), f. SATIRE, ll. TRANSLATION, g]

bizarre [POET, c]

bladdered greatness [CRITIC(s), a]

Blount, Charles [S-S XVIII 79]

Boadicea [HOPKINS]

Boccalini, Trajano [K II 193]

body politic [SATIRE, m]

Bonum quo communius, eo melius [HORACE AND JUVENAL AND PERSIUS, c]

booby, Achilles . . . like a [EPIC HERO, m]

bottle, after the third [POETASTERS, e]

boyish an ambition [EPIC, j]

boyish kind of pleasure [BUTLER, b]

boyisms [CHAUCER AND OVID]

Bracegirdle, Ann [D'URFEY]

Brentford, his other king of [CORNEILLE, PIERRE, b]

Bristol-stone [BOMBAST, b. Cf. CHAUCER, g. CURIOSA FELICITAS]

Browne, Sir Thomas [JK II 756]

Buchanan, George [HISTORY, e]

buffon, un mauvais [POETASTERS, c]

buskin [ANCIENTS, i. PASSIONS (REPRESENTATIVE), i]

butchering, slovenly [SATIRE, b]

buttock, some brand or other on this [ANONYMITY]

caena dubia [POETRY, g]

Caesar, Julius [HISTORY, d]

Cakes and Ale [WALSH, c]

Calderon [K I 60]

Calprenède, La (Gautier de Costes de) [EPIC HERO, d]

calumniating strongly, that something may remain [OBSCENITY, e]

candor [CRITICISM, a, e. DIALOGUE (GENRE), a. DORSET, b. Cf. HISTORY, e. SEDLEY, a]

caput mortuum [DENHAM, b. MANUM DE TABULA, b. Cf. TRANSLATION, e]

carpet-ground [HORACE AND JUVENAL AND PERSIUS, e. OVID, k]

Catastasis [PLAY (PARTS)]

causes: second causes are out of doors [OPERA, a]

cavalièrement [OVID, j]

Chancery, an excellent pleader in the [CRITIC(s), g]

Chapman's *Homer* [CHAPMAN, b. PROSODY, ii]

chapon bouillé [ANCIENTS, s]

Charles V, reign of [POETRY, e]

cheated into passion, but . . . reasoned into truth [STYLE, c]

Chedreux critics [ENGLISH VS. FRENCH, j]

chère entière of women, a [K I 120]

Chetwood, Knightly [N 710]

chess-player, like a skillful [JONSON, s]

chimeras [IMITATION, j]

chronology . . . is but a cobweb-law [VIRGIL, gg]

church and state, poetical [CRITIC(s), d]

church-painters [FARCE, f]

civil people breathing, the most [FRENCH AUTHORS, a]

clipt poetry and false coin [K II 23]

cobweb-law [VIRGIL, gg]

cock's mind in Æsop [CURIOSA FELICITAS]

cold blood, [narrations] made often in [NARRATIONS, b]

cold prose fits [TRANSLATION, j]

colour: a glowing colour and a glaring [VIRGIL, ee]

conceit, sharpness of [FLETCHER, d. JONSON, v. WIT, g]

condition, no man is satisfied with his own [HORACE, m]

contraria juxta se posita magis elucescunt [CHARACTER(s), e]

Cooper's Hill [PROSODY, d]

Selective Index

Selective Index

Luckily, not laboriously [Shakespeare, b]
lysis (λύσις) [Jonson, p]

MacKenzie, Sir George [Dryden, Literary Life, b]
Macrobius [Terence, a-2. Dryden, Literary Life, o]
Madman, easie thing to write like a [Lee, b]
magazine of words, a [Prosody, b]
Magna Charta of heroic poetry [Prosody, jj]
mai esce del bosco [Theocritus, a]
Maimbourg, Louis [Style, a-0]
mal à propos [Tragicomedy, a]
malefactor: I come like a malefactor, to make a speech [Dryden, Works, oo]
malefactor: make a malefactor die sweetly [Satire, b]
Manilius [Chaucer and Ovid. Prosody, s]
man-killers: those ungodly man-killers, whom we . . . call heroes [Homer, b]
man or woman of God's making, scarce a [Present Age, p]
marjoram, sweet [Engllish Language, f]
Martin Mar-prelate [Satire, ll]
materia poetica [Fable, f]
Materiam superbat opus [Virgil, j, k]
mathematical head [Poet, n]
mathematics, a seeming desmonstration in the [Rules, e]
Mayne, Dr. Jasper [Lucian, d. See also S-S XVIII 81]
Measure for Measure [Last Age, c]
Medea [Ovid, c. Cf. Poetic Justice, a]
Medici, Lorenzo de [Golden Ages, b]
medicine [Progress, a]
médisance [Satire, t]
men, a company of warm young [Critic(s), a]
Menippus [Satire, nn, oo]
Merry Wives of Windsor, The [Shakespeare and Fletcher, a]
Messias, the Jews' [Invention, d]

militia, I will never part with the power of the [Dryden, Works, vv]
minds . . . wrought on by the temperament of our bodies [Critic(s), e]
miniature of human life, Tragedy is [Drama: Epic Origins]
modesty depraved into a vice [Decorum, g]
Monsieur Hippolyte [Racine, a]
monster: a faultless monster, which the world ne'er knew [Epic Hero, h]
Montagues and Capulets [English vs. French, z]
Moorfields, gross expressions of [Translation, g]
Morelli, Dr. Henry [Dryden, Literary Life, i]
Mother Hubbard's Tale [Satire, pp]
motion (perpetual) [Narrations, b]
Moyle, Walter [Imitation, h. See also S-S XVIII 78–79]
Musas colere serviores [Poetic License, a. Prosody, ii]
Muses, who ever follow peace [Arts]
mushroom: preferred before a peach [Epic vs. Tragedy, e]
myself: I never writ anything for myself but *Antony and Cleopatra* [Dryden, Works, gg]

ne Hercules contra duos [Epic vs. Tragedy, g]
Nescivit quod bene cessit relinquere [Ovid, g, h]
nicety of manners [French Authors, a]
Nile, like the frogs and serpents in the [Prosody, k]
nobis non licet esse tam disertis [Prosody, c]
non nostrum est tantas componere lites [Horace and Juvenal and Persius, c]
non tu corpus eras sine pectore [Sedley, a]
Northern dedicator, the [Shadwell, b]

Selective Index

Selective Index

versifier: the best versifier of the former age [Sandys]

Versus inopes rerum nugæque canoræ [Obscenity, e]

verve [Prosody, b]

vetus comœdia [Satire, gg, jj]

village words [English Language, f]

Vita proba est [Obscenity, c]

vivorum, ut magna admiratio, ita censura difficilis [Criticism, b]

volat irrevocabile verbum [Epic vs. Tragedy, j]

Vossius, Gerardus Johannes [Opera, h]

vulgar: the great vulgar and the small [Audience, Popular, e]

wakes in one scene . . . slumbers in another [Fletcher]

walk about: the street, the windows, the houses, and the closet, are made to walk about [Unities (Dramatic), Place, d]

warluck [Epic Hero, l]

warm young men, a company of [Critic(s), a]

watchmaker [Poet, h]

Wedderburn, David [Persius, b]

Winter's Tale [Last Age, c]

wit, empire of [English vs. French, h]

wit, scantling of [Chapman, a]

world: I contemn the world when I think on it [Virgil, s]

wrestler, as in a [Fancy, f]

zambras [Opera, c]

zanies [Patronage, a]

Zeal: The zeal of God's House has eaten him up [Collier]

Zimri [Satire, b]

COLOPHON

THE TYPE FACES *used in this book belong to the group generally known as Old Style, though neither is actually a reproduction of the designs of the two sixteenth-century French type designers whose names they bear. The text is set in ten-point Granjon, one point leaded. This face was designed for the Linotype by G. W. Jones and named for Robert Granjon (fl. 1545–1588), though it actually resembles types cut by Claude Garamond, (d. 1561). It is an elegant face, with tall ascenders, and is highly legible, even in small sizes. The title page and display initials are set in several sizes of Garamond Bold, a face not actually based on the designs of Garamond, but having much of the quality of the typography of sixteenth-century France.*

The trademark was designed for Vanderbilt University Press by Theresa Sherrer Davidson and is used for the first time in this book. It is a form of the triskelion encircled by the traditional laurel wreath. Besides appearing in the arms of both Sicily and the Isle of Man, the triskelion has been employed in many cultures, and a form of it was used by the Indians of Tennessee. The Fugitives, the group of poets who flourished at Vanderbilt in the early 1920s, adopted it informally as their emblem. The symbol was originally three legs joined together, and to the Fugitives it was evidently seen as three legs running. It also bears a relation to certain sun symbols, and may have signified the light which the Fugitives were seeking, for they saw themselves as fleeing towards as well as away from something. In some representations, the triskelion is seen as three V's joined together. Theresa Davidson is the wife of the poet Donald Davidson, several of whose books she has illustrated.

The book is printed on Warren's Olde Style paper, manufactured by the S. D. Warren Company of Boston, and bound in Columbia Mills Riverside Linen, stamped in gold. Composition, printing, and binding were done by the Kingsport Press, Inc., of Kingsport, Tennessee.